Am I Dreaming

by

Charles G. Ashford

With Best Wishes
from

Charles G. Ashford

"While all events in my story are true, names have been changed
so as not to embarrass certain people."

ISBN: 0-7596-3882-9

This book is printed on acid free paper.

1stBooks – rev. 6/12/02

Acknowledgement

This book is dedicated to my daughter Susan and my sister Catherine, without whose help and encouragement it would never have been written.

Special thanks must go to Angus Baxter, a well-known Genealogist living in Toronto, for his many years of generous help with family research.

Childhood Days

On the 18th of December 1921 little more than a month before my third birthday, I was baptised into the Catholic faith at St Georges Cathedral in London, England, and given the name of Ronald Brandon.

In the open doorway of a large grey-stone building the elderly gentleman holding me in his arms, handed me to an old lady dressed in black. Closing the door behind her she carried me up a flight of stairs and put me into a cot, leaving me to cry myself to sleep. I must have been at least five years old before I realized the place I lived in was a convent, where children were cared for by nuns of the Franciscan Order.

Built in the early nineteenth century St Joseph's Convent lay on the outskirts of Littlehampton, a small seaside town in the county of Sussex. Fenced off from the outside world by iron railings and privet hedges a front garden with neatly kept lawns edged with flowers, was the only visible sign of colour to brighten the drab surroundings. Sad to say, this cold forbidding establishment on England's southern coast, was the only home many orphaned girls and boys had ever known.

At the entrance to the building a heavy steel studded oak door opened into a spacious office, where the Mother Superior received her visitors. The boys quarters facing the front of the convent backed onto a playground with an iron railing separating them from girls, who lived at the rear of the building. A large refectory in the boys section used as a playroom, also served as their dining room. Their sleeping quarters were up two flights of winding stairs, with a lower dormitory for six to ten year olds and an upper dormitory for boys from ten to fourteen. A seldom used door in the rear wall of each dormitory opened out onto a fire escape, leading down to the playground. At ground floor level overlooking the front of the building was the children's nursery, where infants were cared for by young girls known as novices. Also living within the convent grounds was the resident priest Father Morrissey, who took mass in the tiny chapel each Sunday.

My early years in the children's nursery were quite happy, as I recall. At times an occasional cry of distress was heard when a child was smacked, because they'd wet the bed. And told to stand at the bedside with the wet sheet over their head. Rising at six o'clock each morning we were shown how to wash our faces, brush our teeth, and dress ourselves. Then under the ever watchful eyes of nursery staff we were ushered into the diningroom, for breakfast. Where each child was given a bowl of porridge, with ample helpings of milk. When everybody had finished we left the table, and moved into a classroom adjacent to the nursery. Children between the ages of five and six were then given lessons in the three R's while infants were left in the playroom, until it was time for their midday meal. Returning from a short walk after lunch we were allowed out to play until four thirty p.m, when our final meal of the day was eaten. Evening prayers followed with all present singing Star of the Sea, a well rehearsed hymn, before going to bed. A routine I followed with monotonous regularity in childhood days at the nursery, until I was six and moved in with older boys.

At the age of seven I attended St Catherine's, a school in the town of Littlehampton. Escorted by one of the nuns I walked a half a mile back and forth to school with the rest of the boys, returning to the convent at the end of the day. It was here I observed a vast difference between convent children and those who lived in the town. Each day their mothers met them after school hours. But the only mother I ever knew was the mother superior at the convent, where it was not unusual for one or two nuns in charge to remind me I was an orphan. As I grew older parcels addressed to me would arrive each Christmas and picture postcards were sent at the end of January, which I later discovered was my birthday. Postal orders or stamps to the value of one shilling were also enclosed, but the name of the sender remained a mystery.

It was at this particular time life at the convent changed quite dramatically, and from that day forward I was soon to learn the meaning of fear. I missed the comfortable surroundings I'd long been used to in the infants section when I moved in with older boys, where thirty of us aged from seven to fourteen slept in a large dormitory. Until I got to know the other boys and their nicknames, I found this a rather frightening experience.

Because my surname was Brandon, they called me Brandy for short. On dark winter nights we were sent to bed at six o'clock and when all lights were extinguished we'd listen to ghost stories told by Dusty Millar, one of the fourteen year old boys. I would lie there hidden under the blankets while he spun tales of ugly witches on broomsticks, flying off to haunted castles. Waiting inside were weird monsters and werewolves who ate people, that left me terrified. Waking up later that night I watched as ghostly figures wandered around the dormitory and fearing for my life, stayed beneath the bedclothes.

At six o'clock the following morning I was awakened by Paddy Ryan, the boy who slept in the bed next to me.

"Sister's shouting for everyone to get up, Brandy," he whispered, removing the blankets covering my head.

Still in shock, I sat there staring at him.

"What's the matter?" he asked,"you look as though you've seen a ghost."

"I saw them last night, Paddy," I mumbled.

"You've been dreaming," he chuckled. "Dusty Millars ghost stories must have given you the creeps."

"I'm telling you Paddy, I saw them."

"Aw c'mon Brandy you're having me on" he said, "nobody believes in ghosts any more."

"But there were two of them Paddy," I protested. "I saw them with my own eyes. They were dressed in long white gowns, and walked around the dormitory."

"I suppose you heard them telling jokes to each other," sneered Podgy Barnes, who had been listening.

"What d'you mean Podge, did you see them too?" I asked.

"No I didn't you daft idiot, they were the nuns in charge of our dormitory you saw last night," he laughed. "When they hear a noise they come from their cubicle next to the toilet, and look around the room."

"Oh gosh" I said, "they frightened the blooming life out of me."

Just when I was getting used to my new surroundings a change of staff among the nuns looking after us brought Sister Rose on the scene, who at a stroke altered a routine and way of life we had become used to. Her strict code of discipline upset the existing peace and tranquility of our every day lives, causing havoc between ourselves and the rest of the convent staff. Tall and wiry, she resembled something chiseled out of granite. The piercing grey eyes set in a face both pale and gaunt looked incapable of showing the slightest emotion, but beneath an otherwise calm exterior her tight lipped mouth showed signs of a cruel streak. A sharp pointed nose that was seen to drip earned her the nickname, Dew Drop. Often whispered behind her back by many boys, who had come to loathe and fear her.

On her first morning in charge she strode into the dining-room and stood gazing down at us like some colossus, her entrance effectively stopping the normal hum of chatter that went on among us at the breakfast table. In the deathly silence that followed you could hear a pin drop as those hawkish eyes swept around the room, causing everyone to fidget uncomfortably. In a voice like thunder she demanded we sit still, and pay particular attention to what she had to say. To a subdued audience she informed all present in no uncertain manner, from here on silence will be observed during meals. Pressing home her desire for obedience from everyone she leaned forward menacingly and like a vulture watching it's prey warned, any child caught misbehaving will be severely punished. For some minutes an eerie silence descended on the hushed dining room, no child daring to move until she turned on her heel to leave. Then as if in a gesture of defiance a peal of laughter from the rear of the diningroom, saw all heads turn in alarm.

"Everyone will face the front immediately" she screamed, and with cat-like strides she reached the back of the room.

With lightning speed her huge arm shot out and seized the culprit by his ear, lifting him bodily from his seat. Seething with anger she dragged the unfortunate lad in front of a stunned assembly and ordered him to face the wall, saying; "I'll deal with you later, my lad."

From that moment on I came to know the meaning of fear, as witness to the way the boy now suffered from a red and badly swollen ear. Blood oozed from the lobe, where Sister Rose's nails had dug into it. As he turned his head to glance in my direction, I recognized him as the first boy I made friends with on leaving the nursery section. He was my friend Paddy Ryan, whom they'd nicknamed Smiler. A sturdily built lad of twelve with a mop of red hair, a podgy nose, and a pair of laughing Irish eyes.

He obviously objected to this newly arrived nun Sister Rose, and the discipline she introduced. Like several boys at the convent who had no parents, Paddy and I were often told by certain nuns we were orphans. As such we were unfairly treated by them and often punished for the slightest thing, when given an opportunity. Under intolerable conditions, every unfortunate orphan was made to suffer at the hands of those in charge. Children at the convent with homes to go to were never given the type of punishment meted out to us orphans, fearing they might upset their doting parents.

Breakfast on that particular morning was a solemn affair, eaten in absolute silence. None wishing to stir up a hornets nest, for fear of bringing the wrath of Sister Rose down upon their heads. As soon as the meal finished we left the dining room and filed out into the playground, with the exception of Paddy Ryan, waiting to be punished. Taking our hats and coats from the cloakroom we waited for the nun on duty to take us to school, in the nearby town of Littlehampton. Several among us stood close to an open window of the dining-room, and listened to the swish of Sister Rose's cane as it whistled through the air.

There was Bully Bromwhich, Dipper Dykes, Haystacks Jones, Podgy Barnes, Squeaker Smith, Lofty Towers and myself, arguing as to how many strokes of the cane she'd give Paddy.

"He'll get six of the best" crowed the fat boy, Podgy Barnes.

"He won't feel a blooming thing" choroused Lofty Towers, a skinny lad nicknamed the pipe cleaner. "He's sure to have a book stuck down the back of his pants."

"Ooh! I wouldn't want to be in his shoes" moaned boss-eyed Squeaker Smith, the snitch. "She's got arms like a big navvy."

Huddled together under the open window we heard Smiler Ryan's anguished cry of pain from inside the diningroom. Standing on tip-toe Podgy Barnes managed to peer inside the room without being seen then ducked out of sight, fearing he might be caught and accused of spying. Ashen faced and visibly shaken, he gasped; "Cor blimey they've taken Paddy's trousers off, and his bum's all red."

Turning on boss-eyed Smith the Squeaker, Podgy sneered;

"Dew Drop's lashing Paddy with the cane you were supposed to have hidden, you little runt."

It was at this point Smiler's angonized howls were no more than a whimper, then all was quiet.

"D'you think he'll be alright Brandy?" Lofty asked, a tremor of fear in his voice as he spoke.

"I'll take a peep, but you'll have to keep watch out for the sister on playground duty," I warned him.

A hurried glance through the diningroom window, sent a shiver down my spine. Sister Rose better known as Dew Drop had the sleeves of her nuns habit rolled up above the elbows, revealing a pair of muscular forearms an Irish navvy would have been proud of. Cane in hand she stood over the cowering Smiler as he struggled to put his trousers on, ordering him to hurry up and get dressed. Beads of sweat glistened on her forehead whilst the granite-like face showed not the slightest trace of emotion, turning from grey to red as a result of her exertion.

Moving away from the window fearing I'd be seen I felt a rush of blood surge through my body, and listened to the pounding of my heart. Somewhere in the vicinity the clanging of a bell, warned us it was time for school. My mouth went dry, and my garbled warning to the other boys went unheeded. "Let's go' shouted Podgy; and off they dashed toward the cloak room, with me in pursuit..

Hats and coats we'd hurriedly snatched from individually named pegs were put on in preparation for our daily trek to St Catherine's school all convent children attended, from the age of six to fourteen. This was the one place where I felt a certain amount of freedom, from the everyday fear I lived with while at the convent. Here I could at least enjoy a small part of my childhood, in the company of boys and girls from the nearby town of Littlehampton. One particular friend of mine named Paul Engle, gave me a weekly supply of comics such as the Wizard and Funny Wonder, which I had to hide when returning to the convent. Such things were taboo and frowned on by the nuns, who said they were unfit for young children to read and the work of the devil.

There were many occasions during my walk to school I'd stop to lace up my shoes, and whilst out of sight of our escorting nuns I'd meet up with my friend Paul. Together we'd wander around town. It was on one of our trips to Woolworth's, looking at various goods and toys priced from three pence to six pence, we met the village policeman. A blotchy-faced character with a large scrubbing brush moustache beneath a cherry ripe bulbous nose, nicknamed Spit on the Baton. Fearing the unnecessarily harsh punishment I'd receive from the nuns back at the convent if I was caught, Paul and I headed for the exit. Dodging in and out of busy shoppers, we hurried back to school hoping we'd be in time for roll call. Stopping only briefly to catch our breath, we looked back and spotted Spit on the Batton leaning against a wall gasping for air, his huge belly heaving up and down like a pregnant frog.

Paul's birthday was the next occasion for a another brush with the law, so to speak; a meeting that caused much laughter among the boys at school. Given a clockwork submarine for his birthday, he decided to bring it to school and show his chums. It was agreed we should all slip down to the boating pond on our way to cricket practice, that very afternoon. Without teachers permission we met beside this huge pond, where children of all ages sailed their model yachts. Removing the submarine from it's box Paul wound up the tiny mechanism, placing it gently in the water. Gathering speed it surged forward circling the water, to the delight of many boys gathered there.

"Gosh that's smashing," howled Lofty with delight.

"Why not wind it up again Paul?" pleaded Haystacks Jones.

A jolly good idea came the response from the rest of the lads, with the exception of Podgy Barnes.

"Submarines are supposed to go under water, so why can't this one," he argued.

Disagreeing with Podgy, Gerald Bromwhich the school bully butted in. "Why don't you leave him alone fatty, it's his birthday not yours. Maybe we ought to chuck you in the pond instead of Paul's submarine," he sneered. "You need a good ducking."

Sneaking up beside Bromwhich, a now frightened Podgy was full of apologies and, whinged. "Sorry Gerald, I was only kidding him you know."

Podgy watched in silence as Paul wound the tiny engine of his toy submarine, not daring to offer a word in protest. Waiting until Bully Bromwhich who scared him to death, was out of earshot, Podgy whispered; "Tilt the rudder up, Paul."

Doing as Podgy instructed, Paul placed his submarine back in the water. A gasp of alarm escaped the boy as his birthday present disappeared beneath the murky water's of the pond.

It's tiny propeller whirring madly caused a muddy patch to appear on the waters surface. Paul's look of surprise suddenly turned to tears, as Podgy taunted him.

"The blooming thing has been torpedoed" he shrieked, breaking into a fit of laughter.

A free for all developed among the lads, with fists flying in all directions. Bromwhich wasted no time laying into a squealing Podgy, who he blamed for the loss of Paul's submarine. Meanwhile the noise attracted the attention of "Spit on the Baton" the town policeman, who happened to be on his beat.

"What's the matter sonny?" he asked Paul, who stood crying bitterly.

"I've lost me submarine, mister," wailed Paul.

"You've done what lad?" said the policeman, removing his helmet and wiping a stream of perspiration running down his fat red face. Scratching his ginger mop he gave the boy a quizzical look.

"A submarine did I hear you say son," said the mystified policeman.

Seeing there was no sign of it he questioned the boy further; "But where is it then, son?" asked Spit on the Baton.

Pointing in the direction of the pond's muddy water Paul sobbed, "It's down there mister."

With a considerable effort the portly constable loosened his uniform jacket, and bent his huge torso over the edge of the pond. Scanning it's murky waters he turned toward the lad and sternly declared; "Er'e, are you av'ing me on son?"

"Oh, no sir" cried Paul through his tears, "it's my birthday present."

"It's stuck in the blinking mud" moaned Squeaker Smith, "cause I can't see nothing down here."

"That's because you're boss-eyed you daft bat" sneered Lofty.

Fresh arguments broke out among the boys, as to who was to blame for the loss of Paul's submarine. Raising an accusing finger in Podgy's direction, pint sized Dipper Dykes hollered. "You did that you big fat slob, I heard you telling Paul to make it dive."

With Podgy in hot pursuit young Dykes took to his heels and sought refuge behind Spit on the Baton standing at the edge of the pond, who at that moment was scanning the muddy water in search of the missing submarine. A stifled cry of alarm escaped the boy's lips as he collided with the policeman, sending them both headlong into the pond. A huge column of water shot high into the air, as the pair of them disappeared beneath the surface.

Dykes was the first to surface. Discharging a mouthful of muddy water he drew in great gulps of air and floundered about helplessly, in a desperate effort to scramble out of the pond. A nearby swirl of mud from the depths below marked the spot where Spit on the Baton the village bobby had vanished, leaving a stream of bubbles rising to the surface. Then like some prehistoric monster from bygone days, he made his appearance. Huffing and puffing noises like a wounded walrus escaped his lips, as he waded to the edge of the pond and clambered out. Seeing young Dykes he seized him by the scruff of the neck and shook the frightened boy, as if he were a rag doll, saying; "Er'e what's your blooming game sonny?"

"It wern't me mister" the lad pleaded. "I got shoved in by Podgy."

Looking toward a group of boys standing beside the pond he searched in vain for Podgy Barnes, who had long since disappeared from the scene. Warning the boy as to his future behaviour young Dykes quickly took to his heels, leaving a wet and bedraggled Spit on the Baton to trudge wearily off toward the police station to make his report.

Back at school Dykes was ordered by his form teacher to see Miss Malone the head mistress, nicknamed "Molly" by all her pupils.

A big buxom lady built to withstand the force of an earthquake, her well muscled arms were like the branches of a young oak tree. Waiting outside her study young Dykes shivered convulsively, more in fear of facing the wrath of Miss Malone than the wet clothes he stood in. Answering his timid knock on her door, she sternly replied; "come in."

With a feeling akin to terror his hand shook like a leaf as he reached forward and touched the door handle, causing it to rattle.

Irritated by the noise, the head teacher shouted;"I said come in whoever it is. Or are you deaf?"

Plucking up courage a shaken Dykes gripped the handle, gently pushing open Miss Malone's study door. Open mouthed he stood in awe of the huge figure of the head teacher, glaring at him from behind her desk.

"Well, she growled," peering at him over horn-rimmed reading glasses. "Aren't you going to close the door behind you?"

Unable to move, he stood rooted to the spot. Like the proverbial fly in a spider's web, waiting for the creature to devour it. With mechanical step he forced himself to creep forward and pushed Miss Malone's study door shut, then waited for her to pronounce sentence on him. Removing her glasses she placed them on the desk in front of her, and easing her huge bulk off her high backed chair, advanced threateningly toward the boy. Towering above the petrified Dykes, she thundered; "And what in heaven's name have you been up to, my lad?"

Waiting for the boy to speak she watched a large pool of water spread across her study floor, while it continued to drip from his sodden clothing.

"Sorry miss," a tearful Dykes stammered. "It weren't my fault, I was pushed in by Podgy Barnes."

"Pushed in where?" she demanded to know.

"T'was at the boat pond miss" said Dykes, gesticulating with his hands. Trying to explain to an irate head teacher, how it had happened.

"And what may I ask were you doing at the boat pond" she thundered, "when you were supposed to be at cricket practice."

There was nothing the boy could say in his defense, he therefore chose to remain silent. Losing patience with the boy she ushered the bedraggled Dykes out of her study. Rebuking him as he left she advised; "You'd better go and get yourself cleaned up. I'll speak to those responsible later," she warned.

During an afternoon break the children of class seven were assembled in the classroom, while she lectured them. Deploring their behaviour Miss Malone reprimanded those responsible for disobeying orders, declaring; "All games will be cancelled until further notice."

Turning toward Podgy Barnes whom she had ordered to face the wall, she hissed; "You, my boy will also remain in class during playtime, as further punishment for your part in this dreadful incident."

A murmur of disapproval from everyone present, spread through the classroom as she left. Many were keen sports enthusiasts, in particular Gerald Bromwhich. Pointing an accusing finger in Paul Engle's direction he remonstrated with him; "You're to blame Engle," he sneered. Shaking his fist in a menacing fashion at the boy. "You and your blooming submarine, you stupid idiot."

Stepping forward to protect our friend Paul, Paddy Ryan and I warned Bromwhich; "Lay off him, it's Podgy you should speak to. He's the one who got us all into this mess."

With a shrug of his shoulders, bully Bromwhich wandered off in search of the missing Barnes. The loss of his beloved afternoon sports, was a bitter blow to him. He now faced the prospect of extra time spent in class on lessons, which he hated. Upset at losing a golden opportunity to play cricket instead of wasting his time in the classroom, he plotted his revenge on Molly Malone the head teacher.

Waiting until the tumult and shouting had subsided, Bromwich and his pals had a surprise in store for the unsuspecting head teacher next morning.

"She's late," said Bromwhich irritably, "I wonder where the old windbag's got to?"

"Probably inspecting the loo" said Paddy, with a derisive laugh.

"She must have fallen in," joked Lofty.

Animated chatter among pupils in class seven ceased abruptly, when the door leading from Miss Malone's study into the classroom opened. She stood there like some feudal baron, looking down on his sujects. A formidable looking figure, her piercing blue eyes swept around the classroom. Satisfied she had the attention of the entire class, she addressed them in her usual authoritarian voice; "Good morning children."

As one, the class responded immediately; "Good morning Miss."

Holding everyone's attention she announced: "Each child will answer their name as I call the register."

Having good reason to feel peeved with his head teacher Gerald Bromwich made no secret of his intention to get even with her, and watched her every move. With purposeful step, she strode toward her desk. For such a large person she moved with consummate ease, squeezing her huge body between desk and high chair. With her foot on the bottom rung of the chair she hoisted herself up, and gingerly lowered her huge posterior onto the seat below.

As her broad beam touched the seat a howl of agonized pain escaped her lips, echoing round the classroom. For one of such ample proportions she leapt from the chair with the speed and agility of a scalded cat, propelling herself across the room. With a sickening thud she bounced off the classroom wall, landing in a heap on the floor. Her huge bosom heaved up and down like the roaring tide, as she fought to regain her breath. Then leaning to one side her hand slid down toward the wounded area of her posterior, where she gingerly removed the offending object lodged in her backside. Seeing a large drawing pin in the palm of the head teacher's hand, the children's laughter reverberated around the classroom.

"Will you be needing a stretcher miss?" Podgy Barnes asked, in mock sympathy.

"That's enough from you my boy" snarled Molly Malone, wincing with pain. "We can do without your sarcastic wit thank you."

Rising painfully to her feet she glowered at the class, noting many of them were quite obviously enjoying the joke. From a ghostly white, her face suddenly changed to a bright crimson. Trying to make light of her mishap she moved with determined step, to confront the class. Hands on hips and legs astride like some Sergeant Major on parade, she stood there in silence. With intimate care she studied each child's face, looking for some sign of guilt. Finding none she limped toward her desk and withdrew a heavy stick she used for a cane, and brought it down with a resounding whack on the desk top. Startled pupils sat in hushed silence, as she warned them; "Whoever is responsible for this shocking behaviour, will own up now." Adding, "the culprit will be found I can assure you." With a look of disgust at the silent class she hobbled from the room, saying; "You have two minutes to make up your minds, and if on my return the culprit has not come forward you will all be punished."

Her sudden exit from the classroom, signaled the start of a heated argument among those present. Several of us who were aware of the pranksters' name chose to say nothing, while the rest of the class squabbled among themselves. Secreted away in the far corner of the room Squeaker Smith was seen to whisper in the shell like ear of Kathleen Byrne, his girl friend at the school. A nonedescript shortsighted girl with thick-lens glasses and straight black hair, she had the usual basin crop style of cut, the trademark for girls from St Joseph's convent. While not accepted as one of our group of friends in the know, I felt sure Sqeaker had an idea who'd put the drawing pin on the head teacher's chair, and was now spilling the beans to the girl. Before any of our group could approach the Squeaker to warn him the classroom door opened, and in limped the head teacher, back to her desk. Carefully examining the seat of her chair, she eased her well proportioned rear end gently into place. Massaging it ruefully, with the palm of her hand.

"Well, have you made your minds up now? "she declared.

Hardly had the words been spoken, a hand at the back of the class shot into the air.

"You there with your hand up, come here" cried Miss Malone. A look of triumph on her face.

As if by some prearranged signal, every pupil turned to stare at the informer. It was as I suspected, Kathleen Byrne. Ignoring whispered insults and threats to her person from Gerald

Bromwhich's friends in the class, she hurried toward Miss Malone, who gave her a smile of encouragement.

"Come along now I'm not going to bite you," she reassured the girl. "Tell me, do you know who the culprit is?"

Without further prompting from the head teacher, she spluttered. "Please Miss, it was Gerald Bromwhich." And pointed an accusing finger at the boy.

In that instant Brommy's fate was sealed. Squealer Smith treacherous skunk that he was, had evidently overheard him plotting against Miss Malone, and snitched to the girl. Rising slowly from her chair she hobbled over to a white faced Bromwhich, sitting at his desk in stunned silence.

"So it was you my fine bully boy," she sneered. Seizing the terrified lad by the scruff of his neck, she lifted him bodily into the air. Tossing him into a far corner of the classroom.

"Face the wall," she hissed, "I'll deal with you later my boy."

Work in the classroom ceased immediately, when the bell for our morning break sounded. Under the watchful eye of Miss Malone class seven trooped into the playground, leaving Gerald Bromwhich to face the music. Above the sound of children's voices at play one heard anguished howls of pain coming from the Head Teachers study, much to the delight of many children present. Pleased to know bully Bromwich was getting some of his own medicine, on the receiving end of the weighty forearms of Molly Malone. But in spite of minor upheavals at school such as this, an atmosphere of friendliness existed between convent and town antagonists, and with the passage of time we learnt to value each others companionship. Often reluctant to leave them when it was time for me to return to St Joseph's Convent when my day at school ended, I felt an unwillingness to face the rigid code of discipline demanded of every child, and an on-going fear of those in charge. Yet for all the rules and regulations, and unnecessary harsh punishment from which many of us suffered, there were occasional happy moments in the lives of orphans. Scarce though they may have been. During the summer months we were taken for walks along Littlehampton's stony beaches, or down quiet country lanes in the beautiful county of Sussex. During rare occasions such as this, we managed to escape from under the watchful eyes of our escorting nuns. Only then was it possible for us to forget the convent and the constant day to day fear under which we lived, if only for a few short hours. Then like fledgling leaving the nest for their first flight, these all too short precious moments of freedom were ours to enjoy. There were occasional visits to Arundel Park, home of the Duke of Norfolk, some four miles walking distance from the convent. Although dog tired upon arriving at the park, we enjoyed it's lakes and wooded area's. A home for herds of deer, peacock, rabbits, pheasant, and other wild life who unlike we unfortunates, were allowed to roam unhindered. Here in this truly magnificent setting covering twenty one square miles of parkland, stands Arundel's Norman Castle. Built in 1066 during the reign of William the Conqueror, this ancient monument attracted visitors from all corners of the globe. Alas, our time in this earthly paradise was all too short when the raucus voice of the sister in charge could be heard, demanding we hurry up and prepare to return from whence we came.

☐

A Frightening Experience.

Mid-summer was a time of the year when nun's from various convents were sent on retreat, a period of silent meditation. It also brought about unexpected changes to our daily lives when Sisters Clare and Vincent left the convent, that summer of 1931. A kind and caring couple who could be strict when the occasion demanded yet were so different to some of those in charge of us, who at times were brutal. I myself had good reason to fear the new arrivals who took charge of the boy's domitory, where I and many of my orphan chums slept. Escorting us up to our dormitory we were told to stand by our beds whilst they looked us over as one would cattle at the local market, and seemed none too pleased to find one or two untidy beds.

"Don't you make your beds properly before going down to breakfast?" they asked Lofty Towers, who chose to ignore their remark with a shrug of his shoulders.

His lack of response seemed to infuriate the smaller of the two, who remarked; "I am Sister Anthony and this is Sister Magdelen; we demand obedience from all of you."

Rather surprised they would give her a name like Mary Magdelen, in all innocence I asked her; "But why did they give you that name Sister, wasn't she a wicked woman?"

Her cherry red face turned a deathly white as she came toward me, and angrily hissed; "What is your name, boy?"

Shaking like a leaf I stammered, "It's Ronald Brandon Sister, I didn't mean any harm."

Obviously not the type of person to forgive easily she brushed my protestations aside, saying; "How dare you speak to me in that manner, I'll remember you for this. Now be off with you boy, and watch your tongue in future."

For a moment I stood rooted to the spot, then turning away, hurried to join the rest of the boys. Past experience served to warn me this episode would not go unpunished, retribution would surely follow.

Of the two, Sister Anthony was rather small in stature with ginger hair, the look of an angel, and cold blue eyes hidden behind gold-rimmed spectacles that would bore into your very soul. Given to strutting around our dormitory like some ballerina with her nun's habit pinned up at the back, she became a target for much banter among the boys who christened her the "Peacock." Her companion Sister Magdelen was twice her size. Solidly built with exceptionally large hands and feet, a cherry red complexion that set her face aglow, and a pair of deep-set grey eyes. Aptly nicknamed "Shino," because the carbolic soap she used to wash herself with each morning, made her face glisten in the morning sun. Her strength was such that a well aimed clout round the ear from her ham-sized fist, was like a charge of electricity shooting through your body.

"You're for it now" whispered Lofty, watching the two new arrivals, Sisters Magdelen and Anthony leave the dormitory. "They're sure to be on the warpath, so you'd better watch out. Just look at the big one, she's built like a blooming battleship."

Much too late for regrets, there was nothing I could say or do to alter the situation I now found myself in, for I realized my slip of the tongue would get me punished. Little did I suspect an unguarded moment on my part would give them the opportunity they'd been waiting for, much sooner than I anticipated. I did however begin my summer holidays during that year of 1931, with mixed feelings.

Each morning the sun would appear in a cloudless sky of blue as it had done since early June, promising another prolonged spell of hot weather. Although for want of a good downpour of rain, fields of lush green pastures had now turned a golden brown. During the first week of our August holidays children fortunate enough to have parents, were given leave to spend time at home with them. Whereas orphans like myself who were few in number remained at the convent, never free from ever watchful eyes of the nuns. Adherence to discipline was maintained at all times in the convent, even during holiday periods. It was therefore up to each of us so-called waifs and strays, a name tagged on to us by the nuns, to stick together at all costs.

Daily walks down country lanes or visits to the beaches of Littlehampton and nearby Climping became part of our normal every day routine, during the long hot summer. Whilst strolling along Climping's shore one often unearthed a lost golfball, the result of a wayward drive from the eighteenth tee on the nearby golf course. Providing you slipped past the eagle eye of the nun in charge without being caught, the finder was rewarded, should they return the ball to a club member. Quite often a penny or two was given, depending on the generosity of the golfer in question.

During idle moments I'd nestle down amid a maze of sand dunes beneath a warm midday sun, content to listen to the cry of sea birds, mingled with the sound of waves crashing on the shore. In the midst of daydreams during moments such as this, I'd imagine myself a castaway on a desert island. With sea-gulls wheeling overhead in a clear blue sky, I'd feel warm sea breezes caressing me. But all too soon my dreams would be rudely interrupted by the voice of the nun in charge, echoing back and forth across a wide expanse of empty beach."Come along there Brandon" she would scream, "hurry up and get yourself ready to go back to the convent."

Rising somewhat reluctantly, I slipped my shoes on and joined the rest of the boys ready to leave the beach. A hurried check by the nun in charge, Sister Anthony, to make sure everyone was present, found Haystacks Jones and Paddy Ryan were missing. Ordering everyone to sit down she crept down to the water's edge, and caught them unawares.

"What are you doing Jones?" she asked the startled boy, as the bottle he'd thrown landed with a splash in the water.

His face took on a sickly white hue, when he answered. "Er, nothing Sister he stuttered," just having a laugh."

19

"Well, let's find out what's so amusing shall we," she sneered, sardonically. "You can fetch that bottle you've just thrown in the water for a start, and bring it here to me."

Stripped down to his underwear, Jones waded into the chilly waters of the English Channel. A foaming sea swirled around his lanky frame almost knocking him off his feet, as he grasped at the green bottle. Lifting it clear of the water he turned it upside down and shook it vigorously, in a desperate effort to dispose of it's contents. But to no avail. A piece of paper on which he'd written his message, refused to budge."You can bring that to me also Jones" she barked, as she watched him remove it's contents.

Jones's face turned a shade of green like the bottle he was holding as he approached Sister Anthony, and handed her a sodden piece of paper he'd taken from it.

"What's this you've written on here?" she asked, struggling to open the note Jones had given her. Her head moved slowly from side to side as she read the message the boy had written, then quite suddenly her eyes narrowed. The normally pallid face turned a shade of crimson;

"Did you write this?" she hissed."

"It was only done for a joke, Sister," pleaded the terror stricken Jones. Pausing long enough to catch her breath, she threatened him; "Just wait until I get you back to the convent my boy."

Fearing what might happen to him Jones was far from happy as he entered the convent gates that afternoon, his message intended as a practical joke had backfired on him. Instead of floating away toward the French coast as Paddy Ryan suggested it would, it now lay in the hands of the last person on earth he expected to receive it. With little chance to escape whatever punishment they had in store for him, he prepared for the worst.

Late that same afternoon Jones faced the wrath of Sister Rose, and Sister Magdelen, nicknamed "Dewdrop" and "Shino." Wasting little time "Shino" tore the boys trousers off and held him down, while "Dewdrop" beat him unmercifully on his bare backside. Each vicious stroke of the cane wielded with immense power, left huge red weals across the terrified boy's buttocks. Every swing of her huge arm, brought a scream of agonizing pain from the boy's lips.

Through the open window of the room where his punishment was taking place, the boy's pitiful cries for mercy echoed around the playground. A tremor of fear swept through each of us who witnessed this terrible thrashing the unfortunate lad received, from a vantage point away from prying eyes. A group of boys including Podgy Barnes, Paddy Ryan and Gerald Bromwhich and I, who'd watched this ordeal from start to finish, could not believe nuns were capable of carrying out such a barbaric act. This is surely where the teachings of the good book were tossed aside, we told each other. How could they treat children placed in their care, with such cruelty. Had they never read the passage in the Bible in which the lord said; "Suffer little children come unto me, and I will comfort you."

Evidently not, for there was never a spark of love or mercy shown to any child, from many nuns who had taken holy orders. They seemed to derive some form of pleasure in punishing orphan children, at the slightest provocation. Often referring to the old adage; "the sins of the parents shall be visited on their children." Those among us tagged as orphans, being made to suffer, unnecessarily.

Entering the refectory for our evening meal we noticed our friend Haystacks Jones, shivering in the far corner of the room. His pale tear-stained face, pressed hard up against the wall. This was a day when each one of us who witnessed this act of barbarism, (there is no other way I can describe it,) would long remember. An air of sadness spread throughout the older boys dormitory, when we prepared for bed that night. A feeling akin to revulsion at the inhuman treatment handed out to the unfortunate boy, was evident in our steadfast refusal to speak to either of the nuns that evening. Long after lights out I woke Paddy Ryan in the bed next to me and questioned him; "What did Jones write on the note he put in the bottle?"

21

I heard the sound of his muffled laughter, and his whispered; "D'you really want to know Brandy?" "Yes,let's hear it Paddy, but hurry up before old "Shino" comes round again," I suggested.

Listening to Paddy recite word for word the poem young Jones put in the bottle, caused a chill down my spine. It must have seemed nothing short of blasphemy to Sister Anthony, as she read each line which went as follows;

> Hail glorious St Patrick, came down one day
> And sat at my table, scoffing away,
> Like Oliver Twist, he asked for some more
> But poor old St Paddy, got kicked out the door.

"You're kidding Paddy I whispered," as he finished. "He wouldn't write anything like that, you're having me on."

"No, it's the truth Brandy. I don't know where he heard it, must have been from one of the town kids at school I reckon."

"Blimey, it's no wonder old "Dewdrop" went bonkers.We'll have to keep out of her way for a while, Paddy."

Our whispered goodnights to each other, were said none too soon. On well oiled hinges the dormitory door slid open and the ghostly figure of"Shino" appeared in the doorway, on her nightly rounds. Holding a lighted candle as she moved about, her silhouette cast it's ominous shadow on the wall opposite. Hiding underneath the blankets I closed my eyes and lay perfectly still, feigning sleep. My heart began to beat ten to the dozen, when I heard her creeping ever closer to my bed. Hesitating for a moment, she then moved nearer to me. A slight tug at the bedclothes was sufficient for her to remove the covers from my head, allowing the cool night air to caress my face. I listened to the sound of her heavy breathing as she bent over me, and in the light of her flickering candle studied my face for a while. Assuming I was fast asleep she slowly shuffled away, leaving me to ponder over the day's events and the merciless thrashing Jones received at the hands of "Dewdrop," alias, Sister Rose.

Such was the measure of his discomfort, he found great difficulty in sitting at the meal table next morning, with the rest of the boys. Huge red and blue weals across his buttocks faded with the passing weeks, as did the pain. But, the memory of his terrifying punishment lingered on. This would no doubt remain an episode in his young life he would never forget, leaving him scarred mentally if not physically. Time as always the great healer, allowed those of us who'd witnessed the savage beating of Haystacks Jones to quickly recover from the shock, as the final week of our summer holidays drew to a close. The promise of a warm sunny day for our mystery coach trip to an unknown destination on the morrow, caused excitement to run at fever pitch as night fell.

In the fading light of a summer's evening a gas lamp flickered, casting eerie shadows across a now silent dormitory. Whispered conversation among boys at the far end of the room having long since subsided I listened to the snores of my friend Paddy Ryan, sleeping soundly in the bed next to me. Finding sleep impossible I sat up in bed, and tucking my knees under my chin allowed my mind to wander at will. Where I wondered, would our forthcoming mystery tour take us. Deeply engrossed with thoughts of my own I failed to hear the tread of slippered feet moving furtively up the stairs, until it was too late. Alerted by a noise outside the dormitory I slid beneath my bedclothes pretending to be asleep, and watched anxiously as the door swung open. Through half closed eyes I saw the shadowy figure of Sister Magdelen standing in the open doorway, a lighted candle in her hand. Behind her a distant light from below the stairs outlined the figure of Sister Anthony, who accompanied her. With bated breath I watched the ghostly pair dressed in white night attire coming toward me, fearful of what might happen. With my eyes tightly closed I lay motionless, until the lighted candle held by Sister Magdelen was placed close to my face, forcing me to recoil in fright from it's searing flame.

"Why are you awake at this late hour?" she hissed. "You needn't pretend to be asleep, we were watching you sitting up in your bed."

In the light of her candle I shrank in terror, as the face of Sister Magdelen leered down at me.

"It's too hot for me to sleep," I stammered nervously.

"Oh! is it," she mocked. Then turning to her ever present shadow Sister Anthony, she sneered, "Did you hear that Sister, he can't sleep. We'll have to give him something to encourage him then, won't we."

I heard the rustle of garments in the darkness. Suddenly, two pair of hands reached out, and seized hold of me. Lifting me bodily from my bed they bundled me unceremoniously downstairs to the bathroom, where a bath of cold water had been prepared beforehand. Stripping off my night clothes they took hold of my arms and legs, and proceeded to duck me up and down in the water. My frenzied cries for mercy were stifled with a wet flannel "Shino" pressed against my mouth, to deaden the noise. Any attempt on my part to break free from their clutches proved useless, against such brute force. Every time I opened my mouth to snatch a mouthful of fresh air, they forced my head beneath the water, banging my body against the side of the bath. I felt as if I was going to die, when the bathroom began to cart-wheel around me. Suddenly the ducking ceased, and I found it possible to breath again. They then lifted my tortured body from the water, and in one swift movement, threw me onto the bathroom floor. I landed with a sickening thud, that jarred every bone in my aching body. As I lay panting for breath, Sister Magdelen threw a towel at me.

"Dry yourself boy" she sneered, "then get off to bed."

At the bathroom door she turned to look at me, and hissed, "let that be a lesson to you. Hold your tongue in future. You're just an orphan, a nothing."

Closing the door behind her I heard "Shino" mutter to her partner, before they parted on their final rounds of the night.

"That'll teach him to treat us with respect, Sister Anthony."

Drying my pain-wracked body I crept upstairs to bed. Shivering beneath the blankets with tomorrow's outing all but forgotten I lay there weeping, nursing my bruised and aching body. There was nothing I could do after such a harrowing experience, but cry myself to sleep. At the age of twelve and a half I was rather small in stature, certainly no match against the brute strength of a couple of nuns, determined to make an example of me.

A gentle touch on my shoulder next morning was enough to waken me, and opening my eyes recognized the friendly face of my pal, Paddy Ryan. "Wake up Brandy," he urged, "we'll be going on our outing soon. You'll have to hurry up and get dressed."

Sunshine streamed through our dormitory windows on that bright summer morning of 1931, but I could not bring myself to join in with the laughter and merrymaking of the other boys, getting ready for a day's outing. Removing the blankets covering my body, I noticed a collection of bright red weals on my arms and legs, that had turned blue overnight. As I rose from my bed Paddy came over to me, and asked; "What's the matter Brandy?"

Seeing the bruises on my arms and legs, he gasped;" Oh gosh, who's done that to you?"

Evidently he'd fallen asleep while waiting for me to go back to my bed, and had no idea what had happened to me. But I refused to speak of the punishment I received at the hands of Sisters Magdelen and Anthony, just to mention the suffering I endured caused my tears to fall too easily.

"Never mind Brandy" said Paddy, doing his best to cheer me up. "You'll have your chance to get even with them today. Just you wait and see," he promised.

His words of encouragement helped in some small way, to ease a mood of despondency I'd fallen into. Washed and breakfasted, we were all dressed in our white shirts, grey shorts and socks with white plimsoles, and prepared to board coaches waiting for us outside the convent gates.

25

"Don't forget to bring your football boots with you Brandy, we're playing a game today" Paddy reminded me.

Leaving the convent at eight o'clock that morning two coaches full of excited girls and boys set off on their annual outing, a day they would long remember. At the rear of each coach stern faced groups of nuns watching over us, called for silence while passing through the town of Littlehampton. Sitting with Paddy Ryan, Haystacks Jones, Dipper Dykes, Podgy Barnes, Lofty Towers, and Boss-eyed Smith, I listened to the football team captain Bully Bromwhich, discussing our annual soccer match against the nuns, due to take place that day. Well out of earshot, although we were being closely watched by our escorts who we were determined to beat, Bully's whispered plan of attack received the teams approval.

Down winding country lanes we drove in a northerly direction, across the beautiful county of Sussex. Past quaint little hamlets tucked away among rolling landscapes we sped on through the green hills of the Surrey countryside, and on into the county of Hampshire. Arriving at Aldershot we stopped at a small convent close to Aldershot's huge army barracks, where a group of nuns waited to greet us. Leaving our coaches we were allowed to wander around the outer perimeter of the barracks, to stretch our legs. Walking round the place we stopped to admire a life-sized statue of the first Duke of Wellington, Arthur Wellesley K.G. sitting astride his charger. Described as the most famous British General of the nineteenth century.

Lunch was taken at twelve o'clock that day and by one thirty all had been made ready for our soccer match to take place on a football pitch, inside the barrack grounds. Our team Captain Bully Bromwhich rubbed his hands together with a measure of satisfaction, when seeing a copy of the nun's team. "Here's your chance to get even Brandy," he grinned, "Shino's in goal for the Nun's."

Also included in their team was Sister Anthony, nicknamed the "Peacock." This dainty looking fleet of foot but nonetheless dangerous adversary when roused, was down on the team sheet to play in the half back position.

Prompt at one forty five p.m, the game started in earnest. Right from the kick off we allowed the nun's team to slip through our defence to shoot past our goalkeeper fat boy Podgy Barnes, who was told to let them have the first goal, to give them a little encouragement. From the restart we took control of the game, intent on giving them a taste of their own medicine. Trapping the ball beautifully, our outside left Lofty Towers passed it to Bully Bromwhich. On the blind side of the referee Bully dribbled the ball toward Sister Anthony, giving her a hefty shoulder charge in the belly as she approached him. Knocking the wind out of her sails, he left her lying prostrate and swung the ball out to Haystacks Jones, playing out on our right wing. Dribbling the ball upfield toward the nun's goalmouth he split the nuns defence and passed the ball across to me waiting in centre field.

"It's all yours, Brandy" he hollered, shove it in the back of their net.

We were now one goal all, and soon got a second and third, to make it three goals to one.

Coming upfield with the ball for my fourth goal I waited until Sister Magdelen the nun's goalkeeper nicknamed "Shino" had left her goal area, and came lumbering toward me to collect the ball. From among a section of the spectators, a shout of; "Go for it Brandy," saw me dashing headlong in her direction. Leering down at me as she had done during the night I recalled the pain and suffering I endured because of the brutal treatment she handed out to me, and I saw my chance to retaliate. Like an angry bull seeing red, I rushed toward her as she tried to pick up the ball. Lifting my right foot back I lashed out with all the strength I could muster, determined to score that vital goal. As the ball slipped through her outstetched legs into the net, the toe of my boot made contact with her right ankle. She gave a loud anguished cry of pain, and her shiny red face paled. Then like a deflated balloon she collaped in a heap in front of me, to lay writhing in agony on the damp grass.

"Er, sorry Sister" I mumbled, apologetically. Trying hard to suppress a laugh. "Soccer's a tough game you know," I reminded her.

Rushing back upfield I took up my position at centre forward, waiting for the game to restart. As the referee approached midfield for the kick off, protests from our opponents went unheeded until he spotted the prostrate figure of Sister Magdelen lying in the nun's goalmouth. A shrill blast on his whistle brought the game to a halt.

"What's the matter ref, protested Podgy Barnes, "why have you stopped the game?"

"I think she'll need help up there, he remarked; pointing to the inert form of Sister Magdelen the nun's goalkeeper, stretched out at the far end of the field.

"She's only kidding you," laughed our captain Bully Bromwhich. "I saw her eyelids flutter, so she's just having a rest."

As he spoke three or four nuns appeared on the field from various corners of the ground, and gathered around their injured goalkeeper. Putting her on a stretcher that had arrived on the scene they carried her off the field of play. Ribald comments from convent boys among a large gathering of spectators at Aldershot's Army Barracks, came thick and fast. "Don't forget the flowers" came the cry from one section. Followed by remarks such as; "Make sure they are dandelions."

Shouts of "Well played Brandy," greeted me as I walked off the field and entered the dressing room.

"She won't bother us for a while," grinned Haystack's Jones. "You didn't half give her a wallop, Brandy."

"Serves her right," said Paddy Ryan. "She got a taste of her own medicine, let's see how she likes it."

Throughout the rest of the day little was seen or heard of any of the nuns, who'd travelled with us to Aldershot. The "Peacock," alias Sister Anthony, who had a habit of causing trouble for the boys, was most conspicuous by her absence. It seemed as though she had decided, enough was enough. Right now at least, we were able to enjoy a certain measure of freedom, until it was time for us to return to the convent at Littlehampton.

Sunset was rather late as it spiralled down toward the western horizon, leaving streakes of red and gold across the evening sky. It was now mid-summer and for some reason the evening sun seemed reluctant to bid us adieu as it hovered above the rooftops, threatening to explode at any minute. It's sudden departure left us wandering about in semi-darkness as evening shadows drifted in, prompting one and all to hasten toward our coach. In bouyant mood we hurried aboard and sped away as darkness closed in. Beneath a canopy of stars twinkling in the night sky the sound of our voices raised in song, echo'ed throughout the silent countryside. Huddled together on the rear seat of our coach, a group of nuns listened in stony silence. Each with their hands tucked in the folds of their black habits, they sat tight lipped, looking straight ahead. Sister Anthony the "Peacock" lay slumped in a seat nearby nursing bruised ribs, as a result of a hefty shoulder charge from Podgy Barnes during the annual soccer match. Moaning and groaning she clutched at her stomach, while Podgy Barnes led the rest of our team who were singing to their hearts content. We had at last managed to settle an old score with our adversaries, knowing only too well there was nothing they could do to retaliate. It was accepted by everyone taking part in the game, as one of those accidents one encounters on the field of play, that left Shino and the Peacock nursing their wounds.

Arriving back at the convent later that night we were all rather tired, feeling the day had gone extremely well for us. Much better than we had dared hope for. It was however a pleasant surprise to find a rather subdued nun in the shape of "Dewdrop" (Sister Rose), waiting to greet us some time later in the refectory. Having missed the day's outing she'd already been informed of the unfortunate accident to Sisters Magdelen and Anthony during our annual soccer match, no doubt glad that she too was not in the line of fire. By way of a change she condescended to offer everyone a drink of hot cocoa, instead of chasing us off to bed because the hour was late.

Morning saw a change in the weather. Banks of sullen grey clouds rolled in across an angry looking red-streaked sky, with the sun struggling to peep above the horizon. As the sky darkened rain the size of penny pieces splashed across dormitory windows, leaving criss cross patterns on the dust-laden glass. As the summer holidays drew to a close we welcomed back those of our friends fortunate enough to spend a few weeks with their parents, which coincided with the departure of Sisters Anthony and Magdelen. Their leaving made life for the older boys at the convent more bearable, we now had two likeable nuns, Sisters Clare and Bernadette in charge of our dormitory. Unlike their predecessors who at times were brutal, this kind and caring couple treated us more like human beings. Always willing to lend an ear to any child with a problem. Their very presence radiated a feeling of happiness, where none had previously existed.

Back at St Catherine's school for the start of a new term in September of 1931 I saw many new faces among it's pupils, and as expected the enormous figure of Molly Malone our head mistress was there to greet us at the school entrance. Bell in hand, she waited until she could see the whites of our eyes before raising the heavy object above her head, then her arm sliced through the air in a huge arc. The clanging of her bell could be heard for miles around causing pupils to panic in their rush to get to school, fearing they'd be marked absent.

Mild sunny weather enjoyed thoughout the month of October changed dramatically at the outset of November, bringing bitterly cold winds with a covering of frost in the morning. A setback of little importance to those of us at the convent looking forward to the annual firework display on the fifth of the month, generally accepted as bonfire night. An event in the British calendar celebrating the failure of the gunpowder plot of 1605, when a certain individual named Guy Fawkes conspired with others to blow up the Houses of Parliament. Fawkes himself was captured hiding in the cellar below, and hanged.

Frowned upon by nuns at St Joseph's Convent, displays such as celebrating bonfire night were condemned as work of the devil. Possession of fireworks by any child was strictly forbidden. On the night in question all dormitory windows were covered with seldom used large wooden storm shutters, thus barring our view of this colourful display. But not to be denied, as soon as the night sister left to continue her rounds, shutters were quickly opened by Podgy Barnes. Squeaker Smith was then told to keep a lookout, and placed at the head of the stairs. As darkness fell the night sky echoed to the sound of exploding fireworks, amid a brilliant display of colour.

A huge bonfire in Farmer Williams field directly opposite our dormitory windows, cast an orange glow in the sky above. Skyrockets, roman candles and fire crackers all served to light up the night, providing us convent boys with a breathtaking spectacle rarely seen. A final series of loud explosions from thunder flashes accompanied by skyrockets streaking across the night sky, brought the firework display to a close. Only then was Squeaker Smith allowed to leave his lookout post and tumble back into bed, whilst Podgy Barnes himself hurriedly drew the storm shutters over each window of the now silent dormitory.

November's dreary weather having passed on, we faced an equally cold and miserable month in December. Outbursts of torrential rain tended to quickly freeze over, causing havoc underfoot. From the outset, skies of grey rolled across the landscape blotting out all traces of the sun, the sign of a bleak and bitter winter to come. Midway into the month fragmented formations of dark grey cloud running before bitterly cold east winds, brought winter's first fall of snow. At times drifts of four to five feet clogged the towns highways and byways, preventing children in many outlying districts from attending school. Adding to a cold and inhospitable landscape, snow continued to fall unabated, giving the place a touch of originality for our forthcoming Christmas festivities.

Preparations to celebrate this joyful event were well in advance at the convent, where a wealth of multicoloured decorations festooned our dining-room walls. At the far end of the room a large tree displayed an assortment of coloured fairy lights, twinkling among it's branches of green. A sizable amount of parcels having arrived for some of the children prior to the festive period, were kept for them until Christmas Day, when they shared with their less fortunate orphan friends.

Normally a time of goodwill to all people Podgy Barnes had an unpleasant surprise in store for Sister Rose, on New Year's Day of 1932, the last I was to spend in this house of horrors. On this one special day of the year boys and girls at the convent joined together for an evening concert, given by members of staff. A prelude to our party that evening was a customary bun fight between a team of boys captained by Podgy Barnes, versus the nuns, led by Sister Rose. Scheduled to begin as soon as the concert ended Podgy decided this was an opportune time to settle an old score with Dew-Drop, the only chance he was liable to get throughout the year. He chuckled at the thought of giving her a taste of her own medicine, without having to face the consequences. Eager to let battle begin as the concert ended he wasted no time in getting his team ready, and as the two sides faced each other he waited until he could get her in his sights.

The contest began at a furious pace, both teams hurling tightly packed balls of cotton wool at one another. Although these missiles dipped in french chalk left nothing but a tell-tale white powder mark, they were never intended to harm anyone caught in the line of fire. At least, they were supposed to be the rules of the game. All clean fun, but not in Podgy Barnes book. Inside each missile tucked away in his pocket, he'd placed his secret weapon. A stink bomb he'd been given by his friend in town, made especially for this occasion.

During a spell of heated exchanges, balls of cotton wool flew in all directions, the boys, determined to win at all costs.

Excitement reached fever pitch as Podgy took careful aim, when Sister Rose, alias the Dew Drop, came into his line of fire. With the speed and accuracy of an arrow shot from a bow the missile found it's mark, catching her on the side of her big head. Clasping a hand to her face, old "Dew Drop" staggered against the diningroom wall. A cry of pain was heard to escape from the thin bloodless lips. Slowly, the colour drained from her face as she sank to her knees, where she remained, until helped away by a team member. Minutes later a pungent odour of rotten eggs filled the room, causing one of the boys to remark; "She must have pooped her drawers."

Sullen grey skies and cold easterly winds sweeping up the English Channel gave ample warning of a spell of bitter wintry weather that lay in store for us, as we moved into the second week of January. Indeed our walk to school on Monday of the week that followed was quite hazzardous, owing to icy conditions underfoot caused by heavy falls of snow. Children arriving at St Catherines found their playground inches deep in a thick white carpet of snow, which soon turned into a battle-field. Snowballs flew in all directions until Miss Press one of the teachers who stood in for Miss Malone, put in an appearance.

Wrapped in winter furs, she stood on a cold snow covered playground. Bell in hand she waited ready to call children at play back to their classrooms. Unlike the rest of our teachers at school who were well proportioned, Miss Press was what one might describe as prim and proper. Slimly built and rather dainty, the dark brown hair swept back off her forehead emphasised the paleness of her face and her watery eyes, hidden behind thick lensed glasses. Nicknamed "Eggy" by pupils in her class because she was hard of hearing, they quickly realized deafness was no drawback to her. An expert at lip reading, children were careful not to make derisory remarks when facing her. Glancing nervously at her wrist watch, she stood ready with the bell in her right hand. Then raising her arm as if in protest, she shook it vigorously. It's urgent peals saw pupils hurrying helter skelter, back to their respective classrooms.

After a winter with more than our share of frost, snow, and freezing rain, the arrival of Spring came as a welcome relief. Stirred from their winter period of hibernation by the sun's warmth, primroses, snowdrops and crocuses appeared as if by magic in a vast array of colour. Gardens resounded with the song of the thrush, and chatter of the white vested magpie. Soon a chorous from the chaffinch, skylark and reed warbler along with many songbirds back from their winters retreat in southern climes, joined with the trill of the blackbird. A mixture of April showers and warm sunny spells encouraged forsythia's yellow blossom to suddenly appear, and sticky buds on horse-chestnut trees lying dormant throughout the long winter, began to shed their protective coats for a mantle of green.

A profusion of spring blossom during the month of May had all but faded with the approach of summer, by which time Podgy Barnes had been allowed to simmer down. His threat to get even with the head teacher, long abandoned. All was forgiven it seems, when Miss Malone permitted him to join the rest of the boys out on the playing field, at the start of the cricket season.

Mid-way through the month of July, Miss Edison our Gym Mistress, decided it was time the Morris Dancing team put in some practice, in preparation for our annual school fete at the end of the summer term. As a member of the team I welcomed the chance to get out of a stuffy classroom, to enjoy a breath of fresh air. In the midst of rehearsal our head mistress, Miss Malone, suddenly appeared, and was seen to approach me. As she drew near I could not but help notice her normally stern face wore half a smile, when taking a wooden baton used during the Morris dance from my hand. In a voice loud enough for everyone present to hear, she said; "You won't be needing this Ronald, you're going home to your mother."

Mouth agape, I looked at her in shocked surprise, and stuttered: "but I don't have a mother, Miss. You must be mistaken, I'm an orphan."

Seeing how upset I was, she placed a comforting hand around my shoulder, and said; "The Mother Superior will see you when you go back to the convent, Ronald."

A buzz of excitement spread among my friends from the convent, as word went round; "Hey, did you hear what Molly Malone just said, Brandy's got a mother?"

As though in a dream I heard the bell ring for the end of classes, and leaving St Catherine's school I arrived back at the convent, to be shown into the Mother Superior's study. Rising from her chair as I entered the room, she beckoned me toward her. Taking an envelope from her desk she withdrew a photograph and a document from inside, and handing them to me said; "This is a picture of your mother, who wishes to take you home, and here is your birth certificate. Your name is Charles, Gregory, Ashford, not Ronald Brandon."

"But I don't have a mother," I protested, "I'm an orphan." Sister Rose always made a point of telling me, I had no parents, which left me wondering who I really was.

Waving my protestations aside the Mother Superior rang a tiny bell sitting on her desk, and from an ante room a young nun wearing the white veil of a novice appeared. Taking me by the arm, she led me from the study into the refectory beyond. Sister Rose who took a delight in punishing orphan children, stood at the far end of the room. Her brawny arms, tucked in the folds of her habit. A wry smile replaced the mocking grin usually reserved for orphans such as myself, whom she could not abide. Her half-hearted attempt to appear friendly, did no more than turn her face, into that of a gargoyle.

"You'll be leaving us soon, Ronald," she cackled in her squeaky voice. "We'll be sorry to lose you."

What lies I thought to myself. Refusing to speak to her or even look in her direction, I walked right on in silence. Saying to myself; "And jolly good riddance to all of you."

Home with Mother

Because I was going home to my mother I felt somewhat bewildered and a little scared at leaving the convent, which had been my home for the past ten years. Even though I hated the place where the Nuns never tired of telling me I was an orphan and had no parents, I felt a reluctance to leave. Knowing nothing about my mother or any family she might have I was apprehensive, even a little frightened, wondering what the future had in store.But in spite of this, I looked forward to meeting her. If only to find out why she put me into such a place to be illtreated by these monsters, at a time when I needed her most. Her sudden appearance would no doubt turn my life upside down but at least it established my identity, for which I was grateful. A birth certificate tucked away in my pocket, laid bare the lies of those who told me I was an orphan.

On a bright summer's morning toward the end of July 1932, I bid goodbye to my friends at St Joseph's Convent. Accompanied by a solemn faced nun I was taken into the town of Littlehampton, to catch my train for London. At the railway station the nun chose to eye me up and down disapprovingly, saying; "Now don't move. You will remain here until your train arrives."

Pausing long enough, she rapped out a final command; "Now don't you forget to say your prayers."

So saying she departed, and with her went the last vestige of fear, under which I'd lived from infancy. No longer subject to a strict code of convent rules and regulations, a feeling of joy filled my boyish heart as I watched her disappear from view.

Feeling free to move around without permission I bought a comic from the station bookstall, something I would never have been able to do in the normal course of events. This type of reading material was regarded as an evil influence from the outside world, and strictly prohibited within the convent walls. Undeterred by threats that the almighty would punish me for daring to read such blasphemy, I buried my head in it's colourful pages.

Hearing the rumble of an oncoming train I looked up to see a column of black smoke puffing from it's chimney, and steam gushing from below it's huge steel body. As it drew alongside the frail looking platform where I waited, the tiny railway station itself shuddered. Smoke from the engine's squat chimney had already enveloped the vicinity, shutting out the bright morning sun. As it cleared a perspiring train driver was seen to lean from his tiny cab, wiping his sweat-laden forehead with a large red spotted handkerchief. Soon carriage doors flew open and weary passengers tumbled out, shattering the peace and quiet of a lovely summers morn.

"Is this the train for London?" I asked the man in uniform, who I noticed was carrying a green flag.

"Why, yes sonny" he replied, "but you've plenty of time. She won't be going for another ten minutes yet."

Walking along the platform I peered anxiously into each carriage window, until an empty compartment caught my eye. Entering the carriage I took my seat by the window, and suddenly my thoughts turned to the friends I'd left behind.

Remembering the good times we'd shared together over many years, a feeling of loneliness crept over me. Seeing they were no longer around I wanted to run back to the convent to be with them, but hesitated to do so. Knowing there was no way on earth, I would ever return to that place again.

Carelessly throwing his luggage on the floor of my compartment, I watched the elderly gent who'd just arrived curl up on the seat opposite, and fall fast asleep. He made no move as I brushed past him, and placed his belongings on the seat next to him. Using my small parcel of clothing given to me when leaving the convent, as a pillow, I settled back on the red and black upholstered seats. Admiring several photographs of distant holiday resorts arranged beneath the luggage rack, I listened to the old man's muted snores.

A shout of "all aboard," followed by a shrill note on the Stationmaster's whistle sent two bowler hatted gentlemen strolling aimlessly along the platform, scurrying into the carriage occupied by myself and my sleeping companion. From my seat beside the window I watched the Stationmaster, resplendent in his railway uniform, wave a large green flag. With an impromptu shudder the train jerked forward like a dog straining at it's leash, throwing late arrivals looking for empty seats off balance, as it crept forward. Inching it's way along the platform past groups of people waving goodbye to family and friends, the train slowly gathered speed. On leaving the station a magnificent view of the Sussex countryside lay before me, and a feeling of nostalgia rose within me. Would I perchance ever see such beauty again, I wondered.

Deep in thought as we sped through the rolling downs I kept asking myself; "How would mother recognise me?"

She had no way of knowing how I looked, seeing she did not possess a photograph of me. Shrugging off any lingering doubts running through my mind, I tried to convince myself all would be well. Meeting my mother for the first time in my life would I hoped, pose no problems for me when I arrived at London's Victoria Station. The photograph of mother given to me by the Mother Superior at the convent before leaving, would I felt sure help me to recognise her.

As the train thundered along at breakneck speed, I felt a cold draft from the open carriage window where I was sitting, tearing at my thin summer clothing. Pulling on a leather strap hanging below, I slammed it shut. The noise brought looks of disapproval from two fellow passengers who sat opposite each other in the centre of the carriage, noses buried in the financial section of The Times newspaper. Smartly dressed in pin-striped suits and bowler hats, they no doubt had been away on business and were returning to their offices in the city. Both in similar attire, they could have passed for twins. Seemingly not on speaking terms for neither one uttered a sylable, it was their style of dress that caught the eye, enabling one to make comparisons.

The elderly gent who lay curled up in a corner of the carriage fast asleep when I arrived elected to open his eyes and mumble incoherently, then promptly dozed off to sleep again. Comfortably seated on the far side of the compartment I decided to use my precious parcel of clothing for a pillow, and closing my eyes, lay there listening to the clickerty clack of the wheels as they sped along the railway track.

A squealing of brakes, awakened me with a start. Rubbing the sleep from my eyes I watched the bowler hatted pair fold their newspapers simultaneously, and look straight ahead. Showing little interest in any of the tall grey buildings we passed on either side, as we entered the City of London. A surge of boyish excitement overtook me as the train inched her way forward beneath Victoria Station's glass covered roof, and jerked to a halt. This brought an immediate response from the city gents who smoothed down the jackets of their pin-striped suits, adjusted their hats at a jaunty angle, and moved towards the door. Giving the old chap who had just woken up, no more than a cursory glance, they left without a word. Seemingly annoyed by such discourteous behaviour, the man passed no remark. A simple shrug of his shoulders was gesture enough to say, "who cares."

A look of concern spread across the gentleman's face as I made to leave. He politely asked; "Is there anyone here to meet you sonny?"

"Yes thank you" I replied. "My mother will be waiting for me in the station."

A smile creased his weatherbeaten face, causing it to wrinkle up like a sheet of brown paper, revealing a set of gleaming white teeth. With a nod of approval in my direction, he took his leave. Stepping from the train I followed on behind a group of travellers walking along the platform, hoping my mother would be waiting for me. Reaching the exit I handed my ticket to the uniformed man at the gate, and found myself tangled up among a couple of porters pulling trolleys laden with luggage, amid a jostling crowd. Some of them stood around as though lost and squinted anxiously at a huge indicator, obviously looking for the time of a certain train's departure. Others waited patiently on new arrivals.

Caught up in the crowd and unsure of my bearings, I was close to panic. On the verge of tears I wandered blindly along into the path of a young woman, with her back to me. As she turned I heard her startled cry of "Charles." When she hurried toward me, I realized it was my mother.

Of medium build with dark brown eyes that positively sparkled, she looked a picture of elegance in her smart black coat with soft fur collar. Worn at a jaunty angle, the stylish matching hat she wore, failed to hide her dark brown curls peeping beneath it's tiny brim. Brushing aside her tears she engulfed me in a warm embrace, and as her lips brushed my cheek I smelt the fragrant odour of a heady perfume she wore. Holding me close to her bosom she gave an involountary shudder as a tear escaped from her eye, to trickle down my face. Looking into her tear stained face I whispered; "Please don't cry mother."

Her hold on me tightened, and smiling through her tears, she murmured; "it's been such a long time Charles."

Leaving a noisy overcrowded Victoria Station behind us we walked arm in arm through some of London's narrow streets, where unfamiliar buildings towered above me. Hemmed in on all sides their closeness worried me, fearing they might topple over and engulf us. It came as something of a relief when we boarded a bus for Wimbledon, that thundered over steel bridges spanning the murky waters of the River Thames. Leaving the smoke laden atmosphere of the city for the outer suburbs, we entered the County of Surrey. Here one caught a glimpse of old world cottages, lying in close proximity to each other. Well-tended gardens, white-washed walls and neatly thatched roofs had much in common with the Sussex countryside I knew so well. Alighting from the bus in the picturesque village where mother lived, we walked but a short distance before arriving at her home. A recently decorated red brick house lay back off the road, it's garden displayed a variety of brightly coloured flowers bordering a neatly cut lawn. Opening the front door mother took me by the hand, saying; "This is your new home Charles."

From the rear of the house an elderly man appeared to welcome mother, giving me no more than a cursory glance as we entered the door. Tall, slightly built and thinning on top, a small tobacco stained moustache adorned his upper lip. Sharp featured with deep set eyes, the look on his face was one of annoyance rather than that of welcome. Mother introduced him to me as Mr Marsden my step father, but with no more than a curt nod in my direction, he was gone. Following close behind mother I entered a neatly kept kitchen where a young boy aged about two sat at table, and sitting in a high chair a child of about six months played with the remains of it's breakfast. Mother introduced them as Colin and Edward my new step brothers. Much too young to understand they simply stared at me, wondering who I was. Given time we would soon get to know each other, but first there was the problem of settling into my new home and it's strange surroundings. This I felt would take a little while, because of the strict routine I'd become accustomed to at the convent.

Rising at my usual time of six o'clock next morning an eerie silence pervaded my room, I missed the usual chorous of good humoured chatter among my convent chums. It seemed strange not to hear the sound of a nun's stern voice, demanding silence, or rebuking some child for making a noise, albeit under the threat of punishment for those who disobeyed. But as the days and weeks past by I became accustomed to my new way of life, although there were times when I felt a little lonely and longed for my orphan friends; Paddy Ryan, Haystacks Jones, Podgy Barnes and a few others. It was mother who encouraged me to join the local boy scouts group, that helped me get over the loss of my friends back at the convent.

There was little sign of a break in summer's stiffling weather for the sun rose high in the sky each August morning, to bake dry the parched green fields surrounding our house in the countryside. From my bedroom window I watched several white

41

butterflies fluttering around Mr Marsden's much prized marrows, sip honey from the flowers and deposit their eggs on it's leaves. Beneath a nearby gooseberry bush robins and blackbirds scratched at the sunbaked earth, in a fruitless effort to find a succulent worm. From her kitchen below I heard mother's call and hurried down for breakfast, knowing my step-father whom I did not get on with, had left for work. But it was not until we'd finished our meal and my offer to help mother with the dishes was politely refused, that she surprised me, by saying; "You'll be starting work soon enough Charles. Go and enjoy yourself with your friends" she advised, then added; "I must take you to see your Grandmother in London as soon as it's convenient. She is anxious to see you."

"Oh, do I have a Grandmother?" I said, "when can I see her."

"You also have Aunts and Uncles," she replied. "Some of whom you will probably meet later."

A sudden change in the weather during the first week of September brought gale force winds with heavy showers, preventing my stepfather who was employed in the building trade, from carrying on with his job. Taking advantage of this golden opportunity, mother beckoned me into the kitchen where she was busy with the breakfast that morning, and whispered;

"I've arranged to take you to visit your grandmother today, Charles, your step-father will take care of the children until we return."

My cheerful good morning to Mr Marsden when he came down for breakfast, was rewarded with no more than a grunt. He seemed quite upset and in a foul mood, simply because he was left to look after the children. Not wishing to remain in the house any longer than was necessary, I busied myself helping mother clear away the breakfast dishes. This enabled mother and I to catch a bus to Wimbledon, in time to avoid the early morning rush.

By the time we had reached our destination, the morning downpour was no more than a drizzle as we stepped from the bus. On entering Wimbledon's brightly lit underground station mother and I had to push our way through a crowd of people hurrying around in all directions, like bees in a hive, apparently off to work. Fearing I'd get lost in the melee mother took hold of my hand, guiding me toward a group of people entering a lift. Packed in like sardines with little room to move, I watched anxiously as the huge gates closed behind us. A gasp of alarm escaped my lips, when I felt the ground beneath my feet began to move. Mother's comforting arm around my shoulder put me at ease; "It's taking us down to our train," she said, "so don't get upset."

Without warning the lift jerked to a stop and as the huge gates slid open I hurried out, heaving a sigh of relief. Waiting deep below ground I heard a distant rumble like that of thunder, and a row of lights appeared from a darkened tunnel. Then as if by magic a train appeared. With a swoosh it hurtled past, and with a loud squealing of brakes began to slow down. As it jerked to a halt, loud hissing noises like that of escaping steam could be heard coming from beneath the train. Then silently the carriage doors slid open, allowing passengers to tumble out. Taking my hand, mother hurried me onto the train, saying; "Come along Charles, we musn't miss this train or we'll be late getting to your grandmother's."

No sooner had we settled in our seats and made ourselves comfortable, the doors quickly closed and we were off. As the train sped away at breakneck speed through darkened tunnels into the City of London, it's warmth and gentle rocking motion soon had me nodding off to sleep. Waking in response to mother's urgent call, I heard a voice booming out; "Peckham Rye."

Alighting from the train we found ourselves propelled along by a jostling crowd toward one of the many lifts available, and whisked up to ground level. Outside the station it looked as though the heavens had opened, the rain lashed down by the bucketful. Even so it was a great relief to see the light of day once again, ending my first experience on the City of London's underground railway system, which for me was not a particularly happy one. Peckham lies to the south east of the river Thames, among London's outlying districts. The area in which my Grandmother resided, boasted many beautiful old houses ranging in style from early Victorian architecture, to Tudor, and Gothic. Houses with holystoned front steps, brightly polished front door knobs, and letter slots of burnished brass, matched the crisply starched muslin window curtains. In essence these were accepted qualifications necessary, for one to be part of suburbia's select middle class respectability.

Welcoming us with open arms, Grandmother ushered mother and I into a spotlessly clean kitchen and gave us a much needed cup of tea. Small in stature, her once dark hair now streaked with silver and grey was brushed well back off the forehead, and tied in a bun at the nape of the neck with a black velvet bow. Her finely chiselled facial features, and dark brown eyes, simply oozed with warmth. A dainty lace collar adorned a black dress, hidden from the waist down by a beautifully starched white apron. Indeed she looked every inch the sort of Grandmother, loved by every child. Casting an approving eye over me she smiled, saying; "My goodness Charles, you've grown into a fine boy. Tell me, how were you treated in that convent."

"Not very well Grandma," I replied hesitantly. "They used to beat me quite often, I was always frightened of them."

"Well they can't touch you now dear," she answered sympathetically.

As though reproaching her for putting me in such a horrible place, she turned to mother, saying; "I never did trust those people, anyhow."

It was at this point a young man arrived, accompanied by a pretty girl.

"Come along and I'll introduce you" said Grandma, taking me into a cosily furnished parlour. "This is your Uncle Ernest" she said, as the smartly dressed young man rose from his chair to greet me. In his late twenties he was of medium height with a shock of dark brown hair, parted down the centre. His handsome features and charming smile, were without doubt, inherited from Grandmother. Then, turning to the young lady accompanying him, who suddenly started blushing, Grandma said, "this is Phyllis his fiancee."

Leaving us engaged in animated chatter Grandmother retired into her kitchen leaving the door ajar; the aroma of her vanilla pudding and freshly baked bread pervading the room. From inside the kitchen snatches of conversation between my mother and grandmother with reference to my recent homecoming, could be heard quite distinctly through the partly open door. I first heard Grandmother's voice, calm and precise scolding mother for not standing up to my stepfather, saying; "You should have taken Charles from that place much sooner, never mind his protests."

For a moment there was silence, then I heard Grandmother pleading with mother. "Why don't you bring Catherine home now dear, surely she would be a great help to you?"

Mother's response was cut short when Uncle Ernest decided it was time he left, and knocking on the kitchen door went in, closing it behind him. Sitting there alone, I heard my uncle and his fiancee in hurried conversation with the two women, before bidding them goodbye. Anxious to find out who this girl was Grandmother had referred to, I went into the kitchen and asked her; "Who is Catherine?"

My question earned me a sharp rebuke from mother, whom I noticed had turned a little pale, saying; "You have no business asking questions that do not concern you, Charles. It is also very rude to listen to other people's conversations."

From the tone of her voice I knew she had no intention of parting with further information, which left me wondering who this mysterious person could be. Avoiding an awkward situation from developing between the pair of us Grandmother announced lunch was ready, giving mother time to regain her composure. She seemed most upset that I should want to know the identity of this girl, and refused to tell me about her. During the course of our meal, Grandma suggested mother should arrange for me to visit an Uncle living in Downham, Kent, the following week. Feeling I might have a chance to speak alone with my Grandmother, I waited until the table was being cleared, before saying; "Would you like me to help with the washing-up?"

"Why of course Charles" she replied, and turning to mother suggested she take a rest.

Between us Grandmother and I cleared the dishes from the dinner table and took them into the kitchen, where she closed the door behind us and quietly remonstrated with me, saying; "Your mother was very upset that you should questioned her, Charles. There are some things we grown-ups don't like discussing with our children."

"But Grandma" I protested, "why shouldn't I know who this person named Catherine is. Can't you can tell me?" I pleaded.

Taken by surprise, she seemed quite concerned I should choose to question her on such matters. But instead of scolding me as mother had done, she drew me to the far side of her kitchen, and whispered in my ear; "Catherine is your sister, that is all I can tell you Charles."

I stood open mouthed and stared at her and as her words sank in, I said; "If I have a sister, why won't mother talk to me about her."

Hard as I tried to question her further, Grandmother would have none of it. With a shake of her head she stopped me in mid-sentence, and placed a finger to her lips asking I be silent. Her warning was given none too soon, mother's head popped round the kitchen door, and asked; "Have you finished helping Grandma with the dishes, Charles? It's getting late and I don't want your stepfather worrying."

With a promise to visit her soon, we took our leave of Grandma and set off for the station. Passing beneath railway bridges spanning the road, I noticed huge posters advertising Andrews Liver Salts, Cadbury's Cocoa and Craven'A' cigarettes. This it seemed was the only bright spot in an otherwise dull, and uninteresting part of the town. Life in the city itself moved at a fast and furious pace, but it's subterranean mode of travel both frightened, and excited me. My journey into London during the morning rush hour, had been far from comfortable. Herded into lifts like so many sheep, then to be dropped down into the bowels of the earth was for me, a simple country boy, a frightening experience. But for mother insisting there was no bus available, we were forced to take the underground train at Peckham Rye. Otherwise she said, we would never have made it back to Wimbledon, and then there would be trouble with my stepfather.

Our travelling companions on the journey home, were a noisy group of young men in sailors uniform. Their antics whilst boarding the train brought howls of laughter from the young folk, and looks of disapproval from the elderly. Anxious to find out who these young men were and where they were from, I asked my mother.

"Oh they're in the Navy" she said, then pausing a moment added; "Your father served in the Royal Navy for many years, Charles."

She rambled on talking quite freely about my father which surprised me, so why had she refused to discuss my sister Catherine, I asked myself. Was she living with my father, I wondered. Unaware my question might hurt her feelings, I asked; "What happened to my father?"

Her response was not immediate. Instead she just sat there like some statue, looking straight ahead of her as though she was in shock. For a fleeting moment I watched the beautiful face turn a whiter shade of pale, before she recovered her composure. She could not however suppress a tear, that fell from the corner of her eye. It hovered there for a moment, glistening in the pale light inside our carriage, before rolling gently down her cheek. When at last she spoke, her face wore a pained expression. "Maybe I should have told you long ago Charles," she murmured. "Your father was badly wounded during the war, and never recovered."

Placing my hand on her arm, I whispered; "I'm sorry if I've upset you mother."

"Oh that's alright dear," she responded. "You're not to blame. My loss has at times, been very hard to bear" she confided, then lapsed into a period of silence. No further word was exchanged between us during the remainder of our journey.

The evening sun had dipped below the rooftops by the time our train arrived at Wimbledon's Underground Station, and in gathering dusk I waited with mother beneath the street lamp's eerie glow, for the oncoming vehicle. Stepping aboard a Green Line Bus we sped off into the country, where the twinkling lights of the village welcomed us back home. Alighting from the warmth and comfort of the bus, we hurried to mother's house a short step away. I heard my stepfather's voice from the kitchen, as soon mother opened the front door; "Is that you Carrie. Where have you been all this time?" he grumbled.

Seated in a corner of the lounge I could hear him complaining, telling mother off for leaving him to look after the two children all day.

"But it's only once in a while Percy," I heard her say. "Surely it was not too much for you dear, it's rained hard all day so you couldn't go to work now, could you?"

"Yes I know that," was his curt reply. "But I couldn't put a foot outside the house, and I've got no damned tobacco."

"I'll send Charles up the road to get you some dear," she offered.

I didn't hear his mumbled reply as mother appeared from the kitchen. "Will you slip out and get your stepfather some Nut Brown tobacco?" she asked, pressing the money into my hand.

She no doubt had taken the money from her housekeeping allowance to pacify him, leaving herself and the children short of food. This kind of thing often occurred, because of his precarious job with the building trade. Prolonged spells of wet weather meant meagre wage packets, which were often the cause for much heated arguments between them. Thinking I was out of earshot my stepfather had on several occasions reminded mother that I was not his child, and therefore he was not responsible for my welfare. On one occasion he begged mother to give him the money for a packet of tobacco, then suggested she should encourage me to look for a job.

"He's thirteen, Carrie," I heard him complain. "There are boys much younger than him helping the family out, by doing odd jobs."

This confirmed something I was aware of from the outset, my addition to his family was most unwelcome. As far as he was concerned I was nothing but a burden to him. Although quite small at the age of thirteen I did have a voracious appetite. In all probability a legacy from my convent days, where we had to eat whatever was put in front of us. To avert any unpleasantness mother might encounter I decided to look for a job, and help out with the family budget. If only to stop my stepfather moaning at her, over what he termed as the extra expense I'd burdened him with.

My every effort to look for work during the summer holidays had gone unrewarded, and it was now time for me to attend school. Shortly before the new term began a representative from the Education Board accompanied by the school's head master, met all new pupils with their parents. Mother apparently knew the headmaster for they talked together for quite some time, before she introduced him to me, saying; "This is your new Head Teacher, Mr.Turner."

Tall in stature and sharp of eye he was an elegant dresser, who seemed quietly confident and sure of himself. His carefully groomed hair receding slightly in front and brushed back off his forehead, had a pronounced tinge of grey at the temples. His curteous manner and quiet air of authority, endeared him to pupils and parents alike. Slightly tanned, his brown eyes twinkled as he came forward to meet me. Smiling cheerfully he took my hand saying: "Hello Charles, how are you. Your mother has just been telling me all about you?"

During the course of our conversation, he suddenly asked; "By the way, how do you like being at home with your mother, it must be quite a change for you?"

"Oh! It's very nice here Mr Turner," I replied. "I'm really enjoying myself thank you."

"Then I'll look forward to seeing you at school, Charles," he replied. Shaking me by the hand and wishing me well at my new school, he left. As he walked away I had a feeling mother must have told him about the convent, and wondered why. She had especially asked me not to tell anyone, where I had come from.

With the summer holidays drawing to a close, my search for work was now limited to weekends. Unable to afford the bus fare I travelled on foot for miles around, calling at village stores I told them I was willing to take on any type of work. In howling wind and pouring rain I persevered, in what proved to be a futile mission. With nothing but a couple of jam sandwiches in my pocket I continued to trudge the streets in all weathers, without the benefit of an overcoat to keep me warm. Even the black plimsoles I wore, mother either picked up for a song at Paddy's Market in London, or won them in a raffle. They were much too large for me, and leaked like a sieve. At the end of the day I would arrive home worn out, and soaked to the skin.

Not until the month of November arrived with bitterly cold winds and night temperatures dropping below freezing, did my luck change. A chance meeting with my school chum Gordon Holmes who delivered morning papers for newsagents W.H.Smith & Sons, gave me the opportunity to secure work at his place. Of three applicants who had applied for the vacancy I happened to be the smallest, and as I stood in the manager's office waiting to be interviewed, my knees were knocking ten to the dozen. Eyeing me rather disapprovingly as one would a lame donkey, he remarked;

"You're a bit small lad, do you think you'll manage to cock your leg over the crossbar of one of our machines. The bicycles we use to deliver the papers, are quite big sonny."

"Oh I'll manage that easily sir" I replied, "I've got to get a job because my mum needs the money."

A wave of pity must have swept over him when he saw the hungry look on my face, holes in my threadbare jacket, and the toes sticking out of my black worn-out plimsoles, begging to be thrown in the dustbin.

"Alright lad let's see what you can do" he said, escorting me out of his office. Inside a huge packing shed he pointed to a row of red painted bicycles leaning against a wall, saying; "Let's see you ride one of these, son?"

Anxious to please I gripped the huge handlebars and leaped over the crossbar as though my life depended on it, and landed with a sickening thud in the saddle. The pain started somewhere in the lower region of my crotch, then shot up to my throat causing me to gasp for breath. An array of bright stars blotted out my vision, and in that short space of time I felt sure I'd done myself a mischief. With my pride somewhat dented I hung on grimly to the handlebars of the huge red machine and gritting my teeth, circled the area twice, much to the approval of the watching manager. "Alright lad we'll give you a month's trial. You can start on Monday morning" he said, then broke into a fit of laughter.

My day began with the muffled tones of an alarm clock waking me with a start, at five thirty a.m. Groping around in the dark I managed to switch the thing off, before it disturbed the rest of the family. From my bedroom window I could see the lights of town spreading across the horizon, for it was not quite break of day. Having little time to waste I slipped into the bathroom, and washed my face in water that chilled me to the bone. Slipping into my clothes I crept soundlessly down stairs to the kitchen, where I ate a large slice of bread and dripping mother had prepared for me the previous night. Taking my jacket from a peg on the back of the kitchen door I put it on and without making a sound, lest I wake the sleeping household, hurried out into the cold morning air.

With the wind whistling through a thin summer jacket I wore on that bitterly cold and frosty November morning of 1932, I set off toward Wimbledon. Quickening my stride in an effort to keep warm, my plimsoles tended to slip on icy patches in the road's frozen surface, forcing me to slow down.

Long before I reached W.H.Smiths newspaper office, a luminous glow in the dawn sky ahead warned me of it's presence. Beneath the glare of floodlights inside the depot, people hurried back and forth loading bundles of newspapers into waiting delivery vans. The clamour of men's voices issuing orders or exchanging pleasantries could be heard above that of the vans throbbing engines, waiting to take to the open road. As I stood watching this feverish activity taking place at such an unearthly hour, I was confronted by a tall freckle faced lad.

"Hey, is your name Ashford?" he asked, removing his cap to mop a perspiring brow. "Yes it is" I replied, "what do you want?"

"I've been looking all over the blooming place for you," he grumbled. "I've been told to help you with your paper delivery this morning, so come on or we'll be late. Customers are waiting for us to deliver their papers."

"What's your name?" I asked, noticing his close cropped head of ginger hair.

"Stuarts the name, but just call me Ginger. The rest of the lads do, so one more won't make any difference," he remarked offhandedly.

Signalling for me to follow him we entered a huge loading bay, where a row of red painted bicycles their carriers already loaded with papers, awaited delivery.

"That's yours at the end of the row," freckle face grunted, pointing to the bicycles.

I took one look at the size of the red monsters and stammered; "Have I got to ride one of them?"

"What's the matter, can't you ride a bike?" he said, with a grin.

"Why of course I can" I replied, with an air of bravado.

"But I haven't been on one for some time."

"That's ok" said Ginger, "you'll soon get used to riding it, just watch me."

He gripped the handlebars and in one swift movement that would have done a ballet dancer proud, he cocked his leg over the crossbar with the greatest of ease, and landed gently in the saddle. Admiring the boy's skillful manoeuvres I stood glued to the spot, in silent wonder. He proceeded to hop on and off the bicycle, with the ease of a bird leaving it's perch.

"That's the way to do it," he laughed. Then offering the bicycle to me said; "Here, you get on?"

I stood beside the huge red monster and eyed it warily. To me, a mere strip of a lad, the damned thing looked enormous. For a start, it's handlebars towered above my shoulders. Added to that a large carrier fastened on the front of the machine held a big bundle of papers, I felt sure would block my view ahead. Panniers on either side of the rear wheel crammed with papers posed further problems, if and when I managed to reach the road. Between the two of us, Ginger Stuart and I wheeled the bicycle from the comparative warmth of the loading bay, into the cold morning air.

"Here, take hold of the handlebars" said Ginger. "We'll have to hurry now we're behind time, so I'll hold the bike steady at the back while you get on."

Beneath the glare of street lamps I picked out patches of ice, glistening on the frozen road ahead. Eyeing that huge bundle of newspapers lodged in the bicycle's front carrier with some misgiving, I knew there was no way in hell I'd be able to see where I was going. I felt sure it spelt danger for me, but there was little I could do about it, my ginger haired companion was becoming impatient.

"C'mon Ashford he urged, let's get moving, we're late."

Easing my leg over the bicycle's crossbar, I felt quite comfortable as my foot touched the pedal. But no sooner had my rear end brushed the saddle, an unexpected push from behind sent me hurtling down the road, with the sound of Ginger's laughter ringing in my ears.

Gripping the handlebars, I hung on grimly. My view of the road ahead obscured, by a bundle of newspapers blocking my vision. By screwing my neck sideways, I somehow managed to steer the machine on it's downhill course. Gathering speed on the road's frosty surface the beam of my bicycles front lamp picked out a large patch of ice on the road ahead, and a tremor of fear ran through my body. It was far too late for me to do anything, disaster stared me in the face. Quite suddenly, my front wheel went from under me on the frozen surface, causing me to lose control of the darned thing. I hit the kerbside with a sickening thud, and hanging on for dear life to the handlebars, together we flew through the air.

A huge privet hedge surrounding a nearby garden suddenly loomed up ahead of me, blocking my flight path. Letting go of the handlebars I went sailing on over the top of the hedge, landing with a dull thud onto a well kept lawn. Newspapers fluttered around me, like confetti at a wedding. And brightly coloured stars exploded inside my head like a miniature fireworks display as I lay there, stunned and immobile. From some nearby dwellings a group of spectators who'd witnessed my early morning attempt at aeronautics, gathered around me. The babble of their voices, waking me from my stupor.

"I've never seen a flying bicycle before" laughed one bystander. "Don't think he's had much practice, his three point landing was lousy."

"I must admit he'd make a jolly good trapeze artist," joked another.

Scattered around me, the morning papers I should have delivered to my customers, looked a sorry sight. Then from out of the morning gloom my ginger haired companion arrived, and seeing my plight broke into a fit of laughter.

"What happened to you?" he mocked.

"You should damn well know, Ginger," I replied.

"It was you who blooming well caused the accident, wasn't it," I shouted angrily.

"Where's you're bike then?" he asked.

Turning toward the privet hedge through which I'd made such a spectacular entrance, I spotted my bicycle hanging at a crazy angle among the branches. It's lamp winking at me.

"There's the blasted thing" I snapped, pointing to the machine. It looked for all the world like something out of space squatting there with it's evil eye looking in my direction mocking me, daring me to move. The assembled crowd suddenly parted and the joking and jesting ceased, when an elderly gentleman arrived on the scene.

"Are you alright sonny?" he asked, as I staggered unsteadily to my feet.

Pulling out a few sprigs of the privet hedge that had lodged in my jacket, I felt the lump on my head and replied; "Oh! I'm quite alright now thank you."

"Are you sure there's nothing broken son?" he asked.

"No, I don't think so, I can still move my arms" I assured him, and started brushing off the last of the privet leaves stuck to my coat.

"Let's give you a hand to pick your papers up," he suggested.

Calling on everyone to help, newspapers lying about the gentleman's garden were hurriedly collected and placed in some semblance of order. Meanwhile, Ginger busied himself extricating one badly scratched red bicycle, none the worse for it's recent encounter with the privet hedge, from among it's torn and tangled branches. When the last of my damp and torn newspapers were gathered I thanked the people for their help, then continued on my way. Ginger, who sure was glad to see the back of me, gave a grunt of satisfaction when my last paper was delivered.

"You can take the bike back to the depot now" he shouted, waving me goodbye.

Worn out after such a traumatic experience I was not likely to forget in a hurry, I arrived home a tired but much wiser boy.

With constant practice during the passing weeks, I was able to handle the red bicycle quite easily. In fact I soon learnt all the short cuts on my paper round, which helped me finish much earlier than most other boys. This ruse allowed me ample time to read comics while waiting at the depot, long before they reached the shops.

Around mid-December a temporary slump in the building trade due to a mixture of wet and frosty weather, posed more problems for my stepfather who was put on short time. With mother having to struggle to make ends meet on her depleted housekeeping allowance, I took on an extra job of work at the United Dairies, helping out with Saturday and Sunday milk deliveries. This as I imagined, turned out to be no easy job. Starting at six a.m prompt and finishing approximately at three p.m, my day was spent scurrying around helping the roundsman deliver milk to his various customers. Carrying large wire baskets with a dozen bottles of milk at any one time, was no mean feat for one so small. At the end of a hard day's work for which I was paid the handsome sum of two shillings and six pence, I crawled home tired and exhausted.

There were however a number of men employed by the United Dairies as Company Inspectors, whose job was to check a roundsman's books, while the regular delivery man took his day off. I was, sad to say, rather unfortunate, when accepting a day's work with one particular character among them, who took a delight in playing tricks on boys he hired. Unwittingly, I was to became his next victim, having refused to heed a warning from several boys who'd fallen foul of him.

"C'mon son," he shouted to me as I made to get aboard his milk float. "Let's go" he yelled, and galloped out of the company's depot, giving his poor old horse a sharp crack of his whip, that stung the frightened animal into action. I barely had time to scramble into my seat beside him before he was off at breakneck speed. Shouts of derision from a group of boys waiting outside the depot greeted the inspector as we left, they obviously had a score to settle with him.

"Watch him Ashford they warned, as we galloped past, he'll leave you high and dry."

Shaking his fist at one young fellow shouting insulting remarks the inspector perched high up on his milk float seemed unperturbed, as we drove on. Sublimely indifferent to their taunts and cat-calls, his eyes were glued on the road ahead. He just sat there like an overstuffed statue of Buddha, seemingly immobile.

For a man of such enormous proportions he was anything but athletic, his movements slow and cumbersome. Content to allow the horse to trot at a steady pace he looked to neither left or right or spoke a word, just sat with the reins gripped in sausage-sized fingers of his podgy white hands. Beneath a grease-stained peaked cap strands of sandy coloured hair stuck to his thick red neck, overlapping the collar of his white shirt. Red cheeked and weather-beaten, the ginger moustache on his upper lip bristled like a scrubbing brush. Little was said as we galloped on and I wondered if he was cooking up something to catch me out, mindful of his habit of playing tricks on new recruits. As time went by and nothing untoward happened, I doubted whether a well intentioned warning cry of "Watch him Ashford," from an irate boy at the depot, was genuine. The man himself seemed quite amiable, becoming quite talkative as the morning wore on, even to cracking jokes. Was he by chance lulling me into a sense of false security, I wondered.

Outside a large brownstone house in the late afternoon, he checked his book, and said; "This is our last call son, we can go home after this one."

I was about to place several bottles of milk on the lady's front doorstep, when he shouted; "Don't leave the milk there son, take it round the back. That old dear's rather fussy," he said with a grin.

His friendly attitude gave no warning of the crafty move he had planned, when politely saying to me; "You won't forget to pick up all the empties now, will you son?"

At the rear of the house I found a dozen or more empty milk bottles on the old lady's doorstep, waiting to be collected. Quickly loading them into the two wire baskets I carried with me

I hurried back to the milk float, where the inspector sat waiting for me to return, a short distance away. Reins gripped in one podgy hand and his whip in the other, he waited until he saw me hurrying back with two baskets of empty bottles and burst out laughing.

"You'll have to run faster than that son" he shouted, "It's getting late."

Within striking distance of the milk float I heard the crack of his whip and a shout of "Giddy-up Lass "from the inspector, who lost no time in getting away.

Like a Roman charioteer he took off at breakneck speed, leaving me to struggle back to the dairy on foot with my heavy load. His mocking laughter ringing in my ears as he disappeared from view, safe in the knowledge another victim had fallen into his trap. Footsore and exhausted I returned to the depot to be greeted with ribald shouts of; "I told you so" from Spotty Wilson, who'd fallen foul of him the previous week. Throwing the baskets of empty bottles down in disgust, I waited for the fat slob to appear.

Grinning like a Cheshire Cat he came toward me, his fat grubby hand outstreched, offering me my hard earned money.

"Never mind son" he grinned rubbing his podgy hands together in glee, "You'll sleep without rocking tonight."

Snatching my hard earned money from his sweaty palm, I screamed at him; "You big fat pig, I'll never work for you again," and limped off home.

As Christmas approached a cold easterly wind brought winter's heaviest snowfall to date, and a lack of money in the Marsden household found me once again trudging down to the United Dairies Depot in search of work. Conditions underfoot were not exactly favourable for anyone standing around in such bitterly cold weather, but times were hard and like many other boys, I was sent out to earn a few extra shillings to help my hard pressed family. Grouped together for warmth, our numbers slowly dwindled as each milk float left the depot, and another boy was hired. Finally we were just three in number. From

Spotty Wilson came a warning cry of, "look out lads here comes Fatty."

From out of the depot came big Ginger the crafty Inspector, about to leave on his milk round. His appeals for help from us three boys waiting there, fell on deaf ears. Taking offence because we refused to work for him he made an insulting gesture, giving the three of us a two fingered salute as he galloped away.

A snowball thrown at him in passing by Spotty Wilson found it's mark, hitting the Inspector fair and square on the back of his big red neck. Giving a sharp tug at the reins the horse stopped, bringing the milk cart to an abrupt halt. He turned round just in time to see the three of us scampering out of sight. In retaliation he reported us to the manager of the depot, which led to the three of us being refused further employment at the United Dairies. Although the extra money did help, my situation was not desperate, I had my job at W.H.Smith delivering early morning papers to fall back on. My family could at least enjoy a decent Christmas dinner, then it was a case of waiting to see what the New Year had in store for us.

The Call of the Sea.

An urge to sail the seven seas when just a boy was certainly inherited from my father, who's career in the Royal Navy began at the tender age of sixteen. With schoolboy enthusiasm I was eager to learn about the great oceans of the world, and ships that sailed their turbulent waters. Desperate to continue my studies as we entered the New Year of 1933, it came as a welcome relief when I returned to school, following a period of idleness during our Christmas holidays. Among the school libraries collection of well thumbed books, a seamanship manual caught my eye. Inside I found a wealth of information concerning ships of both the Royal Navy and Merchant Service, to which I had a strong leaning. Whenever possible much of my time was given to studying books describing day to day life at sea aboard cargo vessels and ocean liners, their trade routes and various ports of call. There were also sketches of knots and splices, the ships compass, and a complete A to Z table on the morse code in which I was particularly interested. Whilst every available minute of my spare time was spent in the school library pouring over a dog-eared seamanship manual when others were out playing, I'd already made up my mind I wanted a career at sea, even before reaching my fourteenth birtday.

With my nose to the grindstone studying the rules of the road at sea, I hardly noticed the early months of the year slip by. As the weather warmed up during the first weeks of April, my studies had to take a back seat. Mr Taylor my form master decided he would like me to join the school football team, much to the annoyance of my stepfather who hated the game with a vengeance. Because it was necessary for me to travel to London to play matches each Saturday morning he became disagreeable and objected, saying; "You should be helping your mother out by working, instead of kicking a stupid football about."

Arriving home with my football kit one Friday evening, a look of concern appeared on mother's face."You'd better keep that out of sight, Charles" she warned. "Your step-father will have a long face if he knows you're playing football tomorrow, when you should be working."

"Oh, but I am working mother," I replied. "I'll have already finished my paper round by seven and the game doesn't start until nine," I protested. "There'll be plenty of time."

"Well, you'd better say nothing about it," mother advised. "He'll expect you to be out on your paper round as usual, when he comes home tomorrow, Charles."

Dawn was breaking when I left the house around five thirty the following morning and set off for W.H.Smith's newspaper depot at Wimbledon, anxious to make an early start with my deliveries. I had to walk some two miles to work, and the pavements were glistening with morning dew. Entering the newsagents loading bay, I caught sight of a familiar line of red bicycles stacked with morning papers waiting to greet me. Checking in at the office adjacent to a large packing shed, I wheeled my machine out onto the road. Making sure the load was secure and my tyres were pumped up, a brief glance at the depot clock told me it was six twenty and I was on my way.

Hurrying back home some two hours later to pick up my football kit in preparation for the game, I found the door to my bedroom securely locked. There was little doubt my step-father had done this to prevent me taking part in the football match. Without waking mother who was still sleeping, I slipped into the back garden. Taking a small ladder from it's fastening on the fence I propped it up against my bedroom window, which I'd been in the habit of leaving slightly ajar. Climbing into my room I retrieved the football kit I'd hidden under the mattress, and leaving the ladder propped up against the wall, hurried off to the match.

I arrived on the scene just as the two teams were taking the field and saw Dusty Mason our team's centre half, dashing across the pitch to meet me. "Glad to see you''ve made it Charles,"he grinned, "we thought we'd have to play a man short."

My appearance on the field as centre forward brought a chorus of ribald comments from a group of supporters, belonging to the opposing team, St Mary's, Clapham.

"Where did you find him" shouted a spotty faced lad from our opponents; "In a Christmas cracker?"

This brought a chorous of laughter that echo'd around the field. I was after all rather small for a centre forward at three foot nothing in my stocking feet, but being rather agile could leave the big fellows standing. Then of course there was my ill-fitting football outfit, a subject for much hilarity, causing a near riot between spectators from both sides. The football boots I wore were many sizes too big for me, and turned up at the toes. A pair of baggy white shorts fastened around my waist with a piece of string pinched from the neck of a spectator's dog, dropped down past my knees. Flapping about in the wind, they billowed out like sails on a River Thames barge. A green and white striped football jersey hung in folds around my neck, the sleeves hiding my hands. But in spite of being small in stature I was blessed with two nimble feet, capable of dodging clumsy bull-like charges of the opposing defence while the game was in progress. In doing so I managed to score a couple of goals, much to the delight of our sports master and the consternation of our opponents. As the referee's whistle sounded to end a game, which we won by a margin of three goals to one, I dashed off to the dressing room and quickly changed. Receiving a few words of encouragement from a delighted and enthusiastic sportsmaster, for the part I played in the game, I hurried away.

Anxiously waiting for me to arrive back home, mother sat by the front window watching the road intently, having good reason to be worried. Even before I'd reached the driveway she had the front door ajar beckoning me to hurry in, so I guessed something was amiss.

"Well how did the game go, Charles,?" she asked, closing the door behind me.

"Better than I expected," I grinned, "we gave St Mary's a right drubbing. Beat them three goals to one."

Taking me by the arm she led me out into the back garden, and pointed to the ladder I'd propped up against my bedroom window.

"Fancy leaving that there, Charles," she scolded, "you had better put it back where it belongs, before your step-father arrives. He should be home for his dinner shortly."

Replacing the ladder back in it's original position on the fence, mother suggested I wander off to the village and keep out of the way, until my stepfather had returned to work. He expected me to be hard at work on a milk round for the United Dairies. Mother I felt sure would say nothing to him, fearing the wrath of his tongue. Although the half-crown I earned would be sadly missed for the little extras it purchased, she said she would much rather do without, than have me working in all weathers, getting soaked to the skin. It was quite obvious mother never mentioned the incident about the ladder to my step-father, as he made no further attempt to stop me from playing football. Maybe it was a warning he received from the school authorities, who threatened action would be taken against him. He was told in no uncertain manner he had no right to interfere when I participated in school sports or other activities, which caused a permanent rift to develop between us, that never healed.

Having passed my entrance exam for higher education on reaching the age of fourteen I left the tiny elementary school in the village where I lived, to attend St Joseph's Academy at Lee Terrace in Blackheath, London, for the next two years. A non-coed establishment, it's pupils were taught by Catholic Brothers who insisted everyone attending the Academy, adhered to rules and regulations. Suitably attired in a school uniform of grey flannel trousers and green jacket with the school badge emblazoned on the breast pocket, and a green cap bearing two yellow rings, I was admitted to this seat of learning. The school itself was built of red brick, and lay in one of the more secluded suburbs of town, away from the hustle and bustle of daily life.

Because of ongoing discord that existed at home between my step-father and myself, it was considered necessary I be boarded out near the school itself. Accompanied by my headmaster Mr Turner who was shortly to retire, I was entrusted into the care of a Mrs Beresford who ran a small boarding house. A plump silver-haired motherly type of lady, the tweed suits she wore made her look even larger than she really was. Childless through having lost her husband shortly after their marriage in the early part of the First World War, she devoted her life to caring for young boys such as myself, in her well-run establishment. Proud of her role as foster mother to five or six young pupils, who affectionately called her Ma Beresford. Her black cocker spaniel, Sparky, a firm favourite with her charges, was often the centre of friendly exchanges as to who's turn it was to take it for a walk.

Discipline like everything else at the school, practiced over many years, was strictly adhered to with almost mechanical precision. In their teachings, pride of place was given to the study of religion. This often reminded me of my convent days where one's daily life revolved around catechism. The difference here being, one was not subjected to unnecessary and at times, brutal punishment I had to endure whilst at the convent. Sports such as cricket and rugby were played at various times of the year on nearby school playing fields, under the paternal eye of a Games Master. Tolerated as of secondary importance, the game of football, whilst frowned upon, was never discouraged. Tiny in stature and christened "tich" by my classmates who towered over me on the rugby field, my role as scrum half left me covered in bruises. Accepted as part and parcel of a game where I always managed to come off second best, my time at this school as far as I can recall, was a very happy one. Prior to my departure from St Joseph's Academy in 1935 at the age of sixteen I received a visit from Mr Turner, who acted as my guardian in the absence of mother. Asked what sort of a career I'd like to follow, my immediate reply, was; "I would like to go to sea." This brought a puzzled expression to his face.

"Why on earth do you want to go to sea?" he exclaimed.

Shrugging my shoulders I answered; "Oh, it must be born in me I suppose"

Responding with a kindly smile he answered; "Well if that is what you really want, I'll see what can be done for you."

Returning home shortly after my sixteenth birthday my step-father insisted I take a job as a grocer's errand boy with J.H.Sainsbury's, in the village. Seeing no prospect in wasting my time peddling a bicycle around the village, I wrote a letter to Mr Turner, seeking his help. His response was to inform my mother arrangements were in hand for me to enter a Sea Training College. He advised her, if it was a sea career I wished to embark on, courses in seamanship, navigation, and wireless telegraphy would be made available to me. As I expected my step-father accused me of deserting the family, at a time when he was hard pressed to make ends meet. Mother in her wisdom, decided it would be best to let me do what I had set my heart on, a career at sea. This however tended to cause ill-feeling between Mr Marsden and myself, up until the day I departed, to enroll at the training college.

After a cold and bitter winter with more than our fair share of snow we welcomed the change to spring-like weather, at a time I was destined to leave home, to learn about life in the seafaring fraternity. Venturing inside the portals of a sea training college accompanied by Mr.Turner, I was introduced to the officer in charge. Situated close to London's huge system of docks with the River Thames but a short distance away, from the college windows ocean going ships were to be seen going about their business up and down the river.

Built of white stone blocks the school had at some time in the past been used as government offices, and vacated when it's usefulness expired. Sectioned off into classrooms, each was used in teaching separate subjects. Pupils were allowed out during certain periods of the day for special lessons, such as conducted tours around London's dockland. This enabled them to obtain firsthand knowledge of work carried out on board ships, and examine various equipment used for navigation purposes on the vessel's bridge. By the time our training at the college had finished, pupils were expected to be familiar with the workings of ship's lifeboats, and had acquired a lifeboat efficiency certificate, with a reasonable knowledge of equipment carried in them in case of emergency. To me a country boy it was all so very exciting, just to sit and watch huge cargo vessels sailing up and down the river. All ships operating along the river would according to the rules of the road at sea, give way to large wooden barges moving up and down the River Thames, often seen with sails billowing in a strong westerly wind. It was also interesting to note, each ship had distinctive markings or colours on their funnels, indicating their trade route and the company to which the vessel belonged.

Filled with boyish enthusiasm I prepared for my first voyage to sea in March of 1936, having reached the ripe old age of seventeen. Failing in a last desperate attempt to obtain a scrap of information as to the whereabouts of my sister Catherine, from my mother, I bid her goodbye. Little did I imagine, this would be the last time I'd ever see her.

Accompanied by a Mr Appleton, one of our school instructors nicknamed "Seedy," I was taken to join the S.S Ardmere, berthed in London's King George V Dock. Expecting she was some luxury liner waiting for me at the dockside, imagine my horror when confronted by a rusting hulk ready for the scrap heap. No larger than a cross channel ferry running from Dover to Calais, her name was hardly legible beneath a thick coat of dirt and rust. Looking at this heap of junk, I felt certain she'd never been priviledged to feel the gentle touch of a paintbrush on her rusting steel plates in many a year.

"Have I to ship out on that,?" I asked Seedy, eyeing it suspiciously.

"Oh it's not that bad son," he said, weighing her up and down. "She looks a good solid tramp steamer to me. You could get a lot worse than her, believe me."

"Why do you call it a tramp steamer. There aren't any tramps on board, are there sir?" I asked, ignorant of the fact there were such ships known as tramp steamers.

Suppressing a desire to laugh he tried to explain the situation as briefly as possible, saying; "Large shipping companies had their own regular trade routes. Now and then they hire or charter cargo ships from small companies, without such facilities. Vessel's on hire travel all over the world and are classed as tramp steamers."

"I think you should take a look around the ship while you're waiting to sign on," he advised. "You'll find it quite interesting."

Left to roam about the ship's deck at will I wandered through a huge steel door leading into the kitchen area, known to seafarers as the galley. Approximately twenty feet in length and eight feet wide, a cooking range ran along it's entire length. For a while I stood admiring rows of gleaming saucepans, neatly arranged on a steel grating above the stove. Hearing the steel door behind me open I turned to see who it was and found myself face to face with a huge coloured man, as black as the ace of spades. His melon-sized grin revealed a row of huge white teeth, reminding me of a crocodile about to swallow it's prey.

"What you look for, white boy?" he asked.

Never having seen his like before, filled me with a sense of foreboding. Scared to death, I spluttered; "I don't want anything I'm just looking" and took to my heels. Making a beeline for the saloon, where I'd last seen Mr Appleton the instructor, who'd brought me on board the ship. Unable to find him I panicked and ran headlong into a weatherbeaten old man wearing a dark blue seaman's jersey, sitting out on deck.

"What's the matter sonny, have you lost something?" he asked, squinting through watery eyes.

"No" I gasped, "but I've just seen a great big black fellow in the galley. He fair put the wind up me."

"That's Smokey the ship's cook" he laughed, "comes from Africa. Oh you're alright now son" he assured me, "they don't eat the white man any more, they'll steal from you instead."

"Are you one of the ship's crew, then mister?" I asked somewhat hesitantly. His sun-tanned face cracked wide open in a shark sized grin, showing a row of broken tobacco stained teeth.

"Parker's the name sonny," he announced, holding out a calloused hand. "My friends call me Nosey," he chuckled.

As we chatted away Mr Appleton who'd been searching the ship for me, hurried towards us. "Come on son" he urged, "they're waiting for you to sign on, make it snappy."

Inside the ship's dining saloon he pointed to one of several chairs around an oblong table covered in a green baize cloth, and whispered; "Sit down opposite the shipping master, you're next to sign articles, son."

Smoke from a cigar gripped firmly between the shipping master's teeth, curled lazily towards the ship's deckhead and hung there, above his bald head. He was a solemn faced individual who took his time before choosing to look up from some documents lying in front of him, to study my face as I sat before him. Through the smoke filled atmosphere he gazed at me without saying a word, just chewed on the butt of his cigar. Balanced rather perilously on the end of his bulbous red nose that looked for all the world like an overripe strawberry, was a pair of gold rimmed spectacles. Leaning across the table toward me, he asked; "Are you the young radio op that's joining this ship?"

My response of "Yes sir," was answered with no more than a grunt.

From a black briefcase he withdrew a sheaf of papers, and placing them in front of him, asked; "Your name young man?"

"Charles, G, Ashford, sir," I replied timidly.

His pen moved slowly across the paper making a scratching noise, in rhythm with a dull throbbing sound from the ship's dynamo housed in the nearby centre castle. Without raising his eyes from the paper he was busy signing, his voice droned on; "Your age, next of kin and home address please."

He suddenly stopped writing to look up, and ask; "Do you wish to leave an allotment, sonny?"

His question puzzled me. The only allotment I had ever known was a small vegetable garden, rented from the local council by my stepfather. It was at this point Mr Appleton came to my aid.

"He wants to know if you wish to leave part of your wages to your mother, each month."

"Yes, I'd like to do that," I replied.

"Sign right here on the dotted line," said the Shipping Master. Pushing the document in front of me, he added: "I hope you are aware you've signed on for two years my lad, and thats a long time" he reminded me.

"Why of course sir" I replied, "is there anything wrong with that."

About to sign the paper himself, the Shipping Master gave me that (I told you so smirk) and murmured; "You'll find out soon enough, son."

Rising from the table I rejoined Mr Appleton who waited nearby, and left the smoke filled room.

"Well, what do you think of the ship," my instructor asked, as we boarded the train to take us back to the college.

Having visions of seeing a sleek white painted vessel like those you see in glossy magazines, I replied: "She's not what I expected and she is a bit rusty sir, don't you think."

"Ah, that's because she's been laid up. Once she gets a fresh coat of paint on her she'll be as good as new," he enthused.

Having had an opportunity to see the state of the vessel for myself, his attempt at presenting a glowing picture of a heap of old junk did nothing to boost my confidence. Her razor thin steel plates buckled like a concertina at the touch, and were it not for a multitude of cockroaches holding hands below deck, she'd have fallen apart. Built in 1917 during a time of war the S.S Ardmere a vessel of some six thousand tons with a flush deck and coffin stern, had little to offer in the way of comfort to those who sailed in her. Her crew from many parts of the globe were a motley crowd, to say the least. The native stokers came from Africa while most of it's seamen and officers hailed from ports scattered far and wide, throughout the British Isles. Mainly inhabitants of Scotland, the engineers complained bitterly about the state of her engine. Mention of her speed brought a painful grimace from the chief engineer who when asked about her performance would angrily declare: "She couldn't pull you out of your bloody bed."

Of one thing I could be certain, she was to be my constant companion for the next two years whether I liked it or not. Before leaving the ship everyone signing on was ordered to report on board at eight am, ready to sail on the morning tide. With this in mind I hurried home where mother awaited my return, unaware it would be many a long day before I came back. Recalling the events of my day I told her all had gone well, but I'd signed on for a period of two years.

"Two years Charles," she gasped in astonishment; "My goodness that's an awful long time dear, what will you be doing during that time?" she asked.

"We might come home earlier" I told her, to allay her fears.

As soon as the evening meal ended I decided it was maybe an opportune moment to question her once again, regarding the whereabouts of my sister Catherine. Offering to help her with the dishes I waited until my stepfather was out of earshot, before attempting to broach the subject. Whilst we were alone I seized my chance to put the question quite bluntly to her, saying; "As you are well aware mother, my one desire has always been to see my sister. It would be a nice gesture on your part if you could give me her address, so I can correspond with her while I'm away at sea.

She recoiled as though stung, causing the colour to drain from her face. A momentary look of fear almost akin to terror crossed her face, quickly disappearing as she regained her composure. Facing each other, we stood in total silence. Save for the ticking of a kitchen clock growing louder with each passing second, no sound disturbed the quiet of evening. As on previous occasions my request for information regarding my sister fell on deaf ears, which led me to believe she was hiding something from me. Were there skeletons in the family cupboard she dare not speak of, for her own peace of mind?

Bitterly disappointed over mother's refusal to disclose my sister's whereabouts I turned on my heel, intending to leave her in the kitchen. It was then I heard her anguished cry; "Charles!"

It sounded like a plea for help, forcing me to turn about. I could see she was distraught and on the verge of tears. Her quietly subdued voice faltered slightly when she spoke.

"You must understand Charles there are some questions I find imposible to answer, such as the whereabouts of your sister." Pausing for breath, she continued. "At the moment she is quite well, that is all I am prepared to tell you."

Reaching out she took my hand, squeezing it gently. Her voice hardly more than a whisper, she pleaded; "Please don't press me any further, dear."

Tears she'd fought to hold back suddenly cascaded down her cheeks, prompting me to place an arm around her shoulder. "Please don't cry mother," I begged her, "I didn't mean to upset you."

Through her tears she murmured, "I understand your desire to be in touch with your sister and I don't blame you Charles, but there are some things I simply cannot discuss with you."

Realizing nothing would be gained by pursuing the matter further I decided it was time for me to say goodnight, and edged toward the foot of the stairs.

"I'll have to hurry up and pack now mother" I said, changing the subject, "I'm due to report on board the ship at eight o'clock sharp in the morning."

"I expect you'll need an early breakfast then dear. I'll give you a call at six if that's alright with you," she replied.

Bidding her goodnight I retired to my room and busied myself with packing. Rolling into bed some hours later, I tossed and turned into the small hours before dropping off. In response to mother's early call, I awoke to a cold grey dawn and a howling March wind. Tiptoeing into the bathroom my ablutions on that particular morning were speedily carried out. With as little noise as possible I dressed, then gathering up my bags slipped down to the kitchen. At breakfast mother seemed rather reticent and withdrawn, certainly not her usual chirpy self. Quite casually I asked; "Is there something troubling you mother?"

Pausing for a moment she answered; "No, everything's fine, but why do you ask?"

It was then I detected the first sign of panic, a deep seated fear she was about to lose me again. Then with a sigh she said; "You're going to be away for an awful long time, Charles, but it's your decision and I have to respect that."

"Is my stepfather upset?" I asked, in an effort to change the conversation.

Although I did not see eye to eye with him, it was mother who had to live with him. Her well-being came first and foremost, if she was happy with him I was prepared to suppress my feeling of dislike for him, accepting things as they were. Rebuking me for mentioning it, her response set me at ease.

"The choice is yours Charles," she agreed. "There is no doubt the urge to go to sea lies deep within you and no one can alter that, and I for one would never try to stop you from going." As an afterthought she said; "Two years is such a long time dear, but you will write as often as possible won't you."

Promising to keep in touch I reminded her it would take us some time before we'd reach a port where I could post a letter to her, which according to reliable sources would most certainly be on the West Coast of Africa. Glancing at the clock I noted it was time for me to be moving and as I prepared to say goodbye, a feeling of sadness welled up inside me.

"I must be off now mother, everyone has to be on board by eight o'clock" I said, somewhat reluctantly.

Her arms reached out to me in a farewell embrace and as my lips brushed her cheek, I could see she was about to cry. "I'm going to miss you Charles," she whispered, and as she held me close I felt the warmth of her tears trickle down my face. "Go with my blessing dear," she murmured, "and may the good Lord keep you safe."

Slipping from the warmth of her embrace I picked up my sea kit, and stepped out into the cold morning air. Bracing myself against a blustery March wind driving dark clouds scudding across an overcast sky, I strode toward the bus stop. Sadly I was not to know this would be the last time I'd ever see my mother again, as I watched her waving from the doorway. With a final wave I walked on until out of sight.

Alighting from the bus at Wimbledon Underground Station I sought what little warmth there was to be had, hanging on to a hot mug of tea at the station buffet whilst waiting for my train. Journeying on through London I reached the King George V Dock lying on the north bank of the River Thames and through a thin veil of early morning mist, caught sight of the ship I was about to join. Closer inspection revealed the vessel's name S.S. Ardmere cut into her bow, the letters having long since lost their coat of white paint. Arriving on board just before eight a.m, a young steward directed me to a cabin, situated in the midship area, at the after end of the ship's bridge. Entering the tiny cabin, I knew how Alice must have felt when stepping into wonderland, everything was small and compact. The room itself measured barely six by ten feet, hardly room to swing a cat around. A bunk bed pressed up against the ship's side, looked cold and uninviting. A limited amount of daylight filtered into the cabin, through a tiny porthole. Steel outer covers referred to as deadlights attached to each porthole, were screwed down during stormy weather to keep the sea from rushing in.

In one corner of the cabin a wash-basin with rusting tap, from which water had long since refused to flow, was in danger of parting company from its fragile fastenings on the bulkhead. A tiny closet no larger than that of a sentry box afforded the only means I had, to hang up my clothes. Sizing up the situation I now found myself in, earlier preconceived thoughts of an easy life on the ocean wave soon disappeared. It was much too late for me to do anything but honour my contract. I was set to spend the next two years of my life aboard this rusting hulk, the rats had abandoned long ago. How the vessel managed to stay afloat remained a mystery, for as one member of the crew commented; "take away the rust and she'll fall apart."

Glowing accounts of trips to far away tropical islands one read about were as far away as ever, for me there would be no paradise where I was heading, more like purgatory. Ah, well, I suppose we all have to start somewhere, but damn it all this was rock bottom. I couldn't have sunk any lower if I'd tried. In deciding discretion was the better part of valour and I should knuckle down to it, I set to and unpacked my bags. Wardrobe space was at a minimum, almost non-existent. Not that I expected anything palatial mind you; but the place was so small, a mouse would have difficulty finding a place to hide in this rabbit hutch. A large drawer beneath my bunk seemed an ideal place to pack my small garments. Gripping two brass handles attached to it I gave the thing a sharp tug, and in doing so a large section came apart in my hands. My immediate reaction was to report the matter to the Chief Steward.

"Oh, I shouldn't worry about it son," he laughed, "the damned ship's falling apart, anyway."

In the midst of all the chaos a knock on my cabin door brought me face to face with my opposite number, a young radio operator named Perkins.

"Are you the new Sparks?" he asked.

"Yes" I replied," showing him the broken drawer. "I was just tidying things up in my cabin and I've run into a problem."

"Can you slip up to the radio room when you're ready," he asked, "there's a few things we have to sort out. So don't worry about the breakages, Chippy can see to it later," he assured me.

"Who's Chippy" I asked, thinking it was some kind of joke they played on new recruits.

"He's the ship's carpenter" said Perkins, "you'll find him under the foc'sle head." Then left me to finish putting things to right in my cabin.

Stepping out on deck I mounted a companionway leading up to the boat deck and knocked on a door marked radio room, situated on the port side of the ship. My knock was answered by a shout of; "Come in."

Seated at a small table Perkins the senior operator looked up from some papers he was studying, and welcomed me in. Tall and angular in appearance, he looked every inch a sailor. His suntanned face, creased up in the corners when he smiled. One could tell he'd spent much time in the tropics. Moving to one side he allowed me to squeeze past him into the cabin, which was much smaller than I had anticipated. Barely eight feet square, the room was filled with various pieces of radio equipment. On one wall a mass of dials, switches and clocks covered a large area of the tiny cabin, with barely enough room for a small table and rickety old chair.

"It's a good job we're both skinny" said Perkins cheerfully, "or we'd never get in."

My introduction to the radio room was an eye opener, the use of each piece of equipment being explained to me in detail. In the cabin, wires of varying colour poked out at all angles, attached to a profusion of switches. Numerous dials and flashing indicators, left me somewhat bewildered. As I took my leave Perkins asked;"did you get the drawer in your room fixed?"

"I'm afraid not" I replied, "I really haven't had the time."

"You'd better go and see the carpenter before we sail" he warned, "he'll be too busy later."

Clawing my way through a tangled mass of ropes and wires cluttering up the foredeck, I soon managed to get to the carpenter's workshop under the forecastle head. The place was in darkness, with no sign of life from within.

"Are you there Chippy," I shouted.

A shaft of light pierced the gloom and the door of his workshop slid open, no more than an inch or two. Inside the room a man wearing thick lensed glasses, squinted at me through the door's narrow aperture.

Seeing I posed no threat to the occupant, the door of his workshop opened, and the light spilled out. A wizened old man in torn overalls and open necked shirt stood facing me, and asked; "What can I do for you son."

He had more hair sprouting from his chest than on his head, which was balding and grey. His face was etched with deep lines, and wrinkled like a dried up prune. A legacy of too much time beneath a tropical sun, down the coast of West Africa. Examining the broken drawer I held in my hand, he gave a toothless grin, saying: "There's not much I can do with that my old son, it's knackered."

"It's the drawer from under my bunk and I've nowhere to put my clothes," I told him.

"What, you've no coat hangers?" the bald one said, acting as though shocked.

"I'm afraid I don't have any," I replied. "Is there a place where I could buy some?"

"Don't worry" he said, much to my surprise. "I'll soon find you something to hang your clothes on." From his workshop he brought a handful of rusting nails and offered them to me, with a heavy claw hammer.

"What are these for?" I asked, rather puzzled.

"Did'nt you want some coat hangers sonny?" he declared.

"Why yes," I replied,"but these aren't coat hangers."

"Are they not" he laughed, "and where the hell d'you think you are matey, at the bloody Ritz?".

Refusing to accept his offer of a hammer and nails, I returned to my cabin. As I left, a ripple of derisive laughter followed me. Retracing my steps back along the deck that had now been cleared of obstructions, an uncanny silence filled the air. No longer could we hear the shouting and cursing of men entangled in masses of wire strewn around the deck; all was as quiet as a cemetery. Longshoremen had completed loading their last slings of cargo, battened down the hatches and left the ship. All was now ready for us to sail on the midday tide.

Lunch was taken in the dining saloon earlier than usual, where my appearance was greeted with a jocular remark from Perkins my opposite number. "Come on in Charles" he said "you're lucky there's anything left, we've a right crowd of gannets here."

A chorus of laughter following this remark was not appreciated by Prendergast the ginger haired first mate, seated at the far end of the table. Tall and wiry with a pair of deep set piercing blue eyes he was a miserable sort of fellow, one had the misfortune to sail with from time to time. His short goatee beard of fiery red stubble hid the greater part of a deep-seated scar down the right side of his face, the result of a bar room brawl. When he was angry the ginger hair on his chin would stick up, like the bristles on a hedgehog's back. On the other hand a smile from him albeit a sickly one, was a rarity indeed.

A warning blast on the ship's whistle sent everyone hurrying from the dining room to standby stations; we were about to leave the port. From my position on the wing of the bridge I watched the pilot enter the wheelhouse, and give an order to stand by the engine. Moving over to the engine telegraph the duty officer pushed the levers slowly forward, warning the engineer on duty in the engine room on standby. The noise and clatter from the ship's windlass up on the fore'castle head suddenly ceased, as the last of the ship's mooring ropes were heaved aboard. Tugs secured to the vessel fore and aft took her in tow, easing her gently away from the quayside into the murky waters of the River Thames.

On a cold miserable morning in March of 1936 under skies of grey and drizzling rain, I watched my final link with mother fade into the distance. A stark reminder that she was now far beyond my reach, probably sitting down in comfort at home. Studying the shoreline I looked long and hard at the water that lay between us, before deciding it was much more than the few lengths of my local swimming baths, which was all I could manage. There was nothing else for me to do but knuckle down, and make the best of it.

Along the River Thames a gathering of vessels sailing in and out of the port sounded their sirens in passing, as either a hello or goodbye when ships of various companies chanced to meet. Approaching the river's estuary an order was given to stop the ship's engine, and the S.S Ardmere slowed down to await a launch to come alongside the ship. A stiff easterly breeze blowing in from the north sea tossed the tiny boat about like a cork, making it difficult for our pilot who had descended a jacob's ladder, to board the waiting launch. Standing on the bottom rung of the ladder as the launch arrived he swung about as if on a trapeze, and risking life and limb, managed to land in the tiny craft at the third attempt. With a shout of "bon voyage" and a wave of his hand, he disappeared in the gathering mist and was gone.

A force six easterly wind met us head on when entering the north sea, causing the ship to shudder each time her propeller left the water. Turning to starboard we took a southerly course toward the English channel, where a following wind on our port quarter continued to hamper us as we pitched and rolled our way south.

It was now time for my first watch in the radio room, which consisted of four hourly spells on duty with four hours off in between. On a rota sytem I was on duty from midday to four p.m, eight until midnight, then four to eight p.m. As I entered the radio room the duty operator took off the headphones, and handing them over to me he remarked;

"There's nothing to report at the moment and probably won't be for the next few hours, until we're clear of the channel."

Leaving the door ajar I sat gazing out to sea watching vessels of every description from huge liners to the small coastwise ships passing to and fro, heading for their own individual destinations. In the distance I could see the towering White Cliffs of Dover rising majestically above the windswept waters of the English Channel and in passing, I realized it would be two years before I perchance would see them or my mother, and home. As dusk gathered Perkins my relief arrived in the radio cabin to take over, and announced rather casually; "I suppose you know we're heading for West Africa, Charles."

"Seeing that we'll be away for at least two years, I don't suppose it matters where we go," I replied.

"No, I don't think it does really," laughed Perkins.

"Ah well," I said at length, "there's nothing to report so I'll nip below for a bite, I'm a bit peckish."

The wind had increased to near gale force by this time, forcing me to run for cover as I left the warmth of the radio cabin. Gazing toward the coast, I watched the lights ashore dancing in the darkened sky. From St Catherine's Point along England's southern coast, fingers of light swept across storm tossed waters, and as ever the lighthouse performed it's never ending task of protecting those who sail the seven seas. I was feeling a bit seedy by this time due to a turn for the worse in the weather, and much against an inner voice that bade me no, decided to take a chance and eat my evening meal. Taking my place at the dining table I was about to swallow a spoonful of soup, and was interrupted by a jovial devil may care sort of chap, who sat beside me. A little on the tubby side, a mop of fair hair matched his blue eyes that twinkled mischievously, as he introduced himself;

"Hello there Charles, my name's Gilchrist" he said, offering me his hand. "I'm the second mate."

Seeing it was my first trip across the briny and I was looking decidedly green about the gills, he seemed quite concerned and asked; "Are you alright?"

"I'm feeling a little under the weather right now," I told him.

With the ship pitching and rolling in seas lashed by gale force winds, each time she nosedived into a trough I'd get that sinking feeling. Then as she lifted skyward, it felt as if my stomach was trying to catch up with me.

"You'll have to watch what you eat" he said, rather sympathetically. "The worst is yet to come."

"What do you mean?" I groaned, as my stomach somersaulted.

"I didn't want to alarm you Sparky, but I guess you might as well know what's in store for us" he said, almost apologetically; "I've just seen the weather report, there's some real nasty stuff ahead of us out in the Bay."

There was a note of warning in his voice when he spoke, so I questioned him; "What do you mean by nasty stuff."

"Rotten lousy weather" said Gilchrist, a worried look on his face. "Not like the wind and rain you get at home, oh no, Sparky lad, there's a ruddy force eight brewing out there."

Whether or not it was intended to shock me, his remark certainly managed to do that when next he spoke: "I wouldn't mind that so much," he said, arms outstretched in a gesture of hopelessness, "but the arse is falling out of the bloody barometer."

Ignoring his seafaring language which had never before sullied my ears, I remained silent. How was I to explain to this worldly wise character that yours truly was brought up in a convent, shielded from the outside world and it's devilish practices.

When about to rise from my seat in the dining saloon I felt the ship give a sudden lurch forward and decided to hang on, as her bow dug deeper into storm tossed seas. A roar of laughter went up from those present when the contents of a jar of pickles shot across the table, landing in my lap. It was at this point I rose unsteadily to my feet, and scooped up the pickles. Taking them out on the open deck I hurled them overboard, while the ship continued pitching and rolling head on into mountainous gale-swept seas. Approaching my cabin I received a timely word of warning from Barker the second steward, a real old salt who'd travelled far and wide.

"Batten yourself down tonight young fellow," he advised, "and make sure your porthole's screwed down tight or you'll get washed out of your cabin."

Moving about inside my cabin on unsteady legs, I managed with some difficulty to securely fasten the porthole and deadlight. All this time the ship bounced around like an Egytian belly dancer in the teeth of the gale, while I hung on desperately to whatever I could, until the task in hand was accomplished. Feeling the need for some shut eye I lay prostrate on my bunk, praying the ship's bulkhead would not cave in each time a huge wave thudded against it. With clockwork precision, she buried her bows in the raging seas. Each time her propeller left the water to thrash the air, it shook the vessel from stem to stern like a rag doll. With a force eight south westerly gale blowing we made little headway against mountainous seas, ducking and diving our way across the Bay of Biscay.

"Come on now Sparks show a leg there" came the raucus voice of the seaman who leaned over my bunk to wake me, saying; "It's almost midnight, and time you were on duty."

Water dripping from his sou'wester splashed all over my face, causing me to stagger from my bunk on leaden legs. Sinking into a nearby chair I tried to focus my bloodshot eyes on the cabin door, where the seaman who had just roused me waited for me to get dressed. Wrapped in heavy oilskins and thick rubber seaboots, his craggy face took on a ruddy glow from the light in my cabin. Water continued to drip from the clothing he wore whilst he watched me dress, leaving a large puddle on the floor.

"What's the weather like?" I asked him.

"It's not fit for a dog to be out in young sir," he replied, "and what's more there's a howling bloody gale outside. You'd better put a warm coat on" he suggested, blowing on his fingers.

"Why, is it that cold out there" I said, unprepared for his response.

About to leave my cabin, the old seaman turned and laughed, saying; "Cold, did you say Sparky." Then putting his shoulder to my cabin door pushed and held it open against the gale force wind, allowing a rush of cold air to fill the cabin, and stepped out on deck.

"It's enough to freeze the balls off a brass monkey out here" he hollered and slamming my door shut, he left.

Heeding the old seaman's advice I donned a warm duffle coat and small woollen hat, in preparation to face the elements. Driving rain and a fierce wind hit me head on as I stepped out on the open deck, knocking the breath out of me. It's sheer intensity flattened me against the bulkhead outside my cabin, delaying my dash for cover..

Ahead of me lay a companionway I had somehow to climb, before reaching the comfort of the radio room. Gripping a small safety rail I planned my next move. Watching each huge wave as it crashed on the ship's deck, filled me with foreboding. I began to have second thoughts about my choice of a career at sea.

"What on earth am I doing out here in the middle of nowhere?" I said to myself, as great lumps of water thudded against the bulkhead in front of me. I guess it was too late now for regrets, the die was cast and I jolly well had to get on with it. Releasing my frozen grip on the safety rail I scrambled over towards the companionway, dashing up the steps two at a time. It was at this precise moment this floating scrap-heap gave a funny sort of twist and roll, leaving me hanging on to the handrail by my finger tips. A huge green sea sweeping over the deck below covered me with salt spray as I hung there helpless, too frightened to move. Minutes later I managed to claw my way to safety, reaching the radio room on the upper deck. Soaked to the skin the cabin's inner warmth came as a great relief from the bitter cold and hurricane force winds, that had been my sad misfortune to encounter on this my first trip to sea.

"Hello young fellow you've made it," laughed Perkins, who I was about to relieve. "Take a seat while I give you all the gen."

There had been a distress signal from a small coasting vessel lying off Cape Finisterre, he told me. I could see he'd already marked the area on a chart, lying on the table in front of him.

She had apparently developed engine trouble, and was now wallowing in a heavy swell off the north west coast of Spain.

"I'm afraid we can't do anything for her" said Perkins the duty radio operator, "we're miles out of reach."

Looking at a map of Europe hanging on the wall he pointed to Ushant on the French coast. "This is our present position, Charles," he said. "But I guess they'll have problems up on the bridge, keeping clear of these French fishing trawlers. The trouble is, they have their blasted nets spread-eagled all over the place right now. Never mind that's his pigeon grinned Perkins pointing to the navigation officer up on the bridge, busy pouring over maps in the chart room.

It was just after midnight when he left the radio room, bidding me goodnight. Standing in the open doorway my attention was drawn to a collection of small white lights, dotted around the Bay of Biscay. I had no doubt these were the fishing trawlers I'd heard Prendergast the first mate, complain of earlier in the evening, when asking my companion; "Can you speak French?"

"Why, what's the matter?" Perkins asked him.

"Oh, it's those bloody French trawlers, with their damn nets strung out all over the place," moaned old Prendergast. "Every time I come through this blasted place, it's always awash with the damned fools."

"I told him there was nothing I could do to help him," grinned Perkins. "I don't savvy the lingo any better than you Mr Prendergast," he confessed. And with that he bid me goodnight.

Closing the door of the radio room behind me I slumped down into a battered armchair, our only means of snatching a rest in such a confined space. Looking through an open porthole I winced every time mountainous seas crashed down on the ship's paper-thin steel deck, causing her to roll on her beam ends. Suddenly her bows disappeared into an ever deep trough of foaming green ocean, she seemed unable to surface as her propeller thrashed the air, shaking the very guts out of her. My God, I gasped, as another gigantic wave smashed against the ship's side, standing the old tub on her beam ends. What on earth made me decide to go to sea, I asked myself. Slipping from the radio cabin I staggered out on deck and managed to reach the bridge, where I spotted Gilchrist the second mate busy pouring over his charts.

"Hello young Sparks, what can I do for you at this ungodly hour of the morning" he asked, as I toppled head first into the open doorway of his chartroom.

"God, I feel awful" I said, collapsing into an empty chair near his desk.

"I know what you're going through my old son" he said, with a sympathetic smile. "We've all had our share of it at one time or another. "Stay on dry tack" he advised. "And mind you leave the greasy food alone."

At the very mention of the word grease a sickly feeling hit my stomach, causing it to cartwheel around like a mad thing, completly out of control.

"You'd better stay out in the fresh air" Gilchrist suggested, "the stuffy atmosphere of the cabin will make you feel worse."

Hurrying back to the radio room I sat close to the open door, allowing the cold wind and salt spray to do it's worst. It was either kill or cure, anything to stave off an attack of sea-sickness which I felt sure was inevitable. If my memory serves me right, the next three days were a nightmare. Like a fish out of water I lay motionless on the cold steel deck while huge green seas washed over me each time she nose-dived into a trough, giving my stomach a chance to empty out a little more. Although by nature I was inclined to be quite skinny, my stomach seemed to swell up like a poisoned pup's. In short, I looked like a pregnant broom handle.

At lunch time Barker our second steward, a kindly soul with my best interests at heart, found me stretched out on deck. I simply lay there like a corpse waiting for the hearse to arrive, so he thought he'd do me a favour. Peering closely into my deathly white face, his soothing voice begged; "Ain't yer gonna eat something, Sparky, lad."

I winced involuntarily. "Oh God, no," I groaned.

But there was no stopping him. He went on to say;"We've got some nice juicy pork chops on the menu, son," making a determind effort to coax me into the dining room. "We don't want to waste them now, do we lad?" he chided.

It's effect was to urge me to be violently sick. My stomach spun around like a ferris wheel, and everything I'd eaten in the last two days was quickly regurgitated.

In a state of collapse, I was lifted bodily from my watery surroundings, into the warmth and comfort of my cabin. A sedative from the Chief Steward, who incidentally issued all medicines on board in the absence of a doctor, enabled me to drop off into a much needed sleep. Forty eight hours had now elapsed since I was unavoidably incarcerated in my bunk. During that time the weather had abated somewhat, causing me no further bouts of sickness, although my innards felt they didn't belong to me. Rounding Cape Finisterre off the northwest tip of Spain heavy showers accompanied by a huge sea swell, replaced the gale force winds we'd become accustomed to, causing the ship to roll and swing about like a pendulum. Although my bout of sickness over the past few days had eased off, I'd yet to regain my sea legs. Life became more tolerable once we'd entered calmer waters of the South Atlantic.

Deck chairs which had been stowed away and almost forgotten, suddenly appeared as if by magic. Allowing off duty personnel, to enjoy a well earned spell of sunbathing. Wooden decks encrusted white with salt from rough sea's continuously washing over the ship, were now carefully hosed down after treatment to clean them. It was at this point in the voyage I first met Frederick Collie the ship's Captain, who'd seen service in the Royal Navy, and hailed from the Isle of Man. Small in stature, a large hooked nose covered in a mass of black hair took pride of place on his craggy weather-beaten face. In keeping with his Naval tradition he carried out an inspection of his ship each Monday morning, as regular as clockwork. One would think he was still in command of a naval vessel instead of a rusty old tramp steamer, ready for the scrap heap. His team which included the First Mate, Chief Engineer and Chief Steward stood to attention on deck each Monday morning in their Sunday best, and saluting Herr Capitain, followed him around the ship on his inspection. Gold braid glinting in the morning sunshine they saluted each other in true naval fashion, and dispersed when the meeting had finished. Which I considered was a bit much, for a rusty old tramp steamer.

As an innocent bystander drinking a mug of tea in the ship's galley, I watched the inspection team pass me by and listened to one seaman's description of his captain. "Ere," said Nosey Parker to Jimmy Boyle, "what d'yer think of the skipper with his blooming inspections, he thinks he's still in the Royal Navy, the pompous little sod."

"Couldn't agree with you more Nosey" scoffed Jimmy, "e's nothing but a big ead."

New Horizon's

Beneath a cloudless blue sky the morning sun sparkled like diamonds on the clear blue waters of the Atlantic, as the S.S Ardmere approached the island of Madeira our first port of call. Like a jewel in the crown this island, the largest of an archipelago lying off the north coast of Africa, enjoys a mild climate amid lush tropical and semi-tropical plant life. A wonderland of charm and beauty, Madeira's economy is centered on agriculture and an internationally famous wine. This sparsely inhabited island discovered in 1418 by the Portugese explorer Joao Goncalves Zarcothe, was colonized by his countrymen some years later. Not until the latter half of this century were tourist hotels built in and around the island capital of Funchal, which became a worldwide winter holiday resort. A playground for the rich and famous.

Sailing into the harbour at Funchal, the mere beauty of this subtropical island renewed the urge in me to follow my chosen career at sea which had by this time diminished somewhat, because of a nightmare outward bound crossing experienced by my good self. Slowing down as we neared our berth mooring ropes were passed ashore, and the vessel's steam winches groaning under the strain, heaved the S.S. Ardmere alongside. Fenders placed over the ship's side to protect the vessel's paper thin steel plates, were of little use. The merest bump was enough to send a cloud of rust, beneath the island's clear blue waters. No sooner had the ship berthed, local traders swarmed aboard the old tub, hoping to sell their wares. They brought with them brightly coloured scarves, caged canaries, and small barrels filled with the local Madeira wine. In broken English one of their number cried; "Hey amigo you wanna da nice'a canary, him plenty sing." The crafty fellow knowing only too well, the bird was unable to whistle a note.

With a smile that could hypnotize a crocodile he held the cage in front of his face, and imitated the bird's whistle. Such was the cunning of these islanders many seamen were duped into buying so-called songbirds, only to find out some time later all the damn thing would do was to chirrup, seed! There were of course some seamen who liked to indulge in a drink of the island's renowned Madeira wine, disposing of the potent brew like there was no tomorrow. Waking many hours later, with a sore head.

Having discharged our small assignment of cargo from the vessel's hold onto the wharf for transport up island, it was soon time for us to leave. Saying farewell to the island of Madeira, we headed for the coast of North Africa. Our course taking us within hailing distance of two islands from the Canaries group, Las Palmas and Tenerife. Before the vessel reached Dakar our next port of call in North West Africa, sun helmets were issued to all European members of the crew. With instructions to wear them each day from sunrise until sunset. This was a precaution one had to take to avoid catching sunstroke, because of the extreme heat in tropical climates. Which at times, reached one hundred and twenty degrees in the shade.

Within sight of the port of Dakar, capital of Senegal, cooling Atlantic breezes gave way to strong winds off the African desert, as temperatures soared in the sweltering heat. An economic center for market gardening the port of Dakar has an expanding industry, producing food products, fertilizers, cement, and textiles, and is linked by rail to outlying regions of Mali and Mauritania. Chosen as the capital of French West Africa in 1902, Dakar was occupied by U.S. forces during World War 11, and is today an educational and cultural center.

As soon as berthing was completed, a swarm of native workers began discharging our cargo of coal briquettes from the ship's hold. Throughout the day they toiled working in temperatures well above one hundred degrees, their sweat soaked bodies glistening in the the midday sun were as black as the cargo they unloaded. Having finished discharging a limited amount of cargo for the port of Dakar by nightfall, we headed out to sea for a breath of fresh air. At daybreak we arrived off

Bathurst our next port of call, and dropped our starboard anchor a few cables length away from a little used wooden jetty. Berthing alongside the rickety structure, mooring ropes from the fo'c's'le head were fastened to a steel post buried in the ground, with our stern ropes secured to nearby trees on the beach. At first sight the golden sands and tall green palm trees in this native settlement looked somewhat inviting, to a perfect stranger visiting Africa for the first time.

A row of white painted bungalows occupied by resident Europeans lay within easy reach of the beach with it's cooling Atlantic waters, giving the occupants some relief from the heat of a sweltering African sun. Moderate ocean swells rolling back and forth along sandy beaches in a flurry of foam and white spray, looked the perfect picture of an idylic African setting which tended to deceive. In my one and only trip ashore next day, I came across a collection of corrugated tin shacks and mud huts sheltering many of the local inhabitants. Hidden out of sight, behind a background of jungle greenery. Plumes of smoke from wood fires were my only guide to their whereabouts as I ventured into dense undergrowth, well out of sight of the beach. Quite by chance when facing an off shore breeze, I caught a whiff of human excreta rising from shallow open ditches dug in the ground. This no doubt served as a toilet for natives living in the area. Hurrying back aboard my ship, I decided that would be the last time I'd set foot in Bathurst.

Thankfully our stay here was limited to just a few hours before we headed back out to sea once more, bound for Freetown, the main port of Sierra Leone. Natives living in this part of Africa from the Kroo tribe were hired as cargo handlers by many shipping companies trading along Africa's West coast, for whatever length of time it took to load and unload each particular vessel. As many as one hundred and fifty to two hundred natives were hired, according to the size of the ship and amount of cargo she carried. Food being provided for them while they were on board, which could be as long as two or three months, was cooked by a member of their company. Having none of the usual toilet facilities for natives while they were on board the vessel the problem was taken care of by the ship's carpenter, who built a wooden box like structure from stout timbers, some days before our arrival at the port. This makeshift contraption covered in canvas and fitted with a wooden platform, was placed over the stern of the vessel and secured to the ship with strong ropes. Serving as a toilet for the natives, it enabled the user to perform such duties as he deemed necessary. The butt of many a joke by the seafaring community sailing the southern seas, who nicknamed it,"The West African Ensign."

Steering due south along the African coast the S.S. Ardmere drew nearer the equator, where the intense heat around midday became almost unbearable. As night fell we arrived at Freetown, Sierra Leone, one of many ports along the African Coast without berthing facilities, which meant we had to anchor in the bay. At daybreak a consignment of two hundred native cargo workers came on board the ship, and set to discharging a few hundred tons of cargo into barges for transport ashore.

A slight westerly breeze blowing across the ship brought a measure of relief from the searing heat of the midday sun as darkness closed in, but all too soon we were invaded by swarms of marauding insects. Mosquitoes and flies of every description from a minute midge to the huge cocoa beetle chose to descended on the ship in their thousands forcing me to take refuge in my cabin, which by this time was as hot as an oven. Luxuries such as electric fans were unheard of on this antiquated Noah's Ark, that should have been scrapped long ago. What little cool air did filter into my cabin via a tiny ventilator, brought with it a swarm of mosquitoes looking for blood. Soaked in perspiration I lay prostrate on my bunk beneath a net in this miniature Black Hole of Calcutta, listening to multitudes of unwelcome visitors buzzing around my ears before dropping off to sleep. Waking at intervals throughout the night I was sorely tempted to step out on deck for a breath of fresh air, but the infernal buzzing of these winged monsters seeking entry into my mosquito net discouraged me from committing such a foolish act. Attempting to do so would I felt certain, leave me with lumps and bumps the size of a duck egg.

Morning brought little relief from the night's humid atmosphere as the sun peeped over dense jungle greenery, before heating up the ship's deck. Riding at anchor the vessel rolled slowly from side to side in a large sheltered bay, opposite the sprawling native township of Freetown. Smoke from wood and charcoal fires on shore rose lazily into the clear morning air forming a thin blue curtain above a cluster of trees, circling a group of mud huts spread out along a palm-fringed waterfront. In the foreground taking pride of place stood the town's only licenced establishment, providing food and shelter for one brave enough to enter this cockroach infested domain. An imposing sight against such a squalid background of tin shacks and mud huts, the white fronted City Hotel dominated the skyline. Acting as a landmark for many ships using the port, seeking a safe anchorage.

Across sunlit tropical waters the babble of native voices could be heard coming from the town's market place close to the shore, disturbing the early morning stillness. Congregated around a wooden jetty jutting out from the shore a collection of small boats were loading various tropical fruit such as bananas, coconuts, mangoes, and limes, their ultimate goal being to grab whatever rich pickings were to be had aboard the ship.

Bearing down on the vessel, a barge loaded with two hundred native cargo workers and their belongings, crept nearer. Watching their approach a feeling of dread came over the first mate, Slim Prendergast. Eyeing his recently varnished accommodation ladder hanging over the ship's side, he could not bear to think of the damage this unruly mob might do to his prized possession when they charged aboard, and he shuddered at the thought. Fully realizing the situation facing him, he knew there was nothing he could do to stop this unruly crowd of native cargo workers about to descend on his ship, that would be their home for the next three months.

Hearing the shrill blast of the tug's steam whistle, Prendergast turned to a seaman standing nearby and gestured toward the barge loaded with native workers, being towed toward his ship. "Here comes trouble," he moaned. "Get those fenders over the ship's side as quick as you can, before they cause any damage."

As the barge neared the vessel's side Prendergast's nerves were on edge, visualizing the mess he might have to clean up. Seizing a megaphone he screamed at the captain of the tug; "Ahoy there, slow down, you're coming ahead too damned fast."

Receiving no reply he began waving his arms up and down, motioning the tug with it's barge in tow to slow down. Watching from the wheel-house aboard his tiny craft the native captain mistook Prendergast's madly waving arms, as a sign of greeting. Propelling the huge barge toward the ship he gave those on board, a friendly wave of his hand. Prendergast looked on in horror as the barge with it's human cargo drew closer, heading straight for his newly varnished accommodation ladder, his pride and joy. In no mood for such niceties he roared angrily at the native in charge; "Never mind the crap Sambo, watch my bloody accommodation ladder with that heap of junk you've got there."

Helpless to avert a collision which now seemed imminent he feared the worst, and hurriedly ordered his men to lift the ladder clear of the water. Howls of laughter and cheering aboard the barge were stilled as it made contact with the ship, landing with an almighty wallop it thudded into the vessel's stern end, buckling it's paper thin plates. Sliding halfway along the entire ship's length, it came to rest beneath the upraised accommodation ladder. The impact was like a miniature earthquake causing a tremor to run throughout the vessel; a human cargo of native workers packed in like sardines aboard the barge were thrown in all directions. Shouts of welcome from native stokers among the ship's crew caused further confusion among natives down on the barge, who rushed to clamber onto the ship's accommodation ladder as it was being lowered. Soon a surging mass of humanity fighting each other to be the first on board came close to wrecking the the ship's ladder, as it smashed up against the side of the vessel.   Spurred into action, Prendergast who'd been watching this performance rushed to the ship's side. In an attempt to stop this bunch of natives from the barge ruining his prized possesion as they scrambled aboard, he screamed at them; "What the hell's going on down there?"

Pointing to the tug's captain who seemed oblivious to the damage the natives might cause to his new accommodation ladder, Prendergast screamed; "Hey you there, stop them or they'll break the bloody thing."

Startled by the tone of the first mate's voice, a momentary stillness settled on the barge.   Somewhat surprised, all two hundred natives on board looked up toward the ship's deck, the whites of their eyes popping out like organ stops. For a moment nobody moved, then suddenly the deadlock was broken when one of the natives on board the barge blew a bugle. With excited whoops of joy they scrambled up the ladder, en masse. Racing wildly around the ship with what little possessions they owned, many individuals knowing the ropes, searched for a place to hide their precious belongings.

Standing on the after deck watching the antics of these native workers a group of seamen I grew to know well during the long voyage, were engaged in conversation.   "Nosey" Parker whom I'd already met and appeared to be the oldest among this motley crew, were composed of the following who answered to nicknames such as; "Snowy" White, "Shifty" Sullivan, Jim "The Book" Doyle, and Taffy Davis "The Welsh Nightingale." Last but not least among them were the terrible twosome of Ted "The Plonker" Bigmore, and Paddy "The Spud Basher" O'Rourke. Doyle the youngest and craftiest among them seeing me on the upper deck, sidled up to me saying; "Watch out Sparky lad, we're being invaded. This bloody lot are taking over."

Even as he spoke several natives dashed onto the after end of the ship intent on being first to christen their new toilet hanging over the stern, commonly known as the "West African Ensign."

Uproar and confusion followed as they fought one another for the privilege of using this newfangled toilet, of which they were now the proud owners. On orders from the captain a padlock was placed on the ship's fresh water pump underneath the fore'castle head, as a precaution against any waste of this precious commodity by the natives. A need to conserve fresh water supplies which at times were scarce on the African coast, was of the utmost importance. Natives regarded a water pump with special interest, treating it as though it were a toy to be played with. Like so many children they loved to watch the water splashing over the deck whilst pumping away to their hearts content, but with the risk of a water shortage it had to be locked up.

As was usual, the privilege of allowing seamen to hire a native from the Freetown area to clean out their quarters was permitted, whilst on the African coast. With this in mind they chose one particular native employed by them on previous trips along the coast, who answered to the name of "Joe Beef." A funny sort of name for a native you may think, but then again they all took unto themselves what they considered to be names they could best answer to. True, their African names were more or less difficult to pronounce. The native in charge of the Captain's launch for instance went by the name of "Half Past Five" of which he was quite proud, and whilst employed aboard ship these were the only names natives would answer to.

Splashes of red and gold melted away as the evening sun dipped slowly beneath the far horizon, shedding an iridescent glow across the now silent bay, as the S.S. Ardmere prepared to leave Freetown. Noise from the anchor chain groaning and squealing on it's way down to the chain locker as it was hauled on board, could be heard above the chatter of native voices preparing to bed down for the night. For a moment an eerie silence followed whilst the anchor cable was stilled in the gathering dusk and a pencil of light from the fore'castle head stabbed the darkness; it's beam shining on the water beneath the ship's bow. Hanging just above the surface the ship's starboard anchor covered in mud, swung idly to and fro, as it was being hosed down and heaved into place. Out of the stillness of this tropical night the plaintive voice of Prendergast the first mate was heard informing the Captain who waited on the bridge; "Anchor's a'weigh sir."

"Aye, Aye, mister mate" came his response, as he paced up and down the bridge. "Secure anchors and go below."

Turning to Dawson making his first voyage as third mate, the captain ordered him to push the lever of the engine telegraph to slow ahead, which brought an immediate response from the engineer on duty in the ship's engine room. Moving sluggishly the old tub began to shiver and shake as her propeller thrashed the water, in an effort to get her in motion. With great reluctance she slowly inched her way out to sea until a command from the Captain for full speed ahead, caused the old tub to shudder uncontrollably. When it seemed she would shake herself to pieces, we began to gain momentum and headed out into the wide blue yonder. Even the cockroaches down in the ship's holds, breathed a sigh of relief. Soon the twinkling lights of Freetown seen as no more than a red glare in the night sky, disappeared below the horizon. Caressed by a cool evening breeze our living quarters which were like ovens during the heat of the day, quickly cooled down. Allowing all on board, some measure of comfort throughout the long night.

Waiting for my turn of duty I sat on the boatdeck beneath a star studded tropical sky as the old tub gently rolled from side to side on a lazy ocean swell, and watched fascinated, as a reflection of the full moon appeared to dance upon the Atlantic's velvety waters. My moment of peace and tranquility was rudely interrupted when out of the darkened night "Shifty" Sullivan one of the ship's seamen sidled up to me, whispering; "You'd better make sure your cabin is locked whilst you're on duty. The bloody pirates are on board, Sparky."

"Pirates" I remarked, "I haven't seen any. When did they arrive."

"What do you mean," he scoffed. "Didn't you see that crowd of tealeaves come on board in Freetown, those natives running wild all over the ship."

"Tea leaves, Shifty, what are they," I asked.

He gave an irritated grunt. "They're bloody thieves Sparky mate, that's what they are" he said.

His attitude surprised me. "Oh! they're not that bad are they," I replied.

He seemed genuinely concerned that I should be made aware of the situation which left me in no doubt why, when he again warned; "Listen Sparky, they'll pinch the laces out of yer boots and ave the bleeding cheek to come back fer yer eyelets. So watch em, d'yer ere me son."

Stressing the need for instant action on my part he explained why it was necessary to keep my cabin door locked, saying; "Take heed of an old salt Sparky, I know these buggers. If it moves, they'll lift it."

Thanking him for his concern, I reached my cabin as the gong sounded for dinner. Taking the key to my cabin from a drawer I carefully locked the door, hurrying down to the dining saloon. Our conversation during the evening meal, centered around our next port of call.

At daybreak the following morning we arrived off Takoradi as the sun raised it's head above a cluster of tall green palms around the nearby town of Sekondi, a mixture of old and new buildings on a hilly site extending to a stretch of fine sandy beach. Once a thriving surfport, it soon became commercially obsolete with the opening of a harbour at Takoradi. Picking up a pilot to guide us in we sailed into this modern seaport town in the Gulf of Guinea, a few miles north of the equator. Constructed in the late twenties this deepwater harbour with it's berthing facilities, guaranteed we could at least be sure of a comfortable night's sleep for a change.

Up until now we had lain at anchor at various ports whilst the ship rolled on an ocean swell or bobbed about like a cork, forcing us to literally jam ourselves in our bunks each night to prevent us rolling out. Possessing one of the finest ports in West Africa, Takoradi is the trading centre for the entire area along the Gold Coast. Exporting such commodities as cocoa beans, palm oil, rubber, bauxite, gold, and manganese. Staying long enough to enjoy a swim on Sekondi's beautiful golden beaches and a quick tour of it's shopping area, we left early next morning for Accra, capital of the Gold Coast.

Without the benefit of a harbour in which to accommodate large ships, all vessels calling at the port were obliged to lie at anchor. Ships calling at the port of Accra had their cargo transferred ashore in surf boats, specially designed for the purpose. Manned by a dozen natives these sturdily built craft were paddled through mountainous waves of rolling surf, seen to crash headlong on the sandy shore. Lying at anchor on that first day in Accra, Gilchrist the second mate came to my cabin and advised me to close the porthole at night. A warning I'd already received from "Shifty" Sullivan. He also reminded me to put my cabin ventilator facing the wind, or else I'd be suffocated.

"What do you mean?" I asked him, waiting for the inevitable punch-line.

"Oh, I'm not joking," he said. "After you've closed your porthole and locked the cabin door you'll find the heat will be stiffling, so you will be glad of what little fresh air comes down the vents. If you don't lock up while we're at anchor here in Accra you'll be picked clean, that I can assure you, he warned." With a grin he left me to turn in for the night.

As was customary Morrison the ship's Chief Steward ordered a quantity of fresh provisions through an agent of the ship's company, together with a consignment of beer from the local Accra brewery, which arrived on board the vessel next day. Several heavily laden surfboats loaded with cargo made the gruelling journey ashore through boiling seas, bringing back with them much needed food and beer, to the delight of many seamen. With little to occupy their time during off duty hours and shore leave being out of the question, it was not unusual to find some seamen spending the long evening hours in idle gossip and drink. Spending their hard earned money on bottles of locally brewed beer from the Chief Steward, who'd sell nuts to a monkey. This evidently was the only means of solace for a particular seaman named Parker, who indulged in bouts of drinking when the opportunity arose. Nicknamed "Nosey" by his close associates, who were alas, few in number.

There were times when his heavy drinking left him in such a state of inebriation as to render him absolutely legless, and in such a condition was liable to loose his marbles, so to speak. Suffering periodic bouts of constipation which many of his ilk were prone to do, he turned to medicine by way of change from alcohol, to cure his affliction. This at times was hard to accept, so he compromised by mixing a concoction of the two with disastrous results for one unsuspecting native, who unfortunately happened to be the seaman's mess-man, answering to the name of "Joe Beef."

Purchasing a quantity of black draught from the ship's medicine chest which he kept in an empty beer bottle, Parker decided to sample the potent liquid that very night while quaffing a quota of beer he'd just bought from the Chief Steward. Taking a bottle of beer with his ready mixed bottle of black draught, guaranteed to blow your rear end off, he slipped away to his usual spot on the after deck and sat in his favourite chair, allowing the golden elixir to quench his thirst.

It was late that evening when Joe Beef the seaman's native mess boy went round the ship's deck looking for his friend "Massa" Parker, well aware he had purchased a quantity of beer earlier that evening. Like a shark seeking it's prey, Joe was determined not miss out on a free drink. His friendship with Parker and his voracious appetite for a drink of beer, were his downfall. Finding his old friend stretched out in a chair on the after deck, and stoned to the eyeballs with an array of bottles surrounding him, he took the opportunity to bum a drink. Waking the drunken Parker, he pleaded with him in his pigeon English; "Please Massa, I beg you, give me small beer."

Parker's bloodshot eyes squinted at the native standing beside him; "Hello Joe, d'yer wanna drink" he mumbled.

Picking up the nearest bottle to hand which happened to be his mixture of opening medicine, he offered it to the unsuspecting native.

"Ere yer'are Joe, finish it off" he croaked.

A grateful "Joe Beef" readily accepting Parker's offer put the bottle to his lips and took a huge gulp, then spluttered; "Oh "Massa" that no beer, me not like it."

"Aw co'mon Joe, drink it up" the wily old Parker urged. "Ave another drink it'll do you good."

Giving old Parker an agonized look, he said; "Massa," I go now."

Turning away he hurried off toward the after end of the ship, making a bee-line for the African Ensign.

"Where the hell yer going Joe?" Parker shouted.

There was no reply, nothing but the patter of Joe Beef's feet, pounding along the after deck in a desperate bid to reach the khazi to drop his load.

"Why, the ungrateful bugger" old Parker grunted, as the native disappeared.

Slumping down into his comfortable chair he dozed off, unaware of the commotion he'd caused among native workers. Milling around the ship's stern, they listened in silence to the anguished cries of distress from one of their countrymen.

Suddenly a pair of rough hands seized hold of old Parker, shaking him violently, to wake him out of his drunken stupor.

"Massa" Parker come quick," pleaded the native who had woken him, "Come quick "Massa," Joe Beef, gonna die."

Reluctant to move from a comfortable chair, the old sea-dog cursed the native who had dared to wake him from his slumbers, and peering through bloodshot eyes, he muttered;

"Wa'sa matter Sambo, can't you bloody sleep?"

"Massa come now," begged the hapless native.

Rising unsteadily to his feet, like a ship without a rudder, he weaved his way toward the stern of the ship. Padding along behind him a frightened native chattered away in his own lingo. Pushing his way through a sea of black faces, Parker could see Joe Beef squatting on his haunches in the natives' toilet. It seemed the poor fellow was in great pain and as he gazed heavenward, as though in meditation, the whites of his eyes rolled around, as he pleaded; "Lord ha' mussy. Ooh! Lord ha' mussy!"

Seeing the unfortunate Joe Beef hanging on grimly to the stern rails writhing in agony, Parker turned to face his native companions who looked on helplessly;

"Now yer don't wanna worry bout 'im mate," he laughed, jerking a thumb toward his mess-boy. "He's just having a good shit."

Then holding his nose, Parker complained bitterly; "Gaw'd you don't arf stink Joe, yer must've dropped yer guts."

With a grunt of disgust he made as though to walk away, and turned once more to admonish the poor fellow; "Ah've told yer before about drinking too much beer matey, serves yer right."

As an afterthought he quipped: "don't think yer'll need any more beer this trip, Joe. Yer'd better keep on the water wagon or yer'll get another dose of Montezuma's Revenge."

Morning appeared as a cloudless sky of blue with the tropical sun rising slowly above the far horizon, spreading an orange glow across a wide expanse of still water. Since break of dawn native cargo handlers had continued work loading several surf boats waiting alongside the ship, with the last few tons of goods we had for the port of Accra. Steam winches on board working flat out since early morning discharging cargo from the vessel's holds, ceased their clattering around midday when the job of discharging had finished. Making all haste to leave port, the Captain gave orders to heave up the anchor. As his ship got under way, he gave a blast on the ship's steam whistle warning small craft in the vicinity to keep clear.

Gathering speed the old tub began to pitch and roll in a heavy sea swell, burying her nose in the ocean. With little cargo left in the holds to give her stability, she seemed cumbersome to handle and sluggish to respond to the helm. Veering in all directions we sailed on down the African coast, until arriving at the mouth of the river Niger where we picked up our pilot for the journey up river to Lagos, the capital of Nigeria. Having a natural harbour, ships of many nations called here with much needed imports of machinery and general cargo. Loading exports of palm oil kernels, cocoa beans, groundnuts and hides, before returning to their home port.

Our journey up river was slow and laborious, the vessel's clapped out engine working overtime, made little headway against a fast flowing river. On our starboard hand we passed the Governor's residence, lying in close proximity with the waterfront. A sprawling white painted colonial style building, with neatly tended gardens. Across the river lay the small town of Appapa with up to date berthing facilities welcoming ships of all nationalities, to load exports of raw materials, such as palm oil, ground nuts, cocoa beans and rubber.

Letters from mother waiting for my arrival at Lagos provided all the news from home without mentioning my sister or enclosing her address, which would have allowed me to get in touch with her. Sadly word of Catherine's whereabouts was never mentioned in any correspondence from mother, which was disappointing. It now seemed futile pursuing the matter any further.

Travelling mile after mile in a southerly direction along the West African coast on this heap of rusting junk brought us ever nearer the equator, where temperatures as high as one hundred and twenty degrees in the shade were the norm. With little hope of escaping from the stiffling heat we had to put up with day and night, of several cabins fortunate enough to have electric fans installed in them, not one operated properly. None had sufficient power to blow a fly off the wall, or gave little comfort to the occupants in the steamy atmosphere. Many Europeans among the ship's company took to sleeping out on deck at night beneath their mosquito nets, which proved to be a blessing in disguise.

Life without them would have left us at the mercy of swarms of mosquitoes invading the ship at night in search of a meal.

Time having moved on rather quickly, I suddenly realized three months had gone by since I'd parted company with England's green and pleasant land. Not without some misgiving I found myself getting accustomed to a life on the ocean waves, firmly ensconced aboard this Noah's Ark they called a ship. Now well past it's sell by date she was as many an old sea-dog would say, a pig of a ship in half a gale. Dancing lightly over the waves like some burlesque queen, her mood would suddenly turn violent. Burying her nose in the sea her motion was like that of a belly dancer with a dose of the trots, as she tried to shake the guts out of you. It was at times like this I found out who my friends were, kindly chaps with my best interests at heart. Someone like the second steward who found me lying in the scuppers spewing my heart up, and whispered in my ear; "Ow'd yer like a couple of nice pork chops fer dinner, Sparky lad?"

Yet to all intents and pupposes I was considered a greenhorn, or as many would say, still wet behind the ears. Having so much to learn about life at sea at the age of seventeen, not until I'd spent the necessary length of time on the ocean waves, would I be considered to have gained my sea legs, so to speak. And as one who was brought up in a convent is entitled to be, I was totally ignorant of the ways of a seafarer. Never having heard such language used by men who sailed the seven seas, until now. Not that I would apportion blame on any particular individual, it was simply by chance I was to learn about the seamier side of life when my ship berthed at the port of Lagos, West Africa.

The Seamier Side of Life at Sea

Checking the ship's radio aerial on arriving in Lagos, Perkins the senior radio operator suspected one of the insulators was cracked and needed replacing.

"You might ask the Bo'sun for a couple of his men, Charles, the aerial will have to come down from aloft," he said. "He's an obliging sort of chap."

Standing six feet tall in his stockinged feet, the Bo'sun looked every inch an old sea dog if ever I saw one. Slimly built, with not an inch of fat on his wiry frame, he looked as though he could do with a good meal. Or as one seaman was heard to remark; "I've seen more meat on a butcher's knife."

Bronzed beneath a tropical sun his weather-beaten face was partly hidden by a huge handlebar moustache, sprouting from the upper lip. Hollowed cheeks puffing in and out like a concertina, he ambled toward me like a seal in the mating season. It was then I realized why they'd nicknamed him, the Walrus. The wizened face broke into a smile when greeting me, revealing several discoloured front teeth as a result of chewing plug tobacco.

"What can I do for you Sparks?" he asked. "If it's money you're after, you're out of luck," he said, grinning. "I need your help, Bo'sun. Do you think you could oblige me" I asked.

"Don't they all, Sparks," he replied. "But what can I do for you son?"

"We have a faulty insulator on the radio aerial that needs replacing, could you have it lowered down on deck so that I can see to it,?" I asked.

"Oh hell," he groaned. "I'll have to stop my men before they slip ashore for a bit of black velvet," said the wily old devil.

I gave him a puzzled look saying; "Black velvet, what do they want that for?"

With a nudge and knowing wink, he quipped; "they're after a bit of the other, son."

"A bit of what other "I countered, hoping I did not appear stupid. Stroking his handlebar moustache he gave me a searching look and asked; "How old are you son?"

Uncertain as to his reason for wanting to know my age, I proudly answered; "I'm seventeen, Bo'sun, why do you want to know?"

"Then tell me sonny," he replied, giving me a questioning look; "Where have you come from, a bloody monastery?"

Allowing himself a chuckle at my expense, he said good humouredly; "Alright son, wait until I detail a couple of my men to lower the aerial for you."

Taking me to one side while the work was in progress he did his best not to shock me, while explaining the seamier side of life at sea. But because I was brought up in the kind of background one would describe as sheltered, I found his many nautical expressions hard to comprehend. Certain in the knowledge they could not be found in the good book. Unable to understand much of the seaman's language he used, you can imagine the effect it had on a young innocent abroad, like me. Not only was I at a loss to understand the use of what one might term his nautical vocabulary, I quickly came to realize that life at sea was a world apart from one educated in a convent.

Meanwhile two seamen busily engaged up aloft trying to release the triatic stay, gave a warning shout. "Lookout, below."

From a height of about fifty feet a steel spike hurtled down onto the deck below, barely missing the Bo'sun and myself standing directly underneath. Like a pair of scalded cats, we leapt clear. Then shaking his fist menacingly at the two men aloft, he screamed; "You stupid sods. What the hell are you trying to do, kill us?"

Ashen faced he turned to me, gasping; "Christ Almighty, we were damned lucky there, Sparks. We could've both been killed."

Gazing aloft he carried on a tirade of abuse against the two seamen working up above, shouting at the pair of them; "I know you're after my job," he rambled on, "but you'll not get rid of me that bloody easy."

"Snowy White," the youngest seamen of the two, made an effort to apologize. "Sorry boss" he shouted, trying to placate the infuriated old devil.

"Sorry my arse" hollered the "Walrus" with an air of disgust, and walked away.

Standing aside I waited until the triatic stay was lowered onto the deck then replaced the damaged insulator, moving well out of harm's way as it was being hauled aloft and placed back in position. Thanking the Bo'sun for his help, I left the scene as a further stream of curses directed at the men aloft, erupted from the old man's lips.

"Just look at them Sparks" he bellowed, pointing aloft. "They're sitting there like a couple of vultures waiting to pounce," he sneered.

Back inside the radio cabin I assured Perkins all was well, that the radio aerial had been repaired and should now be in working order.

"By the way" he said, with a grin; "How did you get on with the Bo'sun. He's a funny old cuss, don't you think."

"Oh, I guess you could say that," I replied. "But I'm afraid his language was rather choice."

Perkins gave me a sidelong glance. "What do you mean, Charles?" he asked.

Grinning sheepishly I replied, "He said his men were going ashore for a bit of black velvet, while he himself made reference to the local native girls."

"Oh! take no notice of that old reprobate he'd lead an angel astray, if she cared to listen to him. You have to be careful while at sea Charles, be sure you stay on the straight and narrow." Perkins then went on to lecture me on do's and dont's of one's behaviour while on board ship, pointing out the pitfalls and serious consequences that no doubt would follow. With a friendly wag of the finger he warned; "Take heed of my advice Charles and leave the dusky maidens alone, otherwise you'll come to grief. You are far too young to understand the ways of the world, right now." His final comment had me worried. "Just imagine what your mother would say if you ran into trouble," he warned.

Watching drunken seamen returning aboard ship that night, I was more than grateful for the advice Perkins gave me earlier in the day. I thanked my lucky stars I took the time to listen to him. It brought to mind a well-known phrase I'd often heard; "But for the grace of God, there go I."

As the sun rose slowly in the east next morning, it tended to get hot and sticky as the day wore on. Native workers having risen at dawn were stripped to the waist, discharging the last of our cargo ashore. The task of cleaning the ship's holds would now be undertaken before a fresh consignment was taken on board, when revisiting various ports on our journey up the West African coast. From Lagos we set course for Port Harcourt lying some thirty inland miles from the sea, up a tributary of the River Niger. Navigating it's many twists and sharp bends was a hazardous business; our journey up river was both slow and cumbersome. Reaching a sharp bend in the river, we ran into difficulties. Anxious to avoid unnecessary damage to his ship, the Captain ordered the first mate standing on the fo'c'sle head, to drop his starboard anchor. A cloud of dust rose in the air as the anchor with five fathoms of rusty cable left the ship's chain locker, and rattled down the hausepipe. Hitting the water with a loud splash, it disappeared beneath the river's muddy surface.

Dragging her anchor the vessel's stern swung to starboard and drifting inshore, swept aside all manner of vegetation blocking it's path, along with the natives' toilet fastened to the rails on the ship's after end. Oblivious to the danger he faced by using the toilet at such a critical moment, the native occupant sitting on the throne ended up clinging to the branches of a nearby tree. His cries for help could be heard echoing throughout the jungle.

Seamen watching the performance on the ship's after deck, roared with laughter: "Ask him if there's any coconuts up there?" shouted "Snowy" White.

Arriving on the scene much too late, the ship's carpenter surveyed the wreckage. Seeing the West African Ensign shattered beyond repair hanging in dense undergrowth ashore, he blew his top. "Good grief" he exclaimed, shaking his head in disbelief;

"What the hell's happened here, that's all my bloody work wasted," he moaned.

Catching sight of a native worker waving frantically from a tree top, he asked young Doyle standing nearby, "How did that stupid bugger get up there?"

"I suppose he felt homesick" the seaman laughed, "and slipped ashore for some oranges."

"He didn't have to take the bloody toilet with him, said the carpenter. "I've no timber left to make another."

As the ship pulled away from the river bank the native's cries for help were heard by the Captain, directing operations from the bridge.

"How the hell did he get up there, mister Prendergast?" he asked his first mate.

"They must have forgotten to bring that damned West African Ensign inboard," the mate replied.

"Then we'll have to leave the stupid sod up there," Captain Collie replied. "I'm not stopping my ship to pick him up. He can get a bloody canoe to take him up to Port Harcourt."

Against a backcloth of stars twinkling in the sky tiny fingers of light punctured the far horizon, on our approach to Port Harcourt, the next port of call. Stealthily night spread a mantle of darkness over this tiny township carved out of the African bush, where a bite from the mosquitoe was likened to that of the kick from a mule. No sooner had we berthed at the tiny settlement a row broke out among native workers over the loss of their toilet. The situation was made worse when the ship's carpenter refused to put together a makeshift toilet for the natives, saying to Prendergast the first mate; "I've no damn timber left, let them hang over the ship's side to empty out. That's what they do as a rule."

Leaving the after deck I retired to my cabin for the night, which by this time was hotter than an baker's oven. With the sound of native voices no more than a distant murmur against a background of crickets chirruping in the nearby jungle, I slipped beneath my mosquito net. Feeling relatively safe from the brutes buzzing around my cabin I closed my eyes. The winged monsters would not be dining out tonight.

Through the porthole of my tiny cabin a shaft of morning sunlight pierced the semi darkness, increasing an already oven-like temperature. It was shortly after six a.m. and the sun already high above the horizon in this tropical outpost, had evaporated what little moisture there was from the morning dew. Out on deck native workers were busy removing tarpaulins, covering number's one and two hatches. The clatter of the ship's steam winches hard at work were discharging what little remained of our general cargo, destined for Port Harcourt.

By seven oclock that morning the temperature in my cabin had shot up into the lower eighties, causing me to sweat profusely. Stripping off my pyjama's which by this time were saturated in the cabin's oven-like humidity, I allowed myself the luxury of a cold shower. Taking time to finish dressing, I locked the door of my cabin and took a brisk walk around the ship's deck, before my day's work began. Abreast of the ship's accommodation ladder, a native whom I recognized as the fellow we'd left stranded in the bush the previous day, approached me. Pointing to the ship's bridge, in a mixture of pidgin English he shouted; "Him Captain, no bloody good, leave me in jungle." Gesticulating wildly he went on; "Look me Massa, I plenty scratch. Tear all cloth" he said, showing me his torn shirt and trousers. "Me see Captain now, Massa," he demanded.

His bloodshot eyes swept around the deck as he staggered close to me, belching loudly. It was then I caught a whiff of the native fire water he'd been drinking, and tried to pacify him, saying; "Captain sleep now, better you come back later time."

Reluctant to move away he muttered; "I wait Massa, I wait. Me make plenty trouble for Captain, him bad man."

Standing my ground I barred his way up to the Captain's deck, telling him there was no point in disturbing the Captain at this unearthly hour. Shielding his eyes from the sun he gazed heavenward for some minutes as though seeking advice from his witch doctor, and receiving none gave a resounding belch and shuffled away muttering threats to the Captain's person. Not until after midday did he appear in a more sober frame of mind, when taken before the Captain. Who reprimanded him for failing to do his duty, then fined the native for being absent without leave.

Working throughout the day beneath a tropical sun was thirsty work, needing ample supplies of liquid refreshments. Reason enough for many seaman to hit the bottle, when their day's work was done. Whilst beer was always available on board the ship at a reasonable price, many sought to drown their sorrows in a locally brewed liquor extracted from the sugar cane, aptly nicknamed, "jungle juice." A potent concoction said to have a one hundred percent alcohol content, powerful enough to drive a car. Legend had it the golden nectar acted as an insect repellent, that left mosquitoes non compus mentis. Doubtless another old seafarer's yarn, encouraging them to drink the stuff. Like a moth attracted to the flame of a candle, many seamen were enticed ashore each night to drink the fire water. Returning back on board the ship early next morning, to collapse in their bunks, in a drunken stupor.

With the morning sun an orange ball of fire rising above the eastern horizon, and the local inhabitants still fast asleep, the Bo'sun was busy shepherding his men into a small boat moored alongside the vessel, ready to start the day's work. Anxious to get some rusty patches on the ship's starboard side painted, he urged his men on, like an old mother hen caring for her brood. As usual the terrible twosome Paddy O'Rouke and Ted Bigmore were feeling the effects of their previous night's binge, and complained of having sore heads.

"Serves yer right," laughed the Bo'sun. "Drinking that bloody jungle juice would rot the soles of yer boots, never mind yer guts."

Leaving the two men to commiserate with each other as they painted the ship's side he slipped away, hoping there would be no further interruptions from the rest of his men. As he settled down in his comfortable chair, a howl of pain from Davis, the Welsh nightingale, rent the air.

Bursting into song, he decided to entertain his shipmates with a rendition of "Men of Harlech" while painting the ship's side. Seeing a mango fly settle on his new paintwork, he tried to flatten it with his paint brush and missed the winged monster. Attracted by the colour of the red paint it returned to the scene some minutes later and sank it's poisoned barb in the fellow's rear end, giving him the screaming ab-dabs. Climbing up a jacobs ladder like a scalded cat, he hopped around the deck rubbing his backside.

Leaving the comfort of his cabin, where he sat enjoying a pipe of tobacco, the Bo'sun ambled along to the after deck to see Davis gingerly massaging his rear end.

"What the hell's going on here," he groaned. "Can't I get five minutes peace?"

"Who's bright idea was it to send us down in that damn boat?" Davis shouted.

"Why, what's the matter, Taffy?" the Bo'sun asked him.

"I'll tell you what the matter is," snarled Davis.

"I've just been stung on the arse by a bloody great mango fly."

To a burst of applause from his shipmates, the Bo'sun quipped; "You should be so lucky my son. I've been coming down this coast fer nigh on twenty years, and never had the honour."

Some twenty four hours later, a huge swelling appeared on Taffty's backside, forcing him to languish in his bunk for a while.

Our departure from Port Harcourt next morning came as a welcome relief from the humid jungle atmosphere with it's mosquitos and other nocturnal creatures, one encountered throughout the hours of darkness. Back at sea I stood out on the boat deck for some minutes, enjoying a breathe of fresh air. Moving lazily down the coast the S.S. Ardmere nosed her way south across the equator to Matadi our next port of call, lying on the left bank of the Congo river in Equatorial Africa.

First discovered by the Portuguese explorer Diego Cao in 1487 Matadi was chosen as the main seaport for the Belgian Congo when it was colonized in 1908, because of it's favourable position to the Atlantic ocean. Slowing down at the river estuary we picked up a native pilot assigned to guide us through the many twists and turns of the world's second largest river, until reaching the port of Matadi. With a maximum speed of six knots it turned out to be a hazardous task for the ship when manouvering round many dangerous bends and innumerable whirlpools, with the vessel struggling to stem a fast flowing river. Reaching our destination, as dusk fell, we berthed alongside a clapped out wooden jetty, and faced much the same problems that we did in Port Harcourt when the vessel's lights were switched on during the hours of darkness. Pestered by swarms of mosquitos, and other nocturnal insects invading us. Attracted by the ship's powerful arc lights, cockroaches, cocoa beetles, and praying mantis crash landed on the ship's deck and lay there helpless, until put out of their misery by a passing seaman's size ten boot.

Unlike many parts of Africa colonized by Europeans where the quality of life for the native population was seen to be greatly improved, such was not the case here in the Belgium Congo. Venturing ashore in Matadi during the hours of darkness one was obliged by law to carry a flashlight, street lighting here was vitually non-existent. Failure to do so was punishable by a fine.

There were of course instances, where one might even find themselves incarcerated in one of their foul smelling native jails. Seen from my vantage point aboard ship the following morning, I noticed white walled bungalows with brightly coloured red tiled roofs, occupied by the European community living along the river bank. Huddled together in a small clearing some way back in the undergrowth amid a background of jungle green, were native palm fringed mud huts.

The town's one and only hotel, the Metropole, a fine example of Gothic architecture, stood resplendent among brightly coloured magnolias and lawns of green velvet. A welcome sight for any thirsty seafarer wishing to indulge in a quiet drink to while away the daylight hours, whilst sheltering from the fierce heat of a tropical sun. Having skillfully navigated a course from the ship to within the hotel precinct's, drink was readily available to those in need at any time of the day or night. One also had to be wary of thieves lurking around the darkened streets of town, seeking to waylay any individual from the ship foolish enough to venture out alone.

While in port seamen worked each day from eight a.m. until five p.m, allowing them time for shore leave each evening. Weekends were days of rest, as from midday Saturday until eight a.m. on Monday morning. In spite of the many hazards that lay in one's path when setting foot ashore at night, it did nothing to deter certain members of the crew from rushing ashore to sample the native liquor, an alcoholic drink produced from the sugar cane. This urge to partake of a local brew aptly nicknamed "jungle juice" often proved too great a temptation for many seamen, which for some, had unfortunate results. Forsaking the usual custom of changing out of their working clothes then showering and shaving before stepping ashore, many went without a meal in their craving for just a sip of the so-called golden elixir of life. Very cheap to purchase and extremely potent this concoction boasting an alcohol content said to be one hundred percent, was consumed in great quantities by seamen known to patronize local native haunts.

Drawn to the native fire water, like a moth to a lighted candle, Paddy O'Rourke wasted no time in satisfying his craving, for what he said was the staff of life. Hurrying ashore as soon as the gangway hit the quayside Paddy found his way along a well trodden jungle path to the nearest native village, where he supped the local brew until the tap ran dry. At midday when the sun had risen to it's full height and even the natives sought relief from the sweltering heat of the day, Paddy was seen to enter the town's Metropole Hotel seeking to further satisfy his thirst. Having supped more than his share of the local booze he was seized with a sudden urge to relieve himself and remembering a couple of decorative pots filled with tropical flowers that caught his eye on the way in, took what he considered the easiest way out of his awkward situation. Ah! he thought to himself as he left the hotel in a drunken stupor and came upon the flower pots, this looks a likely place. Seeing the soil was parched and dry Paddy decided the plants were in need of a watering, and promptly obliged by discharging a considerable quantity of diluted jungle juice into each flower pot.

"Why you do that massa?" asked an irate native gardener, looking on.

"S'matter Sambo, ain't yer seen anyone av'in a squirt before?" said Paddy, "I'm saving you a job, sunshine."

Within minutes the local police were on the scene to witness his drunken performance, and promptly threw him in jail.

Venturing ashore later that day Paddy's bosom pal and boozing partner, Ted Bigmore, scoured the nearby village looking for him. Seeking help from the natives, Bigmore was told by them; "Bigman Paddy drink plenty fire water, him go hotel now."

At the hotel the manager informed Bigmore that Paddy had been thrown in the local jail, and was likely to remain there. Going to the local police station, Bigmore demanded to see his pal Patrick O'Rourke, to which they readily agreed. Then promptly threw him in jail, to keep Paddy company.

Early next morning an agent from the company's office ashore boarded the ship and informed the Captain two of his men where languishing in the local calaboose, and would he send someone along to have them released.   Calling on Slim Prendergast, the chief mate, to come to his cabin, the Captain requested he go ashore and secure the release of his two men in jail.

"Can't trust that damned Irishman, O'Rourke, and that useless idiot he goes ashore with, out of your sight for a minute," he complained to the Captain. "I'd leave the pair of them to rot in jail if I had my way," he moaned.

"That's not possible mister Prendergast," the Captain replied. "We'll have to leave this place while there's daylight, I don't want to be steaming down this river after dark, it's too treacherous. You'd better ask the Bo'sun to let you have a man to go with you ashore to bail them out."

Reluctant to accompany the first mate ashore when instructed to by the Bo'sun, Snowy White retorted; "I'd rather go on my own than with that miserable sod. It's him we should leave in jail."

Asked by his shipmates why he was going ashore with Slim Prendergast, he replied; "Paddy's in trouble again, so I've got to go with that jerk to the jailhouse to bail him out."

"What the hell's he been up to now," asked Taffy Davis.

"Drunk as usual" laughed Snowy, "he's had too much jungle juice, I'll bet."

"That's nothing unusual for him," said old Nosey Parker. "A sniff at the barman's apron, and he's sozzled."

Stretched out on number four hatch like a corpse waiting for the wooden box, Sullivan, a grizzled old seadog, suddenly sprang to life. "What the hell's going on now" he asked, rubbing the sleep from red rimmed eyes.

"Paddy and his side-kick Bigmore are stuck in jail" said Snowy,"and I've got to go with Slim to get them out."

"They're damned lucky they can afford to drink" he moaned, "I've a wife and four kids to support, so how the hell can I afford to go boozing?"

"You should to have tied a knot in it when you got hitched up" laughed Jimmy Boyle, nicknamed the Philadelphia Lawyer. Inclined to be sarcastic at times, his verbal wit and offensive criticism enraged old Sullivan.

"What do you know about marriage sonny?" he shouted angrily. "You're too young and still wet behind the ears. I suppose you think kids come from under gooseberry bushes," he sneered. "I bet you're still a virgin," he leered menancingly.

Sullivan's final remark took the wind out young Boyle's sails and left him speechless, when the old fellow quipped; "You haven't dipped yer wick yet, have yer sonny?"

This started a heated argument that threatened to get out of hand, until the Bo'sun's call to resume work left the cocky young Boyle with his pride somewhat dented.

Back ashore O'Rourke and Bigmore were released from a darkened cell in the local jailhouse where they'd spent the night, and staggered out into the light of day. Shielding his eyes from the sun's glare O'Rourke squinted at Slim Prendergast the first mate and Snowy White, waiting to escort them back to the ship.

"Any chance of a drink mister Prendergast?" Paddy asked the mate."Me throat feels like bloody sandpaper."

"You want a drink," sneered Slim. "It's milk you need, you can't get drunk on that."

Paddy nudged his old pal Ted Bigmore. "D'yer hear that Ted, the miserable sod won't let's have a drink."

"Aw c'mon Pat, I've got some jungle juice on board" whispered Bigmore.

Accompanied by the silent yet ever watchful first mate and a sympathetic shipmate in Snowy White, the pair trudged back on board the ship to face Captain Collie, a fearsome looking character who reminded one of Bligh of the Bounty. Of rugged appearance with broad shoulders and short muscular neck, his deeply tanned faced carried a scar running down the left side of a large hooked nose. Being a strict disciplinarian, he would not tolerate ratings from the lower deck misbehaving during the voyage. As a share holder in the company he cared little for the comfort of his crew, and made sure food aboard his ship was never wasted. In condescending to look up from some papers he was studying on his desk, he cast a sidelong glance in the direction of O'Rourke and Bigmore waiting outside his cabin, and asked Prendergast his first mate to show the offenders in.

"Well," he asked the two seamen standing before him; "And what excuse have you to give for your behaviour?"

Shifting nervously from one foot to the other, O'Rourke broke the silence. "Well, t'was like this sir," he explained. "I thought I'd wet me whistle so I nipped ashore fer a quick one."

"So how did you land in jail," the Captain inquired.

Paddy thought for a moment; then said; "Ah! I remember now sir, me tank wanted emptying and I couldn't find a loo."

"So you decided to water the flowers, O'Rourke," Captain Collie retorted sarcastically.

"Yes and he damned well killed them with the rot-gut he was drinking, sir" Prendergast chipped in. "It's strong enough to kill an elephant, never the mind flowers."

"And what happened to you Bigmore?" the Captain asked sardonically.

Bigmore eyed the captain suspiciously as he scribbled a report in his log book, refusing to utter a word.

"What's the matter, haven't you a tongue in that thick head of yours?" Captain Collie asked him, rather irritably. "I suppose you just went there to hold O'Rourke's tiny hand did you,?" the captain remarked. But, much to his annoyance Bigmore remained silent.

"Take the useless pair out of my sight mister," he told his first mate. "They'll be logged a day's pay for being absent without leave, and charged for any expenses they've incurred while ashore. See that it's deducted from their wages, mister Prendergast," he instructed.

Dismissing the drunken pair, he added; "You'll both remain on board until further notice."

Down aft in the seamen's quarters Jimmy Boyle waited for Snowy White to enter the forecastle, grinning like a cheshire cat.

"So what happened to them?" Jimmy asked.

"Oh! Paddy's been serenading the natives. Gave them a rendition of "It ain't gonna rain no more, outside the Metropole hotel."

"And what the hell's wrong with that?" old Sullivan wanted to know.

"There was nothing the matter with the song" laughed Snowy, "he was watering the flowers with his hosepipe at the same time. Said they needed livening up."

"You mean he pissed on em," said old Parker.

"Good for him boyo," quipped Taffy Davis, they must have needed a drink."

Young Boyle began quoting a passage from his gardener's manual, with the remark; "Like most humans," he went on, "flowers do like music."

"But they don't like jungle juice or Irish liqueur either" grinned old Sullivan, who motioned for silence from the rest of his mates as O'Rouke and his sidekick Bigmore set foot inside the fo'c's'le.

"Where's the booze Ted," the Irishman asked his pal; "I'm as dry as a bone."

Leaving the two of them to drink into the small hours, it was long after the nightly chirruping of crickets ceased that the drunken pair finally fell asleep. Each hugging his half empty bottle of cane juice.

Rising in the east like a red ball of fire the tropical sun spread it's warmth across the fast flowing waters of the Congo, embracing a row of white walled bungalows lying along the river bank. Greeting a new day, anguished cries from gulls on the wing woke the ship's Bo'sun from his slumbers. Dressing hurriedly as though the hour was late he stepped smartly out on deck, determined to make ready for an early start to the day.

Making all possible speed his bandy legs would allow him he entered the seamen's quarters on the after deck, and roused the men from their bunks;

"Come on now me lads, show a leg there."

Getting no reply he hollered; "You'd better get out of yer ruddy louse traps now, cos we're sailing on the early morning tide."

"Is the tea made?" Taffy asked, rubbing the sleep from his eyes.

"You want me to bring tea," said the Walrus in mock surprise; "Where d'you think you are son, the bloody Ritz?"

Sullivan and Parker made a beeline for the galley in search of the native mess boy, and found him sitting on a bench talking to his countryman, the cook.

"Where's our tea, Joe Beef?" Parker asked the boy, who sat there gazing at the kettle.

"I come quick now Massa. Him water no boil before dis time," he told the seaman.

Seeing the ship's African cook busy over his hot stove, Sullivan shouted; "Morning Snowball, what's fer breakfast?"

Beads of perspiration running down his face, the cook turned away from the hot stove and grinned. "OK boys, today I give you curry rice."

"Cor blimey, not again," moaned Sullivan. "D'yer hear that" he said, turning to Parker; "It's another dollop of duck shit and hailstones. That chief steward must think we're bloody coolies."

Complaints the men made to the Chief Steward fell on deaf ears. The chief, like the captain, also happened to be a shareholder in the company.

"Take it or leave it," he told them bluntly. Dissatisfied with his offhanded attitude a deputation led by Jimmy Boyle representing the seamen, took their complaint to the Captain. An eloquent speech by the professed sea lawyer outlining the men's grievance, fell on deaf ears. "Eat it or damn-well starve," was Captain Collie's prompt reply.

Leaving the humid jungle atmosphere and primitive conditions we encountered in the Belgian Congo, we sailed back up the West African coast. Calling at several ports we'd visited on our journey south, small amounts of cargo were taken on board as we ventured north. Fully loaded by the time we arrived at our final destination of Freetown, native cargo workers hired to work on board the ship returned to their homes ashore. Clearing up the mess they left behind was cause for loud cursing by the seamen, who had to spent long hours washing the ship down with a strong solution of disinfectant. Once we were clear of the African coast, Atlantic breezes tended to cool down the vessel's steel deck as the day wore on. Which were hot enough to fry an egg on. Evening came upon us suddenly, the sun no more than a splash of red and gold slipped ever so gently beneath the western horizon. Lulled by the gentle motion of an Atlantic swell my thoughts were not of the palm fringed coast of Sierra Leone we'd left behind, but of my first visit to America, as we set sail for New York.

A Glorious Sight

Beneath a star studded tropical night sky a full moon bathed the S.S Ardmere in radiant light as she rode a gentle ocean swell, groaning beneath the weight of a cargo of cocoa beans in her holds and mahogany logs lashed down on the open deck. It was shortly before midnight that I left my cabin and mounted a companionway leading to the wireless room, where I was due to begin a four hour stint of duty. Perkins the operator on watch answered my knock and opened the door of a tiny cabin that served as the radio room, and invited me in. Motioning for me to take a seat he handed over the headphones, saying; "There's nothing to report, so you should be O.K for a while."

From a small locker next to the transmitter he picked up a book he'd been reading, and sighed wearily; "I guess I'll hit the sack."

With a cheery goodnight he closed the door behind him, leaving me with my thoughts.With the headphones clamped to my ears, I sat listening to an incessant chorus of dots and dashes bouncing over the air waves, for the next four hours.

Alone in the dead of night I sat cramped up in the tiny radio cabin swaying from side to side in rhythm with the ship, as she swung first to port and then starboard.

Riding a moderate ocean swell she pitched and rolled along on the Atlantic's glassy waters, headed in a nor'westerly direction toward America. I also had brought a book with me to read in the radio room to while away the lonely hours between midnight and four a.m, referred to by many who sailed the seven seas as the dead watch. The reason being that men stricken down with tropical diseases, tended to kick the bucket during these unearthly hours. Ending up in a canvas bag with a couple of steel firebars for company, then dispatched to a watery grave. Glancing at a calendar hanging in the radio cabin, I noted with some surprise we were now into the month of June. Having left England in early March I'd spent the last few months sailing up and down the West African Coast, suffering much discomfort from a bout of malaria and on-going periods of prickly heat from which there is no escape. It seemed one had to put up with such conditions when visiting tropical countries, where each and every day was alike.

With a symphony of dots and dashes pounding my ears, my thoughts were of mother and home. Why I asked myself did she never mention my sister Catherine in any of her letters, choosing only to talk about other members of the family. Meanwhile I was content to carry on with a routine of bed and work counting the days until reaching New York, where I expected a letter from mother would be waiting for me.

After a tedious journey of almost three weeks, by which time even the cockroaches were fed up, the S.S. Ardmere arrived at the mouth of the Hudson river in New York. An early morning mist quickly dispersed, giving way to bright sunny weather. Slowing down to allow a pilot to board the vessel we continued up river, anchoring opposite the Quarantine Station to await clearance from the Port Health Authorities. Most noticeable was a hive of activity taking place on the river, where ships of various shapes and sizes were seen moving into position. This unusual performance prompted the Captain to remark; "There's something going on here, I've never seen such a large collection of ships."

Waiting on the river were several ocean going liners and small coastal craft, decked out with flags of every conceivable colour. At a prearranged signal it seemed all hell had broken lose when every ship in the vicinity opened up with loud blasts on their siren's; the noise was deafening.

A cry of "There she is" from the duty officer caused a flurry of excitment, with every member of the crew rushing to the starboard side of the vessel. Out on the horizon the silhouette of a huge liner, drew ever closer.

"It's the Queen Mary" Perkin's shouted, with boyish enthusiasm.

The Cunard Company's latest addition to the fleet had just arrived in New York, on her maiden voyage. Decorated with a multitude of flags flying from stem to stern, her gleaming white paintwork sparkled in the early morning sun. Her three huge red and black funnels, giving an added dimension to her enormous size. Majestic in her every move she looked a wonderful sight as she moved gracefully up the Hudson river, with all the aplomb of a Queen. This surely, was one of the proudest moments in the history of the British Merchant Service. Not forgetting the men who built her, at John Brown's shipyard on the river Clyde, Scotland. Passing the Statue of Liberty her siren's boomed out a vibrant salute to attendant ships.

In response, she received a deafening chorus of welcome from every vessel in the area. It was a privilege indeed to have witnessed such a great spectacle, as the arrival in New York of the Queen Mary on her maiden voyage.

Our stay at the Quarantine Station duly ended with the arrival of the Port Health Doctor for his customary inspection of African members of the ship's crew, carried out on vessel's entering the port from tropical countries. Lining up on deck native firemen and stewards waited for a short arm inspection before the vessel was allowed to berth, a precautionary measure against risk of contagious diseases being brought into the country.

As the doctor passed down the line each man was asked to take out his Ding-a-ling, and squeeze it. At the far end of the row a young native stoker was struggling with the zip on his trousers, when suddenly his ding-a-ling flopped out. Hanging there, like a length of black rubber hose. Seeing it's enormous size, the doctor remarked good-humouredly; "I guess you weren't behind the door when they were dished out."

A melon-sized grin spread across the stoker's face, and proud as a peacock he replied; "Oh no sah, ah's born wid dat."

"Somebody trod on it as he walked away, Doc," choroused an onlooker among the seamen.

Doubled up in a fit of laughter, the doctor exclaimed; "Wait until they hear this one at the hospital. They'll be in stitches."

Given clearance by the Port Authorities, the S.S. Ardmere continued on her journey up river to her berth. Passing Manhattan Island I stood in silent awe, marvelling at the size of it's skyscraper's. Tallest of them the Empire State Building stood head and shoulders above them all, in isolated splendour. It was by any stretch of the imagination, a wonderful sight to behold. Looking back on the many large buildings I'd seen in London, their dingy appearance was no match against these lofty giants. Moving up river we approached Brooklyn Bridge which connects the Bore with Manhattan, and were taken in tow by escorting tugs who shepherded us gently into our berth. Thus ended a long and tedious voyage from West Africa, which had taken just over three weeks. Much longer than expected, owing to engine failure in mid-Atlantic.

With nothing but water to drink when the ship arrived in New York several members of the crew couldn't wait to get ashore, eager to satisfy their craving for a glass of lager. Like so many lemmings hurtling over cliff tops, they were in a hurry. Anxious to quench their thirst, en-masse they charged toward the ship's gangway. When about to set foot on American soil their path was blocked by none other than Prendergast the first mate, who held up his hand like a London bobby stopping the traffic in Picadilly Circus.

"Sorry lads" he leered, "no shore leave until Custom's have cleared the ship."

"Wha'dya mean chief," said a surprised Snowy White, "can't we get a lager."

"Not until they know what you've got to declare," sneered Prendergast.

"Yes, we declare you're a bloody nuisance mister," jeered old Sullivan. "That's all we've got to say."

Howls of derision, curses, and threats to his person were hurled across the deck at Slim Prendergast, as dejectedly the seamen trooped back to their quarters.

"Maybe we ought to keep you all on board, "Prendergast shouted, as they disappeared into the fo'c'astle. "How will that suit you, my lads?"

They were not kept waiting too long however, before the ship was finally cleared. A sharp knock on his cabin door was answered by O'Rouke, who found himself face to face with an American Custom's Officer.

"Good morning sir" said Paddy trying to create a good impression. "Won't you come in?"

"Good morning boy's" echoed the officer, "don't mind me, just carry on as usual."

Taking a folding stick and flashlight from his bag the customs officer began tapping the vessel's bulkhead, then shone his torch behind some pipes and into small crevices. Using a tiny mirror attached to the stick, he was able to detect hidden contraband. When the officer had finished searching the seamen's cabin they were asked to open their suit cases, allowing the official to check the contents. O'Rouke then showed him a small holdall, and detecting a hint of Irish brogue in the officer's voice, winked at his pal Bigmore.

"So it's from Africa you are, now?" said the customs officer.

"Yes and a stinking hole it is to be sure" says Paddy, putting on the blarney.

"Well let's forget the formalities," said the customs officer. "Murphy's the name, boy's"

Quick as a flash, O'Rouke held out a grimy and somewhat calloused hand, offering it to the official. "Patrick O'Rouke at your service, Mr Murphy," he said with a grin.

Touching his forelock in some form of salute he shook the officer's proffered hand, saying; "Well now Mr Murphy it's grand to meet someone like yourself, from the old country."

The officer studied him for a moment, and in his broad Irish accent cagily asked; "And what about you now Patrick, have you anything else to declare."

From beneath his bunk O'Rouke dragged a large canvas kitbag, that had seen better days. Tipping it up, he emptied the contents on his bunk. "There ye'are Mr Murphy sir, that's me lot," said Paddy. Glancing at the untidy heap of clothes spilling out of the bag, the officer lost interest in it's contents. There was nothing more than a pair of seaboots, much the worse for wear, a cracked shaving bowl, cut-throat razor, and a faded photograph of some distant relative inside. Never having to undergo such a thorough search before Paddy was inquisitive, and asked the officer; "And what would you be looking for Mr Murphy?"

"Well I guess you don't have any," said the officer, "the place is clean."

"And what in the Lord's name would I be wanting to hide" said O'Rouke, acting the innocent.

"Surely you've heard of Irish Sweepstake tickets now boy's," grinned the official. Paddy's eyes lit up in mock surprise. Here was an opportunity for him to get even with first mate, Prendergast. The man who had the audacity to stop him going ashore, for a much needed drink. Turning to his pal Bigmore he winked, saying; "Did you hear that now, Ted. This here gentleman's looking for Sweepstake Tickets, of all things. Now what was it, you were telling me about them."

"Oh it was nothing much," said Bigmore, "just a conversation I heard before we arrived here," he confessed.

"About what?" asked the officer, interested in what he had to say.

"Why don't you tell him, Pat," said Bigmore, "you can explain it better than me?"

"Well t'was like this Mr Murphy, Sir," said Paddy. Trying hard to make it sound none too serious, yet holding the man's attention. "Me mate here was coming off the bridge a few nights ago, having done his spell at the wheel. Passing along the deck he heard these voices talking, and they mentioned Irish Sweepstake tickets for this month's Derby. He couldn't see too much through the porthole, Mr Murphy, Sir, because the curtains was partly drawn."

Hesitating long enough for the officer to say; "Well go on, and what did you see?" O'Rouke continued. "Now you'll never

125

believe who me pal saw Mr Murphy. I tell you it fair shook i'm up it did. T 'was that Prendergast, the first mate."

"There you are officer" said O'Rouke, rambling on with a touch of the blarney. "You can't trust any of them, Sir. All these foreigners taking tickets out of the country and robbing the poor Irish folk, what do you think of that, Mr Murphy."

"H'm," said the officer. "The fellow you speak of Patrick, was that him I passed as I came up the gangway."

"Ah, for sure officer he was the very one, him with the three gold stripes on his coat sleeve. The very man, Mr Murphy," echo'd Paddy's mate, Ted Bigmore. "And more than likely waiting for his contact on the shore, to collect the tickets," sir.

"Thanks for the information boys," said Customs Officer Murphy as he left the cabin. "I'll not mention your names."

"You're a sweet talking sod, Paddy" grinned Bigmore, as soon as Murphy was out of earshot. "I've never heard such bull-shit."

"Ah but it'll sort that bloody Prendergast out, Ted, then we can scarper ashore."

Meanwhile, customs officer Murphy joined his companion, who'd been rummaging through the African stokers' quarters. The pair walked along the afterdeck toward the ship's gangway, where Prendergast, was busy talking to a longshoreman. Exchanging their usual "good morning" courtesies as they approached, Slim asked; "Is there anything I can do for you gentlemen?"

"Well" say's Mr Murphy, "come to think of it there is. We've searched the crew's quarter's and if you'd oblige us, we'd like to make a start on the officers' cabins."

"Search the officers" said Prendergast, "what for, they don't usually bother with us."

"Oh, it happens now and again that we get special instructions," said the Customs Officer, following Slim up onto the boat deck.

"But what are you searching for," Prendergast wanted to know.

It was at this particular moment, O'Rouke and Bigmore decided it was time for them to hit the road. Strolling nonchalantly toward the gangway they heard their arch enemy, Prendergast, arguing with the two customs officers outside his cabin on the boat deck.

"But I haven't got any damned Irish Sweepstake tickets," the first mate protested angrily. "Why do you keep on asking me what I've bloody-well done with them. I can hardly afford a tram ticket on the wages I'm being paid here."

Suppressing an urge to burst out laughing, Paddy and his sidekick Bigmore hurried ashore. In the seclusion of the customs' shed roars of Cockney and Irish laughter rent the air, as the pair rolled around in hysterics. "That's stopped his gallop," said Bigmore. "Who does he think he is, trying to stop our shore leave."

"Aw' c'mon Ted," said Paddy, "let's get a drink before I die laughing."

Following a cursory examination of Prendergast's cabin the tumult and shouting simmered down, with the first mate still protesting his innocence. Although professing to know nothing about the Sweepstake Tickets they assumed he was smuggling into the country, customs officials insisted he remain on board until further inquiries were made. It seemed O'Rouke had managed to convince customs' authorities the first mate was indeed a regular carrier of contraband, and thereby put the boot in Herr Prendergast. Sidelong glances from his fellow officers at the lunch table that day, made the first mate feel distinctly uncomfortable. Things got completely out of hand when Morgan the Chief Engineer jokingly asked him; "D'you have any sweepstake tickets to spare, Mr Mate."

This was too much for the enraged Prendergast. Rising from the table he pointed a finger at Morgan and leered;

"Why don't you stuff an oily wad in your big gob chief, you're too damn nosey."

This brought a huge smile to the face of Captain Collie, nicknamed the "Manx Tiger."

Charles G. Ashford

Not wishing to get involved in a heated exchange of words I left the warring couple to sort things out for themselves, and hurried along to the gangway. When about to slip away unnoticed my path ashore was blocked by the Bo'sun, referred to as "The Walrus."

"Ullo there Sparks" he said, "Off ashore are you."

"Just going to take a quick look around town, Wally," I assured him.

"Well, don't hang around the docks Sparky boy," he warned. "They'll cut yer blooming throat for five cents."

"Oh, I'll slip up town then, maybe it's safer there."

"Smart young lad like you will 'ave to watch the ladies," he advised. "You're only seventeen son, so you don't want to catch a dose of the pox now do you?" he said, with a sly grin.

"The pox" Wally. Do you mean chicken pox," I said, somewhat alarmed. "I've had measles and mumps when I was younger, but I've never had that. Is it dangerous?"

His face took on a purple hue, and he almost exploded.

"Dangerous did you say son, it could ruin you fer life. This place is rotten with it. Take my advice son and give the pretty girls a miss, c'os if you go with them your thingy could drop off. You could even go blind lad. Now you wouldn't like to go back home to yer mum without a thingy, carrying a white stick, would you now?"

The very thought of walking about without a thingy and having to use a white stick, tap tapping my way along the pavement because of blindness, sent a feeling of horror coursing through my body.

"I'll keep clear of them, Bo'sun" I promised him, "I'll just have a quick look around the shops."

Taking a taxi I hi-tailed it up town to the large department stores, visiting Gimble's and Macy's on fifth avenue. Heading for Times Square I was about to hail a taxi, having decided I'd had enough for one day, when the plaintive cry of a familiar voice assailed my ears.

"Oi there Sparks, where yer dashing off to. Come ere an ave a drink?"

"Good grief" I muttered to myself, "how unlucky can you get."

Sitting on the sidewalk as large as life, clutching a large jug of cider or some other concoction, were none other than Paddy O'Rourke and his side kick, Ted Bigmore. They'd apparently been painting the town red. How they managed to reach such a sophisticated area in the state they were in, was beyond comprehension. Their usual hunting grounds were the nearest pub outside the dock gates, so I guess they must have taken a taxi.

Making an excuse that I needed to get to a toilet, I shot away like a bat out of hell. As expected the pair of them did not return aboard ship until late that night, and were soon in trouble with the law. Helping themselves to the remains of a leg of lamb from the ship's galley they offered the bone to a Customs and Excise guard dog, hoping to coax the animal on board the ship.

While our stay in New York was somewhat limited, I did manage to squeeze in another visit to many of the big stores on my last day ashore. Keeping an eye out hoping Paddy O'Rouke and his partner Bigmore were nowhere in the vicinity I hurried along Fifth Avenue. By-passing Broadway, and Times Square, I hopped aboard a trolley car on my way back to the ship. Not forgetting to post a letter home to my mother, in reply to the one I received from her on arrival here.

Before returning aboard ship I visited the nearest drug store and purchased a small bottle of disinfectant, mindful of the Bosun's recent warning about catching galloping dry rot or some other contagious disease, that frightened the life out of me. Unfamiliar as I was at the time with much of the seafarers' jargon, I was to all intents and purposes still a greenhorn. Otherwise I would never have allowed the Bo'sun to scare me, with a list of unimaginable diseases I'd be likely to pick up.

A change of orders cutting short our stay in New York was not unexpected, tramp steamers like the S.S. Ardmere having no regular trade route were liable to be sent all over the globe to pick up cargo. It therefore came as no surprise when the vessel was ordered to leave New York harbour, on a morning cloaked in heavy mist. Loaded down to her plimsol line with a full general cargo the old tub met the choppy waters of the North Atlantic head on, her paper thin steel plates groaning beneath the weight. Like most of her crew, she was reluctant to make the long arduous trip back to Africa.

Taking a south-bound route our journey back across the Atlantic's southern waters was smooth and uneventful, with never a ship in sight. It was also boring. Just catching sight of a flying fish skimming over the Atlantic's unruffled waters at first light of dawn, was enough to give rise to a bout of excitement. Leaping from the ocean, many caught in the fresh southeast trade winds were blown onto the ship's deck. Forever on the lookout for a tasty meal, Rusty the ship's cat had a plentiful supply of fresh fish for it's breakfast.

Battered by strong head winds whistling through the rigging off Africa's west coast there was a dull thudding sound as the old tub dipped her bows into a deep trough, limping into Freetown, Sierra Leone, our first port of call. Waiting to meet us were the same old invading hordes of native cargo workers, waiting to pick us clean. First aboard was Joe Beef, offering his services as the seamans' mess boy. Forgiving old Nosey Parker who'd subjected him a dose of the trots on our previous trip, when offering him a drink of a purgative known as black draught, in mistake for a beer, he warmly greeted the old sea dog.

"Hello Massa Parker" said Joe, saluting him. "I wait you long time, sah. Me your mess boy one more time. You give no more bad beer, please sah;"

"Alright Joe, take your gear aft before the rest of the bandits take over" said Parker, rising from his huge teakwood chair, as though a tribal chief. Walking along to his quarters, he informed the rest of the seamen Joe Beef had been hired as their mess boy again.

"He hasn't come for another dose of the shits, has he," laughed Snowy White.

"He might put some of the witch doctor's jollop in your tea this trip, Nosey, so you'd better watch out."

Within the hour two hundred native workers swarmed aboard and like an army of ants they ran amok over the entire ship's deck, seeking a place to hide their belongings. Several seen to make a bee line for the fresh water pump beneath the fo'c's'le head found it chained and padlocked, the key given to their head man with restrictions on it's use. By nightfall things had settled down and with some semblance of order restored, the S.S. Ardmere heaved up anchor and slipped quietly out to sea. Standing on deck, I watched the lights of Freetown fade in the distance. Further along the coast sporadic spurts of flame from bush fires, lit up the night sky. Flickering in the inky black of night for a moment, they were gone. All that could be heard was the rush of water slapping against the ship's side as she carved her way south, riding the Atlantic's silken waters.

A build up of overnight cloud left a morning sky of grey, a sure sign the rainy season was about to commence. Yesterday's oppressive heat was now replaced by a stiff breeze, bringing ominous black clouds in it's wake, scudding across the horizon. A period of violent thunder, followed by vivid flashes of lightning, warned of the deluge that followed. Suddenly, the wind increased, and down it came. Huge droplets of rain the size of penny pieces hit the deck, bouncing around as though on springs.

Leaving the stiffling atmosphere of the radio room for a breath of fresh air I made my way to the bridge, where Gilchrist the second mate paced restlessly up and down. Soaked to the skin and evidently worried by a sea mist that had developed to cloud his vision, he slipped into the chart-room to dry himself off. As further heavy showers lashed the vessel he quickly donned his oilskins before returning out on the open bridge, to face the elements. Nerves on edge he strode up and down the starboard wing of the bridge until a ferocious downpour accompanied by flashes of lightning, drove him back into the wheel-house. Unable to see his way ahead because of the ensuing deluge, the tension caused him to break wind. Startled by the noise, the native bridge boy busy polishing his brass looked up in surprise, saying; "Master, your arse he go talk."

Seeing a look of guilt spread across the second mate's face, Taffy Davis standing at the helm burst into a fit of laughter. Feeling embarrased, Gilchrist chose to ignore the native's remark, and stepped back out onto the starboard wing of the bridge. He had no doubt this episode would be relayed to all and sundry down in the seamen's forcastle by the helmsman, at the earliest opportunity.

Berthing late that afternoon at Takoradi, one of the Gold Coast's larger seaports, work began on discharging the S.S. Ardmere's 200 tons of kerosene. Taking little more than an couple of hours, off duty crewmen had scant time to slip ashore for a drink. Surprisingly this did not worry the likes of O'Rouke and Bigmore, who'd already had their shore leave suspended by Captain Collie, for running amok in Matadi. Instructing Joe Beef their native mess boy to purchase a quantity of local brewed Palm Wine from the nearby village they quietly congratulated each other on making such a crafty move, and waited for the boy to come back aboard, believing all was well.

Night had fallen by the time I finished my evening stroll around the deck, when in the glare of the vessel's arc lights I watched Joe Beef the seamen's African mess boy stagger up the ship's gangway. Bent double with a heavy load on his back he stepped aboard as a dark clad figure hidden from view on the lower deck stepped out of the shadows and stopped him, on his way to the seamens' quarters on the after deck..

"What you got there, boy?" said first mate, Prendergast, taking the startled Joe Beef by surprise.

Dropping his sack on the deck, Joe Beef opened it up for the mate to peer inside. Bending low Prendergast thrust his head into the open sack and reeled back as though stung.

"What the hell is this," he yelled; "It stinks to high heaven."

"Him tombo sah" said Joe Beef, a puzzled look on his face. "Him good Africa palm wine, sah," he proudly announced.

Screwing up his face in disgust, Prendergast snorted; "Where d'you get this stinking concoction from, the bloody sewer? It's enough to poison a donkey."

"Dis not for me sah" pleaded Joe Beef, and pointing to the sack holding two large calabashs of the horrible brew, he stuttered; "Him for big Massa Paddy sah. He speak no go shore-side, get plenty headache. Him tell me, Joe Beef go bring plenty Tombo."

"Ah, so that's his bloody game" sneered Prendergast, and gave the two jars of palm wine a hefty kick, sending the contents spewing out all over the deck.

Rousing the seamen from their quarters, Prendergast ordered O'Rouke and Bigmore to get buckets and brooms to clean up the mess. Under his watchful eye they toiled long into the hours of darkness, scrubbing the deck clean. Only then were they allowed to slink off to their quarters, without as much as a sip of the jungle juice they craved.

Our departure from Takoradi next morning was delayed by a violent thunder storm with gale force winds sweeping along the coast, bending tall palm trees in it's path like an archer's bow. It was almost midday when we managed to leave the harbour and head in a southerly direction towards Lagos, our next port of call. As so often happens with tramp steamers, our expected visit to Port Harcourt was cancelled at the last minute, with our cargo of kerosene for the town being transferred to a small coasting vessel.

Leaving our berth alongside the wharf at Appapa we were requested to anchor up one of many swamp infested creeks in the vicinity, to await further orders. Surrounded by dense jungle as far as the eye could see with suffocating night temperatures that defied description, a goodnight kiss from any one of thousands of mosquitoes invading this swamp infested area was guaranteed to give you a dose of the screaming abdabs. Why, I kept asking myself, was I stupid enough to think a life at sea among these green jungle horrors was my forte. I could so easily have been swanning around on a bicycle at home working for Sainsbury's, the family grocers.

Waiting in that stinking green hell for what a seemed a lifetime, but was only a matter of weeks, we finally left our jungle hideaway. Running short of coal we were ordered to proceed to Durban, South Africa, to replenish our depleted stock, and await further instructions. Arriving in the port after an uneventful four day passage down the African coast, we at least had the benefit of a cool ocean breeze, a breath of clean air, and able to stretch our legs with a stroll along the dockside. Other than that there was little for me to do except watch a group of native convicts arrive each morning, to work on the new breakwater.

Chained to one another with leg irons the prisoners were guarded by three native warders armed with assegai's, as they toiled throughout the heat of the day beneath a blazing sun. Short breaks were given for a tin mug of water, but an unscheduled stop in between was rewarded with a quick response from a warder. The tip of a spear prodded their backsides, or they would feel the stinging lash of the white overseer's bull whip. Transport in and around the area we were informed was either by a rickety old banger that invariably threw in the towel when you were halfway to your destination, or a more sedate form of travel, the rickshaw. Jog-trotting at a steady pace, a half naked Zulu wearing a feathered head-dress and little more than a jock strap made of leopard skin covering his loins, would perchance take you to your destination.

Preparing to go ashore I approached the Dutch overseer who'd just boarded the ship, and asked; "How much do I pay the chap with the rickshaw?"

"Chap he answered," giving me a rather puzzled look. I knew then he did not understand what I meant.

"My friend and I want to go up town, how much do I pay him" I said, pointing to the Zulu?"

"Oh, the kaffir" he laughed aloud. "Never give them what they ask for, just give em half."

"But he's a big fellow" I said, "supposing he starts arguing."

"Kick his arse," was the man's quick response.

That most certainly was not the type of situation a skinny seventeen year old greenhorn, wished to get mixed up in. A second glance at the fellow's rippling muscles on his huge torso, caused me to quickly change my mind. Why, the fellow might take me to some lonely spot and eat me, I feared. I decided after all I could quite easily see all I wanted to of Durban from the safety of the ship's deck, and as luck would have it, our stay here was limited to the time it took the ship to bunker. Before leaving Durban Captain Collie decided to fill the vessel's ballast tanks, to give the old tub some stability. Soon we were on our way to God knows where, the Captain being the only person with a clue as to our next destination, but would not inform anyone.

Abreast of Capetown the ship was buffeted by strong south easterly winds and a huge sea swell that tossed the old tub about like a piece of cork, as she pitched and rolled her way up the east coast of Africa. Each time a following sea swept under her stern the vessel lurched forward, burying her nose deep in the ocean. Without warning the after end would rise clear of the water to shake the vessel from stem to stern, her propeller thrashing the air like some wild thing. Fearing this might cause serious damage to his ship, Captain Collie requested the Chief Engineer report to him on the top deck.

"Can't you ease the engine revs down Chief?" the Captain asked him, when he appeared on the bridge. "You're shaking the guts out of her."

"I've already told that idiot on watch to ease the throttle down when she takes a nose-dive, I can't do more than that, Captain."

"She'll fall apart if we don't watch out," the captain moaned. "There's only a layer of rust and the rats holding hands down below, that's keeping the bloody ship afloat," he went on.

The situation went from bad to worse, when the ship was halfway up the East African coast. Checking the fresh water tanks the ship's carpenter discovered our supply of drinking water was running short and reported the matter to the Captain, who decided to make an emergency stop at the nearest port to hand, Mombassa. Lying close to the equator this is Kenya's main port with a natural harbour where ships arriving with general cargo for the port, took the opportunity to replenish the vessel's supply of fresh fruit and vegetables. An overnight stay was more than sufficient for any human being in the oppressive heat of this tropical cauldron, where daytime temperatures reached one hundred and twenty degree's in the shade. At night the hot and sticky atmosphere encouraged armies of nocturnal creatures to invade the ship from outlying swamps, making life intolerable for all concerned. A point emphasized by a remark from an irate seaman, saying; "They've got hobnail boots on."

The final leg of our long boring journey took us across the Indian Ocean to Colombo, capital of Ceylon. It was late afternoon when the ship dropped her anchor, in one of the many beautiful bays surrounding the island. Staying no more than a few hours we again replenished our depleted supply of fresh water, before setting off to our next destination, where ever that might be.

From the deck of the S.S. Ardmere I surveyed the town's palm fringed beach with it's stretches of sun-kissed golden sand, caressed by the clear blue waters of the Indian ocean. How I envied the young native children frolicking about in the surf, while I had to be content to pace the deck of this rusting hulk. With scant relief from the stiffling heat.

As evening approached the sun appeared as a red ball of fire hovering on the far horizon for no more than a few fleeting seconds, then surrendering to fast approaching hours of darkness, it slipped out of sight. In the inky blackness of a moonless night we hoisted our anchor and slipped back out to sea, hugging the Indian coast on our journey north to Calcutta, capital of Bengal. With no suitable berth the ship was secured to bouys in midstream on the Hoogli river, using the ship's anchor cable. Within a short space of time, a flotilla of heavily laden barges arrived alongside the ship. After much arguing among them as to who would be discharged first, order was restored among Indian barge crews, when the first mate threatened to cut them all adrift. Work on discharging large quantities of rice and gunny bags from each of these craft went on ceaselessly during the following weeks, loading much needed commodities in short supply on many cocoa plantations throughout West Africa.

On this my first visit to India I was appalled to see large families of poorer class Indians living in such squalid conditions on board these barges, where poverty and deprivation are accepted as a way of life. Even the water they drink and wash in, is from the polluted waters of the river, where vultures are seen to feed off dead bodies that are allowed to drift up and down it's length for days on end. While class distinction is much in evidence in this vast country, the only means of earning a living for many of the poorer classes such as the untouchables, is by begging. Is it any wonder when strangers visit this country they are often surprised and saddened, as I was, when accosted in the street by infants in ragged clothes, begging for money. Arms outstretched they approach a stranger, with a cry of; "Baksheesh Sahib."

Much as I would have liked to further explore this historic city of Calcutta which started as a trading post for the then British India Company way back in 1690, the place had lost it's appeal following my one and only venture ashore. This land of fragrant perfumes, silks and spices, not to mention Rajahs and their beautiful palaces written about in children's storybooks had, for me, suddenly ceased to exist. The bubble burst so to speak, when I first set foot ashore. The aroma of eastern promise replaced by a pong of stale curry, and a strong odour of cow - muck lying in sun-baked village streets.

It was with a feeling of relief and sadness I left the city of Calcutta some weeks later with the cry of hungry children ringing in my ears, mindful never to return. Our journey via the

Cape of Good Hope to the West Coast of Africa was anything but hopeful for those of us aboard the S.S Ardmere, when the weather turned nasty abreast of Capetown. Lying deep in the water she fell victim to a strong south easterly gale lashing the ship, spewing heavy seas over her rusting deck. Rounding the Cape, a huge sea swell caused her to dance about like a marionette. At times she buried her nose into seemingly bottomless troughs and I feared she would turn turtle, never to resurface. But the old tub did her best to maintain a top speed of five knots, when at the same time shaking the guts out of us. It was with a feeling of relief we reached Duala, a seaport in the Cameroons on Africa's West Coast, administered by the French.

Whilst exporting large quantities of minerals, hides, timber, and other raw materials, the area has vast banana plantations. Duala's railway being of strategic importance, links it to Yauonde, the capital. Lying in the Gulf of Guinea close to the equator, one is glad to seek shelter from the intense heat during daylight hours. With this in mind, canvas awnings giving adequate protection from the tropical sun, were put up around the bridge and crews' quarters.

With the bulk of the ship's cargo of rice being discharged here in Duala taking forever, we suffered in this sweltering heat from dawn till dusk. Like many African ports lying up jungle infested rivers Duala had it's nightly patrol of winged monsters, inducing one and all to sweat it out each night beneath mosquito nets, in oven-like conditions. Trying to sleep in temperatures exceeding one hundred degrees throughout the hours of darkness, was like asking for manna from heaven. Luxuries such as electric fans were unheard of on this ship, and even to suggest the idea of having one installed for one's comfort, was liable to cause the captain to have an apoplectic fit.

After what seemed an eternity the loading of cargo for the ship was finally completed with a consignment of mahogany logs bound for the U.S.A, securely fastened down on her deck. It was with unbounded joy I felt the old ship's engine tremble beneath my feet the night we sailed for Takoradi, having spent some three weeks in seeking relief from a tropical sun so fierce, it could have dried up the sea. Although Takoradi's position in the equatorial Gulf of Guinea boasted much the same tropical atmosphere as our last port of call, we were able to enjoy the benefit of cool sea breezes, instead of the unbearable jungle heat of Duala.

Daybreak saw the sun peeping above the horizon sending an orange glow across the ocean's stillness as we slipped into Takoradi harbour unnoticed, where a handful of natives waited to take the ship's mooring ropes. By mid-morning native dock workers arrived to discharge what little remained of our cargo of gunny bags from India, and clean out number one and four holds which now lay empty. Consignments of cocoa beans lying on the quayside were hurriedly stripped of waterproof coverings, and work on loading the S.S Ardmere began in earnest. Toiling from early morning until long after dusk natives worked through the choking heat of each day with a short break for a meal at noon, until the job was completed by the end of the second week. It was now time for us to set course for our final port of call.

Sailing due north under blue skies with just the hint of a breeze off the Atlantic Ocean, the journey by all accounts took much longer than anticipated due to engine failure. This saw us limping into the harbour at Freetown, Sierra Leone, for much needed repairs. Our orders were to move up a narrow creek with swamp and jungle either side, where we dropped anchor close to a rickerty wooden jetty. From his vantage point on the boat deck Captain Collie watched a small tug towing a string of barges loaded with chrome ore toward his ship, and sensing they were not under control shouted a warning, instructing the tug to slow down.

Wringing his hands in despair when the order was not carried out, he winced as the loaded barges thudded against the ship's side. The impact caused the vessel's paper thin plates to bend like an archer's bow, shaking the vessel from stem to stern. A column of red dust was seen to shoot into the air and drift astern, leaving a brown carpet on the creek's muddy surface.

"Is there no one looking after my ship mister?" he asked Prendergast his first mate, who seemed at a loss for something to do.

"Get the Bo'sun to put a couple of men on the port side to watch these stupid natives," he moaned. "They'll sink my damn ship if you let them. Just look at this idiot" he growled, as another barge slammed against the ship's side.

Seamen Parker and Sullivan were detailed off to ensure the next load of barges caused no further damage to the ship, and waited for them to come alongside with fenders ready. Missing his target by a mile the tug captain in charge of the operation was unable to avoid a head on collision with the ship as it rattled her plates, bouncing off the vessel's side in a shower of rust. Watching from the boat deck Captain Collie vent his anger at the two seamen, who stood there laughing.

"They've damaged my blasted ship" he screamed, "and you damned fools stand there grinning like a pair of Cheshire cats."

Sullivan spread his hands in an apologetic gesture; "It's only the rust that's fallen off Capt'n."

"Rust be damned, we could have sprung a blasted leak," he bellowed.

"They've saved us the bloody job of chipping it," Sullivan muttered to his mate.

"It'll give the weevils a breath of fresh air," grinned Parker. "They've been dying to escape."

Whilst the loading of the ship was taking place in this God-forsaken, swamp infested green hell, out in the middle of nowhere, I fell victim to the dreaded Malaria. In a moment of madness I threw caution to the wind when taking a moonlight stroll on the boat deck, and forgot to use a mosquito repellent I kept in my cabin. Halfway round the ship I received a goodnight kiss from one of many thousands of tiny winged monsters, buzzing about in the warm night air. It was no more than a pin prick, but I soon learnt the little devil had the kick of a mule.

Some twenty four hours had passed when I began to feel a little dizzy, my head started to spin around like a top and an uncontrollable bout of shivering gripped my body, cartwheeling me into space. Buckling at the knees there was nothing I could do to save myself from falling as the steel deck came up to meet me, while I drifted aimlessly into oblivion. Entombed in a place of darkness from which there seemed no escape, a pinpoint of light suddenly appeared to lead me out of a long tunnel, where soft white clouds brushed my face in passing. Regaining consciousness I was vaguely aware of a dark skinned man at my bedside saying to the person standing next to him; "I'll have to give him an injection."

A voice I recognized belonging to Perkins our senior radio operator, tried to reassure me all was well, saying; "You'll be alright, Charles."

A whiff of surgical spirits assailed my nostrils as the native doctor wiped my arm with a piece of cottonwool, and muttered; "Just a little jab, Mr Ashford."

I tried to remain calm as the needle bit into my flesh, then felt myself slipping into a bottomless pit. I was just another victim of the dreaded malaria, a disease I was told, few survived.

It has often been said death comes suddenly to people afflicted with tropical diseases, favouring neither young or old. Malaria and blackwater fever are a curse to the European community where in many instances the victims indulge in bouts of drinking, brought about by sheer boredom. Sometimes an accumulation of all three. In any event death can come swiftly, for many there is no time to linger while relatives and nurses tiptoe around making comforting noises. How I lived to tell the tale when so many young men who'd gone before me simply perished, I will never know. During the next six years I was to suffer with this dreaded disease.

It was late December of 1938 when the S.S. Ardmere once again sailed into New York, where bitterly cold easterly winds iced up our snow covered decks like some skating rink. The ship's Captain had by law to report I had a tropical disease to the Port Health Authority, who insisted I be sent to hospital immediately. From our berth in Brooklyn I was quickly transferred to the Long Island College Hospital and left to await a visit from the doctor, in a small ante room.

"Hello, can I help you?" asked the young man, who'd popped his head around the door in passing. "And where have you come from" he asked, looking me up and down.

"I've just arrived on a ship from Sierra Leone, West Africa," I informed him.

"You look ill. Are you suffering from some malady?" he asked. Mention of the word Malaria, saw his face light up in surprise. "Malaria did you say sir. Would you care to come this way, please."

I was taken into a laboratory where a group of young men similarly attired in white coats were busy conducting some sort of experiment or other, among a collection of test tubes and bunsen burners.

"We have a visitor from Africa suffering with a tropical disease," my guide announced to his fellow workers. "Malaria, no less, I believe. Is that correct sir?" he asked me.

My answer was lost in a tinkle of glass being swept aside, as they gathered around me. Then like werewolves baying for a victim's blood, they took samples from my fingers. I became a human pin cushion. But for a kindly nurse who happened to be passing by and released me from the clutches of these young students, I would have been bled dry. I was then taken to a ward in the hospital and placed under observation, until the ship was ready to leave New York. Visits from sympathetic old ladies who brought me presents of cookies, candy and magazine's, made life delightfully tolerable.

"So you're from Africa" my visitor would say. "Why, it must have been awful for you out there, what with the heat and all those wild animals roaming about."

Comfortable in my new surroundings I soon adjusted to the luxury afforded me in hospital, and wished my ship would sail off without me. Sadly, this was not to be. Like black clouds suddenly appearing on the horizon Captain Collie and his bosom pal first mate, Prendergast, appeared at the far end of the ward.

Peeping from beneath my blankets I watched as their beady eyes scanned the room, looking for me. It was just a matter of time before they arrived at the foot of my bed, where they stood exchanging glances. Prendergast's face went from white to crimson, when seeing the huge assortment of goodies I'd been tucking into.

"I hope the company isn't paying for this lot" he grumbled, "just look at all the chocolates he's been eating, Captain."

Several glossy magazines and papers lay on a table at my beside with a half empty box of chocolates and packets of cookies, donated by kindly old dowagers on their weekly visits.

Removing a blanket covering my head, Prendergast grunted; "Come on son you've been here long enough, you'd better dress and get back on board. We're leaving on the morning tide."

"You've cost the company enough already," Captain Collie whinged. "You're not staying here a moment longer in the lap of luxury."

Back on board the ship that night I dreamt the Captain and first mate were shipwrecked, many miles away. Adrift in an open boat that leaked like a sieve they held hands and sang let's be buddies, as it slowly sank beneath the waves.

Awakened next morning by the noise of the ship's steam winches heaving our mooring ropes aboard, I lay in my bunk thinking of what might have been. Cursing my luck and Captain Collie for dragging me back aboard this heap of junk, I watched the skyscrapers on Manhattan's skyline fade in the distance. With New York and the Hudson river far astern of us, we reached the open sea. Only then did I realize life could have been so much easier if those two jerks had left me in hospital, to be spoilt by the old ladies who visited me.

A cold blustery north east wind and a following sea caused the vessel to pitch and toss about like some wild thing, dipping her bows into every trough. Off Cape Cod a blinding snow storm delayed our arrival at Boston until the following day, when our deck cargo of mahogany logs was hurriedly discharged ashore. Leaving on the morning tide we then sailed on to

Philadelphia, where a small cargo of kerosene was taken on board. At the end of January amid showers of snow, rain and a good deal of fog we left Philadelphia for Norfolk, Virginia, to replenish our dwindling supply of coal, which by this time were pretty low. Arriving in Norfolk the following morning bunkering the ship took no more than fours hours, allowing the S.S Ardmere with a full compliment of cargo to leave the port. Creaking and groaning under the weight of a full consignment of general cargo, she ploughed on into the cold unfriendly waters of the Atlantic. By taking in a southerly route we hoped to avoid running into any bad weather that lay in our path enroute to the West Coast of Africa, which at the earliest would take us the best part of three weeks with our top speed of six knots.

Due to make landfall within the next few days, I wondered if mother had taken the time to write. Her letters having been few and far between over the past six months worried me, for I had no way of knowing if all was well at home. In a matter of weeks my two year contract with the company was due to expire, bringing to a close an exciting chapter in my life. Remembering my upbringing as a child in the cloistered atmosphere of a convent, I had during my two years at sea come to learn about life as it really was, seeing for myself much that amused or shocked me. I would doubtless return home a much wiser young man.

As expected there was no letter from mother on my arrival in the African Port of Freetown, Sierra Leone, a disappointment I sought to overlook, knowing I was soon to be on my way home. It was not long before I started packing my personal belongings and prepared to board a waiting launch with several members of the crew, about to leave the rusty old tub that had been our home for the past two years. Memories of my time aboard the S.S. Ardmere both good and bad flashed through my mind in a trice, but I had to confess there were no regrets.

On landing ashore all member of the ship's crew due to be relieved were accommodated at the City Hotel, a large white fronted building on the edge of town, equal in status to that of a second class boarding house back home. A swashbuckling Greek who imagined he was Errol Flynn, ran this hotel, treating his native staff like a bunch of pirates, which of course many of them were. The place was comfortable to a degree, if you didn't mind flies doing the breast stroke in your soup. In the lounge a radio purchased from some hard up seaman providing music from a bygone era, was the only source of entertainment the hotel offered to it's guests. The alternative was to spend an evening listening to the ceaseless banging of jungle drums, or a rendition of "O Sole Mio," from Paddy O'Rourke in a drunken stupor. Otherwise you might as well plug your ears with cotton wool and try to get some sleep, not forgetting to spread a mosquito net over your bed.

Having experienced several bouts of malaria during my time in Africa I was most anxious not to jeopardize my chances of a passage home, and made a point of using a mosquito net each night. There was no way I wished to end up in a native hospital. Paddy O'Rourke however, seemed immune to the mosquitoes deadly bite, which left me wondering if it was the amount of local brewed jungle juice he'd consumed that deterred them. Along with his buddy Ted Bigmore they danced the night away with the native girls in the nearby village, to the non-stop rhythm of the tom-tom's.

From the window of my hotel next day I watched the rusty old tub that had been my home for the last two years sail away, leaving me with a wealth of experience gained during my time aboard. Witnessing firsthand many amusing incidents among drunken seamen after a night on the tiles, so to speak, reminded me of a quotation from one of many books I'd read; "If only we could see ourselves, as others see us."

With little first-hand knowledge about life at sea from the outset I was to all intents and purposes an innocent abroad, when signing on the S.S Ardmere at the tender age of seventeen. Coarse language used in everyday life on board the ship was hard for me to grasp, due to my convent upbringing. I later learned to live with such remarks, often spoken in a humorous manner.

My long awaited passage back home arrived after two weeks. As I stood with some of my shipmates on the waterfront, we watched the silhouette of a ship out on the horizon grow larger with each passing minute. Back at the hotel, lunch was served amid a hubbub of excitement. Our main topic of conversation centred on the question, how soon would we be on our way home. It was late afternoon when we received word from the company's agent that we were to take passage aboard the M.V. Accra, lying at anchor in the bay. To whoops of delight everyone hurriedly packed their bags, and leaving the City Hotel were taken down to a small jetty, where we spent several hours waiting for a launch to take us out to the ship. Late that evening I stood on the boat deck as she prepared to leave, her poweful engines throbbing beneath my feet, as they burst into life. Soon the twinkling lights of Freetown slowly disappeared in the gathering gloom as the vessel picked up speed, and headed out to sea.

Waking early next morning to the cry of sea-gulls on the wing waiting for the usual bucket of garbage from the galley, I lay still for a while and listened to the waves slapping gently against the ship's side. Above my cabin I could hear crewmen going about their morning chores hosing down the ship, brooms scraping the wooden deck. Rising slowly I washed and dressed and left the cabin for my morning walk, before venturing into the dining room for breakfast.

We were now three days out from Freetown and approaching Cape Finisterre the northernmost point in the Bay of Biscay, when the weather quickly deteriorated. Struggling to maintain a steady speed of fifteen knots against gale force winds, a relatively calm sea had suddenly whipped up waves of mountainous proportions, which at times threatened to swamp us. It's ferocity easing in intensity, on reaching calmer waters of the English Channel. It was on the sixth of March of 1939 I caught my first glimpse of England's southern coast, since leaving some two and a half years earlier. Entering Plymouth Sound the M.V Accra was taken in tow by attendant tugs, shepherding the vessel into her berth. Shortly after receiving clearance from Customs and Port Health Authorities I was given a railway ticket to London, and allowed to disembark. Hailing a taxi I asked to be taken to Plmouth railway station, and whilst waiting to reach my destination, my thoughts were of mother and home.

A Sad Homecoming.

"Here you are sir, Plymouth Station"said the taxi driver, helping me with my luggage. Paying him in excess of the fare he'd asked for, I took stock of my surroundings. Like most seaside towns in England during winter time the place was deserted, except for a handful of sailors from the nearby naval base, going on leave. At the ticket office a pale faced individual in a crumpled railway uniform scrutinized the travel voucher I'd given him, and pushing his black peaked cap to the back of his head, he took a good look at me. For over a minute or so his watery eyes studied my suntanned face as if to satisfy himself I was not on the wanted list, then asked; "And what can I do for you?"

"I'd like a ticket to Victoria Station please. That's if you're not too busy" I replied, tongue in cheek.

Looking at the green form again he produced a railway ticket from a drawer in his desk and once again eyed me with suspicion, before parting with it.

"Go to platform four over the bridge, the train will be here in half an hour," he drawled. Somewhat reluctant to part with the information.

A relic of past grandeur, when railways were a joy to behold, I found the waiting room at Plymouth station nothing but an empty shell, both cold and uninviting. On a wall covered in graffiti, a once ornate mirror hung from it's rusting chain at a grotesque angle, shattered beyond recognition. Travellers seeking to rest awhile would find little comfort inside, other than an overpowering smell of urinal, a drunken visitor's calling card. Out on the platform a machine that once held penny bars of Nestle's chocolate stood empty, the red paint peeling from it's rusting iron frame. Huddled up in a warm dufflecoat against biting March winds, I was obliged to paced up and down the station platform in an effort to keep warm, whilst waiting the arrival of my train.

With a pennant of white steam gushing from it's funnel, the train for London puffing into Plymouth station, was music to my ears. Time being of secondary importance the huge engine slowed to a snail's pace as it neared the platform, and ground to a halt. Carriage doors swung open as tired passengers tumbled out and trudged wearily toward the station exit, glad of an opportunity to stretch aching limbs. Stepping aboard I stowed my luggage in a rack above the seat, brushing off the footprints left by previous passengers from the red upholstery, before sitting down. Toffee papers and cigarette ends littered the carriage floor, whilst an odour of stale tobacco prompted me to open the window for a breath of fresh air. Some five minutes later the stationmaster's whistle spurred a uniformed railway guard into action. As the train jerked forward he hurried along the platform slamming several carriage doors shut, the noise reverberating throughout my compartment like a clap of thunder. Waving his green flag to indicate all was clear, a cloud of black smoke issuing from the funnel obscured my view of Plymouth Station as we left.

Frozen stiff after waiting on that cold and cheerless platform without shelter, warmth from the train's heating system slowly penetrated my body. Patches of morning fog hiding much of southern England as we travelled north, had dispersed by the time my train arrived in London. Alighting at Victoria Station a column of dense black smoke issuing from the engine drifted up toward it's glass covered roof, thick with layers of dust and grime accumulated over the years. The light of day failing to penetrate badly blackened areas. Carrying two heavy suitcases containing all my worldly goods I inched my way through bustling crowds, toward the exit. Conveniently parked outside, I took a taxi to the Embankment Underground Station where I caught my train to Wimbledon, then a local bus home.

With mother having failed to answer any of my letters during the final months of my time abroad, I approached the house with some misgivings. Could it be because of my insistence in begging her to divulge my sister's whereabouts, or

149

did she have some dark secret she desperately wanted to hide. Carefully considering many unanswered questions throughout the past months I was still in the dark as to her reason for not wanting me to have my sister's address, when arriving back at the home, I'd left two and a half years earlier. I had hoped she would at least explain why she had not written for the last six months of my time abroad, now that I had returned from my first voyage.

Knocking gently, I stood back from the door waiting to see the look of surprise on her face, to find me standing on her doorstep unannounced. An infant's cry from within the house gave no indication that anything was amiss, when I remembered mother had two small children to look after, when I left. As the front door swung open I was surprised to see a young woman standing there, holding an infant in her arms.

"Is Mrs Marsden in?" I asked.

The young lady shook her head. "I'm sorry sir" she said, "I think you've come to the wrong house, there is no one living here by that name."

"Well, this is 32 Merton Road isn't it?" I remarked, "my mother was living here when I left to go to sea."

"I'm afraid I can't help you" she said, apologetically."Why don't you ask next door. She must have known Mrs Marsden, as she has lived here for some time."

Somewhat bewildered I turned away, as she closed her front door. Mother's next door neighbour, Mrs Barnes, wasn't a wealth of information either. Simply saying she'd left the area some six months earlier, and whilst on friendly terms with her, had no idea where she had gone. The situation I now found myself in was nothing short of desperate; there was no one to whom I could turn. My inquiries at the local council offices having also proved fruitless, a feeling akin to panic, seized me. Not only had mother deserted me, she'd left me homeless. It was something I had not bargained for, when returning from sea.

Saddened, and bitterly disappointed by mother's disregard for my welfare, I retraced my steps to London, and sought help from the police. Giving them the last known address of my grandmother Mrs Adams, whose London address was Rye Lane, Peckham, they promised to contact her. But as my last glimmer of hope faded when they told me she was no longer living there, I was advised to seek refuge at the sailor's home where I could obtain temporary shelter. With what limited means of support I had and little prospect of discovering mother's whereabouts, I had no choice but to accept their advice.

A grim and forbidding greystone building guarded by iron spiked gates they called the sailor's home, was certainly no hotel. If anything, it was a replica of New Gate Prison as seen in the olden days. The accommodation was not particularly comfortable but with no alternative I had to remain there for the time being; it was either that or sleep on the streets. Pressing a rust encrusted button on the front door of the building, brought an immediate response from an elderly man who reeked of stale tobacco, and stared at me through pink rimmed eyes. Welcoming me in with a toothless grin, he rubbed his pale white hands together in an effort to keep them warm. Poking around a dimly-lit office he produced a tattered ledger and handing it to me, said; "Sign here for your room son, its five shillings a week."

Giving me the key to my room, he proceeded to lecture me on the pitfalls one encountered in such places saying; "Put yer boots, one under each leg of yer bed. That way, they can't pinch them, son."

Entering my room, I was shocked to find the window protected by steel bars. I had no way of knowing whether this was to prevent intruders from breaking into this house of horrors, or stopping the inmates from throwing themselves out. Maybe in a fit of depression, or a bout of the D,T's. Suffice to say, no sane person stayed too long here, where one was assured of a quick passage to the nut house if they dared to linger.

From the ground floor I climbed a wrought iron staircase up to a corridor with a row of small cubicles, with a communal washroom and lavatory at the far end. Carrying a horse blanket the old man had given me, I entered the tiny room to which I had been allotted. Sparsley furnished, it had an old iron bedstead and a tattered straw mattress, referred to as the donkey's breakfast, by members of the seafaring community. In one corner of the room stood a small washstand with a cracked and discoloured basin, that had seen better days. On the floor shattered beyond repair lay a mirror, it's rusting chain left hanging on the wall.

A cold March wind whistled through gaps in the window of the room where I was to sleep, turning it into an ice box. Eyeing the razor thin straw mattress with suspicion I felt certain an army of bugs nestled inside, waiting to attack me as I slept. Bearing in mind the damage these blood sucking creatures could cause to one's person, I chose to leave my clothes on.

Wrapping a blanket around the mattress to stop the red devils escaping I used my jacket for a pillow, and covering myself with my overcoat, laid down to sleep. Then a series of unearthly screams from some demented drunkard on the lower landing chasing pink elephants, disturbed the entire fraternity of this glorified doss house, in the dead of night. Finding sleep impossible, I lay in a comatose state until morning. Daylight brought scant relief to my pain-racked body, after a night of torture on a bed of iron. Needless to say, I was filled with an urgent desire to remove myself from this damp and depressing establishment as soon as possible. The night's performance by some drunken inhabitant only served to hasten my speedy departure from this doss house, without so much as a bite to eat.

Depositing my luggage at the nearest railway station I took the tram to Leadenhall Street, in the city of London, where I sought employment with one of several shipping companies in the area. Like a lost sheep I wandered past tall office buildings, keeping an eye open for a likely doorway I might squeeze into, if only to get a warm. Stopping in front of a greystone building the brass plate attached to it's frontspiece caught my eye and, like a magnet, I was drawn toward the shiny object. A closer inspection revealed the name of a shipping company on the plate, one of which I'd heard glowing reports. With nothing to lose, I decided to take a chance, and mounted the steps.

Preventing myself from being trapped in the revolving doors as they spun around, I slipped in unscathed. Approaching a young receptionist in the foyer I explained to her I was destitute, and in desperate need of work. Taking pity on me she directed me toward a room crowded with people whom I recognized as seamen, by the clothes they wore, and was told to wait there.

"What's happening?" I asked the fellow standing next to me.

"We're hoping to sign on a ship" he replied, "there's very little work to be had at the moment."

My practiced eye knew in an instant to which department various members of this diverse gathering belonged, by their mode of dress. Stewards and cooks in the catering department were seen wearing a collar and tie, whereas seamen were easily recognized wearing dark blue jersey's. Among those employed as deckhands were a mixture of Liverpool or Cockney characters with one or two quietly spoken men from Scotland's far flung islands, the Outer Hebrides and Orkneys.

Questioned as to my presence in the office by a young clerk at the inquiry desk I was ushered into a well-lit ante-room, my feet sinking into luxurious carpets, warm to the touch.. An elderly gentleman seated behind a large oak desk pointed to a chair, requesting I be seated. He was tall and well proportioned, with a welcoming smile that put me at ease immediately.

"Are you in the company's employ, young man?" he asked.

"I'm afraid not, sir," I replied, and informed him I'd just arrived home following a long engagement abroad.

'Well now, what can I do for you?" he asked almost apologetically.

Explaining the unfortunate position I now found myself in through no fault of my own, I set about convincing the gentleman I was homeless and in need of help. Showing him my discharge papers from my last ship he left me for a moment to consult with a colleague in an adjoining room, and quickly returned. Dispensing with formalities, he politely asked;"How soon can you be ready? We have a vessel due to sail shortly, hopefully we can accommodate you."

Accepting his offer I duly signed aboard the M.V. Seafox, an intermediate class motor vessel of approximately five thousand tons gross weight, carrying a dozen passengers. Freshly painted she was loaded with a general cargo bound for West Africa, and lay waiting for her crew to join her. Within forty eight hours I would once again be back on the high seas a sadder but wiser man, promising myself come what may, the search for my sister Catherine would continue on my return to England. Time they say, is a great healer. Sadly, the hurt caused by my mother's sudden disappearance left bitter memories that would never be erased. She had for some unknown reason decided to cast me aside again, as she'd done when I was an infant.

Early morning sunshine glistened on the vessel's white paintwork as I stepped aboard. Seamen were busy clearing her decks of dunnage, prior to leaving the Port of London. Nearby lay two attendant tugs secured to the vessel fore and aft, waiting to tow her out into the river Thames. A signal from the pilot directing operations from the bridge saw the tugs heave the ship away from her berth, and as the lock gates swung open, she entered the river. In midstream our escorting tugs held us against a fast flowing tide until the ship's engines took over, then slipped their tow wires and headed back into dock. With reasonable weather ahead we made good time in reaching the English Channel, where a fresh south westerly breeze caused us to pitch and roll.

Our passage through the Bay of Biscay being moderately calm the vessel reached Madeira on schedule, where we stayed for a few hours. Moving on we visited the islands of Tenerife and Las Palmas, where passengers were allowed ashore for a short period of sightseeing. Having no cargo to discharge in the port, our stay was limited to the time it took the ship to refuel the vessel she then headed on her way south to Sierra Leone, West Africa.

Reaching Freetown our first port of call on the African coast, we prepared for the usual invasion of native workers about to descend upon us. Strategically placed in position astern and secured to the ship's rails by stout ropes, the native's toilet referred to in seafarer's jargon as the West African Ensign, waited for it's first customer. No sooner had the first batch of native cargo workers stepped aboard there was trouble, squabbling broke out among late comers careering madly around the ship's deck seeking a place to hide their belongings. Many arguments getting out of hand were soon settled by the head man in charge, who beat the culprits with a heavy cane, often seen to bounce off their thick heads.

Leaving Freetown, the M.V. Seafox visited many ports along the West African coast, to which I had become familiar during my first voyage of two and a half years. Without doubt it helped broaden my outlook on life, seeing how the other half lived, so to speak. Nothing surprised me any more, even the men I sailed with. The everyday routine of life at sea became habitual, while among the ship's crew one always found a joker or studious type of fellow, who spent his off duty hours with a book. With a reasonable knowledge of Board of Trade rules and regulations, he was the one chosen to speak up for his shipmates if things went awry. Nicknamed the "Philadelphia Lawyer," he was seen as no more than an agitator by the captain, who had to deal with him. Others nicknamed "plonkers" seized every opportunity to get inebriated, and wandered around in a state of semi-consciousness, having no idea if they were coming or going.

A favourite tipple among many, was a brew made from sugar cane referred to as "jungle juice," which they purchased for one shilling a bottle. This potent mixture the natives called "fire water," was rumoured powerful enough to drive a car. Each port visited had it's own concoction of palm wine, guaranteed to remove paint from the ship's side. It's vile smell would put a donkey off it's oats.

It was in Takoradi a thriving port on the gold coast that the evil brew proved the downfall of several seamen, partaking of it's delights. Drinking more than was good for them they decided the cooling effect of the ocean's bracing waters, to be most beneficial for them. Hurrying down to the beach, they invaded the private enclosure of the local European Yacht Club. Stripping naked they danced along the shore in a drunken frenzy, with a performance good enough to have brought an encore at the Follies Bergere. Shouts of encouragement from the native populace attracted the attention of local European residents, who threatened to have them thrown in jail. Not wishing to sample the inside of an African prison, the seamen dressed rather hurriedly and left.

The early morning sun beat down on the ship's steel decks, as only it can in the tropics, not a breath of wind stirred the Red Ensign on her stern. Leaving their quarters on the after deck a group of red-eyed and befuddled seamen staggered out into the light of day, following their late night escapade. The captain waited for them to appear, then demanded to know who among them had visited the local Yacht Club. Receiving no response he conferred with a native policeman who'd arrived on board at daybreak, a burly looking character dressed in blue tunic and shorts. With the mannerisms of a witch doctor he eyed each man suspiciously, and from his trouser's pocket produced a grey sock. Holding the tattered sock at arms length he asked; "Who belong him."

A roar of laughter followed as Sniffy Wilkinson stepped forward and examining the sock, shook his head, saying; "Him no belong here. Him smell like Arabs underpants."

With a sweep of his arm Sniffy tossed the sweaty sock over the ship's side, and addressing the policeman in Pidgin English, said; "White man on shore side not like sailorman. Him no good, make plenty palava for seaman," much to the Captain's astonishment.

Denying all knowledge of the incident, the seamen said they were on board the ship throughout the night. Sniffy then demanded an apology from the owners of the Yacht club, which brought a smile to the Captain's face. Warning all seamen as to their future conduct while ashore he informed the policeman there was little he could do, his ship was set to leave port later that afternoon.

The day was hot and uneasy with banks of dark cloud drifting up over the horizon when the vessel prepared to leave the harbour at Takoradi, facing the threat of a tropical storm. Banks of ominous black cloud drawing ever closer engulfed the ship in a torrential downpour, a reminder the rainy season was upon us. In the space of ten minutes there were two violent rain storms, with bouts of thunder and lightning for good measure. Squalls of heavy rain soaked native workers trying to cover numbers three and four hatches with tarpaulins, as the last slings of cargo were dispatched ashore. Amid peals of thunder reverberating across the darkened sky the M.V Seafox slipped out of harbour, into the storm tossed waters of the South Atlantic.

Daybreak saw us berthing at the town of Appapa opposite Nigeria's capital of Lagos on the Niger river, where vessels from around the globe are familiar with it's modern wharf and railway terminus, adjacent to nearby swamp and jungle. In a clearing some distance from the wharf stands the Seaman's Mission, equipped with a small bar, library, and billiards table. A meeting place for many seamen who'd been shipmates together at one time or another, and will perchance meet again to share a drink or two, to talk of old times.

Staying long enough to replenish our water supplies we left the port at midday, and headed south toward the equator. Nightfall saw us anchored off the island of Fernando Po, lying in the Bight of Biafra, a mountainous region covering one thousand square miles. Exports of coffee, cocoa beans and large quantities of timber cut from the forests, provide the island with it's main source of revenue.

First light of day brought a sudden gasp of alarm from the officer on watch, seeing some two hundred mahogany logs in the form a raft being towed toward his ship. Apparently out of control, there was nothing the skipper of the tug could do to stop them crashing against the ship's side. The impact shook the vessel from stem to stern rousing the entire ship's company, who at the time were sound asleep. Securing them alongside the vessel native cargo workers proceeded to heave them aboard throughout the day, stowing them down in the ship's hold. As the tropical sun peeped above the horizon a colony of fruit bats left the island where they had spent the night, and flocked to feed on the mainland.

With two thousand tons of timber safely stowed in the ship's holds we left Fernando Po for Duala, main seaport of the French Cameroons. A railway system linking the port to Yaounde it's capital, carried the country's vital exports to vessels waiting in the harbour. A shipment of cocoa beans hurriedly dispatched aboard allowed us to leave and sail north to Lagos, our next port of call. It was here we listened to the overseas broadcast from the B.B.C back in England, and heard of the rumblings of war. Political unrest caused by Hitler's claims to territory on Germany's borders, had finally come to a head. Annexing Bohemia and Moravia from Czechoslovakia in the early part of 1939, he maintained the Polish port of Danzig belonged to Germany. It was quite obvious Prime Minister Neville Chamberlain's efforts to appease Hitler when signing the Munich agreement in September of 1938, had proved useless. With Europe once again in turmoil, the threat of war loomed ever closer.

Out in darkest Africa where the mere mention of hostilities were for the moment of no concern, work on loading the ship went on unabated. It was now late August and the rainy season having run its course, we again experienced searing daytime temperatures and humid nights. Taking our leave of Lagos, the M.V.Seafox bypassed the port of Takoradi where earlier incidents by members of the ship's crew had upset the local European community, and sailed north enroute for Freetown on September 1st, 1939. Our morning broadcast from the B.B.C was suddenly interruped by a solemn voiced announcer, saying; "With Hitler's forces having invaded Poland, Britain had no alternative but declare war against Germany."

Orders instructing merchant ships to cover white paintwork with grey, and darken brasswork, caused near panic. Pots of grey paint and brushes were hurriedly issued to all able-bodied personnel, each and every man was pressed into service in a desperate effort to cover the vessel's white superstructure. Even the ship's name painted on her bow and stern, had to be quickly obliterated. News of Britain declaring war on Germany soon spread like wild fire among native workers aboard, who became restless. Adding fuel to their desire to leave the ship as we approached Freetown, their home base. Within sight of the port the ship was stopped by naval vessels patrolling outside, and escorted through a submarine defence system to a safe anchorage. Preparations for such an emergency had been in operation by the authorities for some time, fully aware Hitler's U-Boats were already prowling the oceans. No sooner had the anchor rested on the ocean bed boats of every description drew alongside the vessel, allowing panic-stricken native workers to pick up their belonging and hurry ashore. Especially when rumour spread, German submarines were already lurking in the vicinity.

Now under the jurisdiction of the government all British Merchant ships had to wait on instructions from naval authorities, as to when they could leave port. Anchored at a safe distance behind Freetown's submarine defence system a naval officer arrived on board the vessel as darkness fell, with our orders to sail. In the dead of night we weighed anchor and slipped out to sea, with orders to observe a total blackout. Following in the wake of our naval escort the M.V. Seafox sailed through the port's submarine defence system to the open sea. A mile or so from the shore, a coded message winked out from the darkened bridge of our escorting destroyer."You may now proceed to your final destination with all possible speed, and good luck."

With all lights extinguished including those used for navigation purposes, the vessel gathering speed sailed off into the dark of night. Lookouts placed in strategic positions were instructed to keep an eye open for enemy U-boats, as we zig-zagged our way home. Alone, we prepared to face the unknown.

It was now late September 1939 and with the war in progress we had orders to steer clear of Ushant, on the French coast. Encountering little sign of activity to indicate a war was in progress when arriving in the English Channel, my thoughts once again turned to mother and home. Would I be able to find her I asked myself and in doing so, meet my sister Catherine.

But as often happens, the most carefully laid plans will go awry. Abreast of Land's End a naval patrol vessel from Plymouth approached the ship with a change of orders, and much to my dismay our original destination which should have been the port of London, was switched to Liverpool, in Lancashire. This change of destination forced me to postpone for the time being, an intended search for my missing family.

Sailing in a northerly direction the M.V. Seafox was ordered to alter course, and rounding St David's Head we passed through St George's Channel to enter the Irish Sea. As night fell small coastwise vessels sailing back and forth on regular trade routes across the Irish Sea, added to the problems of lookout men on board the ship. Showing not a glimmer of light in the inky darkness several were seen to cross our bows without warning, forcing us to alter course to avoid a collision.

Daybreak found us steaming up the River Mersey to the port of Liverpool, the busiest port in the northwest of England. Lining the river, silver coloured barrage balloons suspended on long wire cables hung over the area like guardian angels, protecting strategic positions from the threat of low flying enemy aircraft. Sailing along the City of Liverpool's busy waterfront, many historic structures caught the visitor's eye.

Prominent among them, is the Liver Buildings. Perched on top of it's green encrusted dome are the statues of legendary Liver birds, from which the city derived it's name. Running from north to south along a seven mile stretch of waterfront, Liverpool's docks are serviced by an overhead railway system. Stations at various intervals along its entire length, permitted dock workers, seamen, and people connected with shipping, access to vessels berthed there. Passenger liners owned by Cunard White Star, Pacific & Orient, and C.P.R, berth at Princes Landing Stage, centre piece of Liverpool's vast waterfront. Reducing speed abreast of Harrington Dock attendant tugs took the vessel in tow, shepherding us safely into our berth. Only then were we informed the passenger liner Athenia, evacuating women and children overseas, had been torpedoed and sunk by a German U.Boat at the outbreak of war. Hearing of this terrible tragedy brought home to many of us, the real meaning of total war.

With the formalities of berthing and clearance by the Port Health Authorities completed, members of the ship's crew were free to go ashore. Leaving my personal belongings locked away in my cabin I took a taxi into town, and at the local police station asked where I might find suitable lodgings during my stay in the area. Directed to the Sefton Park district on the outskirts of town I arrived outside a large brownstone house and spoke with the landlady, a Mrs Linden, who agreed to give me board and lodgings. Thanking her, I cleared up some business that needed attending to back on board, returning to the good lady's house with my bags the following day.

Located on the outskirts of Liverpool the neighbourhood was fairly quiet with public transport available at regular intervals, allowing one reasonable access to the city centre. Enjoying a short period of leave, I soon settled down with her family of two teenage boys. Conscripted into the army they were at present home on leave, and like thousands of young men before them waiting to be shipped abroad, knowing they might never return. Although I was not subjected to rules and regulations as were men in the armed forces, I nevertheless found myself unable to move as freely as I had done in time of peace. My movements being somewhat restricted, due to the war. Plans for a trip south in my quest to find mother and hopefully my sister Catherine, were left in abeyance for the time being.

As the war at sea developed it became more hazardous with the enemy's use of magnetic mines in shipping lanes around Great Britain, enemy U Boats continuing to cause havoc to our merchant fleet. Ships sunk while carrying vital war supplies across the North Atlantic from America were replaced where possible by vessels snatched from the scrap yard, and pressed into service. Unfortunately, I had to sail aboard one of these rusting heaps of junk before my leave had expired.

A Taste of War.

To all intents and purposes we were a country at war, yet life in England continued apace in the same easy manner. It was most noticeable, however, an exceptionally large number of young people seen in uniform, had been conscripted into the services. Whilst people employed in shipyards, aircraft factories and other essential war work, were exempt from being called up into the armed forces. All available ships, including many that had lain idle during the depression, were hurriedly rushed into service, in order to make up for losses to our depleted Merchant Fleet. Since the outbreak of war the number of ships lost was extremely heavy, due to the increased activity of Germany's U Boats around Britain's coastal waters.

Told to report to the shipping office in Liverpool when my leave expired I was sent to join the S.S.Benbry a vessel of five thousand tons dead weight, built in the early nineteen hundreds. The condition of this dilapidated heap of rusting junk, left much to be desired. Rescued from the breaker's yard and hurriedly pressed into service, the ship was given several coats of paint to cover her rusting hull, in an effort to disguise the paper thin plates. Equipped with an antiquated method of navigating she had steel cables running along either side of her afterdeck leading from the bridge to the rudder astern; a system referred to as chain steering. Rumour had it she was bound for New York, a perilous journey in mid-winter on any ship. But crossing the North Atlantic on this heap of junk was in my humble opinion, akin to commiting suicide. At best her top speed of six knots left her at the mercy of the elements, should we run into stormy weather. Without a scrap of cargo in her holds to steady her, she was more likely to capsize.

In the early light of an October dawn a watery sun peeped from behind a formation of angry black cloud, giving rise to strong north easterly winds and driving rain. Buffeted about as she entered the Mersey's cold choppy waters the S.S. Benbry struggled to follow in line astern with merchant ships heading out to Liverpool Bay, where an escort of several destroyers waited to convoy vessels leaving the port across the Atlantic. When formed up into columns of three our naval escorts proceeded to shepherd us away from the main shipping lanes in the Irish sea, where enemy U-boats waited to strike. Increasing speed in an effort to keep up with the rest of the convoy, volumes of black smoke poured from the funnel of the Benbury. This brought a stern warning from the convoy's C.O, reminding us we were making our position known to enemy submarines in the vicinity.

Out on the Atlantic ocean's stormy waters with nothing but ballast in the ship's holds to steady us, we found great difficulty in keeping station with the rest of the convoy. As a result of complaints from faster vessels who considered us a danger to them, the officer in command of operations ordered us to take up station at the rear of the group. Late on the evening of our third day at sea the weather turned nasty, and with a force eight gale blowing our escorts instructed ships in the convoy to disperse. Breaking away in orderly fashion each vessel then set course for their final destinations, zig-zagging our way across the North Atlantic. Bidding farewell and safe passage to all vessels in convoy our escorting destroyers left to return to base, and within half an hour we found ourselves alone. Ships that accompanied us for the past three days were soon out of sight, no more than a smudge on the far horizon. Preparing to face the elements and U-boat menace if and when called upon, extra lookouts scanned the North Atlantic's unfriendly waters for signs of a periscope. But for a few anxious moments during an otherwise uneventful voyage, we reached the safety of American shores.

On a bitterly cold November morning in 1940, we arrived at the mouth of the Hudson river. Faced with overcast skies and a curtain of fog hanging over the estuary added to our difficulty in locating the pilot, who guided the S.S Benbury to an anchorage off Ellis Island. Immigration and Port Health officials boarding the ship, checked our papers were in order and carried out an inspection of the crew, before allowing the vessel to proceed up river to her berth. Moving at a snail's pace we inched through the fog ladden atmosphere toward Brooklyn's Erie Basin dock, passing the Manhattan and Williamsburgh suspension bridges. Within half an hour of the ship making fast, longshoremen began loading war supplies on board. Working in shifts they toiled night and day in order to get the ship back out to sea, a task completed within a period of ten days.

Taking advantage of an unlimited supply of unrationed goods unavailable back in England, I decided to go ashore on a shopping expedition. Visiting Macy's it was my misfortune to bump into Paddy McGrath, a seaman from the S.S. Benbry. Passing the time of day he told me he was newly-married, and asked for my help in purchasing some articles of underwear for his young wife. As a single man of twenty-one I was no more learned than he as to the type of lingerie women wore, although he imagined I was. Having seen the frilly garments advertised in glossy magazines, I had some idea what they looked like. In offering to assist him, I was about to experience one of the most hilarious, not to mention the most embarrassing moments of my life, inside Macy's department store.

Somewhat apprehensive I approached the lingerie counter with Paddy in tow. A charming young salesgirl smiled, and dutifully asked; "Can I help you sir?"

Explaining the situation my companion found himself in, she smiled demurely; "Oh! it's alright sir I understand," she said shyly.

Placing pieces of female apparel in a variety of colours and sizes on the counter she picked out a delicate pink slip and panties, and asked; "What size would you like, sir?"

Turning to Paddy, a big raw boned Irish lad, I said; "Do you know what size she takes, Paddy?"

His face paled for an instant, then looking around the store he pointed to an enormous lady standing nearby, saying; "Oi tink she's loike her over dere."

The crunch came when Paddy was asked by the young lady, "what size brassiere, would you like for your wife, sir?"

Well I ask you, what else would you expect of somebody straight from the green fields. Whose only previous contact with a female, was milking Daisy the cow. Already in stitches over Paddy's lack of finesse, roars of good natured laughter errupted from two young girls at the lingere counter, when they heard his next remark.

"Is that them tings dey wear here?" asked Paddy, cupping a huge pair of hands to his chest.

"Oh! you mean a bra" I said, rather embarrassed by the method he used to explain the articles of clothing he required.

"Well," I asked him, tongue in cheek. "What size does your wife wear?" Paddy.

Showing not the slightest embarrassment, he again cupped two enormous hands to his chest and gave a sickly grin, saying; "About dis big."

Falling about in hysterics while searching for a bra that was suitable, it took the girls some considerable effort to regain their composure. Anxious to get back to the ship I watched in silence as the salegirl wrapped up the articles and handed them to Paddy. In his haste to get away from the fifth floor of Macy's department store, he made my day in achieving the impossible. With giant strides he took a flying leap onto an escalator on it's downward journey which I found most amusing, and watched him claw his way to the top. With a sigh of relief as he disappeared from sight I left the bright lights of Fifth Avenue behind and took a taxi back to my ship, feeling I'd been dragged through a hedge backwards. Glad of an opportunity to explore what the City of New York had to offer, I will always remember Paddy's hands frantically trying to describe what size lingerie he needed to take home to his wife. Why I asked myself did I volunteer to accompany this farmer's lad on a shopping trip, to buy his wife's unmentionables. When details of my escapade reached the ears of all and sundry during the lunch hour aboard ship next day, it was greeted with hoots of laughter. Johnson the second mate, exclaiming; "You could get a write up in the New York Times with a report like that, Charles."

Loaded down to her gunnels with war material the S.S. Benbry left the bright lights of New York behind on a cold winter's morning in mid-December of 1940, and sailed north for Nova Scotia to await a convoy. Hugging the coast all the way up, our journey was slow and laborious. As night fell all lights had to be extinguished, remembering we were now moving back into a war zone. With a strong head wind and heavy seas impeding our progress north, the ship staggered into the Canadian Port of Halifax. Where we were ordered to join a collection of Merchant ships mustered in the outer harbour and dropping our anchor astern of them, were told to wait for the arrival of a naval escort. Even though thousands of miles from the war in Europe, all ships lying in the harbour area were ordered to maintain a strict blackout. A precautionary measure against an attack by enemy U.Boats, known to be in the vicinity. Scupper deep with a cargo of ammunition and other war material there was every chance we might never reach England, without the protection of the Royal Navy.

On the morning of our sixth day in Halifax a naval escort was seen to arrive, but it was not until nightfall all ships were told to prepare to leave. At a given signal each vessel hoisted it's anchor and headed out of the harbour to await instructions. In all, a total of forty ships loaded with war supplies gathered outside the port, were ordered to form up into five columns of eight. Screened by our escorting destroyers we left Halifax under cover of darkness, prepared for any emergency that might arise during the voyage home. Fresh northerly winds tending to increase in strength the day after leaving harbour made things extremly difficult for slow cumbersome ships such as the S.S.Benbry, to keep up with much faster vessels across the North Atlantic. By the end of the fourth day at sea manoeuvers of any kind became almost impossible for the vessel to carry out in the teeth of a gale and mountainous seas, with a forecast of worse to come. It was at this point the convoy's commanding officer ordered all ships in convoy to disperse, requesting each vessel make all possible speed to their respective destination.

Receiving a warning from the naval authorities before leaving Halifax that the German battleship Graf Spee was operating in the South Atlantic, the captain decided to take a northerly route across the Atlantic. Choosing to face the elements, rather than take the risk of being sunk by the German marauder. Within a couple of hours, we were on our own. Out of sight were our naval escort and the rest of the merchant ships that had been in convoy with us, a short time ago. In a desperate bid to keep the ship's head up to windward against a storm force nine gale, every ounce of speed was squeezed out of her clapped out engine, causing volumes of black smoke to pour from the funnel, giving away our position to the enemy.

With a normal top speed of six knots, reduced by half, we were a sitting duck for any U-Boat lurking in the area. Faced with raging seas and winds now reaching hurricane force that tossed the ship about like a rag doll, we strained every nerve to ride out the storm. Battened down in a tiny radio cabin I hung on for dear life to anything that would keep me upright, every time her stern corkscrewed out of the water like some wild thing. There were moments when I feared the ship might turn turtle, and offered a silent prayer for our safe passage home. Battling against mountainous seas for days on end and having to exist on sandwiches hurriedly snatched from the galley, was soul destroying.

Earlier in the voyage, with nothing better to do to pass the time of day, the subject of religion cropped up. A rather delicate matter to discuss aboard any ship, was quickly pooh-poohed by old Creswell the Bo'sun as a load of hogwash. Professing to be an atheist, he insisted that sort of thing was for people who allowed themselves to be brainwashed. But in moments of peril at sea such as this, men whatever their creed, offered a prayer to their maker for salvation. Seeing this avowed unbeliever on bended knee at the height of the storm, I asked him; "What are you doing down there?" Bo'sun.

"Oh, I'm looking for something I've dropped on the deck," he replied.

It was then, I quipped; "It wasn't a Bible by any chance?" Bo'sun.

Mumbling to himself, he hurried away. No doubt realizing he'd been caught out. Quite unexpectedly the violent weather abated, leaving the raging seas as flat as a mill pond. With hardly a ripple on the surface, a one hundred mile an hour gale had suddenly been reduced to a mere whisper, and a strange silence pervaded the ship. All one could hear was the gentle slapping of the sea against her paper thin plates, now the storm's fury was spent. Thinking we had survived the worst of it was a relief to many of us, until a warning from the navigation officer renewed fears for our safety.

"Oh we're not out of it yet" Johnson announced solemnly, when I stepped into his chartroom that night. "There's more to come. We're in the eye of the storm right now," he confided.

The lull in the weather allowed safety wires to be rigged along either side of the deck fore and aft, with all movable objects being securely fastened down. Some twenty four hours later we were through the eye of the storm, and once again faced the fury of wind and sea. At dusk that day the ocean quickly changed from the calm of a child's paddling pool, into a raging storm. Huge seas lashed the ship, almost standing her on her beam ends. Unable to forge ahead, we seemed to be waltzing with death. With each move forward she buried her nose into the ocean's foam-laced green waters, pitching headlong into bottomless troughs. Gyrating from one side to the other in an effort to rid herself of water lodged in the well-deck, a gigantic wave suddenly hit us. With a thunderous roar it hurtled down on her boat deck, sweeping our starboard lifeboats away like so much driftwood. Solid steel davits measuring ten inches in diameter from which the boats were suspended, were left useless. Twisted and bent like the hapless stem of a flower, drooping over the side of it's vase. Terrified out of my wits, I stood in awe at the ocean's fury. It's devastating power, filled me with the real meaning of fear. Witnessing a catastrophe such as this left one with an ever present reminder, never take the sea for granted. It's moods are unpredictable.

Forced to use the greater part of our coal stocks it was agreed we either burn the wooden hatchboards to keep the ship moving, or heave-to. Thankfully neither was ever necessary, for by some miracle the wild tempestuous weather of the past weeks slowly abated, allowing us to limp up the River Mersey into Liverpool. In retrospect a journey that should have taken ten days in the normal course of events, lasted a nightmare of twenty eight. The outcome of it all left me in a state of shock, and nervous exhaustion. The long hours spent in the tiny radio cabin during an unforgettable voyage, left me wondering why the hell I had chosen a career at sea. Without a second glance at the now rusting hulk that had miraculously survived hurricane force winds to bring me safely home, I stepped ashore in early January of 1940 with a song in my heart and a prayer on my lips to my creator.

Seeing little of the surrounding area when travelling home in the blackout served to remind me, if indeed it were necessary, I was back in the war zone. It did of course effectively outline, it's futility. Stress and mental strain suffered during my voyage that at best could be described as disastrous, had left it's mark. I was exhausted.

The most surprised person to welcome me back home was Mrs Linden the landlady, who answered my knock on her door that evening.

"My goodness Charles, where have you been?" she exclaimed. "I expected you home long ago."

Not wishing to sully the good lady's ears with coarse or vulgar expletives one hears and learns to accept whilst at sea, I couldn't begin to describe to her the frustration, fear, and panic I felt in the teeth of that storm. I decided to satisfy her curiosty by simply saying the ship's crew were fed up when the vessel pitched and rolled around in a frenzy, somewhere out in mid-Atlantic. Fearing for their very lives as mountainous green seas thudded against the ship, almost capsizing her. She most certainly could not have understood if I tried to explain to her, why life lines were placed from fore to aft for one's safety during violent and stormy weather. Or of the fear that rose within me when the vessel corkscrewed about, like a drunken belly dancer. It would be hard for me to describe our days and nights being soaked to the skin, living on hard tack until the storm abated. Then a strange silence, with only the faintest sound of water brushing gently against the ship's side. Only then as the storm's fury and violence abated, did we manage to stagger home.

No, I reasoned with myself. Landlubbers did not understand the ways of a sailor's life at sea. Far better for me to simply tell the dear soul, we were unavoidably delayed.

It was now June of 1940 and British forces were being evacuated from Dunkirk, following the capitulation of France. Overwhelmed by invading German forces, Belgium was helpless to stop them sweeping around the Maginot Line, giving Hitler a free hand in Western Europe. It was at this point he turned on Britain and unleashed his heavy bombers in raids on the City of London, the heaviest since the outbreak of war. In one particular raid, the city was severely burnt by incendiary bombs. The Guildhall and many old churches being destroyed.

My return to sea during this period saw me once again back and forth across the Atlantic to the U.S, in a bid to bolster our flagging war supplies. By the time I returned to Liverpool in January of 1941 the aerial warfare had intensified, with the bombing of many of our major cities. Therefore my plans to travel south in search of my mother during a short period of leave, were once again put on hold. It was about this time I was befriended by a young lady working in Liverpool, and during an exchange of greetings she told me her name was Marjorie Hulbert. From the outset we enjoyed each other's company and our romance blossomed, but all too soon the time for parting came. Once again a call to duty saw me sail away, promising to write to her.

From the end of June 1940, Britain had stood alone against the might of Germany and her allies. Were it not for a Lease Lend Bill signed by President Roosevelt in early March of 1940, our beleaguered country might have been in dire straits. Along with unlimited supplies of war materials they agreed to send us fifty U.S World War I Naval destroyers and several merchant ships, to help make for up the heavy losses suffered by our decimated Merchant Fleet. Several hundred British seamen were then drafted to various ports in America to join these Merchant vessels referred to as Liberty ships, bringing them back to the U.K.

My disappointment at not being chosen to renew an acquaintance with the bright lights of the U.S. increased, when sent to join the M.V. Kinersley on a voyage back to West Africa. An intermediate cargo and passenger ship under the command of a Captain J.J. Smyth, a nervous shoot on sight individual nick-named, "Two Gun Pete." In company with a small convoy of merchant ships, our escort of naval frigates remained with us for three days. Once clear of home waters, orders were given for the convoy to disperse. All vessels were then instructed to make all possible speed to their final destinations. Ships using normal South Atlantic trade routes no longer feared an attack from the German Battleship Admiral Graf Spee, scuttled at the entrance to Montivedeo harbour. While she was free to plunder ships at will, no merchantman was safe. To risk challenging this powerful raider bearing in mind the armament she carried, was akin to suicide. Her supply ship Altmark being used to transfer British seamen to German Prisoner of War Camps, now lay at the bottom of a Norwegian fiord in Narvik. Destroyed by the Royal Navy.

Determined to be ready when coming to grips with the enemy J.J.Smyth, or Two Gun Pete, as our Captain was better known, insisted his gun's crew received regular spells of practice. A four inch gun mounted on the ship's stern was of little use as a deterrent against a surface raider such as the Graff Spee, a single shot fired in anger against her would have been suicidal. Tempting providence, the very sight of a ship on the far horizon or a piece of driftwood floating by, would be reason enough for our gallant J.J. to order his gun's crew to stand by for action. With complete disregard for a naval gunnery officer in charge of the ship's gun crew, who found it useless to try to reason with him. Pointing out his supply of ammunition was being wasted unnecessarily he told the Captain a need for caution was imperative, in such a dangerous situation. The man in question a retired naval Petty Officer, was simply told to obey orders.

It was now early February of 1941 and as the morning sun peeped above the far horizon, it's shimmering light sparkled like diamonds on calm tropical waters. In the distance the Spanish island of Tenerife stood out beneath a sub-tropical sky, a volcano in the foreground long since extinct, towers skyward. Like some giant from bygone days, it's blackness outlined against a sky of azure blue. By-passing the island because of it's friendly overtures with Germany, one recalled much happier times when visiting this island paradise.

Nearing the French administrated colony of Senegal on the coast of West Africa a hoarse cry of ship-ahoy was heard from a lookout man, posted high above in the crow's nest. The silhouette of a large naval vessel drawing ever closer, caused a flurry of excitement on the bridge. Binoculars appeared as if by magic, and half a dozen pairs of eyes scanned the distant horizon. Without considering the danger to his ship or the men who sailed in her, Two Gun Pete threw caution to the wind. In a death or glory attitude to show his total distain for the intruder, he ordered his crew to man the gun.

As the distance between the two ships narrowed and the heavy armament of the vessel bearing down on us was plainly visible, one could not fail to see she was a Battleship. Tension increased by the minute out on the gun platform where a nervous gun crew waited, realizing one false move on their part would be fatal. Within range of the naval vessel's guns, a signal from her bridge requested we heave-to and be recognized. Meanwhile, the gunnery officer suggested the Captain should allow his guns crew to stand down. Adopting a threatening attitude against such a powerful adversary was, he confessed, tantamount to commiting suicide.

Heading toward us at full speed the battleship suddenly altered course and swung away to starboard, allowing a sigh of relief to escape the lips of Captain Smyth. In passing we caught sight of the vessel's large French tricolor flying from her stern, and identified her as the Richelieu, one of two Allied battleships patrolling the area. Watching her disappear we resumed on our course for the port of Dakar, our destination on the coast of West Africa. Many among the crew feared she might have been a German surface raider, one of many known to be roaming the high seas. Looking back it was foolhardy if not downright stupid for the Captain, to have the audacity to challenge a battleship. There is no doubt whatsoever we would have been blown to pieces by her twelve inch guns.

If by chance our gallant Captain had survived after performing his heroic deed and managed to take to a lifeboat, rest assured he'd be sitting next to his bosom pal Cherryblossom, the native Chief Steward. Insisting all aboard sang Land of Hope and Glory in defiance of the enemy, as his ship slid beneath the waves.

As the midday temperature reached 120 degrees in the shade, the S.S. Kinersly entered the sun-drenched port of Dakar the following day. In the naval dockyard across the bay lay the French battleship Cardinal Richelieu our guardian of yesterday, replenishing her fuel supplies. While our stay in port was long enough to top up our water supplies we left that night under cover of darkness, setting course for Freetown, Sierra Leone. Dropping anchor in the harbour on arrival a consignment of native cargo handlers were hurriedly shipped on board, and as dusk fell the vessel slipped quietly out to sea.

Steaming south along Africa's west coast we arrived off Takoradi at daybreak, some two days later. It was here I fell victim to one of my frequent attacks of malaria, that had plagued me since I first set foot in Africa some five years previously. Taking an early morning stroll on deck a feeling of nausea followed by a bout of shivering, gripped me. A violent headache saw me hurry back to my cabin, where I collapsed on my bunk before passing out. In my delirious state I experienced moments of terror when falling into a darkened pit, and catching hold of some imaginary object to stop my descent, grasped at thin air. Round in circles I travelled, chased by monsters of varying shape and colour. Standing before me they began to scream and taunt, pointing to a black abyss below.

It was at this point a sickly smell of ether hit my nostrils, as the needle bit into my flesh. A noise like the bark of a gun being fired hurt my ears, then all was quiet as I floated away on a sea of comfort.

"You'll be alright now," said the young nurse standing at my bedside, when I awoke.

"But where am I," I asked, looking round the brightly lit room where I lay. But even before she had a chance to reply, I realised I was in hospital. The sight of a mosquito net hanging over the bed was enough to jog my memory, bringing to mind what had happened. I'd once again fallen victim to the white man's bogey, malaria.

After weeks of careful treatment from nurses and staff I was pronounced fit enough to leave the hospital in Takoradi, which made the time for parting difficult. It was like losing friends, one had grown to know and love. No praise of mine is high enough to describe the care lavished on patients, by nurses and staff at the hospital. When leaving I was given a medical card stating I suffered from malaria, should it be required in an emergency. Handing it to me the young nurse warned; "You are no doubt prone to suffer further attacks of malaria in the future, so make sure to carry this card on your person."

As with anyone unfortunate to have suffered from a tropical disease such as malaria, black water fever and dysentry, I had lost a considerable amount of weight, and was in no fit state to travel. But as often happened when seamen fall ill while abroad, the company responsible for their welfare had them shipped back home on the first available boat. However, a period of convalescence recommended by the hospital was approved by my company, who transferred me to the Hotel Metropole, at Sekondi. Whilst there I was able to enjoy a period of peace and comfort in this establishment lying close to the shore, run by it's Greek owner named Alexis. A heavily built swarthy looking character with a black beard covering most of his handsome features who greeted me on arrival, and instructed one of his native servants to take my bags to my room. Whilst the pair of us sat drinking a glass of orange juice and exchanged a few pleasantries, until it was lunch time. From my window at the hotel, a beautiful view of the ocean lay before me. A mile or so out to sea I watched giant Atlantic rollers sweep in, gathering speed as they crashed on the shore, spraying the beach in a flurry of white foam.

Adapting to my new surroundings, I soon settled in. Rising early each morning to slip down on the beach for a swim, before the heat of the day sent temperatures soaring. Lying there for a while with cooling waters of the Atlantic tumbling over my feet and the sun's warmth caressing my body, I would then amble back to my hotel for breakfast. With little to occupy my time I'd while away the hours until lunch time, reading a book from the hotel library. Scanning local papers for news of the war in Europe, was nothing but a waste of time. Why I ever bothered is beyond me, for there was never anything of interest to read. Time being of little importance I enjoyed each day as it came, without a care in the world. Talk of war among Europeans living out here in Africa was a non starter, they appeared more concerned with events happening in their own daily lives. Nightly entertainment at the hotel with a movie show sponsored by the proprietor, were dependent on ships arriving from the U.K. Inviting local residents to initial screening of the latest films, helped keep the hotel on a profitable basis. Newsreels covering the war in Europe continued to arrive at regular intervals aboard passenger vessels, stirred little interest in many Europeans who preferred to ignore them.

Seamen arriving from all corners of the globe were often seen to frequent the Metropole, the town's only decent hotel, spending off duty hours drinking ice-cold beer in a shady courtyard. No-body ever heeded the scruffy old grey parrot languishing in it's cage high above them, as they sat chatting away. Even tidbits from the crew of an American freighter visiting the port, failed to get so much as a squawk out of him. Head tucked under his wing, Scruffy the African grey parrot chose to remain silent.

Drinking more than their share of the local beer, men arriving at the hotel from an American frieghter sat in the courtyard arguing and cursing each other. Their unsavory language frowned upon by Alexis the Hotel owner, feared they would drive his local clientele away. Much to his delight the American vessel's stay in port was short lived, and with it's departure we witnessed the arrival of the passenger ship M.V.Abosso with the latest newsreel of the war in Europe and a supply of new films.

It was now late February 1942 and with Singapore having surrendered to superior Japanese forces earlier in the month, the European community gathered in the hotel courtyard next evening to watch the latest war film. As darkness fell a hushed audience watched with bated breath as the whitewashed wall of the courtyard serving as a cinema screen, burst into life. Pictures of the Japanese fleet leaving the scene after Pearl Harbour watched in eerie silence, suddenly turned to roars of laughter from the back of the courtyard. Scruffy the parrot who for many a long day had sat in his cage in silent contemplation, let out a bloodcurdling squawk; "You God-damned son of a bitch," it hollered, when Admiral Tojo was shown inspecting his fleet on their return to Japan.

Amid scenes of hysterical laughter, parrot and cage were quickly removed from it's perch and deposited in the darkened doorway of the hotel lounge. Calling on the native boy responsible for looking after the bird, the proprietor demanded to know why it had not been taken indoors earlier.

"Oh, I forget sah," pleaded his native servant.

"Well, you can forget your damn wages this week," shouted the infuriated proprietor. "You've spoilt the film show for my customers."

Looking around the empty bar of his hotel that evening, Alexis cursed the American seamen responsible for the parrot's blasphemous behaviour, worried lest he lose some of the local clientle who objected to the bird's foul language. There was only one option open to him if he valued his local customers, he had to get rid of the bird. There and then he decided, he would sell it to any interested seamen who happened to drop in. It annoyed him to think the parrot had not spoken a word until now, having been in his possesion for the past eighteen months.

Occasional bouts of dizziness experienced since leaving hospital slowly subsided during the weeks that followed, bringing a marked improvement to my health, which was at a low ebb. Early morning walks along the beach and light exercise, gave me back much needed strength to my weakened body. Lazing around enjoying a life of comparative ease, the war in Europe was the furthest thing from my mind. Mention of it in the local papers was that brief it could have been a figment of one's own imagination, for it was thousands of miles away. As the weeks rolled slowly by with never a word from the company responsible for me, it looked as if they'd all but forgotten about me. In all honesty, I was in no hurry to give up my African paradise. But having sampled the good life for the past couple of months, it came as something of a shock when returning to my hotel for lunch some days later, to find a letter from the company awaiting me. Brief and to the point the message read. A passage home has been arranged for you on the M.V. Accra, due within the next day or so. Please report to this office as soon as possible.

Somewhat reluctant to relinquish the good life I had an idea it was some pimply faced pen pusher at the company's office back home, who'd found my file hidden among the archives. In deciding I was indeed a burden to the company, he'd arranged for me to be brought back into the field of play, so to speak. Obviously in no hurry to report back to the office in Takoradi until the last minute I figured another day would make little difference one way or another, and continued with my normal routine. An early morning dip in the South Atlantic's warm tropical waters before breakfast, saw me take my time over dressing. I was however less than eager to report too early at the company's office, knowing time was on my side.

"Ah, there you are Mr Ashford" said the manager grinning good humouredly, "I'd almost forgotten about you. Come with me and I'll get a boarding pass for you," he said, shepherding me into an adjoining room. "The M.V Accra arrives the day after tomorrow, we'd like you to get on board as soon as you can" he advised, handing the document to me. Then uttering the usual words of wisdom office managers are apt to give their employees, when about to depart, he wished me bon voyage and was gone. Lost in a hubbub of native voices, deep inside his stuffy overcrowded office.

Warmth from the morning sun shining through the open curtains of my hotel room, woke me with a start. A farewell party the previous night, had left me heavy eyed. Seeing the hour was late gave me little time to take a hurried breakfast, knowing I had to get on board the ship as early as possible. Waiting in the hotel foyer, Alexis the proprietor came to bid me goodbye.

"I'm sorry to see you go my friend" he announced sadly, "You've become part of the fixtures. And I must say I've enjoyed your company," he remarked.

Thanking him for his hospitality, I replied; "Nothing is forever, my friend."

A spontaneous wave of the hand was all I could manage as my taxi left, distancing me from that remarkable character. Soon the hotel and my tropical paradise I was so reluctant to leave, had faded from view. A feeling of depression hit me on arriving at Takoradi harbour, when the ship that was to take me back to England came into view. She looked a forbidding sight in her coat of dark grey paint covering the hull and superstructure, and appeared top heavy. A sure sign she'd roll the guts out of you in bad weather. Leaving the taxi with my baggage I was stopped by the purser's assistant as I reached the top of the ship's gangway, who asked: "Your name please."

"Mr Ashford" I replied, hoping he might say there was no berth for me. But it was not my day.

Glancing at the list of names in his hand he turned to a native steward standing nearby, and spoke to him in pidgin English, saying: "You take him Cabin No 41 on B deck, Moses."

"Yes sah, I unerstan" said Moses, giving him a melon sized grin. Motioning me to follow him down a companionway, he directed me to my quarters. Small and reasonably comfortable, a large notice pinned in a prominent position over the wash basin caught my eye. All port-holes and dead-lights must be closed each night at dusk, the notice read, failure to do so will entail heavy penalties.

As evening approached the tropical sun's parting rays sprawled across an ocean streaked with red and orange, and slowly sank beneath the western horizon. With all lights extinguished the M.V.Accra slipped silently out of Takoradi harbour as dusk fell, on a northerly course for Freetown, Sierra Leone. From the boat-deck I watched pinpoints of light on the shore flicker in and out like fireflies in the jungle, and suddenly disappear. Sailing close to the African coast we were obliged to alter course within hailing distance of Sherbro Island, and arrived at Freetown as dawn was breaking. Naval vessels patrolling outside the port escorted the ship through the area's boom defence sytem to an anchorage in the bay, where native workers were quickly dispatched ashore. Picking up a small amount of cargo the vessel was told to wait for orders, and as evening approached we prepared to leave. Dusk was upon us as the anchor was hauled aboard, and as night closed in, were told to follow astern of our naval escort. Clear of Freetown's boom defence system our escort bade us bon voyage, and our course was set for England and home.

It was early in March of 1942 that I arrived back in Liverpool, to overcast skies of grey and bitterly cold winds gusting along the river Mersey's choppy waters. Spring had yet to arrive in this part of the northern hemisphere, still languishing in winter's grip. Facing such bitter weather, I longed for the blue skies and warm tropical beaches I'd left behind. Standing on the open deck waiting for berthing to be completed, a bout of shivering forced me to seek the warmth of my cabin. Having just recovered from a recent attack of malaria while in the tropics, the damp atmosphere of northern climates had an adverse effect on me. As soon as we were given clearance by the Port Health Authorities I hurried off the ship, and without a backward glance, headed for home. Sure of a warm welcome when arriving.

"My goodness what a lovely surprise" said the landlady, answering my knock on her door. "You're nice and sun-burnt, did you have a good trip, Charles?"

Comfortably seated in front of a blazing fire I told the good lady I'd been plagued by another bout of malaria, whilst on the coast of Africa. It was due to the many weeks I had to spend in convalescence that prompted her to remark.

"But you look so well, Charles."

Given time to settle in, I had every intention of taking a trip to the south of England in an effort to find my mother, without whose help my chances of ever meeting my sister Catherine were slim indeed. A bitterly cold March wind with intermittant showers of rain greeted me next morning when arriving in the City of Liverpool, in seach of warmer clothing. Like the rolling of a drum the rain beat a tattoo on my protective umbrella, as I hurried to catch a bus into town. Alighting in the city centre I walked the short distance to Lord street the main shopping area, seeking shelter from the wind that cut through the paper thin clothes I wore, like a knife cuts through butter. Within easy reach of warmth and shelter inside a brightly lit store I felt myself buckle at the knees, and realized there was no way I'd make it. Gripped with a feeling of nausea I lurched forward reaching for an imaginary door handle, and grasped at nothing but thin air. With a sickening thud the pavement came up to meet me and a million stars exploded inside my head, then mercifully darkness enveloped me, bringing a welcome relief to my fever wracked body.

An Unforgettable Journey

Pursued by demons and hordes of grotesque looking animals of varying shapes and colour, I ran blindly on. As they closed in on me I fled into a darkened forest, only to fall headlong into a yawning chasm, from which there seemed no escape. Down I plunged into a bottomless pit, their screams of demonic laughter taunting me as I fell.

A cool hand brushing my fevered brow, served to wake me from a nightmare experience one is bound to suffer, from a bout of the dreaded malaria. Bathed in a pool of my own perspiration I lay perfectly still, the slightest move caused the bedclothes to squelch.

"Where am I?" I asked the young nurse standing beside my bed, for I remembered little if anything, that must have befallen me.

"You are suffering from a bout of malaria," she replied, "and are being cared for in the tropical ward of Liverpool's Royal Infirmary."

I remembered walking through the city's shopping centre, and must have passed out. Fortunately for me, I was carrying my medical card, and taken to this hospital."

Wincing with pain when I touched my bandaged head, the nurse smiled, saying; "You've had a bad fall Mr Ashford, but try to sleep now, doctor will see you in the morning."

Heavy curtains drawn back across the window of the ward, served to wake me from my fitful slumbers. I felt all the old aches and pains of yesterday course through my fever-wracked body, as the effect of a morphine injection wore off. In a semi-stupor I heard the moans and groans of other patients in the ward where I lay, unfortunates like myself suffering from various tropical diseases. Many had dysentery, an infectious disease rampant in backward countries, where drinking water and sanitation leave much to be desired. Lying in a horizontal position with the foot of their beds slightly raised, sufferers are administered periodic enemas to flush out the bowel. Around midday the ward sister resplendent in her neat blue uniform, escorted two white coated gentlemen to my bedside.

"Ah, you're awake" said the elder of the two, "How do you feel now Mr Ashford?"

"Not well at all," I replied. "I've suffered the most horrible nightmares."

"Malaria will cause you to hallucinate whilst the fever rages" the elderly gentleman remarked, somewhat sympathetically.

It was then he introduced himself, and the young man with him. In a voice with a pronounced Scottish accent, he said; "My name is Professor Yorke and my partner here is Dr Adams. We are specialists in tropical diseases. Tell me, how long have you suffered with this malady?" he asked, a note of anxiety in his voice.

"About six years," I replied, recalling my first attack in 1936. "I've been plagued with periodic bouts of malaria throughout these years," I informed him.

Conferring with his partner, he said at length; "Well young man we have a new treatment for malaria, which has proved successful. This, I feel confident, will rid you of the disease from which you are suffering. In the fullness of time you should make a complete recovery," he said. And with a kindly smile, left.

A course of medicine ordered by the professor was administered night and day with monotonous regularity, for a period of six weeks. Feeling weak due to losing so much weight, I was allowed to leave the hospital when my treatment finished and given a clean bill of health, then told I was cured of the disease. Hopefully, I could now look forward to a life free from the ravages of malaria that had plagued me for six long years. Before leaving the hospital, I paid Professor Yorke a visit to thank him personally for the care and attention he gave to so many, who suffered from tropical diseases.

Rising from his chair as I entered his office, he shook me warmly by the hand, saying; "You're well on the way to recovery. A little pale, but that is only to be expected after what you have been through." Studying me closely for a minute, he asked; "How do you feel in yourself?"

"Rather weak, otherwise quite well" I replied.

A look of concern clouded his face, when saying: "I'm afraid I must warn you" he went on in a most friendly manner, "any future visits to the tropics should be avoided at all costs."

"But why doctor?" I asked, unaware of the danger I faced.

Without mincing his words, he warned; "Although you are now free of the malaria virus, to risk further infection could be fatal, should you visit any place where the disease is prevalent. I therefore strongly advise you to keep clear of tropical areas, for health reasons."

He seemed most concerned for my future wellbeing, insisting I heed the warning he'd given. Thanking him, I left the hospital.

Deep in thought I returned to my lodgings on the outskirts of Sefton Park, to consider my options. Although I had now fully recovered from a recent bout of malaria, I'd lost a considerable amount of weight and looked as thin as a rake. Clothes that fitted me snugly, hung on my emaciated body like a scarecrow.

My poor state of health gave rise to a look of concern from my landlady, when I arrived at my lodgings. Her kindly voice, asked; "Whatever's happened to you, Charles, come on in and I'll get you a nice cup of tea?" Then in her broad Lancashire accent, she said, "Aye lad, tha looks awfully thin. Why, I've seen more meat on a pigeon."

Sinking into a comfortable armchair, my thoughts revolved around Professor Yorke's warning and his concern over my health. What was I to do, I wondered? In his letter to me it clearly stated, he was of the opinion I was unfit for further sea service. With a war in progress I was not allowed to pick and choose ships I sailed on, or their destinations. If I was compelled to follow his advice to the letter, I'd have to give up my sea career. Without consulting my employers or the shipping office, neither of whom had bothered to get in touch with me since entering hospital some months previously, I decided to find myself suitable employment ashore. This allowed me ample time at weekends to visit my girl friend, living across the river at Birkenhead, in the county of Cheshire. Together we visited the beautiful City of Chester with it's old Roman walls and fine Tudor style timbered houses, lying at the head of the River Dee estuary. With my health improving I decided to venture south once more in search of my mother who for some unkown reason had left the area in which she lived, shortly before I was due home from my first trip to sea in 1936.

It was in May of 1942 some six years later when I took this first opportunity available to me since the outbreak of World War II, to visit my mother's last known address, in an effort to trace her. Packing a small travelling bag I took an early morning train from Liverpool's Lime Street Station and arrived at Euston Station in London around midday, where a late spring sun, failed to penetrate a heavy curtain of smog hanging over the bomb scarred city. Most noticable were many fine buildings burnt to the ground, leaving the country's capital in a deplorable state. Travellers visiting London at a time like this would find little to enthuse about, in a city with smoke blackened and bomb scarred buildings dotted about the landscape. Many streets were empty, with nothing but the remnants of derelict houses; the occupants having long gone. From Kings Cross underground station I journeyed via Victoria to Wimbledon, a happy hunting ground of mine as a young boy.

Booking into one of many boarding houses in the area I planned to spend a couple of weeks making inquiries as to my mother's whereabouts. I fervently hoped, at this point in my life, she would finally agree to put me in touch with my sister Catherine. Travelling around for miles each day on numerous buses to out of the way places, what little information I was given led up a blind alley. Footsore and weary I'd return to the boarding house each night thinking, my luck will change tomorrow, but tomorrow never came. As the second week of my search drew to a close, I realized there was nothing to be gained by prolonging my stay as, once again, I'd drawn a blank. With a heavy heart I packed my few belongings, and returned north to my lodgings.

Having rid myself of malaria I had no wish to resume my career at sea, especially after the warning I'd received from the specialist, when leaving the hospital. With funds running low I arrived back at my lodgings on the outskirts of Liverpool toward the end of May, hoping to find myself a job ashore. Fully aware since the outbreak of war, shipyards in the area were working flat out, repairing naval and merchant vessels damaged in action. For someone such as myself in need of suitable employment, this seemed the ideal place.

Wasting little time I boarded the local ferry that took me across the river Mersey into the town of Birkenhead. Close by the ferry was the ship repair yard of Rollo Grayson & Clover, where a few discreet inquiries gained me access to the company's main office, and an interview with Mr Mercer the stores manager.

Like many north countrymen he was tall and heavily built with a ruddy complexion, from working long hours outdoors. A bowler hat worn at a rakish angle, pulled down over a mop of unruly ginger hair, hid laughing blue eyes that creased at the corners when he smiled. An understanding sort of chap, whose easy going manner made it possible for me to talk with him while he lent a sympathetic ear to my plight. He readily agreed to offer me a job in the shipyard, instead of turning me away.

Waiting in line with hundreds of men and women employed at the yard next morning I went through the process of clocking on, and watched late arrivals jostle each other to get into the yard before the gates closed at seven thirty. Within minutes the pounding of a blacksmith's steam hammer hard at work, and clatter of pneumatic drills shoving red hot rivets into steel plates of ships under repair, reverberated throughout the yard. Serving behind the counter in the stores department I worked alongside a young lady named Margaret, who was one of several women employed at the shipyard doing light work, handing out nuts and bolts of various sizes, copper piping, packets of steel and brass screws, necessary for carrying out repairs.

Built like a battleship, Margaret was a buxom lass who could hold her own with any man, and in spite of carrying so much excess weight was quite nimble. Serving her customers with speed and precision, she wore overalls and industrial gloves to protect her carefully manicured hands, her blonde hair covered with a multi-coloured scarf, hid a multitude of curlers. Pale of face with deep blue eyes, the heavily rouged lips would pout provocatively when upset. She would not however put up with backchat from any fellow worker seeking to take advantage of her, as proved when a young lad was sent to the stores for a roll of felt by the shipwright, with whom he worked. Unaware he was treading on thin ice, the young fellow approached Margaret who at the time was serving in the stores, and in his broad Yorkshire accent asked; "Aye lass, is this where ah gets felt?"

Taken aback, she glared in astonishment at the big farmer's lad standing in front of her, and lifting a huge forearm the size of a pit prop, replied; "Come round here sonny and you'll feel the weight of this."

Amid roars of laughter from a group of workers waiting to be served the red faced young lad hurried away, returning some minutes later with the shipwright who'd sent him to the stores. When hearing of the lad's stupid remark, he apologized to the young lady, and collecting his order strode off. Cursing the hapless fellow, following in his wake. Instances such as this, gave an added touch of humour to one's life, at a time of nerve jarring tension, when the City of Liverpool suffered a period of indiscriminate bombing.

Working seven days a week from dawn to dusk, left little time for the simple pleasures of life such as going to the movies. It was also dangerous to venture out after dark, due to nightly bombing raids on the nearby City of Liverpool, and the town of Birkenhead where I lived. So for the time being, my girl friend and I decided we would spend our evenings together at her home, where we listened to the radio. Reports of heavy losses at sea due to the submarine menace, did nothing to bolster one's confidence when the country stood alone against the enemy. Also mentioned was the plight of people on the Island of Malta, who were under siege. Facing an enemy, determined to starve them into submission.

It therefore came as no surprise when I received a letter marked urgent, on arriving home from work one evening. Inside was a neatly typed message from the Ministry of Shipping in Liverpool, requesting I report to their office immediately. Arriving at the shipping office around ten a.m next morning I was told to see a Mr Repp, the senior shipping clerk. Normally busier than a hive of bees, with endless queues of seamen hanging about looking for jobs, the shipping office on this particular morning was deserted. But for the inscrutable figure of an old man sitting at his desk arguing the toss with an irate seaman, the place was as quiet as a graveyard. A gut feeling instinctively told me something was amiss; why should men suddenly avoid the place as though it were infected with the plague.

Seated behind a roll-top desk a pasty-faced individual whom I felt sure had never ventured further than on a trip across the River Mersey, was arguing with an elderly seaman. Scribbling a note on a scrap of paper he handed it to the seaman, saying; "Take this to Dr Reeves for your medical, and make he sure signs it."

"But I'm not fit for sea any more Mr Repp," the old man said. "I'm blind in one eye."

"Oh that's alright" said old Repp, sarcastically. "Don't let that worry you. The doctor's always so inebriated you could have a leg missing, and he wouldn't notice it."

My God I thought to myself, I haven't a snowball's chance in hell of staying ashore with this nut, and handed him the letter I'd received. A sardonic grin split old Repp's face in half when he read it; "It's over there" he said, pointing to the door marked, Manager 's Office. Taking the letter from his claw-like hand, I knocked on the door as instructed. Above the rustle of papers from within, an authoritive voice rapped out; "Come in."

A smartly dressed elderly gentleman who at first sight I took to be an ex-naval man, sat at a large polished desk. Looking up from a manuscript he was studying, he asked; "And what can I do for you, young man?"

"I've been instructed to report here" I told him, placing my letter on his desk.

Examining the document carefully, he gave a half smile saying; "H'm, you've been adrift for quite a while, what's happened to you?"

"I've been in hospital at the Liverpool Royal Infirmary for the past few months, receiving treatment for malaria" I replied.

"Oh dear, the gentleman exclaimed. "But you're alright now I take it?"

"I'm afraid not," I answered. "I've a letter from Professor Yorke the specialist who attended me while I was in hospital, suggesting I give up my sea career. One more voyage to the tropics could prove fatal, he warned me.

"Ah, but you'll be alright in other parts of the world, won't you sonny," he grinned.

Reading the specialist's letter in detail he gave an impatient grunt, and handing it back to me, said; "Give it to Mr Repp next door, he'll sort it out for you."

Back in the main office I waited to see Mr Repp, who was back behind his roll-top desk. Like a judge handing out sentences he took a delight in ordering men to join ships, knowing many were unfit to go to sea.

"Are you Mr Ripp?" I asked tongue in cheek, and waited for his response.

His watery eyes glared at me over the top of horn-rimmed spectacles, and white- faced he snarled at me; "The name's Repp, if you don't mind, Mr Ashford."

Specks of white froth oozed from the corners of his thin bloodless lips, and leering at me across his desk he mocked; "Well, what did the manager have to say to you?"

"He asked me to give you this" I replied, placing the letter I received from the hospital on his desk.

A scrawny hand reached out to snatch at the document, and whilst reading it carefully sneaked suspicious glances in my direction, perhaps thinking I'd written the letter myself. With a contemptuous grunt he threw the doctor's report into his waste paper basket, and a sardonic smile spread across the hawk-like face.

"Didn't you know there was a war on?" he leered. "If you think you can wriggle out of it with a phoney doctor's note, you're sadly mistaken sonny. You either go back to sea or get shoved in the army, take your pick."

Remembering discretion to be the better part of valour, I decided it best not to goad him into having a fit by telling him where he could shove it, and kept a still tongue in my head. Seeing I was unresponsive to his snide remarks, he rambled on; "There's a ship waiting for you over in Birkenhead Docks, our doctor will be here to examine you before you sign on at ten o'clock tomorrow morning," he snapped. "Make sure you are here on time."

"Where is she bound for?" I asked.

"You're not supposed to know," he scowled. "Didn't I tell you there was a war on" he said, quite sarcastically. "Report back here to sign articles at ten tomorrow morning."

Back at my lodgings I realized I had no option but to sign on the vessel next morning. Old Repp's veiled threat left me no alternative; "You'll either join the ship or be drafted into the army," he'd warned.

After this morning's performance, I'm sure he'd be delighted to see his threat carried out. I had no choice but to follow his instructions. There was no way I wanted to be shanghied into the army.

My dear old landlady, bless her, was quite upset at the way I'd been treated.

"You should not have to go to sea, after the illness you've suffered, Charles," she confided.

"There's a desperate shortage of men to man the ships" I told her. But knowing little about life at sea, she failed to understand the situation.

Rising early next morning I dressed with meticulous care and gathered together a few odds and ends I had forgotten to pack the night before, taking with me some photographs. One in particular was a faded picture of mother, I treasured. After an early breakfast I prepared myself for the task ahead, for the day was already hot and sticky. But even as I left the house that late July morning of 1942, the sun had yet to rise to it's full height. In no great hurry to reach my destination I sauntered leisurely down to board a tram, that would take me to Liverpool's Pier Head. Packed in like sardines, my journey on that rickety old tramcar was anything but comfortable.

Outside the shipping office at Canning Place, a group of seamen deep in conversation cast questioning glances in my direction as I entered the building, and I wondered why. The moment I stepped inside and took stock of it's emptiness, I suspected something was afoot. Large as life old Repp sat there behind his desk in vulture-like pose, waiting for his next victim. Otherwise the place was deserted. It was so quiet, you could hear the woodworm chewing away inside the old devil's desk. Seeing me arrive he rubbed his thin bony hands together gleefully, and like the proverbial fly caught in the spider's web, I saw myself as another victim caught in his trap.

The bloodless lips parted and an insipid smile creased the palid face, revealing rows of yellow tobacco stained teeth. Pointing to a door marked doctor, he sneered; "He's waiting for you in there, sonny."

A tall balding man, Doctor Reeves was well past his prime. So scruffy in his mode of dress, he might have been mistaken for a vet. The room in which he examined me reeked of stale liquor, and horse linament. Belching loudly he asked; "D'you wear glasses?"

"No, I can see perfectly well thank you," I responded.

With a cursory glance in my direction, he squinted through bloodshot eyes, and announced; "All right, you'll do."

In between a series of muted grunts and groans his pen scratched out a note, which he handed to me, saying;. "Give that to the clerk."

Glacing at the message which I found illegible, I took it to the wily old Repp who snatched the paper from me. Scanning the note he grinned sardonically, saying; "You're fit enough so sit over there, the Shipping Master will arrive shortly."

Seamen I'd seen waiting outside the building a little earlier, entered the shipping office as soon as the Shipping Master arrived. He was a man in his late fifties dressed in a navy blue suit, who took his seat behind a large oak desk. Spreading a sheaf of documents on the table in front of him he called everybody to order, and in a hollow voice read out a long list of Board of Trade rules and regulations. Emphasizing penalties stated therein, for anyone found infringing them. With the usual formalities of signing on completed, he issued the following statement; "The M.V.Waimarama is berthed at Vittoria Dock over in Birkenhead. All personel will report on board the vessel at eight a.m tomorrow morning.

"Blimey, they don't give you a chance to ave a dash across the prairie," moaned a disgruntled stoker.

His comment brought a stern rebuke from the Shipping Master, who reminded him; "There's a time and place for everything young man." Then eyeing him coldly, said; "I suppose you do realize there is a war going on."

With little time to worry about the predicament I now found myself in I made my way home, mulling over the events of the past twenty four hours. The speed with which they occurred, left me bewildered. I had just been declared fit to return to sea by an inebriated horse doctor, and had no choice but to give up my job in the shipyard. Come tomorrow morning, I'd be off to God knows where. Had I dared to protest and requested to be examined by a medical board, I have no doubt I would have been saved from going back to sea on medical grounds. But being patriotic, I allowed my heart to rule my head and stepped blindly forward, unaware the path ahead was fraught with danger. Little did I realize I'd embarked on a voyage from which very few would return; nonetheless, my course was set, so who was I to reason why.

News of my imminent departure in the morning came as something of a shock to my landlady, poor old soul. She imagined I would at least be given a week's grace to get myself ready.

"My goodness they haven't allowed you much time, Charles" she murmured.

"There's a war on dear" I answered, moving toward the foot of the stairs. Hesitating I turned, and in a gesture of despair asked; "What was I to do; they threatened to shove me in the army if I'd refused to join the ship."

Climbing the stairs I entered my bedroom, and looked at a half-filled suitcase lying on the floor. Why, it was only yesterday I had a premonition a situation such as this would develop. My initial meeting in the shipping office with old Repp warned me to be on guard, ready for any emergency. Having finished packing my bags, I visited my fiancee who lived in the nearby village. Saying goodbye was an emotional affair, with tears falling profusely when she learnt of my sudden departure. Assuring her there was no cause for alarm I returned to my lodgings, and made ready for an early start next morning.

A knock on my bedroom door, and a whispered, "It's time to get up, Charles," wakened me with a start. As the morning sunlight filtered through a chink in the curtains I lay still for a while, watching sunbeams dance along it's golden rays. July an exceptionally hot month was drawing to a close, with the dark clouds of war overshadowing the beauty of gardens ablaze with colour.

Taking my time to wash and dress, I picked up my bags and slipped downstairs to the kitchen, where the aroma of freshly toasted bread greeted me. At the breakfast table Mrs Linden bid me her usual good morning, but our conversation, meant to be light-hearted and topical, was somewhat edgy due to my sudden departure. As we sat talking, the ringing of her front door bell caused the good lady to exclaim; "Ah, that'll be your taxi, Charles."

Not wishing our parting to be a long drawn out affair I placed my luggage in the cab, and with a brief farewell embrace I was gone. Driving past our sun-drenched local park rekindled memories of walks along it's tree-lined avenues and sitting beneath the shade of a horse chesnut tree, feeding pea-nuts to a host of little brown squirrels. But all too soon the cavernous entrance to the Mersey Tunnel loomed ahead of me. On display throughout this brightly lit thoroughfare beneath the River Mersey, posters advertising Craven "A" cigarettes, Fry's Cocoa, and holidays at Blackpool caught the eye. Prominent among them, were notices warning people to be on their guard. Some even brought a smile, saying "Walls have Ears, or "Loose talk Costs Lives." One I found most amusing because of the situation I now found myself in, asked; "Is your journey really necessary?" Right now I would most definately say, no.

Leaving the tunnel that had taken me from the City of Liverpool into the town of Birkenhead, my journey ended at Vittoria Dock. Pointing to a vessel lying nearby, my taxi driver exclaimed; "That's her there," and drove up alongside the ship.

A vessel of fifteen thousand tons, the M.V. Waimarama's superstructure towered skyward, like a huge grey ghost. The vessel's name normally seen in white lettering on her stern, was hardly distinguishable beneath a coat of dark grey. Struggling up the gangway with my luggage, a hurried glance around the ship's deck brought a gasp of alarm. She's a damned armed cruiser I said to myself, noting her heavy armament. Newly painted gun turrets welded to her deck fore and aft, were mounted with surface and anti-aircraft guns of every description. Like an army of ants dock workers were frantically loading general cargo into the vessel's holds, in an effort to catch the evening tide.

With extra personnel on board from the army and navy among the ship's compliment of men, there was no doubt in my mind something very secretive was going on, that the ship's crew knew nothing about. Every man jack of her original crew, mainly from Stornaway in the Outer Hebrides or some other far flung island in Scotland, had long since disappeared. Not to attend the Highland Games I might add. They'd more than likely heard where the ship was bound, and scarpered. Whatever it was they'd heard on the grapevine they didn't intend hanging around to find out if it were true. Although we'd been informed the vessel was bound for Australia an air of mystery hung over the ship's destination, especially when one noted the heavy armament installed on the ship. I somehow had a gut feeling we were heading for trouble and this would be no ordinary voyage.

As a late evening sun dipped below the horizon the loading of the ship was completed, it was now the turn of the M.V.Waimarama to leave her berth and move to the river entrance and await high water. Heavily laden our draft was such we were unable to leave the dock until near the top of high water, when the locked gates holding us fast in the dock basin slowly parted. With our passage into the river now clear, the pilot gave an order to let go of our moorings fore and aft. It was now the turn of attendent tugs to ease the vessel past the lock gates into a fast flowing river Mersey. As her engines burst into life the vessel swung sharply to starboard, facing the open sea. With the ship picking up speed the pilot ordered our tugs to let go of their tow-ropes fore and aft, we were then on our way. So began a nightmare voyage, I was to remember for the rest of my life.

Arriving off Holyhead on the Isle of Anglesey our pilot taking his leave bid us bon voyage and descended a jacob's ladder placed over the ship's side, boarding a launch that had arrived to pick him up. With darkness closing in he was whisked ashore leaving the M.V.Waimarama making all possible speed to an unknown destination, to embark on one of the bitterest convoy battles of the Second World War. Destined to send her to a watery grave, taking many of her crew with her.

Awakened for duty around midnight the ship started to pitch and roll in the heavy swell, caused by a stiff breeze and following sea. Reaching the bridge I entered the wheelhouse and glancing at the compass I noticed we were heading in a northerly direction to God knows where, whereas our normal course for Australia was south. Rumour spread like wildfire we were heading north to join a Russian convoy.

Recently installed heavy armament plus the inclusion of Army and Naval personnel to man the guns, gave weight to this supposition. Our arrival at the port of Gourock in Scotland the following evening, was cause enough for concern to every member of the ship's crew. Lying at anchor ahead of us were a group of thirteen merchant vessels of similar design, accompanied by a large oil tanker. All heavily armed with extra surface to air missiles and apparently waiting for orders from the Naval Authorities, as to their final destinations. Patrolling nearby in a mist-shrouded background, lurked the ghostly grey shapes of naval escort vessels forming a protective screen around them. In the fading light of evening a morse lamp winked out, instructing the Waimarama to take up an anchorage close to the vessels waiting there. Reaching our allotted position where an order to drop the anchor was given, there followed a rattle of steel cable sliding down the hausepipe. With a loud splash the anchor hit the water, and came to rest at a depth of six fathoms.

Daybreak on the morning of August 2nd 1942 saw a curtain of mist hanging over the Firth of Clyde, and with the aid of binoculars it was possible to get a clear view of the number of vessels anchored nearby. Weighing up the situation one could not ignore this concentration of fire power on heavily armed merchant ships, to realize there was trouble brewing. The unanswered question was, but where? Soon after breakfast the Captain ordered the ship's company to muster on deck, and set alarm bells ringing. Seamen gathered together on the ship's foredeck, could only hazzard a guess as to our final destination.

Rumours that we were bound for Murmansk quickly spread throughout the ship like wildfire, until the Captain appeared on deck. Calling for members of the ship's company to pay attention, he read out a message he'd received from Naval headquarters in Gourock.

In stunned silence the men listened whilst he read out the following message; "The M.V. Waimarama has been detailed to join a convoy code named Pedestal, bound for the relief of Malta.

Before he could utter another word loud protests from members of the deck crew, rent the air. "We've been bloody shanghied," they shouted angrily. "Why didn't they ask for volunteers?"

Calling for calm the Captain continued, by saying: "The people of Malta are at this moment facing starvation. It is therefore of the utmost importance, or I should say imperative, that this convoy gets through at all costs."

An undercurrent of discontent predominant among the seamen suddenly subsided, when he pleaded with them; "Surely, there is no man among you who would have these unfortunate people starve."

In the silence that followed nought was heard but the mournful cry of gulls, wheeling above the vessel. With a brief word of thanks the Captain dismissed the ship's company, allowing them to continue with their normal duties. As the day ended the sun seen as a golden ball of fire, streaked with flashes of orange, slipped slowly beneath the far horizon. Before night closed in, an aldis lamp flashed out a coded message requesting each vessel to heave up anchor and move out to sea. In semi darkness a ghostly grey collection of heavily laden merchant vessels, slipped stealthily away from the Port of Gourock in Scotland, to rendezvous with their naval escorts. In all, a total of fourteen ships comprised of the cream of the British merchant fleet, in company with the American vessels Almeria Lykes, Santa Elisa and the oil tanker Ohio, set sail for Malta on the night of the 3rd, of August, 1942. Commander A.G.Venables

R.N, in charge of the convoy took passage aboard the merchant ship Port Chalmers while the main body of our naval escort under the command of Admiral Syfret, met the convoy off the Clyde later that night.

Steaming at a speed of fifteen knots our journey thus far being uneventful, we arrived off Gibraltar in the early hours on the 10th of August. Convoy and escorts slipping through the Straits under cover of dense fog. It was late on the afternoon of the 10th that our position was made known to the enemy but by that time our convoy of merchant ships bound for Malta carrying urgently needed supplies, was well into the Mediterranean. Pedestal a code name given to this vital convoy was then joined by a large naval task force from Gibraltar consisting of two Battleships, three Carriers, six Cruisers, and two dozen destroyers. Outnumbering the merchantmen they were escorting, by three to one.

Early on the morning of the 11th of August enemy aircraft spotted the convoy and thereafter shadowed us continuously, in spite of special attention paid to them by our carrier-borne fighters. At midday on the eleventh, when approximately 550 miles from our destination, Spitfires from the carrier H.M.S. Furious flew off to their base on the Island of Malta. At 1.15 p.m that afternoon the aircraft carrier H.M.S.Eagle was hit with four torpedoes fired by U.73, successfully penetrating our defensive screen.

Violent explosions were heard over a wide area as the missiles struck the vessel amidships, setting her on fire and putting her out of action. Drifting helplessly astern she listed badly to starboard, while planes waiting to take off on her flight deck slid into the water, followed by members of her crew. Burning fiercely she began to sink. Slowly at first, then almost reluctantly slipping beneath the Mediterranean's blue waters. A column of water shooting high into the air from the crippled vessel's engine room, as she disappeared. Within eight minutes she was no more.

Escorting destroyers managed to rescue 900 out of her compliment of 1160 men, including her Captain, L. D. Mackintosh. At dusk on the evening of the eleventh the convoy experienced it's first air attack. A large formation of German bombers and torpedo bombers swooping in from the west, escaped the attention of our fighters in failing light. However all salvo's missed their intended targets, while a concentrated barrage of anti-aircraft fire from the guns of every ship in the convoy, accounted for several of the enemy.

At dawn on the morning of the 12th of August renewed enemy attacks were intercepted by carrier-borne fighters some distance from the convoy; few if any, managing to slip by them. This however proved to be a preliminary skirmish by the Luftwaffe and its allies, their most ferocious effort so far. Abreast of their Sardinian airfields around noon on that day a combined force of some eighty torpedo bombers, dive bombers and fighter bombers, in a perfectly timed raid zoomed in on the convoy. The attack in which little damage was done lasted for over an hour, our only casualty being the merchant vessel Deucalion, which was forced to leave the convoy and later destroyed by the enemy, off the Tunisian coast. Further attacks by a force of German dive bombers quickly followed, only to peter out before any serious damage could be inflicted.

Not to be outdone several enemy dive bombers sneaked in out of the morning sun and by diving in low among the convoy, one of their number raked the boat deck of my ship the M.V.Waimarama with a volley of cannon fire. Taken by surprise I dived headlong beneath a nearby lifeboat and lay there unable to move, watching the wooden deck being ripped to shreds. Caught unawares by this sneak attack the Captain's steward emerged from the wheel house, with tea tray in hand. Descending the companion ladder from the bridge he stumbled and fell, landing with a sickening thud on the boat deck below, and lay perfectly still.

Emerging from his place of shelter following the attack, an engineer seeing him fall, shouted; "Are you alright?" and rushed to assist him.

Stunned and badly shaken, the steward slowly raised his head. In shocked silence I watched a jagged gash above his right ear pumping out blood, spreading onto his chest, turning the front of his white shirt crimson.

"Where the hell did that sneaky sod come from?" he groaned. "The square headed bastard nearly had me."

Passing through the main enemy submarine concentration that afternoon numerous attacks were made on the convoy, with many torpedoes being fired at our ships. Were it not for the vigilance of our escorts or the precise timing of several emergency turns made by the merchantmen, serious losses could have occurred. Throughout the remainder of the daylight hours, repeated attacks by enemy aircraft were driven off by concentrated fire power from all ships in the convoy. At times the sky turned black with exploding anti-aircraft shells, blotting out a brilliant August sun.

Late on the afternoon of the 12th a warning to all ships in convoy of an apparent enemy attack, sent battle weary gun crews into action. Nerves on edge following continuous night and day attacks, we made ready once again to meet an onslaught from superior enemy forces. Shoulders strapped firmly into the harness of anti-aircraft guns, grim faced personel stood by to fend off further enemy attacks. Then out of a setting sun they came, huge formations of them swooped down on the convoy with a thunderous roar. On they came like a plague of locust intent on devouring everything before them, squadron's of high level and dive bombers unwavering in their determination to obliterate every Merchant ship in sight. Their objective was to stop the life saving cargoes of food and oil, destined for the starving population of Malta.

Continuous attacks by torpedo and dive bombers lasted throughout the afternoon, petering out as the convoy reached the Skerki Channel late that evening. Changing formation from four columns into two when passing through the channel at 8 p.m. on the night of August 12th, a torpedo struck the oil tanker Ohio. Although badly damaged she managed to remain with the convoy. In repeated enemy submarine and E-boat attacks, affording the convoy little respite, two further merchant vessels, the Clan Ferguson and Empire Hope were lost. Also hit was the Brisbane Star, who eventually managed to limp into Malta. Rounding Cape Bon at midnight, it became apparent enemy E boats were operating in the area. At 1a.m. on the 13th of August, a violent explosion was heard some way ahead of the convoy. Minutes later we passed the cruiser H.M.S. Manchester, hit by a torpedo fired from close range, she was down at the stern and out of action. Marauding E-boats slipping in and out of the convoy during the hours of darkness unleashed a series of torpedoes, damaging the H.M.S Manchester's propellor shafts.

Between 3.20 and 4.30 am on the morning of the thirteenth further crippling attacks by enemy torpedo boats, accounted for the loss of another five merchantmen. Following some distance astern of the main body four of them, the Wairangi, Almeria Lykes and Santa Elishia and most probably the Glenorchy, were all sunk. A cruel blow indeed after the convoy had ventured so far with great success, yet the battle continued unabated throughout the night, with special attention being given to the tanker Ohio. Determined at all costs to destroy her valuable cargo of much needed oil before reaching Malta, they attacked her ceaselessly. In her wake remnants of once proud ships and their gallant crews who joined battle with the enemy, were left ablaze. Throughout the dark of night red balls of fire strung out amid a sea littered with wreckage, lit up the far horizon. From the deck of the Waimarama I surveyed this horrific scene of death and destruction unaware that I, too, would be in the same predicament, in but a few short hours.

No place to Hide

In circumstances favourable to the enemy, attacks by Italian E-Boats from their base at Pantellaria dominated the hours of darkness. An exchange of gunfire during these skirmishes, saw tracers criss-crossing the night sky. From time to time parachute flares enabled escort vessels to seek out enemy torpedo boats sneaking in among the convoy, dispatching some of them to a watery grave.

Daybreak on the morning of August 13th brought scant relief for the battle weary crews of merchant ships, that remained in convoy. Within striking distance of enemy airfields in Sicily, we now faced a bigger threat of attack from dive bombers. Rising at 7a.m. to snatch a hurried breakfast I left my cabin for a stroll around the open deck before going on duty at eight o'clock, and from the deck of my ship I surveyed the remnants of our battered convoy.

A combined attack by submarines and E-Boats during the hours of darkness, had claimed at least six merchant ships sunk and two damaged, not to mention the number of escort vessels destroyed or badly disabled. It was therefore surprising to find how many had managed to survive, during a night of mayhem.

Taking advantage of a lull in the ongoing battle for supremacy of the Mediterranean and command of the Island of Malta, I chanced to relax in the early morning sunshine. Everything seemed so peaceful after a night of carnage, fresh on my mind. It was hard to imagine how any of us engaged in this do or die battle for survival, had come through unscathed. Cautious and forever on guard against a surprise enemy attack at any given time, gun crews waited for the next onslaught, which was not long in coming.

Climbing a companionway leading up to the bridge I entered the wheel house at 7.55 a.m. as red warning flags were hoisted from the foremast of every ship in convoy, signalling an enemy air attack was imminent. From the wing of the bridge a strangled cry of alarm from the duty officer was cut short when a formation of JU.87 dive-bombers, sweeping in for the kill, struck the M.V. Waimarama with a stick of bombs, igniting her deck cargo of high octane. Almost simultaneously a series of violent explosions rocked the vessel, turning her into a raging inferno. The force of the blast lifted me off my feet, throwing me up against the rear wall of the chart room. Momentarily stunned I lay helpless, as flames engulfed the area. Rising unsteadily, I found breathing difficult in the intense heat. Acrid fumes from burning oil and timber choked me as I fought for breath, and looked on helpless, as the fire encircled me.

With lightning speed flames swept through the vessel's tinder dry wooden structure, chartroom windows caught in the blaze cracked viciously as they melted away, turning to molten liquid in a cauldron of fire. Trapped in a roaring inferno creeping ever closer, death stared me in the face, but what could I do? There was nowhere to run, and nowhere to hide. Gasping for air in the stiffling heat escape seemed virtually impossible, and terror clutched at my heart. Fearing my life was destined to end in a dramatic and painful end, I beseeched the Lord to help me in my hour of need, believing I was about to die. On bended knees, I offered a silent prayer to my maker and begged him: "Lord if my time has come, please let it be quick."

Scenes from childhood flashed swiftly through my mind while I stood there, waiting for the flames to devour me. I pictured my first meeting with mother at London's Victoria Station, when a boy of thirteen. Then came a fleeting glimpse of Grandma whispering in my ear; "Catherine is your sister, Charles." Never having set eyes on her, I asked the Lord to spare me.

Caught in a combination of fear and deep emotion, vital seconds ticked away as my lungs screamed out for air. The intense heat and dense smoke from the burning oil, all but choked me. Below decks a series of violent explosions rocked the ship when her cargo of ammunition ignited by fire swept through her holds, tearing the very heart out of her. Quite suddenly a rumbling sound from the port side of the bridge attracted my attention and as I gazed toward it, the scene that caught my eye caused my heart to skip a beat.

It was as if my prayers had been answered, and the hand of Providence was reaching out to guide me. For one fleeting moment an impenetrable curtain of fire between myself and salvation parted, and in those vital seconds I had a clear view of the port wing of the ship's bridge. As yet untouched by the raging inferno, a miraculous avenue of escape lay before me, some thirty five to forty feet away. Hope anew welled up within me. If only I could make it, I told myself. But first I was to run the gauntlet through a dense wall of fire, conscious that in desperate situations such as this when every second counts, one has little time to lose. It was a matter of life and death.

Picking up a steel helmet from among debris littering the chartroom floor I placed it firmly on my head, and raising my eyes heavenward offered a prayer to a merciful Lord who had seen fit to spare me. Placing both hands over my face for protection, I inhaled what little air there was in the smoke filled atmosphere. Holding my breath, I dashed headlong through a rapidly lengthening curtain of fire.

Sheer terror urged me on through a wall of searing flames, licking hungrily at my bare flesh. Fighting every inch of the way through a solid wall of fire, with the sickly smell of death in my nostrils, I choked back a need to scream with pain and stumbled blindly on. In a desperate bid to reach safety on the wing of the bridge. It seemed I had entered the gates of hell when rushing through this inferno and dense smoke, to suddenly emerge from a circle of death. Feeling a breath of cool air touch the bare flesh on my hands, I'd somehow managed to come out alive, but not unscathed. Excruciating pain shot through my hands, now swollen twice their normal size, and badly burnt. But there was no time to waste for I feared the ship itself was in danger of sinking beneath me, serving only to hasten my need to escape.

Frantic cries for help from men trapped below decks were cut short by agonized screams of pain, as the fire engulfed them.

It made my blood ran cold, but I was helpless to do anything to relieve their suffering. My own life hung in the balance. I dared not remain aboard any longer than was absolutely necessary. The ship was loaded with ammunition and might blow up at any moment. My feeling of relief in knowing I was clear of the raging inferno and might possibly escape further injury, was short lived. A glance over the ship's side was enough to renew the fear for my safety, the only avenue of escape appeared to have been cut off. Ignited by high octane from the ship's deck cargo, fuel oil spewing from the stricken ship had caught fire, setting the water ablaze. The situation now staring me in the face was desperate indeed. To remain on board and burn to a cinder, or take a chance to escape from the blazing oil.

With extreme difficulty I removed the steel helmet from my head, ridding myself of whatever clothing I could, and placing my trust in the Lord that I might survive, dived headlong into an ocean ablaze with fire. Surrounded by a sea of pain, I plunged deep into the water in my struggle to survive. Swimming strongly beneath the water, constantly aware of agonizing pain shooting up my arms with every stroke, I kept on going. Failure to put as much distance as possible between myself and the blazing oil surrounding my ship, could be fatal. Holding my breath until my lungs were ready to burst I finally surfaced, coated with fuel oil that clung to me as I emerged above water. Although some distance away I could feel the heat on the back of my neck, coming from the fire. Looking back at the stricken vessel blazing fiercely from stem to stern I realized how lucky I was, to have made such a miraculous escape.

Suddenly a series of violent explosions from ammunition stowed down in the vessel's holds rocked her, encouraging me to swim away from the ship as far as I possibly could. Unable to use my badly burnt hands I turned on my back and propelled myself away from the ship, by kicking out strongly with both legs until I could go no further. Exhausted I lay there watching the crippled vessel in it's final death throes, when an enormous explosion below decks shook her from stem to stern. With a gigantic shudder her huge steel masts that had survived many a storm at sea caved in, and toppled like nine-pins. Spewing out clouds of dense black smoke over a wide area, she suddenly disappeared in a ball of fire.

While in no immediate danger I drifted past huge mounds of fire foam and chunks of wood bobbing about on the water, all that remained of the doomed vessel. Amid a sea littered with debris covering a wide area, a pall of black smoke towering skyward, marked the spot where the M.V.Waimarama had fought so bravely. Taking with her, most of her gallant crew. But for the grace of God I, too, could have perished along with them.

Mingled with the intermittent chatter of anti-aircraft fire a distant rumble of exploding bombs could still be heard, as the battle raged on. But as the day wore on and the sound of gunfire diminished, an eerie silence descended over these troubled waters. Strenuous efforts to put distance between myself and the wreckage of my ship, had left me exhausted. Closing my eyes I lay still, drifting among the debris of battle, now scattered over a wide area of the Mediterranean. Nerves on edge I listened for the slightest sound, believing there was every possibility I'd be rescued.

Worn out and dog-tired due to a lack of sleep since passing Gibraltar, I had just dosed off when a noise like that of a light breeze rustling through the trees, startled me. Afraid to make the slightest move fearing it might be the enemy, I lay perfectly still as though dead. In the stillness of time that followed I chanced to peep through my good right eye, and gazed in awe at an amazing sight that lay before me. No more than a stone's throw away, the ghostly figure of a young woman appeared to be hovering just above the water. Emanating from her being, flowed a bright iridescent light. A gossamer white robe fastened with a girdle of brilliant azure blue adorned the sylph-like figure, who with outstretched arms beckoned me to her.

My reaction was one of fear. Was it just a figment of my imagination, I asked myself. Suppressing a need to cry out for help, I closed my eyes and lay perfectly still hardly daring to breathe. Assuring myself that whatever it was I had seen, would suddenly go. Allowing minutes to tick away in which time I felt the image might have disappeared, I chanced to peep again.. Lo and behold the apparition was still there as before, positioned just above the water beckoning me toward her with greater urgency.

"My God, I'm hallucinating," I told myself; "It must be the sweltering heat of the sun that is driving me crazy."

While in the presence of this awe-inspiring being, an indescribable feeling of calm surged through my body. A sea of pain from my injuries slowly receded, allowing me to move with greater freedom. Anxious to get closer to this apparition or whatever it might be, I instinctively began to swim again. With consumate ease I put extra effort into each stroke determined to narrow the gap between us, but it was not to be. The faster I swam the further away she drifted, seeming all the while to beckon me toward her, until I could swim no further. Thoroughly exhausted I gave up and closing my eyes lay motionless, resting my tortured body.

Startled by the sound of voices breaking the afternoon stillness I turned to my angel-like being for guidance, and found she had gone, and the pain that had left my aching limbs, returned. The mumbled conversation I'd heard being much too distant for me to understand a word of it, I decided to keep quiet. It might be the enemy searching for survivors I said to myself. We were close enough to the Italian island of Pantellaria when my ship went down, and the very thought of being taken prisoner frightened me. I had no wish to spend my time rotting in a prison camp.

Echoing across the Mediterranean's silent waters a peal of laughter broke the silence; "You daft bugger that won't help, they'll probably shoot us if they see that," the voice went on.

Recognizing the speaker as one of my own countrymen was music to my ears. Ignoring a rush of pain to my hands with some difficulty I managed to remove the whistle from a pocket in my life jacket, and blew on it as loud as I could and waited for some response.

Following a lengthy period of silence which in effect was probably no more than a couple of minutes, back came a voice: "Who the hell are you?"

Careful not to alarm them, I shouted, "I'm a survivor from the convoy."

"Keep blowing" the voice replied; "We'll make our way over to you."

Surrounded by huge mounds of fire-foam I was hidden from view but with the sound of my whistle to guide them, two startled young men appeared as if by magic from among a collection of floating debris. Seeing I was covered in fuel oil the elder of the two stammered; "Where the hell have you come from to be in such a mess, and what colour are you supposed to be," asked his partner. "Black or white?"

"I'm from the M.V.Waimarama," I told them. "The ship was sunk by dive bombers. And what's more, like you I'm white and British."

Hanging on to a large bulk of timber from the sunken ship they propelled themselves through the water toward me, looking at me as though I were from another planet. Shaking his head, unable to believe his own eyes, the elder of the two said; "My God you were damned lucky to get off that ship alive."

Apparently they were naval gunners attached to the Waimarama for the voyage to Malta, manning an Oerlikon gun mounted on the port wing of the bridge. Just before the Waimarama was hit by a stick of bombs at five minutes past eight on the morning of the 13th, they'd opened fire on a formation of J.U.88's coming out of the sun, hell bent on sinking the ship. As the bombs struck the ship setting her deck cargo of high octane afire, the men dived overboard and swimming clear of her watched, horrified, by the speed in which the ship sank.

Arthur a man in his thirties and the elder of the two naval ratings, was a reporter for his local paper in peacetime. As an eye witness to our encounter with the enemy he gave a graphic account of the action and described the sinking in detail, saying; "Steaming toward Malta at a speed of thirteen knots, the merchantman M.V. Waimarama was singled out for attack by three German dive bombers. A near miss from the first, was followed by a direct hit with a salvo of bombs from the second. No ship on earth could have withstood such punishment and survived" he assured me, and went on to say; "Missiles landing fore and aft of the bridge caused a tremendous explosion. It was at this point my shipmates and I, manning an Oerlikan on the port wing of the bridge, leapt into the water and swam for our lives. From a safe distance we watched a huge ball of fire appear, followed by a towering column of black smoke. Her masts telescoped inwards like matchsticks, crumbling into the heart of the roaring furnace below. Her deck cargo of high octane had already ignited in a sheet of flame, sweeping the ship from stem to stern. Violent explosions raked her as fire quickly spread to the ammunition in her holds, causing her to vibrate convulsively."

Listing to starboard she suddenly righted herself and sank in seconds leaving a large patch of blazing oil on the water with a pall of dense black smoke, almost blotting out the sun. We later learned a third Junker's bomber following up behind was caught up in a mighty explosion from the stricken vessel, disintegrating in mid-air. It seemed almost unimaginable that anyone could possibly escape such mass destruction. Sadly, most of the ship's crew perished as a result of a shattering explosion in which few were expected to survive.

Meanwhile my two companions seeing I was unable to use my badly injured hands, placed me between them on a cabin door they'd salvaged from the wreckage. This helped us to make headway through the water more quickly but with the enemy on all sides, where we were heading, I had no idea. Having earlier divested themselves of the top portion of their naval uniforms the scorching heat of a Mediterranean sun at it's height, played havoc with their salt encrusted bodies. While the pair were busily engaged submerging themselves below the water to keep cool, I watched a dark smudge on the horizon grow larger with each passing minute.

"I think there's a ship over there" I shouted excitedly. Studying the distant object for a moment Arthur turned toward me, a look of elation on his sun scorched face;

"By god you're right son" he cried, and started waving his arms about as though we'd just won an important victory.

"She's coming this way" his partner shouted, "I hope they've seen us."

Her outline now clearly visible as she drew close, sent Arthur's companion Nobby Clarke into raptures.

"It's one of our L-Class frigates, I can tell by her superstructure" he exclaimed.

"She must be looking for survivors" said Arthur. "Let's try to attract their attention."

While the pair of them waved frantically I placed my whistle between swollen lips, and blew as hard as I could. Our moment of ecstasy at the thought of being rescued suddenly evaporated, when the sound of distant gunfire saw the vessel alter course. Her propellers thrashed the water wildly as she wheeled to starboard, and our would-be rescuer headed in the opposite direction. A deathly silence that followed was broken by an all too familiar sound, of an aircraft approaching.

With bated breath we watched as it skimmed low over the water, heading in our direction. Her markings were now clearly visible to us, when Arthur yelled a warning;

"Duck for God's sake, it's a bloody Jerry."

None too soon I released my hold on the floating bulk of timber I'd been clinging to, and dived beneath the Mediterranean's debris-covered waters. A short burst of cannon fire raked the wooden plank above us; its deafening noise sent shock waves echoing below. Remaining submerged until my lungs felt they would burst, a desperate need to take in fresh air forced me to surface. Gasping for breath I swam toward the bulk of timber floating nearby, and hung on for dear life. White-faced and badly shaken, my two companions surfaced simultaneously.

Shaking his fist at the now distant enemy aircraft, Nobby Clarke screamed; "You murdering bastard. Trying to kill us when we're helpless."

Turning to Arthur he gasped, "that son of a bitch was using us for target practice."

"Hell, that was a bloody close call. I thought our number was up," said Arthur. "We'll have to keep a sharp look out, in case the bastard decides to come back."

Having almost burnt us to a cinder the sun began to cool down as it slipped toward the western horizon, but nothing stirred in the vast emptiness of these troubled waters. Not even a sea bird winging it's way home and any chance we had of being rescued, looked slim indeed. Fearing I might spend the night in these waters, sent shivers through me. My injuries hurt so much I was in need of something to relieve the awful pain, and prayed that rescue might be near at hand.

"I wonder what the time is" Nobby remarked, almost casually. "We seem to have been in the water forever."

It was then I chanced to look at the watch on my wrist, why I'll never know, for it was useless. Burnt beyond recognition, the steel strap had left a red weal on my forearm. Likewise the watches belonging to both my companions were waterlogged, so we had no way of knowing the time of day. We did however notice the heat of the day was fast receding. The sun taking on a reddish hue slipped gently toward the western horizon. In gathering gloom a tiny white light bearing down on us at a considerable speed caught our attention, which turned out to be a ship. Unaware of her identity caused us some concern for our safety but as she drew closer, silhouettes of her crew moving around the foredeck were clearly distinguishable. "I think it's one of our escorts" exclaimed Arthur, excitedly. "We're going to be alright now, lads."

Her propellers thrashed the water violently as she slowly moved astern, and shuddered to a halt. Caught in the vessel's backwash we slowly drifted toward her starboard side and seeing us in the water, the officer in charge ordered a scrambling net to be lowered over the side. Leaning on the rails he addressed us like long lost friends; "Nice to see you safe boys, hop aboard."

Surprised by his jocular remark, Arthur quipped; "What the hell do you think we are matey, bloody monkeys?"

A chorus of muffled laughter from members of the ship's crew standing nearby, was quickly stiffled by the appearance of a senior officer.

"You'd better send a line down for our friend here," Arthur advised. "His hands are badly injured."

As darkness closed in my two companions were helped aboard whilst I lay motionless in the water, until assisted by a member of the crew. Securing a canvas belt beneath my arms they hoisted me up on deck, and gently placed me on a stretcher. In the beam of a tiny flashlight held by one of ship's crew I noticed the red and gold bands on the sleeve of a uniformed officer attending me, whom I imagined was the ship's doctor. Conversing with a seaman in attendance, he said; "I'll need to give him a jab, so you'd better cut open his trouser leg."

With a deft stroke, the blade of the seaman's knife sliced through the oil-soaked fabric and a shiver ran through my body as a cold swab touched my bare thigh, and the smell of medical spirits assailed my nostrils. I felt the needle bite into my flesh and a numbness pervaded me, relieving my pain to render me unconscious.

At daybreak, the vessel carrying me to safety came under a concentrated attack by enemy aircraft and the noise from her guns wakened me with a start. Lying in a dimly lit room aboard the escort vessel H.M.S. Ledbury, I had no idea what was happening. Bandages covering my hands and face allowed me little space to see properly and in the dim light I saw rows of rescued seamen lying around me, filling every available inch of space.

Nightfall brought scant relief for the battle weary ships' crew harrassed by raiding E-Boats, exchanging sporadic bursts of gunfire throughout the hours of darkness. Racing to aid the crippled tanker Ohio still afloat after receiving a terrific pounding, Ledbury was joined by the destroyer Penn, and minesweeper Rye. Together they towed the stricken vessel in the direction of Malta. Constant enemy air attacks during the next two days saw Ledbury's anti-aircraft guns working overtime. Mess tables shook violently each time they opened up, waking myself and many other injured survivors, who slept on them. Lying heavily sedated in semi-darkness I recoiled with fright when seeing ghostly figures moving around the mess deck, which were no more than the ship's gun crew wearing white flash hoods. A safety precaution carried out, when handling ammunition. All three vessels, including the stricken tanker, kept up a continuous barrage of anti-aircraft fire in fending off a desperate attempt by the enemy, to destroy the Ohio's precious cargo.

By dawn's early light on the morning of the 15th of August, I wakened to a tremendous burst of cheering. Having fought off air attacks since the afternoon of the thirteenth, the Ohio and her naval escort arrived at the besieged Island of Malta in a sinking condition, to be welcomed by thousands as she entered Grand Harbour. No time was wasted in salvaging the 10,000 tons of fuel oil she carried, which helped in the island's bid to hold out against further Italian and German air attacks. Out of a convoy of fourteen merchant ships a total of five; the Port Chalmers, Rochester Castle, Melbourne Star, Brisbane Star and the severely damaged tanker Ohio, with the assistance of H.M.S. Penn and Ledbury, reached their destination. The remainder were destroyed by enemy action. Many like my comrades aboard the Waimarma never stood a chance when her cargo of aviation spirit and high explosives ignited as the bombs struck, leaving her ablaze from stem to stern.

As the cheering and shouting died away those among us lucky enough to survive, lay at peace on board the H.M.S. Ledbury. Alone with my thoughts in the aftermath of a bitter battle, I waited to be transported to hospital. With all available lights switched on in the mess deck, through slits cut in the bandages covering my face, I surveyed a scene of carnage, created by man's inhumanity to man. Bodies scattered around haphazardly were packed together like sardines down in the Ledbury's mess deck; their bloodstained bandages hiding horrific wounds. Nothing stirred in the quiet of this peaceful morning save for the anguished cry of pain from a wounded soul, waiting his turn for a sedative.

A squeal of brakes at the quayside signalling the arrival of an ambulance saw medical staff hurrying aboard to attend wounded survivors from the convoy, each in turn waiting to be carried to the vehicle. Bumping and bouncing it took off along narrow mountain roads no more than cart tracks, shaking the living daylights out of you. The journey often interrupted by sporadic enemy air raids ended at an army hospital, near the tiny village of Imtarfa. Skidding to a halt on the gravel driveway our arrival alerted hospital staff who carried the badly wounded on stretchers, into a ward set aside for Naval and Merchant seamen.

Entering a brightly-lit room inside the hospital a strong smell of ether attacked my nostrils, as I waited to be attended to. I recall no feeling of pain as a needle was jabbed into my flesh, just the sound of voices that trailed off into a distant mumur, until the morphine injection took a hold. I felt myself falling slowly at first, gyrating in ever-decreasing circles. Gathering speed I plummeted into space, to watch my tormented body dance crazily before me. As death reached out it's clammy hand to touch my cheek, I recoiled in horror. Once again I felt searing flames ravaging my pain-wracked body with the smell of death pervading the air around me, and as the fire spread my screams for help went unanswered. There followed an eerie silence, then once more all was still.

Night had fallen by the time I'd regained consciousness to feel a cool sponge brushing my fevered brow, and a woman's voice whispered; "You're quite safe now, everything's going to be alright."

I tried to touch my face but my hands were held fast by a cumbersome dressing, pinning them to the bed. Looking up into the face of a pretty young nurse, I asked;

"What have they done to me?"

"You're very ill so you must try to get some rest," she murmured. In a semi-stupor I peered through sleep-laden eyes and watched her disappear down the ward, then darkness claimed me once again.

Wakened by the rattle of a medicine trolley trundling past my bed, I found myself in a brightly lit hospital ward. An oblong-shaped room, painted in shades of white and pastel green, lay before me. Nurses busily moving around beds on either side of the room attended casualties from the latest convoy, code named Pedestal, to arrive at this battle-scarred island. Small lockers at each bedside held the personal belongings a patient may have been lucky enough to bring with him, which in many cases was nothing more than the clothes they stood up in.

Suspended over the bed a mosquito net protected one from nightly attacks by swarms of tiny midges who's bite unlike that of the deadly mosquito was irritating, forcing one to scratch themselves continuously.

Like many occupants in the ward I counted myself among one of the luckiest people alive, to have survived the carnage and loss of life. As happened to many of my shipmates on board the M.V Waimarama, during one of the fiercest fought convoy battles of the war. As comrades in arms we all fought the good fight and, as a result, I now suffered with severe burns to my hands. Staring death in the face, I was among the more fortunate to survive. It was nothing short of a miracle I escaped from a blazing inferno, which was all that was left of my ship. Because of an incapacity to feed and wash myself I was dependant on the good graces of hospital nursing staff, for my daily well-being. Instead of taking things for granted in this every day life of ours, which I now found impossible to cope with, this feeling of inadequacy came as a tremendous shock to me,.

Alone with my thoughts, a gentle female voice asked; "Would you like a drink, Mr.Ashford?"

Forcing open my good right eye it was just possible for me to see the young nurse at my bedside, holding a large cup. Bending over me she placed a small tube from the receptacle against my lips, allowing me to siphon up the liquid in my own good time. A look of compassion and tenderness for those in her care, flowed from the pretty elfin-like face, her soft brown eyes had a look of pity as she watched me grimacing, every time I tried to move my injured hands.

"Is the pain too much for you?" she asked, wiping away drops of water dribbling down my chin.

"Yes, it's getting much worse" I replied. "But I'll be alright" I assured her.

Smoothing down the sheets she drew the mosquito net over the bed, saying; "I'll be back in a moment," and hurried away.

Minutes later she returned to my bedside accompanied by the ward sister who lifted the bedclothes and proceeded to rub my leg with a cotton swab, saying; "Just a little jab Mr Ashford."

An involountary shudder ran through my body as the cold swab touched my bare flesh and a hypodermic bit into my thigh, and almost immediately the sea of pain on which I floated, slowly subsided.

"That'll be alright" she announced abruptly, replacing the blanket.

Bleary eyed I watched as she hurried back down the ward leaving the young Maltese nurse to tidy the bedclothes, and replace the mosquito net over my bed, before I passed out.

Early morning sunlight filtered through the glass panelled doors opposite my bed, when the tinkling of glass on a medicine trolley near at hand, roused me from a fitful sleep. A clock on the wall opposite gave the time as six thirty, but even at this early hour hospital staff were busy dressing wounds, and administering medicine to those in need. It was not long before the young Maltese nurse attending me appeared at my bedside carrying a small bowl of warm water, soap, and towel, and placed them on my locker.

"Good morning, did you sleep well?" she asked.

Smiling at her, I answered; "Yes thank you, I slept like a top."

Dipping a small white flannel into the water she moistened my face, taking great care not to wet the dressing covering my left eye. From a pocket in her uniform she took a small bottle of liquid and poured a little on my head and gently massaged it in, so that she might soften a mass of black fuel oil lodged in my hair. With deft strokes she ran a small comb through the tangled mess, completing my morning ablutions, as the ward sister arrived with the medicine trolley.

"We'll give you a morphine injection as soon as we've dressed your hands, Mr Ashford," she announced. "That will help to ease the pain."

I recollect moments of acute agony as the saline water flowed through the oilskin gloves I wore, tearing at the bare flesh on the back of my hands. And once again those same excruciating spasms of agonizing pain I'd experienced when escaping from the blazing ship, ran through my body. So intense was my suffering I was never aware a needle was biting into my flesh, as I lapsed into a semi-stupor. What happened to me after that is a mystery, but the memory of that fateful voyage will remain with me forever.

So Much Red Tape

British Military Hospitals throughout their long history have maintained a rigid code of discipline, in times of peace and war. Here on the beleagured island of Malta where hunger and death walked hand in hand was no exception, army rules and regulations reigned supreme. Red tape aptly described as Bull Shit by the majority of young servicemen stationed here, was strictly adhered to. Nursing staff in the upper echelons of this service were not slow in pulling rank on all junior ratings, often adopting a mightier than thou attitude. Like the Matron in charge of this hospital who was a fine example, demanding all and sundry jump to attention at her command.

Shortly after I arrived at the hospital she entered my ward, determind to make her presence known. This dominating personality standing six feet tall and heavily built, rumbled up the ward like a Sherman Tank. Her dark blue uniform and white lace bonnet, setting her apart from the rest of the nursing staff. Entering the ward at her usual time of ten o'clock each morning, she took centre stage.

Calling hospital orderlies to attention, she addressed them in a manner befitting the best traditions of a sergeant on parade, with the following; "We have an important visitor arriving shortly to inspect the hospital, so I expect the place be neat and tidy," or words to that effect. "Now I hope I have made myself clearly understood" she barked, with emphasis on the word "clearly." Then turning on her heel, she marched out of the ward.

Smiling at the young nurse who at the time was dressing my wounds, I remarked nonchalantly; "That I assume, was the Matron in charge."

I watched her bright young face cloud over for an instant, and as quickly, the radiant smile reappeared. With a shrug of her tiny shoulders it seemed she was trying to express her feelings, concerned with the position in which she found herself. Having no choice but to obey orders, accepting whatever Matron said was law. Then in answer to my question, she repeated a phrase I felt suited the occasion, when she whispered; "Noblesse oblige."

Skillfully changing the subject, she asked; "Have your family been notified you are here?"

Hesitating, I replied, "No I'm afraid not. I lost touch with my mother some years ago." Then as an afterthought added; "But I do have a sister, but have no idea where she is."

The brow furrowed, and a look of concern crossed her elfin face. "You've no idea where she is?" she said, in shocked surprise!

Reaching out to me in a sympathetic gesture her hand touched mine, with a feeling of tenderness, as though I were just a child. Then, as if to put me at ease, she whispered; "Oh, I'm sure you'll find her one day."

Tidying my bedclothes she made ready to leave, and with a cheerful smile, said; "I'll have to go now, sleep well."

Atten—shun, came the Sergeant Major's voice from the far end of the ward, next morning, and with the usual salutations and much acclaim, our long awaited important visitor put in an appearance. All service personnel in the ward able to stand on their feet or on crutches, stood to attention whilst being inspected.

Accompanied by matron and a retinue of hangers on I heard them coming down the ward where I lay in bed, unable to see them quite clearly until they were almost on top of me, because of blurred vision. Standing head and shoulders above the rest of the group, the visitor approached my bed. I could see he was an elderly man in khaki uniform, who stood gazing down at me. Red faced, with large bushy eyebrows protruding from beneath a peaked cap, his walrus moustache twitching slightly. Breathing heavily he leaned toward me, and I caught a whiff of stale tobacco, as he hollered in my ear.

"And how are you feeling, my lad?"

Heavily sedated with injections of morphine, I replied.

"Damned awful. How are you,?" And moaned, as another spasm of pain shot through my arms.

Turning to one of his uniformed cohorts dripping with gold braid, he asked; "Who is this young fellow, and why hasn't he been shaved?"

Examining the chart hanging at the foot of my bed, the gold braided one turned to his superior, and announced rather brusquely; "He's in the Merchant Service sir."

"H'm," grunted red face, and turned away.

His hangers on followed him as he moved to a bed next to me, occupied by Naval Marine White, nicknamed "Knocker." Lying prostrate with a couple of days' growth covering his face, he gave a nervous cough as Red Face drew near. Then struggled into a sitting position. A gold braided member in the party whom I later learned was his Adjutant, picked up the seaman's chart from the foot of his bed, and read out the following; "Name, White, in service with the Royal Marines. Admitted August 14th, shrapnel wounds to right arm and leg."

"Why haven't you shaved today?" Red Face asked the pale faced, Knocker White.

Receiving no reponse, he turned to a young Naval officer in attendance; "Put him on a charge" he announced abruptly, "we don't need this sort of thing in the services."

This to my mind was a typical example of red tape, at it's worst.

Later that evening, I incurred the wrath of none other than the Matron in charge of the hospital. A woman of immense stature, she came charging up the ward like an enraged bull, intent on goring the matador. At the foot of my bed she stopped, glared at me, and thundered: "Your behaviour today was absolutely disgraceful."

"But what have I done to warrant such attention," I asked.

"You were extremely rude, to a very important visitor," she rapped out.

"What would you have me do dear lady," I replied indignantly, "kiss him?"

I thought she was going to throw a fit. Her ashen grey face turned the colour of beetroot, as she fought to catch her breath. Inhaling great gulps of air, her huge bossom rose and fell, like the heaving waves on a storm tossed sea.

"Didn't you know who he was?" she screamed.

"Oh, was I supposed to?" I asked, feigning a look of hurt surprise.

"That gentleman was Lord Gort, G.O.C. Malta," she crowed indignantly. "And you had the nerve to make insulting remarks to him."

"What would you have liked me to do, the sailor's hornpipe?" I taunted.

"You don't have to be so vulgar," she snapped back at me.

Stamping her foot on the floor in rage, she rambled on; "You Merchant Seamen are nothing but trouble. I'll be glad to see the back of you."

Infuriated by her remarks, I rounded on her. "Many of my comrades perished, trying to save the likes of you from starving," I reminded her. "So maybe you should thank your lucky stars you're still alive. You are so indoctrinated with rules, regulations, and red tape, you go raving mad when your authority is challenged."

My final comment all but knocked the skids from under her, when I added fuel to the fire, by saying;. "Didn't anyone ever tell you, an army marches on it's stomach? These men are hungry and need food," I retorted, "not an extra dose of discipline."

Mouth agape she studied me for a moment, with a look of distaste. "You," she said at length, "have got to be the nastiest person I've met in a long time."

Seizing an opportunity to further annoy her, I remarked; "thank you for your kind words madam" and added, "I need them like a hole in the head."

With a toss of her broad shoulders, she turned and marched from the ward in silence. As the door slammed behind her, cheering erupted around the ward. Out on the verandah a cockney voice piped up; "Good on yer mate, it's about time someone took her down a peg."

But for an occasional air raid disrupting the peace and tranquility, our everyday lives returned to normal. Since our verbal exchanges Matron was most conspicuous by her absence, giving my ward a wide berth. Outnumbered by a large contingent of merchant seamen, she doubtless feared a backlash from the men who'd risked their lives, to relieve Malta's starving people. Whilst a small proportion of food from our decimated convoy had managed to get through, it did at least ease the threat of starvation.

As with the island's population, hospital patients also suffered through a lack of nutrition. The only means of supplementing a meagre diet was to eat local grown grapes and tomatoes. But in doing so one risked severe abdominal pain, followed by a dose of the trotters. Commonly known as Malta Gut.

The sound of a medicine trolley rumbling down the ward told me it was time to get my hands dressed, which had become a regular feature of my daily life. Confined to bed for so long it came as a pleasant surprise to hear the ward sister, say; "You can get up as soon as I've finished dressing your hands, Mr Ashford."

Carefully removing the oilskin gloves protecting my hands she covered them with a thin layer of vaseline gauze, and bandaged them up. Assisted by the young Maltese nurse, whose kindness and devotion to duty I shall be forever grateful, I was able to shuffle a few shaky steps around my bed. As time passed I progressed along the ward, without the need to grasp each bed for support. Soon the day arrived when I found myself as free as a young fledgling about to leave it's nest, and managed to pace up and down the ward unaided. Just to be able to feed myself in spite of having both hands heavily bandaged, was a blessing in disguise. I was however still dependant on the services of my wonderful Maltese nurse, who each day washed my face, removed fuel oil from my hair, and dressed my wounds.

Before leaving my ward to visit the hospital recreation room, they insisted I wear a suit of regulation blues. Many sizes too large, my trousers had to be rolled up at the bottom, and fastened around the waist with a piece of string. My jacket would, I felt sure, have disgraced a scarecrow.

"You may take a walk around the grounds if you wish, Mr Ashford," said the sister in charge. Suppressing a desire to burst out laughing.

"Why are we all dressed in this manner," I asked. "Must we all wear this ridiculous garb."

"Ah, that's in case you get lost" she joked.

"There's not much fear of that" I retorted, "where the hell would I hide in this outfit?"

In accordance with regulations all hospital patients were obliged to wear hospital blues, and because of this it was taken for granted by one of those regimental buffoons, that I was part and parcel of her majesty's forces. Wandering around the hospital I was addressed as "Oi you," by this fellow with stripes on his arm. Answering him in like manner I replied; "And what can I do for you, mate?"

Acting as though shell shocked, he suddenly found his voice. "First of all" he sneered, "I'm not your mate. I'm your Sergeant Major sonny. In future you'll address me as sir."

"Oh that's nice of you" I said, "but when were you knighted that I have to call you sir?"

Fixing me with a cold stare he pointed to the three stripes surmounted by a crown on his sleeve, and sneered; "What the hell do you think these are, Scotch mist?"

"Oh, they look very decorative Sir, Sergeant Major," I replied sarcastically. "But what am I supposed to do, kiss them?"

Before he'd time to recover from the shock of my caustic remark, I'd taken to my heels. Disappearing down a network of corridors inside the hospital, I soon lost trace of him. As a result of this episode, I gathered all Regimental Sergeant Majors and N.C.O's as per the rules and regulations were to be addressed as sir, by the rank and file. Failing to include the word "Sir" in answer to their questions, was tantamount to insult. Rank and number of individuals being all important, had to be memorised by heart. Lo betide anyone who failed to give their number when requested, before they had time to cough.

Taking my first steps outside the hospital since my arrival, I could not help but admire the rugged scenery. Behind a backdrop of barren hills, white vapour trails were seen criss-crossing the clear blue sky. It was wonderful once again to touch the soft green grass beneath my feet, with freedom to move around unaided. Knowing but for the grace of God, I would never have survived to savour this moment, I determined from now on to enjoy whatever life offered. Studying the island's wild terrain with it's many vineyards dotted around the hillside, resembled a giant patchwork quilt. Suddenly the morning stillness was shattered, by the familiar sound of aircraft. Accompanied by my two companions, whom I learned were attached to the Royal Engineers, we strolled toward the outer perimeter of the hospital grounds, marked by a small stone wall. From our position on the top of a hill, the ground sloped gently away into the valley below.

Among a cluster of well camouflaged huts and outbuildings lying adjacent to a small aerodrome, groups of men could be seen moving around. Even as we watched, fighter planes were taking off at short intervals from the airfield, evidently to repel intruders heading our way. Fascinated by the speed with which these fighters took to the air and climbed with such consummate ease, I became oblivious to the hullaballo going on behind me. It wasn't until I noticed my two companions had suddenly disappeared that I became aware of a Military Police Sargeant built like a Japanese sumo wrestler, bearing down on me. "Oi, are you bloody deaf?" he hollered, in a voice that had given thousands of raw recruits the screaming ab-dabs.

"Are you shouting at me?" I asked, giving him a look of mock surprise.

Tiny rivulets of perspiration oozed down his ruddy face, and his upper lip sporting an Errol Flynn moustache, twitched convulsively. Pointing to a notice displayed nearby he sneered; "The sign says out of bounds sonny, and that means you. Can't you read, or are you blind as well as bleeding deaf?"

"I am not, as you so crudely put it "bleeding deaf" I retorted indignantly, when his tirade of abuse subsided. "I don't know who you think you are, and furthermore, I resent being spoken to in such a manner."

Momentarily shocked that I should have the audacity to answer him back, he thrust a hand in his trouser's pocket and produced a whistle. A series of shrill blasts brought a couple of his cronies rushing to his aid. In a vice-like grip they frog-marched me toward a large building. Then pushed me inside a stuffy office containing a desk cluttered with papers, where I was ordered to wait.

Left to perspire in oven-like temperatures for what seemed an eternity, a thickset fellow wearing army uniform with two stripes on his sleeve, kicked the door in.

"You're wanted mate" he gloated, jerking his thumb toward an adjacent building.

"I'm not your mate and don't wish to be. Now where am I supposed to go" I asked.

Ordering me to follow him, I entered a large office. A cloud of tobacco smoke clung to the ceiling where an obsolete fan hung dejectedly, at a lopsided angle. As with the rest of the office furniture it had seen better days. Sitting at an ornately carved desk, an young officer busily manicured his nails. Immaculately turned out, he looked your typical old boy upper crust type, neatly attired in a uniform that fitted him like a glove. Seeming to have all the time in the world he persisted in flicking an imaginary speck of dust from his sleeve, before speaking to me.

Flipping through some paperwork the Seargent Major handed to him, he leaned back in his chair and eyed me suspiciously, tapping the tips of his fingers together. Inspecting

226

my ill-fitting suit of regulation hospital blues, an expression of utter distaste spread across his face. I got the impression he thought I was something the dog had dragged in.

"Well, my man, you seem to have blotted your copy book" he said. "What have you got to say for yourself?" he asked.

His question caught me by surprise. Shrugging my shoulders, I asked; "And what would you like me to say, mister?"

My reply must have ruffled his feathers somewhat, for he snapped; "Now look here my man, this is a serious charge laid against you, by Sergeant Wilkins, here."

From his desk he picked up a copy of army rules and regulations and began to read them out and proceeded to reel off a list of offences, I was alleged to have commited. Refusing to obey an order and insulting behavior to an N.C.O., were among many others. Breaking off from a catalogue of presupposed charges he stopped to ask; "And what is your number?"

Without a second thought I gave him the first number that came to mind, that of my home telephone 3424952, which I rattled off. During an enforced silence in the proceedings a scratching noise made by his pen as he wrote down the number I had given him, sounded like half a dozen rats trying to absconed. With a smile on his face that would have done credit to a Cheshire cat, the sergeant who had laid these spurious charges against me, stood to attention beside the desk.

Glancing up at me with arched eyebrows, the young officer caught me unawares with his next question; "What regiment are you attached to?" he asked.

Feigning total surprise, I stammered; "Oh! I'm not in any regiment. I belong in the Merchant Service," and waited for the repercussions.

The big sergeant instinctively stiffened. His jaw dropped open as though he'd been hit by lightning, knocking the sloppy grin from his face.

The officer turned on him."Why did you bring this man before me without asking for his particulars," he declared.

Caught with his pants down, so to speak, the Sargeant stuttered; "Well sir, he's wearing blue's so I took it for granted he was in the forces."

The officer's sarcastic response took the wind out of his sails; "If a donkey is put into uniform it doesn't necessarily mean it's in the army, does it Sergeant?"

"Er, no Sir" he stuttered," standing to attention.

In a quick about turn the young officer adopted a more courteous manner toward me. Going so far as to apologise for the abject stupidity of his subordinates. At least I reminded myself, I was more fortunate than the young soldier I had befriended earlier. Castigated for a derogatory remark against the Matron, calling her a silly old fart, (which in essence she no doubt was,) earned him seven days in the glasshouse.

Having made my peace with the officer who in a typical gentlemanly fashion apologized for his subordinates utter stupidity, I took my leave. Lunch having been long overdue I hurried back to my hospital ward in search of a morsel of food, and almost collided with my old adversary, Sergeant Wilkins. Whom I'd just crossed swords with. Glowering at me he hissed; "I'd love to get you in the army."

My immediate reply shook him; "Sod you and your Army, mister," I shouted angrily. "You can keep your bull shit." Before he had time to reply I'd beat a hasty retreat, and was long out of sight. Thankfully, never to set eyes on his likes again. Whether he'd been waylaid by some young soldier he taken a delight in bullying, I'll never know, or care. Maybe he'd been secretly shipped off the island for his own good.

Adopting a rebellious attitude against army rules and regulations, eventually led to my premature departure from hospital. Transferred to a convalescent home run by a couple of bible punchers, stuck in the middle of nowhere, I endured a further month of boredom. Isolated on a barren hilltop, I was put out to grass.

Fed up with this nomadic life style, my persistant request for a move nearer civilisation caused many unexpected problems for me. Unaware I'd be jumping out of the frying pan into the fire, I reluctantly agreed to move to the harbour area when promised an early flight home. Taking temporary residence at the Bristol Hotel, situated on the waterfront in Valetta harbour, was without doubt a tactless blunder on my part. In my desperate haste to get away from this hungry, bull shit dominated island, I fell for the three card trick. Exposed to daily air raids the hotel itself was already crawling with all manner of civilian no-hopers, drafted in by the authorities. Classed as undesirables, they awaited their turn to be repatriated. Nightfall brought a stark reminder of the fatal mistake I'd made. From the comparative comfort of a convalescent home, I now found myself confined within the four walls of a sleazy hotel in the bomb riddled harbour area of Valletta. Back among the dust, rubble, and grime of this beleagured city.

The moment I arrived, an air raid warning sent people scurrying for shelter. Inside the hotel itself, a staircase hewn out of solid rock spiralled down into the bowels of the earth. Corridors stretching for a considerable distance underground, punctuated at intervals by rooms of enormous size, housed countless Maltese families. Here in a cold damp atmosphere beneath the rock, I stood shivering. Cursing my luck, and those who'd lured me into this dump.

"Some bloody army whallah's feeling trigger happy" said the old chap standing beside me in the air raid shelter. "Most probably a false alarm" he grumbled, as we waited for the all clear to sound.

Dressed in cast off clothing donated by a relief organization for distressed seamen, the canvas shoes from which his toes sought to escape, were well past their sell by date. On the other hand, I considered myself rather more fortunate than my companion. Because of enemy action, I lost every stitch of clothing I owned, when my ship was destroyed. Arriving in Malta, naked as the day I was born. My sudden departure from hospital in khaki battledress was reason enough for me to pay a visit to Gieves the Naval tailors, where they fitted me out in civilian clothes. Suitably attired in grey flannel trousers and green checked hacking jacket with brown leather buttons, I considered myself quite presentable.

Confined to a damp and bone chilling air raid shelter beneath the Bristol Hotel in Valetta harbour, the distant wail of the all clear signal could be faintly heard. At one o'clock in the morning a collection of cramped and frozen bodies crawled out from dimly lit passages beneath the rock, up a winding staircase to their respective hotel rooms.

"Maybe we'll get some sleep now" I said to my companion.

"Huh, you'll be lucky" he grimaced rubbing his hands together, in an effort to restore the circulation.

Bidding him a brief goodnight I closed the door of my room, and ate what few grapes I'd managed to salvage from the evening meal. Thoroughly exhausted after a day of travelling, I slipped out of my clothing and into bed. Finding a comfortable position between the lumps and bumps of a worn-out mattress, was not easy. My problem was trying to avoid bedsprings protruding through the mattress cover, from puncturing my body. Sleep came in snatches, throughout the remainder of the night. Ever alert I listened for the moaning sound of an air-raid siren that never materialized, having to scratch myself at regular intervals throughout the night.

Too weary to get out of my bed and discover the reason for my discomfort I waited until the pale light of dawn filtered through the tattered remnants of lace curtains draped across my window, and decided I'd had enough. Easing myself out from among the half dozen or so springs poking through the matress in my bed I threw back the sheets, and soon discovered the cause of my problem. A squadron of fleas had been feasting on blood I could ill afford and were now hopping around in all directions, looking for some means of escape.

At breakfast that morning I complained to the hotel manager, a balding Maltese character with a pock-marked face and sad brown eyes, who listened impassively.

"Ah, so you get the bite, mister," grinned the bald one. "You eat plenty garlic my friend, they not touch you" he said.

When he spoke I caught a whiff of his garlic breath, and decided it was not for me.

Slipping aboard the M.V. Melbourne Star berthed in Valetta harbour, a word in the ear of a friendly Chief Steward, and I was in possesion of a small quantity of D.D.T. a new insecticide. Before retiring to bed a liberal dusting on my sheets was sufficient to ensure I had a good night's sleep. Waking next morning I found a multitude of fleas had succumbed to the deadly powder, and now lay motionless. With a regular supply of D.D.T close at hand I was prepared to tolerate living in this flea pit for the time being, but thankfully I did not have to remain there much longer.

Relief came late one evening in mid December of 1942 when I was told to get ready to leave the island of Malta and be flown to Gibraltar. My enforced stay of five long months on the island was coming to an end. Arriving at Luqua, one of Malta's heavily defended airfields in the early hours of the morning, I boarded an American D C Douglas aircraft. Climbing above banks of heavy cloud we were able to avoid contact with a formation of enemy fighters, known to be in the vicinity. At first light Gibraltar's lofty peak at the western end of the Mediterranean, could be seen rising above the morning mist. Distant silhouettes of naval vessels patrolling outside it's harbour, were the only indication a war was raging in the area. Strategically placed, the Rock, to which it was often referred, remained a thorn in the side of the Nazi's. Along with the island of Malta, it remained a stumbling block to Germany's complete domination of the Mediterranean. But whilst the inhabitants of Gibraltar are steadfastly behind Britain, many people on the island of Malta were known to lean heavily in favour of their near neighbours, on the Italian mainland.

Within minutes of touchdown we tumbled onto the tarmac, delighted to feel the morning sun on our frozen limbs. With normal formalities one is accustomed to at all airports being

Charles G. Ashford

waived aside, we were dispatched to the Winter Garden Hotel, situated high up on the Rock. It was here I enjoyed the luxury of soaking in a hot bath, my first for many months. After lunch at the hotel I set off to explore the main shopping area, where an abundance of cheap duty free goods were to be had. Outside on the sidewalk, cafe tables and chairs were set out in continental fashion, a favourite meeting place for local gossip. Around three o'clock each afternoon the traditional cup of tea was taken, by off-duty members of the armed forces stationed here. Seated at one of it's several tables I joined a group of young service men, waiting to be served. Hovering in the background a waiter approached my table, and asked; "Can I take your order sir?"

"I'd like tea and some cakes please," I replied.

Within minutes my table was laden with a large pot of tea and a plate of the most delicious cream cakes I had set eyes on, for many a long day. Spellbound, I could only sit and admire their decorative colour, and fresh cream filling. When about to stuff myself with a tasty morsel I remembered seeing the young children in Malta, begging for food. Filled with a sense of guilt I stayed my hand, secretly wishing the cakes would suddenly disappear. Then a peal of laughter rang out, from a nearby table.

"Don't look at em" laughed the young soldier seeing me hesitate, "eat em, or you'll ave the bleeding rock apes pinching em. Go on, get em down yer," he went on, stuffing a chocolate eclair into his mouth.

With the eyes of several of his pals watching, I bit into a cream slice. Resisting the temptation to dispose of another I rose from the table, and sauntered back toward the Winter Garden Hotel.

At seven o'clock that evening the melodic strains of a dinner gong saw my fellow travellers, make a dash for the diningroom. Laid out on white linen tablecloths, cutlery and glassware sparkled beneath two brightly illuminated chandeliers. Like a plague of locusts, some thirty odd starving seamen who'd just arrived from the island of Malta, descended on the place. Intent on devouring every scrap of food, in sight. While a main course of roast beef, fresh vegetables and saute potatoes was being served, the clatter of knives and forks suddenly ceased. Stilled by the wailing of an air raid siren.

The huge dining room doors were thrown open by a couple of army red caps ordering residents go to their respective air raid shelters, some distance from the hotel. Much to the dismay of a large group of hungry seamen who'd just arrived from Malta, this raid on Gibraltar, their first for six months, proved to be a false alarm. It did however manage to delay for some two hours, the first decent meal we were about to enjoy for months. Night had closed in by the time the all clear sounded and with the Rock in total darkness, we stumbled along a well worn footpath back to the hotel.

Prior to my departure in late December of 1942 an influx of Merchant Seamen rescued from ships torpedoed in the Atlantic, were put ashore in Gibraltar. Many who'd been adrift in open boats for days on end, suffered untold privation. Casualties among the survivors were extremely heavy, many having had nothing to eat for days. Few among us who'd seen and experienced the horrors of war, had any immediate desire to be repatriated back to England. Only to face the same hazards again. However our taste for the good life was short lived. Nothing is forever, as the saying goes.

For many of us idling away the hours in peace and tranquility at this British naval base in Gibraltar, the end came all too soon. Seen as no more than a blot on the far horizon as the early morning mist cleared, it posed no immediate threat. But as the dark grey shape drew closer, we discovered it was a large troop-ship. Edging ever nearer like an angry black cloud preceding a storm, she entered the harbour. Her name undecipherable beneath the grey paint was later identified as the Llanstephan Castle, one of many passenger ships now carrying troops.

Her arrival in Gibraltar set the scene for a period of feverish activity when some two to three hundred merchant seamen staying at hotels around the peninsular, were drafted aboard the vessel. Survivors who were rescued out in the north Atlantic's bitterly cold weather had little opportunity to sample the good life some of us had already enjoyed, their time at Gibraltar suddenly cut short. Some twenty four hours later we sailed from the harbour under cover of darkness, following astern of a naval escort, and passing Gibraltar's submarine defence, set course for home.

Leaving the Mediterranean's blue skies and warm sunshine far behind us we faced the Bay of Biscay's stormy waters, whipped up by bone chilling easterly winds. Back in winter's grip the Llanstephan Castle all twenty thousand tons of her, ducked and dived her way across mountainous seas. On approaching home waters extra lookouts chosen from among many survivors who'd volunteered, were placed at vantage points throughout the ship. Vigilance against surprise attacks from U-Boats hunting in packs around our shores, had to be maintained at all times. Steaming toward Land's End at a speed of 16 knots, fingers of light stabbed the darkened skies at regular intervals. Seen from a distance of eighteen miles Eddystone Lighthouse flashed out a message of welcome, beckoning us home. Changing course when abeam of Land's End saw us leave the shelter of England's southern shores along the English Channel, to face strong westerly winds, as we entered the choppy waters of the Irish Sea.

Shadowed by our naval escort we zig-zagged our way through banks of fragmented sea mist toward Firth of Clyde, arriving at the Scottish coast as night was falling. Slowing down until the first light of dawn, we dropped anchor off the Port of Gourock. The sound of the vessel's anchor cable rattling down the hawspipe, at that early hour, echoing over silent waters.

Rising at daybreak on the morning of December the 20th 1942 I stepped out onto the deck of the Llanstephan Castle anchored on the Firth of Clyde, and surveyed the large expanse of empty water around me. Instinctively I recalled a time in the not too distant past when these same waters were host to a small collection of merchant ships and men'o'war, who set out to do battle with the enemy. Many among these heroic crews who never returned were on a mission of mercy, to save the starving population of Malta.

Vividly I now recall my nightmare voyage that had it's beginnings from this very place, on a journey fraught with danger. Taking me, so it seemed, through the gates of hell and close to death, but for the grace of God I would not have survived. Looking back there is nothing I prefer to remember except for the wonderful care provided by a young Maltese nurse who attended my wounds. Also the pleasure I had of meeting George,(Screwball) Buerling, Canada's greatest fighter pilot of world war two. We were introduced during a concert given by the R.A.F. in aid of the children of Malta.

It is said he flew a couple of feet above Malta's main street upside down when escorting the beleagured oil tanker, Ohio, into Valletta harbour.

For the many of my comrades who perished their loved ones have nothing, but sad memories. Of those who survived some will no doubt be reproached for being drunk when home on leave, trying to erase the memory of that horrendous voyage. The man in the street would do well to try and imagine what it's like to be adrift in an open boat in the middle of nowhere, and not judge him too harshly;

When you see him in the street
Rolling round on groggy feet,
Don't scorn him
For being on the spree,
But did you ever make a trip
On a dark and lonely ship,
Through a submarine,
Or shark infested sea.

Put Out to Grass.

On a damp grey morning in December of 1942, I arrived at the Port of Gourock aboard the troopship M.V Llanstephan Castle, from Gibraltar. Taking passage with me were three hundred and fifty British merchant seamen, whose ships had been destroyed by enemy action. Before the first light of dawn, we dropped anchor opposite the tiny holiday resort of Dunoon.

It was from here a convoy of fifteen merchant ships carrying food, medical supplies and war material, set out on a voyage to relieve the beleagured island of Malta, some five months earlier. Now all was still as we entered this quiet backwater of the Clyde, nothing moved except the ghostly grey shape of an escort vessel returning to base. Braving mist and rain a group of survivors aboard the troopship, Llanstephan Castle, stood out on her open deck until daylight, waiting for a glimpse of their native land.

A fragmented mist along the coastline slowly thickened as drizzling rain continued to fall incessantly, hiding what little there was to be seen of a bleak Scottish landscape. Returning to my cabin on "B" deck, some of my comrades slept peacefully on, unaware the ship lay at anchor back in the U.K. Possessing little but the clothes I stood up in and a couple of gifts I'd brought back home for my fiancee while in Gibraltar, there was nothing I could do but wait until the call for breakfast.

It was loud enough to waken the dead. Cabin doors flew open and heads popped out in alarm as the trumpeter marched along the corridor on "B" deck, playing the wake up call, reveille.

"D'yer have to make such a bloody racket, we're not deaf," shouted a irate seaman from his cabin doorway.

"I was told to make sure you were all awake," the steward replied. "Everyone has to be off the ship by ten o'clock."

236

"We heard you mate" scoffed Sullivan, a cocky young fellow from Liverpool. "Why don't you jerks go and wake the skipper up," he demanded.

"Take your complaints to the chief steward, he gives the orders around here" said the trumpeter, and hurried off to waken others.

A word in the ear of the Chief Steward at the breakfast table, only made matters worse; "It's a wet nurse you fellows want," he retorted. "Where the hell do you think you are, on your Daddy's yacht."

At ten thirty that morning some two hundred survivors aboard the troopship were ferried ashore, and taken to the seamens' mission. Issued with railway warrants that would take them nearest their home town, everyone received a lunch box to see them through the journey. Boarding waiting buses and taken to Gourock railway station, a bleak and desolate place at this time of year, I stood in the drizzling rain with a party bound for Liverpool.

Seeking shelter in the station's waiting room I found the place reeked with the stench of urinal, broken seats lay on a floor littered in fag ends and crumpled newspapers. Grime and dust clung to windows covered in graffiti, allowing a minimum of light to penetrate a damp and smelly interior. Walking up and down the station platform to keep myself warm I asked the man in the ticket office; "What time is this train due."

"Fifteen minutes laddie" he replied, and carried on reading his morning paper.

Beneath sullen grey skies and drizzling rain that soaked me to the skin I watched the approaching train belching plumes of black smoke from it's squat chimney, steam gushing from beneath the huge steel belly, as it ground to a halt.

In a bid to rid myself of the wet clothing clinging to my body I hurried into the nearest carriage, on the heels of my fellow travellers. Shedding our wet outer garments and hanging them on luggage racks to dry, little notice was taken of two old ladies sitting in a corner of the compartment.

"Did ye ever see the like o' that afore," say's one.

"Och, tak nae notice" said her companion, "what will ye hae them do, sit in their wet clothes. Close your eyes lass, and ye'll see nothing."

Cold and hungry I could not wait to get at the food inside my luncheon box, and a much needed cup of tea would have to wait until we reached the station buffet. Not a word was exchanged between us as one after another we opened our luncheon boxes, tucking into cheese and ham sandwiches.

Slowing to a crawl approaching Glasgow's Central Station the sound of childrens' voices out on the railway track, was cause for alarm. Half-eaten sandwiches were put aside, as everyone scrambled to take a look out the carriage window. Several poorly-clad children with arms outstretched, begged for food as they ran after train, shouting; "Gie us a crust mister."

It was like a scene from Oliver Twist in the Dickensian era, and hard to believe such a thing could happen in this day and age. In a spontaneous gesture, everyone in the carriage gave the children whatever food they had. Sandwiches by the dozen passed out of the windows were greeted with loud cries of thanks, from the hungry bairns. Shocked by the lack of clothing on one or two of them, one elderly fellow gave up dresses he'd brought home for his own grandchildren. With cries of delight, several older children followed the train until we pulled into the station at Glasgow, then disappeared as suddenly as they had arrived.

Alighting from the train I bid goodbye to my fellow travellers who'd accompanied me from Gibraltar, and left them to continue my journey south. At the ticket office I was told the train standing at platform four was due to leave for Liverpool in fifteen minutes, and advised to hurry aboard. From Glasgow's Central Station the train rattled on past bleak highland hills and deep green valleys in the Scottish countryside, arriving at Liverpool's Lime Street station toward evening. A waiting taxi drove me through a maze of traffic in the town centre to the Pier Head, where I boarded a ferry and crossed the river Mersey to

Birkenhead. Berthing at Woodside terminus I took a bus to my lodgings in the village of Bebington on the outskirts of town, where I arrived unannounced on the doorstep of my new landlady, a kindly soul who welcomed me back home.

A comely woman, Mrs Godfrey a widow in her late fifties, managed to eke out a living running a boarding house, in the tiny Cheshire village of Bebington. She had a pretty face with dark brown eyes, matched by the warmth of her welcoming smile. Taking my coat and gloves off in the hall I went into the kitchen, where she waited with a cup of tea. Seeing the bandages on my hands, she exclaimed; "My goodness what happened to you, Charles."

Rather than go into detail I told her my ship was destroyed by German dive bombers on a voyage to Malta, and my injuries had kept me in hospital for many months.

"Are they going to be alright" she asked, a worried look on her face.

"That is for the Ministry of Pensions to decide, Mrs Godfrey" I replied, showing her the letter I had received from them. "They have asked me to report to their office in Liverpool as soon as possible, which doesn't sound very encouraging."

"Will they send you to hospital?" she asked.

"Not if I can help it" I replied, "I've spent these last five months in a flea bitten hospital ward in Malta."

"Thank goodness you've arrived back in one piece" she declared, "there's been so many young people who have sacrificed their lives for that awful Hitler."

"There'll be many more before this lot's over" I sighed. "It's going to be a long hard struggle."

Leaving her to prepare the evening meal I settled down and listened to the evening news on the radio, something I'd been unable to do these past months. We heard that Allied Forces had invaded North Africa, and the Eighth Army under General Montgomery was sweeping from El Alamein across North Africa. This chain of events was followed by an announcement on the B.B.C, that the tide of war had turned against Germany's armies in Africa and on the Russian front. As I finished my cup of tea, the aroma of our evening meal drifted in from the kitchen, reminding me I was hungry. At the table I suggested going over to Liverpool next day to visit the Ministry of Pensions, to which Mrs Godfrey readily agreed, saying: "Well, I suppose it's best to get it over with, Christmas will be upon us shortly and they'll probably be closed for a couple of weeks."

Looking out of my bedroom window next morning I was not surprised to see shrubs and rose bushes in the garden appear like so many statues, shrouded in mantles of white. A layer of heavy frost covered the ground, the forerunner of a hard winter to come. I shivered at the thought of it and recalled those warm sunny days and Mediterranean skies of blue, wishing I were there.

It was Mrs Godfrey calling me for breakfast, that broke my train of thought.

"We've got quite a covering of frost this morning, Charles," she exclaimed, as I sat at the table. "You'll have to wrap up well when you do go out" she advised, and added, "Will you be visiting your fiancee?"

"But why do you ask Mrs Godfrey," I said, "Is there something wrong?"

"Why no, Charles. It's just that she came round asking if I'd heard from you, a few weeks after you left. But I haven't set eyes on her since," she said. "But I'm sure she'll be pleased to see you back safe and sound."

"Maybe I ought to wait on the outcome of my interview with the Ministry of Pensions," I told her. "I'd better leave that visit until tomorrow."

Glancing at the clock on the kitchen wall I reminded the good lady it was time I was leaving for my appointment, promising I'd be home for lunch. Muffled up in a heavy overcoat against the biting wind of a cold winter's morning, with careful step I made my way to the bus stop. Hurrying aboard when the vehicle skidded to a halt on the frosty road, I welcomed the warmth and comfort afforded my frozen limbs on the journey.

Alighting from the bus at Woodside, I stepped aboard the local ferry that took me across the Mersey. Buffeted by stiff north easterly winds, deterred none but the bravest among the passengers, who risked venturing out onto the open deck. Huddled against a heater in the vessel's lounge to keep warm, I stayed there until embarking at the Liverpool landing stage. The first thing that caught my eye as I stepped off the boat was the Liver Buildings with the fabled Liver Birds perched on top of it's green encrusted dome, overlooking the waterfront. Close by, the Mersey Docks and Harbour offices, a magnificent piece of Gothic architecture, had many beautiful features to be seen inside. As with many cities throughout the land Liverpool, one of the country's largest seaports, has it's share of noteworthy buildings. Many of which were damaged during the blitz in 1941.

Wandering past large department stores in the city centre, I meandered through a maze of narrow streets at the back of town in my search for Orleans House, offices of the Ministry of Pensions. In a nondescript part of the city I finally found the place I was looking for, tucked away behind a row of bomb damaged dwelling houses. Smoke and sulphur fumes from the chimneys of nearby factories had with time discoloured the white stone frontage, giving it a greyish appearance.

Entering the building, I handed the letter I'd received from the Ministry to the young lady in the foyer, who showed me into the conference room. Around an oval-shaped table sat three gentlemen, who appeared to have been in the middle of a lengthy discussion when I knocked on the door, and were now silent. The eldest, a silver haired gentleman who wore a smart grey suit and gold rimmed spectacles, politely asked;

"Can we help you?" young man.

"I've been asked to report here" I stammered, handing him my letter of introduction.

A puzzled look creased his forehead as he withdrew the letter from it's envelope, studying it very carefully. It was almost as if he'd suddenly remembered writing to me. The look on his face changed to a smile, as he said;

"Why of course, Mr Ashford, we've been expecting a visit from you, but had no idea when you'd arrive back in this country." Pointing to a chair opposite him, he requested I be seated.

Introducing himself and his two colleagues as medical practitioners, he said they were acting on behalf of the Ministry of Pensions, to assess the extent of my war injuries. From his briefcase he withdrew a sheaf of papers and studied me for a moment, before saying; "May I see your hands, Mr Ashford?"

Carefully removing my gloves I placed them on the table in front of him, palms down. I heard his sharp intake of breath as he began to examine them, and watched as he shook his head. Running his fingers across the back of my hands, which were still in the process of healing, caused me to wince with pain.

Apologizing, he said; "I'm afraid they are going to take a considerable time to heal Mr Ashford, the skin is quite tender. This is not a graft taken from your body, but a new method they are using known as tulle-gra."

He then went on to say; "We are not satisfied with the progress of your injuries, as your present condition suggests."

Then the elder of the two, whose name I learned was a Dr McArdle, referred to the convoy in which I'd sailed in August of 1942, code named Pedestal, and remarked; "I must say, from what little information we were given concerning the fate of your convoy and it's mercy mission to Malta, you are a lucky young man to come out of it alive. According to this report you suffered third degree burns to both hands, restricting movement of your fingers. You will no doubt have great difficulty in using them effectively, for some considerable time to come. I would however recommend a spell of physiotherapy, when your wounds have healed sufficiently."

It was at this point Dr. McArdle made the decision of his panel known, saying; "We are all agreed the damage to your hands may be irreversible." Pausing a moment to check the papers on his desk, he continued on a sombre note;"Because of the severity of your injuries, we are of the opinion, you will not be fit to work in the foreseeable future. We have therefore decided to award you a full disability pension."

Hearing this news I was stunned and sat staring into space, unable to believe what the doctor was saying. I myself knew there was no way I'd be fit to work for the next few months or so, but to be thrown on the scrap heap as unfit at the age of twenty-three, was something I was unable to accept.

Without saying a word I left the conference room and hurried out of the building, my sea career in the balance. The way ahead looked uncertain but deep within me there remained an irresistible desire to fulfil my boyhood dream, of a career at sea. I determined there would be no lack of enthusiasm on my part in taking up the challenge, should the opportunity arise. Meantime I would make an appointment to visit my family doctor, seeking his help in speeding my recovery.

Wandering through streets littered with rubble from the nightly air raids on the city, I found myself back at the waterfront. Pacing up and down the landing stage at Liverpool's Pier Head, I waited to board a ferry that would take me across the river Mersey to my home in Bebington. Along a seven mile stretch of the river I stood watching ocean-going ships loaded with war supplies, moving in and out of the docks. Some lying at anchor, waited their turn to berth. Vessels leaving the dock, having discharged their cargoes, were returning overseas empty. With little in their holds other than a few tons of ballast to steady them on the voyage to America, they faced the fury of the North Atlantic's bitter weather, and gale force winds. But in spite of all the hazards one faced while at sea during times such as these, I would have preferred to be on board the ship with them, instead of being a spectator on the shore.

Stemming a fast flowing tide and buffetted by near gale force winds, the ferryboat struggled to make headway across the river from Birkenhead to her berth at Liverpool's pierhead, where I waited to board her. Hitting the jetty with a sickening thud mooring ropes hurriedly thrown ashore by members of the crew held her fast, to prevent any serious damage. Along with several passengers waiting to embark I hurried aboard, seeking shelter from the winter weather, and cold easterly wind. From a window in the ship's lounge I watched her acrobatic manoeuvres as she fought against wind and tide, back across the river to her berth at Woodside Terminal, Birkenhead. Wasting little time I hurried ashore as soon as she was made fast and took a taxi to my lodgings at Bebington.

As I entered her lounge Mrs Godfrey looked up from the book she was reading, and smiled. "Ah, you're back, Charles," she said; "Can I offer you a cup of tea?"

"That would be most welcome" I replied, taking off my heavy overcoat. "It's jolly cold out there."

"Will you excuse me a moment," said Mrs Godfrey. Rising from her chair she disappeared into the kitchen, returning moments later to join me with a cup of tea.

"Well now Charles" she said, "tell me, how was your day?"

"Not good at all" I replied, shaking my head.

"What do you mean, Charles" she remarked, a look of concern on her face. "Did they say you'd have to go back into hospital for some sort of treatment?"

"It's of a more serious nature than that, Mrs Godfrey," I assured her. "They've told me I won't be able to work in the foreseeable future. It seems as though I've been thrown on the scrap heap, if you please."

"But I thought they were short of men," she insisted.

"Yes, Mrs Godfrey, able-bodied men are badly needed at sea right now, I must agree with you. But try explaining that to the Medical Officer at the Ministry of Pensions. Until they are satisfied my hands have sufficiently healed, there is nothing I can do."

"Oh I'm sure something can be done for you," she exclaimed, "Isn't there some treatment they could give you that would help you recover?"

Maybe my family doctor could advise me," I suggested, "I'll have to see him as soon as possible."

"What about your fiancee, Charles," said Mrs Godfrey, "don't you think you should see her and tell her what's happened, I"m sure she'll understand."

"Yes I suppose I really should pay her a visit, I'll go this evening" I countered, in an effort to change the subject. "She must be wondering where I am, don't you think?"

"Shipping companies are not allowed to disclose movements of their vessels, as they did in time of peace," I told her. "The war has changed all that. Why even our letters to each other are censored, in case information useful to the enemy, is disclosed. In any event, the mail is so slow in reaching us abroad."

"But didn't you tell her your hands were injured while you were in hospital at Malta," Mrs Godfrey asked. "Surely someone would have written a note for you, in your condition."

"I'm afraid she hasn't received a letter from me since the day I left," I told the good lady. "She's not likely to be overjoyed about that, I'm sure. But let's wait and see what happens when I visit her tonight."

"I hope she will understand the awkward situation you are in, Charles," said Mrs Godfrey with a sigh.

At six o'clock that evening I switched on the wireless to listen to the latest information, on the war in Europe. The B.B.C. announcer was in buoyant mood as he read the news. I could almost feel the excitement mounting in his normally subdued voice, when he announced: Allied troops have continued their advance through North Africa, and Admiral Darlan Commander-In-Chief of Vichy French Naval forces, has been assassinated."

At last the tide of war had turned in favour of the Allies on both Russian and North African fronts, easing tension in the Mediterranean. Ships carrying much needed food and medical supplies were now reaching the people of Malta. At long last, the enemy's stranglehold on the island, by which they hoped to force the people of Malta into submission, was broken.

As soon as the evening news had finished I switched off the radio, and hearing Mrs Godfrey announce tea was ready, entered the dining-room. On the table set out for two was a plate of freshly cooked ham, instead of the usual spam or meat loaf. "How on earth do you manage to get food like this?" I asked her, pointing to the ham.

Grinning good-humouredly, she remarked; "What is it they say, about careless talk costing lives, Charles?"

Not wishing to pursue the matter, knowing like everyone else in the country she was subject to rationing, I could not understand how she managed to rustle up the most appetizing meals. Was the butcher a close relative of her's, I wondered.

As the meal ended Mrs Godfrey asked; "Did you enjoy the ham, Charles?"

"Most enjoyable, I replied. Reminded me of food they serve up in New York's resturants" I remarked.

"Ah yes, I'm going to miss the little luxuries you used to bring home Charles, they were a great help. I really appreciated them," she said.

I agreed with her, saying; "But who knows what the future holds."

Bidding her goodnight, for I knew she would have long been abed before my return, I left the house. Outside the night was bitterly cold, not a glimmer of light was to be seen in the darkened streets. My fiancee's house lay some half a mile distant on the outskirts of the village, where no-one but the local warden would be up and about at this hour in the black-out.

An only child, Marjorie Hulbert lived with her widowed mother in a small detached bungalow, lying back off the main road in a secluded cul-de-sac. A pale moon had risen above the thickly wooded copse near by, illuminating the road on which she lived. Her house lay in total darkness, showing no sign of life. My knock on the door, brought an immediate response from within.

Holding the door ajar no more than a couple of inches, a voice I recognized to be that of her mother's, asked;

"Who are you, and what do you want?"

"It's Charles Ashford, Mrs Hulbert," I responded. "I've just arrived home from sea."

I heard her sharp intake of breath, and a half-strangled cry of, "Oh!" just a moment, Charles."

Safety chains attached to the front door were let go, and from inside the darkened doorway, she asked me in.

Closing the door behind her she drew a blackout curtain across and switching on the light, illuminated the darkened hallway. I must have startled her for she looked pale and drawn, as though she'd seen a ghost. Inviting me into an adjoining room, Mrs. Hulbert called up to the bedroom;

"Are you there Marjorie?"

There was a momentory pause, then in a faltering voice she said; "Charles is here to see you dear."

From up the stairs I heard my fiancee's gasp of surprise, and the sound of her footsteps coming down the stairs. In the hallway a whispered conversation with her mother ceased abruptly, and the lounge door swung open. Ashen faced, she stared at me for a moment and shaking like a leaf, she whispered: "Where on earth have you come from, Charles. The War Office informed me you were missing in action, presumed dead?"

"Good Lord, who gave you that information?" I asked.

From a drawer in her desk she withdrew a large brown envelope. This arrived some months ago" she said, handing it to me.

Printed in bold black type, the letters O.H.M.S stared up at me. An official document from the War Office inside simply stated; "We regret to inform you your fiance, Mr Charles Ashford, has been reported missing in action, presumed dead."

There were no details explaining what had happened, just a curt apology.

She sat there refusing to look in my direction, as though I were to blame for all that had happened. Her pretty face flushed with anger, she turned to face me;

"I'm sick of this damned war Charles," she said bitterly.

The remainder of her sentence was cut short when her mother appeared from the kitchen, carrying a tea tray.

"Take off your coat while you have tea with us, Charles," Mrs Hulbert suggested. "It's a cold night, and you'll feel the benefit of it when you leave."

The sight of my bandaged hands, brought gasps of alarm from the pair of them.

"Whatever's happened to your hands?" Marjorie cried.

"I'm very lucky to be here I replied. Most of my comrades perished, during the voyage to Malta."

A trifle puzzled by my remark, she quickly replied;

"I don't understand what you mean, Charles."

Briefly, I explained that my ship had been sunk, during a voyage to Malta. The injuries I sustained were of little consequence, compared to the loss of life suffered by the ship's company.

"You will be returning to sea, I suppose," she ventured to ask.

"I'm in receipt of a disability pension as from now," I replied. "My future is in the lap of the Gods."

A worried look creased her brow. "Does that mean you won't be able to work again, Charles?" she asked, a note of dread in her voice.

Uncertain if she were prepared to accept the situation, I replied; "Not in the foreseeable future, I'm afraid."

For an instant we faced each other in silence, and in the blink of an eye her facial expression changed. Pale and drawn, her voice sounded hollow as she spoke.

"I'm sorry Charles, there is no way I'll marry an invalid," she murmured. "Our engagement is off."

"But Marjorie I'm not a cripple" I protested, "it's only a matter of time before I'll be fit to work again."

"I'm not prepared to take that chance," she confessed. "We're barely surviving on the meagre wage I earn, and a pitiful allowance mother receives from her widow's pension."

Nothing I said would alter her decision. Her mind was made up. Rising from the chair, I took my overcoat from her mother waiting in the hallway.

"I'm sorry Charles there is nothing I can do to change her mind," she said with a sigh.

"Oh, that's alright Mrs Hulbert" I replied. "It's not your fault, I realize that."

At the front door I took my leave of her, and wishing her well made my way home. A waning moon shed a watery light on the ice covered pavement, where none but the bravest would dare to venture on a night such as this. With careful step I inched my way home and as expected Mrs Godfrey's house was in darkness, showing not a glimmer of light. Inserting my key, the door slid open at a touch and a flow of warm air brushed my face as I stepped inside. Closing the door behind me I felt my way along the darkened hallway to the foot of the stairs, where I slipped my shoes off and crept silently up to bed.

From Mrs Godfrey's room I heard the sound of her heavy breathing, a buzzing noise like that of a bee extracting honey from the flowers. There lies a happy soul at rest I said to myself, would I be that fortunate. Closing the door of my bedroom so as not to disturb the good lady from her melodious slumbers, I quickly undressed and slipped between the sheets. Unable to sleep I lay there tossing and turning for quite some time, wondering if there was a form of treatment available to heal my injured hands. Should I seek my doctor's advice or look for information at the local library, I kept asking myself?

Around eight thirty in the morning the ringing of the telephone wakened me. Rubbing the sleep from my eyes I put on my dressing gown and slipped downstairs, reaching the lounge as the phone went dead. An aroma of freshly made toast lingered in the kitchen but of Mrs Godfrey my landlady, there was no sign. She had in fact gone out shopping and had left a message on the kitchen table, telling me she would be back in time for lunch.

Having decided to pay a visit to my doctor who lived some distance away in town, I snatched a hurried breakfast and made ready to leave the house. With overnight temperatures having dropped below freezing, a downpour of hailstones in the early hours of the morning hid much of the landscape, beneath a blanket of ice. Stepping out into the chill morning air wrapped in a heavy winter overcoat, my path to the nearest bus stop some twenty minutes away, was if anything hazardous. Finding little protection from a bitterly cold east wind I waited to board the bus as it slithered to a stop, spraying waiting passengers with a shower of hailstones. Hurrying inside I managed to find an empty seat and quickly sat down, before it took off for it's journey into town. Slipping and sliding at frequent intervals on the icy road, it frightened elderly passengers into leaving the vehicle long before reaching their destinations, many refusing to go any further. One irate passenger going so far as to accuse the man in charge of the vehicle of reckless driving, saying to him; "I could do better than that, with my eyes closed. You're not safe to be left in charge of a bloody pram," he sneered.

Not wishing to get embroiled in what might develop into a free for all, I slipped away to keep my appointment at the doctor's surgery, some two blocks away. Giving my particulars to the receptionist I sat waiting until my name was called, some twenty minutes later.

"Dr Richards will see you now Mr Ashford" the young lady said, showing me into his consulting room.

A man in his late fifties Dr Richards was well built with a good head of hair, greying at the temples. He had that middle-aged air about him, as he welcomed me.

"What can I do for you Mr Ashford?" he said with a genial smile.

"Is there any advice you can offer me to help heal these hands of mine, doctor," I asked. I then proceeded to tell him how I came to be injured on a ship carrying a cargo of aviation spirit and high explosives, destroyed by enemy action.

Examining them for a few minutes he said; "The damage to your hands is not as serious as it looks, they can be healed with time and patience. So I suggest you purchase a bottle of saline water and two sponges from the chemist and bathe them in the solution, exercising your fingers with the sponges at the same time."

Thanking him for his timely advice I bid him goodbye and set off for my lodgings, where Mrs Godfrey waited for me to return.

"Ah, you're back in time for lunch Charles" she said, with a smile. "How did you get on at the doctors, was he of any help to you."

"A darn sight more than that lot at the Ministry of Pensions," I replied. "He advised me to bathe my hands in warm saline water three times a day and exercise the fingers, while squeezing the sponges."

"Take this with you Charles" she said as I made to go up to the bathroom, and handed me a small white bowl, saying; "It will do to bathe your hands in."

Christmas was only a matter of days away but with rationing as tight as ever, Mrs Godfrey was most anxious to get her shopping done early. Luxuries such as tropical fruit and many other commodities imported from abroad in peace time, would again be missing from the dinner table during this festive season of 1942, with the war dragging on into it's fourth year. The bombing of our towns and cities having ceased since the Allied offensive of late October forced Rommel's army in North Africa on the retreat, the tide of war in Europe had now swung in favour of the allies.

Needless to say our conversation at the dinner table that day centred on Christmas, with the good lady saying;

"I suppose you'll be wanting to buy a present for your girl friend, Charles. Was she surprised to see you last night?"

"Shocked, would be more appropriate," I replied, showing her a letter she'd received from the War Office, saying I'd been killed in action."

"Oh dear, how upsetting for her" said Mrs Godfrey, a look of concern on her face; "what did she have to say?"

"She's broken off our engagement," I replied.

"Why, is there someone else?" she asked.

"Not that I'm aware of Mrs Godfrey, she simply informed me she was not prepared to marry an invalid."

"You're well rid of her then, Charles, she has no feelings for you," the good lady replied. "There are far better fish in the sea than were ever pulled out" she remarked, trying to console me.

"If that's the case" I laughed, "maybe I've just rid myself of a shark."

Skillfully changing the course of our conversation I mentioned how the war had affected our lives, more than we cared to admit. The country was getting back on it's feet toward the latter end of 1939 after a decade of stagnation, mass unemployment, and poverty during the 1920's, when suddenly it slipped through our fingers and disaster struck again. Through the stupidity of one power crazy idiot we were back where we started, at war again with Germany. Imports of foreign foodstuffs became scarce and food was rationed, as the country switched production from peace to war.

While America was forced by the turn of events to enter into the conflict, we had to go cap in hand to them for aid, and stood alone when Europe was overrun by Hitler's armies. Even so, nothing would deter the British population from enjoying the festive season of Christmas, albeit with a little tightening of the belt.

Throughout this period I kept to the daily routine of exercising my hands in a warm saline bath which I found rather painful and difficult to start with, especially when trying to clench my fists, as instructed by the doctor. As the days and weeks slipped away the treatment was proving successful, because I was begining to move my fingers with ease. Something I'd not been capable of before. Much to my surprise my hands had now healed sufficiently enough for me to dispose of any unsightly bandages covering them, and attend dances at the Overseas Club in Liverpool. It was there by chance I met a wonderful young lady named Gladys Lovell whom I danced with throughout the night, little realizing she would become my wife some eighteen months later.

Together we shared many of the same interests in life and met whenever time permitted from her job at an aircraft factory where work continued around the clock, on a twenty four hour basis. Unfit for work myself at the time because of my war injuries, she understood my predicament and tried to help in every way she could to encourage me, in regaining full use of my hands. Prompted by her confidence in my ability to succeed, I approached a former employer of mine at the shipyard of Rollo Grayson and Clovers and secured a job I'd previously held in the stores. A further morale booster came in the form of a letter from Jack McDonald an old shipmate of mine living in New Zealand, congratulating me on my speedy recovery. Giving me his home address, he wrote; "When you get back to sea, don't forget to see my Mum if you're lucky enough to be visiting Wellington."

By early spring of 1943 life took on a new meaning as the shadow of war receded and air raids, accepted as part of our daily lives, were no more than a memory one chose to forget.

Often recognized as our first day of summer, Whit Sunday the 12th of May, brought with it warm sunny days. Across the landscape the sun once more shone on trees bursting into blossom and flowers emerged from earthbrown nurseries, to bask in it's warmth. On that Sunday morning it was noticeable more people than usual were making their way to St Michael's, when church bells in the nearby village called the faithful to prayer. For while the dark clouds of war no longer threatened this green and pleasant land, many of us saw fit to offer a prayer for our neighbours in Europe, who still suffered at the hands of the enemy.

Return To Sea.

Discharged from the Merchant Service in December of 1942 due to war injuries I now worked in the stores department of ship repairers, Rollo Grayson and Clover of Birkenhead, to supplement a disability pension I struggled to live on. Working seven days a week with the clatter of rivet guns ringing in my ears I found the job boring, and realized I was not cut out to waste my days languishing in this dust-laden atmosphere. Day after day heavily laden merchant ships sailed past my place of work no more than a few hundred yards away and seeing them, I grew restless and longed to be back at sea. At night I lay awake wondering how best I could to get away from the shipyard, without running into difficulties. All shipyard employees were subject to the Essential Works Act, which forbid anyone from leaving the job.

By the end of July 1943 I had become so unsettled in my work at the shipyard, I left without saying a word to anyone. Taking the train to Liverpool I entered the shipping office at Canning Place and requested an interview with the officer in charge, so I could be given an opportunity to return to sea. Because of a desperate shortage of seamen to man the ships, the company were prepared to allow me to continue with my career at sea provided I received permission from the Ministry of Pensions. Without wishing to lose precious time, I wrote them a letter to the effect I wanted to go back to sea. In their reply I was warned any such action on my part would be at my own risk, and I would lose my disability pension.

Feeling this would be no great loss I reported back to the shipping office in Liverpool, taking with me the Ministry of Pension's letter and my seaman's discharge papers. Within a matter of days I signed on aboard the M.V.Monarch of Bermuda a passenger liner of twenty-two thousand tons, with a top speed of twenty-one knots. Built in the early nineteen thirties for the

Furness Withy Line, she was taken over by the Ministry of Transport at the outbreak of war, and now served as a troopship.

The Allied invasion of Sicily on the tenth of July 1943 saw the fall of Mussolini and his ruling Fascist Party in Italy, leading to that country's surrender in September. Because of the serious situation in the Mediterranean at the time it came as no surprise to many aboard the Monarch of Bermuda, to learn she was bound for the Egyptian port of Alexandria in the Middle East. I had cause to remember only too well my last visit to this same Mediterranean theatre of war, some twelve months earlier. Engaged in a desperate do or die battle for survival, I came within a whisker of certain death. Since that never to be forgotten chapter in my life, the fortunes of war had turned full circle. It was now the Nazi aggressors, who were on the receiving end.

With control of the Mediterranean firmly in Allied hands our Middle East forces were preparing to invade the mainland of Italy itself, when my ship arrived in the harbour at Alexandria. At the begining of September 1943, the Monarch of Bermuda with a contingent of troops from the Eighth Army on board, slipped out of the harbour under cover of darkness, and headed out to sea. With an outline of the Italian coast clearly visible on the horizon, by dawn's early light enemy spotter planes keeping a check on our movements were seen off by Allied fighters, covering our entrance into the port of Taranto. Intermittant bursts of small arms fire could be heard from the shore, as the vessel berthed. Amid scenes of destruction in the wake of Italy's retreating army, sunken ships littered a picturesque harbour. With the aid of a small motor launch we managed to get our mooring ropes ashore, easing the ship alongside a deserted wharf.

With little enemy activity in the area other than a couple of sneak bomber raids, troops quickly disembarked and moved further inshore. Our departure from the port of Taranto under cover of darkness, had to be undertaken with a certain amount of caution. Naval minesweepers shepherding the vessel clear of sunken ships lying in our path, in and around the harbour area. Standing out on deck I watched with bated breath as we followed astern in the wake of our escorts moving first to port and then to starboard on a zig-zag course through a minefield, until the ship was well out to sea. In the weeks that followed the Monarch of Bermuda returned time after time from Alexandria to Taranto, ferrying troops to the battle zone. Italy's surrender in early September of 1943 saw British and American forces landing near Naples, preventing a German army already in possesion of the capital city of Rome from overunning the country.

Withdrawn from service at the end of October 1943 the Monarch of Bermuda left the Egyptian Port of Alexandria and sailed unescorted through the Mediterranean to Gibraltar, on her way back home to England. In sight of Malta, I recalled the scene of a bitter battle for possession of this strategic island, twelve months earlier, and remembered those who perished aboard my ship, in a convoy, code named Pedestal.

Slipping through Gibraltar's narrow Straits into the North Atlantic, the weather gradually changed from sunshine to skies of grey, with gale force winds and mountainous seas, entering the Bay of Biscay. Pitching and rolling around like a drunken Polynesian hula-hula dancer, the Monarch of Bermuda did everything except turn turtle during the next twenty-four hours, diving ever deeper into huge troughs she struggled to break surface. At one point I felt sure we were a gonner when her lifeboats tried to kiss the ocean several times, regaining some stability when entering calmer waters in the English Channel. Abeam of Land's End the ship was intercepted by a reconnaissance aircraft of Coastal Command out on patrol, requesting we identify ourselves before being allowed to proceed on our journey north to an unknown destination. Cloaked in a blanket of fog, the Irish Sea was as usual a hive of activity. Coastwise vessels criss-crossing our bows without warning during the hours of darkness, added to the repsonsibility of men on lookout duty.

First light on the morning of November third 1943 found the Monarch of Bermuda steaming up the river Mersey, gateway to the port of Liverpool's seven mile system of docks. Looming up out of a mist shrouded waterfront, attendant tugs took the vessel in tow, shepherding her into her berth at Gladstone dock. A fleet of ambulances waiting at the dockside, transferred wounded servicemen to hospitals in and around the city. Signing off the ship late that afternoon I lost no time in packing my bags, and hurried ashore. Relieved that a three month stint of duty in the Middle East was over, I took a taxi to my lodgings in Bebington village, and was welcomed back by my landlady, Mrs Godfrey.

"Thank goodness your home" she exclaimed, when I set foot inside her front door. "Your lady friend phoned several times while you've been away asking if I've heard from you, so will you let her know your back home Charles."

As soon as I'd finished unpacking, I dialled Glady's number. Her casual hello changed to a cry of delight, when hearing my voice.

"Charles where are you" she asked, somewhat anxiously. "I've received no word from you since you left, and wondered if something had happened to you."

"My ship arrived back home today," I replied. "I'm sorry to hear you haven't received my letters dear, but with the mail being censored, delivery takes forever these days."

"When will I see you?" she asked.

"Barring an earthquake, this evening" I laughed.

I heard her sigh of relief, as she rang off. Mrs Godfrey's call from the kitchen to say tea was ready, cutting short our conversation.

"Is everything alright Charles" the good lady asked, as I took my place at the table. She no doubt remembered the problem I faced with my previous girl friend, and with this in mind asked; "There's no bother I hope, Charles?"

"Just a technical hitch Mrs Godfrey," I assured her. "Some letters I wrote her while abroad have been delayed. She will I'm sure, receive them in due course."

"Does she mind you going back to sea," Mrs Godfrey asked?

"I have no option while the war is on, but I've promised her I'll find a job ashore as soon as it's over. There are many openings I can explore," I replied.

Rain was falling in a steady drizzle that evening, when I set off to visit to my girlfriend. The house in which she lived was on the outskirts of Bebington village, some twenty minutes away. Wrapped up against a cold and damp November night it was more by instinct my footsteps led me to the young lady's house, where no glimmer of light was to be seen, in the blacked-out street. The sound of heavy bolts and safety chains being withdrawn in answer to my knock, echoed throughout the darkened night. A note of caution in her voice as she held the door ajar, my girl friend asked; "Is that you Charles?"

"Yes it is dear," I replied. "Can I come in, it's jolly cold standing out here?"

Having just returned from a voyage to the Middle East where day temperatures soar up to and above one hundred degrees, the cold November night gave me the shivers.

"Mind your step as you come in" she whispered, drawing a heavy curtain to one side.

"It's as black as the ace of spades in here" I laughed, groping around in the dark. "I can't see a thing."

"Here, take my hand," she giggled.

Soft to the touch, her warm hand clasped mine, as she closed the front door.

"Ooh, you're frozen" she gasped, "come and warm yourself by the fire."

About to move along the darkened hallway she paused, to say; "Hold still a moment Charles, I'll have to draw the blackout curtain across the door. If old man Philips our A.R.P. warden see's a chink of light, there'll be hell to pay."

From an adjoining room, a shaft of light pierced the gloom. Barely audible, her mother's voice sounded a trifle nervous. "Who's at the door Glady's?" she asked.

"It's Charles," her daughter replied. He's just arrived back home, and has come to visit us."

A woman in her early sixties, she rose from her chair by the fireside as we entered the lounge, and came to meet us. Slightly built she had an abundance of jet black hair swept back off her forehead, fastened at the nape of the neck with a velvet ribbon. Round of face with hardly a wrinkle in sight life had, it seemed, treated the old lady kindly.

Beckoning me to be seated in the warmth and comfort of her lounge, I sat chatting with Gladys while her mother busied herself in the kitchen, making a cup of tea. Tray in hand she returned within minutes and setting it down in front of us, she said to her daughter; "Your father's not home yet dear, and it's getting late."

"It's only seven o'clock" Gladys replied, glancing at a clock on the mantlepiece. "You know he always works late at the Insurance office on a Wednesday, when he has to wait for his collectors to pay in," she reminded her mother.

With a mumbled apology Mrs Lovell went back into her kitchen where she was preparing her husband's dinner and began singing: "Just a Song at Twilight," which echoed throughout the house. She was a cheerful soul and like most women of her generation accepted being tied to the kitchen sink, once they were married.

At his usual time of eight thirty p.m. every Wednesday, Mr Lovell arrived home, after a long day at the office. Hearing his car tyres crunching on the gravel driveway, she slipped into the lounge just to make sure she'd remembered to put his slippers to warm by the fire.

A heavily built man in his late fifties Mr Lovell was pallid of face and overweight, due to a lack of exercise and long hours spent behind his desk, as manager of an insurance company. Coming from the south of England as a stranger to the region he kept to himself, returning south for his summer holidays each year, to stay with relatives. Like many of his ilk who treated their partners as servants, the emancipation of women, a status they fought so hard to achieve, might never have taken place as far as he was concerned. A woman's place he insisted was at home, looking after their menfolk.

Called upon to serve his country in the first World War, he was assigned to the Royal Navy. His criticism of the Senior Service and anyone who sailed the seven seas as a career was, he said, not to be trusted. Objecting to his daughter courting a seaman he did his best to turn her against the idea, saying; "You'll live to regret it, they've got a girl in every port."

Despite her father's opposition to her associating with me, she refused to listen to his continual outbursts and agreed we should get engaged. Our time together was severely limited to a period of no more than the two weeks' leave, to which I was entitled. Relying on the good graces of her employer at a nearby aircraft factory, to allow her time off work, we went ahead and made plans. By doing so we were able to enjoy two weekends exploring the ancient City of Chester situated at the head of the River Dee estuary, a delightful spot in the heart of the Cheshire countryside. An attraction for vast crowds of tourists who flocked to the area during the summer months, are the old Roman walls, and quaint Tudor style timbered houses in the middle of the shopping area. While in Chester we decided to buy the engagement ring at a jewellers in the city, and celebrated the occasion with luncheon at one of Chester's top restaurants.

Some twenty-four hours before my leave was due to expire a letter reminding me I had to report for duty, arrived with the morning mail. Luck perchance was on my side on this occasion when they instructed me to join the M.V. Port Huon, a twin screw vessel of approximately nine thousand tons. Built in 1927 for the Port Line, her trade route lay between the U.K and New Zealand. Boasting a top speed of thirteen knots she was considered fast for a cargo vessel of that era, compared to large passenger ships which were barely capable of reaching twenty knots when flat out. Undeterred by rumours she was bound for a certain war zone I gambled on the outside chance she could be heading for New Zealand and signed on the ship, unaware she was due to sail the following day.

I now had the unenviable task of telling my girlfiend, who was engaged to me, that I'd signed on a ship and was due to sail in the next twenty-four hours. Visiting her that evening I took with me some flowers I'd bought earlier in the day, and wondered how she would take the news of my sudden departure.

Her smile of welcome turned to dismay when she heard I'd signed on a ship, that was due to sail on the morrow. She seemed quite upset. A look of pained surprise spreading across her face. "They haven't allowed you much time Charles," she protested.

For a minute or so she remained silent. Then resigned to the fact there being a war on, and I had no option, she relented. "Well, I suppose you had no choice but to obey orders, Charles, I'm not blaming you."

Having got over that hurdle, I now had to face a barrage of questions from her father.

"So you're off to sea again" he remarked, when I entered the lounge later that evening. "How long is it for this time, six months. Huh, don't know why you bother to come back here" he snapped, quite sarcastically.

As I sat there listening to her father's uncalled for nasty remarks Glady's could see I was getting upset, and placed a finger to her lips, motioning me to keep quiet. I realized there was no point in getting into an argument with him, he only saw the gloomy side of life.

It was almost midnight when I rose to go. But before leaving I told her not to expect a letter for at least four to six weeks, owing to the time it took for overseas mail to pass through censor. Then having said our goodbye's I set off home along blacked-out streets, moving furtively over frost covered pavements with the wind whistling around my ears. Turning into the street where I lived, a couple of stray cats fighting for the leftovers from an upturned dustbin, stopped to glare at me. Maybe thinking I was after a share of the spoils.

The house was in darkness so I carefully slid my key in the front door, and let myself in. Not wishing to disturb Mrs Godfrey who could be fast asleep at this late hour I took my shoes off, and slipped quietly upstairs to my room for some much needed shuteye.

At seven o'clock next morning I drew my bedroom curtains aside, and looked out on a cold grey November morning. A dense curtain of fog blotted out the landscape, reducing visibility to no more than a few hundred yards. It was enough to depress all but the hardiest, but on this particular morning I felt a glow of satisfaction deep inside me, realizing I'd soon be basking in warm sunny weather. My immediate task however was to finish packing for the long voyage ahead, and search among my personal papers for the address of Jack MacDonald, an old shipmate of mine, from New Zealand.

Nicknamed "Kiwi," he had a sense of humour second to none and was a great favourite with the sheila's; a term he used with reference to the girls. He was first and foremost a born practical joker, and a barrel of fun. Oh, what swell times we had together, no matter what part of the globe we visited. It could be New York or Timbuctoo for that matter, he was always good for a laugh. I well remember his parting words, when leaving the last ship on which we sailed together; "If you should ever take a trip to New Zealand, don't forget to call and see my mum. She'd be glad to meet you Charles."

Rummaging around among my personal papers I finally unearthed his address, hastily scribbled on a sheet of Cunard White Star notepaper. Jack McDonald, 69, Kinghorn Road, Strathmore Park, Mirama, Wellington, New Zealand. Slipping his address in my wallet for safe keeping, I made ready to join the ship later that morning.

"There's a thick fog out there" said Mrs Godfrey, when I came down for breakfast. "Will the ship sail without you if you're late" she asked, rather nervously. "You don't suppose they'll take someone in your place, do you Charles?"

263

"Time and tide wait for no man, Mrs Godfrey," I replied. "But never fear I'll be on board when she sails" I assured her, slipping upstairs to fetch my bags.

Nerves on edge she paced up and down the room, peering out of her front window from time to time. "Ah, this is your taxi Charles" she cried, as it pulled into her driveway.

Leaving my luggage at the front door I walked over to where she was standing, to say goodbye to the woman who had treated me like a son. Drawing her to me as one would when bidding farewell to a loved one, I kissed her on the cheek, and whispered; "Thanks for everything, I'll write you as soon as I can."

Saying goodbye to your nearest and dearest can at the best of times seem hard, so I dared not wait a moment longer. I could not bear to see that look of sadness in her eyes, or witness the inevitable teardrops that were sure to fall.

Hurrying inside the waiting taxi I caught sight of her through the rear window, and waved a final farewell. Standing in the half open doorway with a heavy shawl about her shoulders she looked a lonely figure, reluctant to say goodbye. As my taxi pulled away from her house she slowly raised her right arm aloft and waved, in a brave attempt to bid me au revoir.

Driving on the road that morning was slow and laborious due to poor visibility, delaying my arrival at the dockside where my ship the M.V.Port Huon was berthed. Newly-painted in a battleship grey she lay there fully loaded, and as I stepped aboard I noted her hatches were battened down ready for sea.

With the afternoon tide in full flow the ship's company were ordered to stand by stations, ready to leave the port. Pacing up and down the ship's bridge our pilot looked anxiously toward the river entrance, patiently waiting for the incoming tide to level with the water in the dock. As the huge lock gates swung open, a shrill blast on the Dock Master's whistle spurred his men into action. Attendant tugs fastened to the vessel fore and aft towed the deeply laden M.V.Port Huon stern first clear of the dock entrance into the river, swinging her round to face the incoming tide. Dispensing with the services of both tugs and pilot the ship gathered speed and sailed on down river until reaching the Mersey estuary, where we rendezvoused with several ships in convoy. Like a mother hen fussing over her young brood of chicks, the ghostly grey silhouettes of the convoy's escort circled the waiting ships, forming a protective screen around them. As the light faded an aldis lamp on the bridge of the escort vessel in charge flashed out a coded message to all ships, requesting they form up into three columns before proceeding south through the Irish Sea. Although U-Boat patrols in and around the Western Approaches had produced scant returns of late, our naval escort remained with us until we were well out into the North Atlantic, before the order was given for the convoy to disperse.

Acting on impulse the captain of the ship increased her speed to thirteen knots and headed in a southerly direction, distancing herself from vessels capable of no more than six to eight knots. Within the hour the rest of the convoy were seen as no more than a smudge on the horizon, but the question on everyone's lips was, where are we bound for. Information regarding shipping movements was of course a matter of national security in time of war, no one but the captain of the ship and his navigation officer being aware of our destination. Rumours via the galley wireless spread like wildfire throughout the ship giving our final destination as Gibraltar, which proved unfounded. Passing the Canary Islands, a former base for Germany's submarine supply ships, until diplomatic pressure from Britain forced the Spanish government to refuse them entry, word leaked out that we were heading for the naval base at Freetown, Sierra Leone.

Staying long enough to refuel and replenish the ship's fresh water supply we waited until nightfall to slip out of Freetown, steering a westerly course en route for Panama via the Windward Passage. Sailing alone across the South Atlantic for days on end without catching sight of another vessel, or even a glimpse of a submarine's periscope to break the monotomy, we zig-zagged on and on toward our destination. Each morning at daybreak the tropical sun would raise it's golden head above the far horizon and our constant companion, a lone albatross, would join us, dipping and swaying in time with the ship's foremast as the Port Huon scythed her way through the ocean's glassy surface.

Approaching Panama's Atlantic seaport of Colon as dusk was falling, we encountered our first sign of life since leaving the West African port of Freetown. A small fishing boat, who's crew of two waved to us in passing. This narrow strip of land in Central America was signed over to the United States by Panama in 1903 for the purpose of building and running a canal, over eighty kilometres in length with sea approaches connecting the Atlantic and Pacific Oceans.

Built above sea level with lock entrances at each end, the canal being their main source of revenue, was opened to shipping in August of 1914. In constant use by ships of all nations, Panama's famous canal has a system of locks covering a distance of fifty one miles, estimated to vary between three hundred to one thousand feet wide, with a minimum depth of forty one feet. Relying on the canal for the larger part of her economy, Panama's revenue is bolstered by exports of bananas, shrimps, coffee, and copper. Against this, communications in the region, like those of their neighbours, are very poor.

Passing through the locks at Gatun on the Atlantic seaboard, the M.V.Port Huon sailed through it's artificial lake forty feet above sea level to Culebra Cut. Traversing a series of locks at Pedro Miguel and Miraflores, we arrived on the Pacific Coast, berthing at the Panamanian Port of Balboa. In all a journey of seven and a half hours from east to west from the Atlantic into the Pacific Ocean, past mosquito infested swamps, with jungle on either side, we had now completed the first leg of the long journey that lay ahead of us.

Delayed for several hours while minor repairs were carried out in the engine room we took this opportunity to refuel the ship and replenish our water supplies, which were running low. A quantity of fresh fruit and vegetables were also taken on board, in preparation for our journey across the Pacific to Auckland, the capital of New Zealand. It was late the following evening when the M.V.Port Huon made ready to leave Balboa, with the sun appearing as no more than a red glow on the western horizon as she nosed her way out into the Pacific ocean. Once clear of the harbour all lights were extinguished, with extra lookouts placed at vantage points around the ship. As in home waters our orders were to leave nothing to chance when venturing out of Balboa Harbour, the waters of the Pacific being just as dangerous as the Atlantic. Japanese submarines were known to be scouring the area in search of merchant vessels, whom they deemed, easy prey.

Alone on the open deck some hours later I stood beneath a night sky studded with stars brighter than flawless diamonds, all seemingly within my grasp. A warm southerly wind caressed my face as the vessel gathered speed, leaving a trail of white phosphorescent bubbles in her wake. The lights of Balboa harbour had long since disappeared astern of us when my body suddenly stiffened, and I gasped in alarm. Heading for the midship section on the vessel's starboard side a stream of white florescent bubbles, homed in on us. Grabbing hold of the ship's rail for support, I welcomed the feel of cold steel in my sweating palms. That familiar tightening of the stomach one gets when going into action had the perspiration trickling down my spine, waiting for the inevitable explosion I felt sure would follow.

"My God, I've had it this time," I muttered.

Closing my eyes I said a quick prayer and braced myself, but nothing happened. Out of the corner of my eye I watched this stream of gleaming white bubbles veer away from the ship's side, and head toward the bow. Releasing my grip on the rails a surge of pent up emotion escaped my lips, and I sank to my knees, muttering: "Oh, hell, it's nothing more than a shoal of porpoises."

Shaking from the after effects of my nervous ordeal, thinking we were about to be torpedoed, I walked unsteadily back to my cabin and lay on my bunk, exhausted.

The tropical sun glinted on glass-like waters of the Pacific Ocean when I awoke next morning, and stepped out onto the afterdeck for a breath of fresh air. Leaping up from beneath the ocean as the ship sliced her way through it's turquoise blue waters, flying fish, aided by a light breeze, scooted out of harm's way. Out on deck seamen were busy with their daily chores, chipping rusty patches on bulwarks, wire brushing, painting or splicing eyes on new mooring ropes. The ship's cook in his white hat, left the steamy atmosphere of his galley, and sat watching off-duty stokers playing cards, until it was time for him to serve lunch. Up on the bridge, the morning coffee came as a welcome break, and during this time I chanced to ask the navigating officer what our E.T.A was.

The early days passed peacefully enough without so much as a cry of "ship ahoy" from the man on lookout, scanning the ocean in search of enemy periscopes. There were times when the sight of an ugly-looking water spout appearing on the horizon broke the monotony, causing a ripple of excitement among the ship's company. Other than this there were few, if any, other incidents worthy of mention, during a most enjoyable crossing.

Daylight off-duty hours were spent playing games of deck golf, keenly contested by those taking part. A large number of them won by Morgan, our chief engineer. Who's succesive wins against a seamen known as "Shifty Walker," were viewed with suspicion. Insisting they were fixed, he decided to take matters into his own hands. Now it was common knowledge to all on board, old Morgan had a chamber pot hidden beneath his bunk.

"Let's pinch the old bugger's piss pot" suggested Shifty, to his mates.

"What are we supposed to do with the bloody thing?" said Sandy Wilson, "drink out of it?"

"Leave it to me" said Shifty, giving his shipmate a sly wink.

"The crafty devil's up to something," said young Peters a third member of the gang, nodding in Shifty's direction.

At eight o'clock that evening the vibrant tone of a dinner gong, woke old Morgan with a start. Rising wearily from the settee where he'd been sleeping, he wandered off to the dining saloon. As soon as he was out of sight a shadowy figure moved stealthily into the vacant cabin, and seizing old Morgan's chamber pot, melted into the shadows.

Spreading across the eastern horizon, a ribbon of light heralded the dawn. Rubbing the sleep from his eyes McIntyre the first mate, left the warmth of his chart room where he'd been pouring over his maps and wandered out onto the open bridge, to stretch his aching limbs. Glancing up at the foremast he caught sight of a white object fastened to the yard-arm, swaying back and forth with the movement of the ship. Producing a whistle from his trouser pocket McIntyre gave a shrill blast, alerting the man on standby duty, who hurried up to the bridge.

"What's that hanging up the foremast, Harris?" he asked the young seaman who appeared on the bridge.

"Dunno' sir, I ain't ever noticed it before," he mumbled.

"You must be walking round with your eyes closed, a blind man can see that. Get it down and bring it up here to me," he ordered.

Insisting it was nothing to do with him, Harris left the bridge and sauntered for'ard. Releasing the yard-arm halyards he lowered the heavy object down onto the main deck, bursting into a fit of uncontrollable laughter; "Why it's old Morgan's piss pot," he muttered. Tucking it under his arm, he hurried away.

Grinning like a Cheshire cat, Harris took the object d'art decorated with coloured ribbons into the chartroom, and handed it to Mr McIntyre.

Printed in large black lettering on either side, were the words; "The Morgan Cup for Deck Golf."

His face wreathed in smiles, McIntyre turned to the young fellow, and asked; "Is this the work of your crowd, Harris?"

"It wasn't me mister," said the young seaman, "I don't know nothing about it."

Doubled up in a fit of laughter, Limpy Roberts, the helmsman, let go of the wheel, allowing the ship to veer off course.

"Watch your steering, Roberts," MacIntyre growled, "you're heading back to Panama."

"Sorry Mr McIntyre," grinned Limpy. "I'd just like to see the look on old Morgan's face when they hand him the piss pot, for a golf trophy."

"So would a lot more people on this ship, Roberts," he smirked, disappearing into the chartroom.

During a coffee break that morning old Morgan's chamber pot decorated with coloured ribbons, was given to him by McIntyre the first mate.

"Your prize for deck golf, chief," he grinned.

"And how did you get hold of it" old Morgan asked?

"Found on deck this morning by one of my men," said McIntyre, "have no idea where it came from."

"People should mind their own bloody business," the old man snarled. "I'll have a word with the skipper over this" he warned, and shuffled away.

It was quite obvious the old devil failed to carry out his threat, because the culprit was never brought to book. He did however refuse to take part in another game of deck golf, which was substituted by the game of Chinese Checkers.

After a relatively boring journey across the Pacific from Panama we arrived off the coast of New Zealand, a country made up of two islands separated by the Cook Strait. As the first light of dawn coloured the eastern horizon on New Year's Day of 1944, the M.V. Port Huon sailed into Auckland harbour. Situated on the North Island, this thriving community has an extensive trade in shipping. Exporting sugar, timber, glass and steel. It's climate, beautiful scenery and undulating hills, reminded me of my own County of Sussex back in England. All too soon our time with such friendly people who made our stay enjoyable, came to an end. While reluctant to say goodbye I looked forward to our next port of call, and made ready to leave Auckland as night fell. Dodging in and out of fragmented clouds the moon played hide and seek with us until reaching the open sea, then beamed down on us at full strength.

Keeping within sight of the coast we made our way south, checking our position against infrequent flashes of light from beacons stationed on shore. Dawn appeared as a reddish glow reflected off cumulus clouds hanging over the port itself, on our entering the harbour at Wellington. Lying to the south of North Island, New Zealand's capital is often referred to as "Wet and Windy" by the seafaring fraternity. Yet the city has much to be proud of. Below a bank of fluffy white clouds on the distant horizon, a backdrop of stately pine forests circled the town. The city's parks and gardens are filled with the fragrance of magnolia's, wisteria, and countless other plants. It is here one can listen to the joy of bird song or sit watching colourful butterflies and dragon flies on the wing, flitting over lily ponds. At vantage points around the park Polynesian sculptures are placed in settings of rare beauty, creating an atmosphere of warmth.

It was midsummer in the Southern Hemisphere and as expected, the weather tended to get hot and sticky toward midday. Even so work in the ship's holds carried on apace, in spite of the day's searing heat. Pausing long enough to mop perspiration from sweating brows longshoremen toiled away, discharging our general cargo. With the approach of evening, toil-worn workers drifted home. And a stillness descended on the vessel. Cargo winches ceased their incessant chatter, and lay silent.

Seen as a translucent orb of light in the night sky as I left the ship, the moon cast eerie shadows across a row of brownstone houses in the tree-lined avenue of Kinghorn Road. Knocking on the door of number forty nine I waited for a response, expecting to meet Jack McDonald an old shipmate of mine. Strains of music coming from inside the house suddenly ceased, and the front door opened.

A comely woman in her late forties stood before me, an abundance of black hair brushed well back off her forehead hung over her shoulders. Traces of lissome beauty from days of her youth remained, masking the sadness in her dark brown eyes.

271

Recognising me from photographs sent earlier by her son Jack, arms outstretched, she greeted me.

"Why it's you Charles" she cried with girlish delight, "how lovely to see you. Jack has written so much about you, please come in."

Ushered into her cosy lounge I sat beside a large bay window draped with white lace curtains, overlooking a steep hill. A photograph of Jack and I on board the troopship Louis Pastuer, taking pride of place on her mantelpiece.

"When is Jack due home I asked?" hoping I'd have an opportunity to meet him.

Her face paled and she fell silent, reluctant to answer my question. Instinctively, I knew something was wrong.

It was some time before she spoke, then in a voice barely audible, whispered; "He won't be coming back Charles."

"But why" I asked. "What has happened to him?"

Reaching into her desk she withdrew a buff coloured envelope with O.H.M.S. printed on it, and handed it to me. I knew from past experience letters of this sort were never bearer's of good tidings. An eerie silence seemed to hang over the room, while I read the document. Nothing stirred save for the ticking of a Grandfather clock out in the hall, growing louder with each passing second.

Addressed to Mrs Jean MacDonald the letter from an Under Secretary at the War Office was dated February 1943, and simply stated; We have reason to believe your son Jack MacDonald reported missing at sea, must now be presumed lost.

Handing the letter back to Mrs McDonald who looked sad and near to tears, I offered my condolences. Fearing I might have upset her, I made ready to leave.

"There's no need for you to go Charles," she said. "Stay and have tea with me, we can talk awhile."

A Generous Offer.

In her spacious lounge at the rear of the house Mrs McDonald invited me to be seated and slipped into her kitchen, returning minutes later with a tray of tea. Having by this time recovered her poise, she seemed anxious to talk. Pouring me a cup of tea, she paused to ask; "How do you find New Zealand, Charles. Rather like the old country, don't you think?"

"Yes it does remind me of England" I replied, "especially the county of Sussex."

"I was born in the fishing village of Yarmouth, and left when just a young girl," she said. "The place is famous for it's kippered herrings. I don't suppose you would have any on the ship, Charles?" she said with smile.

"I'll ask the cook in the morning, and if there are any on board you shall have some," I promised.

Where she lived as Post Mistress in the little town of Mirama, the good lady was a much loved personality. The tiny general store come post office which she ran from day to day, kept her in touch with the local inhabitants. Widowed early in her marriage, she somehow managed to struggle on, caring for her son Jack, until he reached adulthood. Losing her seafaring husband so early in life came as a bitter blow, but with help from her many good friends and a little pinching and scraping, she managed to pick up the pieces of her life and carry on. Invites to social functions such as the village fete, local dances and whist drives at the church hall, gave her little time to brood over her loss.

Addressing me personally she said; "At times like this we all need help, Charles. But one can always take comfort in the knowledge, time is a great healer."

The room seemed strangely silent as she finished the sentence, her voice trailed off into a whisper. No tears were shed, just an anguished look from a mother who had suffered the loss of her only son. Sitting motionless as though hypnotized she gazed into space, trying to recall precious moments from the past.

"Are you alright Mrs McDonald?" I asked.

Her face had paled considerably, and I wondered if she was about to pass out. With an effort she pulled herself together, managing to withold a tear perilously close to spilling over her red rimmed eyes. Gradually a little colour returned to the pallid cheeks, for it seemed the past was haunting her, nudging her with memories she could not forget. Like a ghost that would not go away. Assuring me nothing was amiss, she gave a wan smile. "I'm alright now Charles," she murmured. It's just this feeling of loneliness that upsets me, but I'm so glad you came."

"I am also pleased to know you Mrs MacDonald," I replied. "It's such a beautiful country you live in."

"You don't have to be so formal Charles," she insisted. "Why don't you call me Jean, all my friends do?"

Noticeably more at ease she brought out an old family album, showing me photographs taken in happier times. Married in her teens she lost her seafaring husband some years later, and struggled to bring up their only son. Pictures of them holidaying together through the boy's early childhood, portrayed them as a close-knit family. It came as no surprise when her son Jack decided to follow in his father's footsteps, taking up a career at sea. Photograph's taken of him during his early years aboard the sailing ship Pamir and many others, were carefully placed in order. A picture of myself aboard the Port Huon during my visit to New Zealand, had yet to find it's place among her many souvenirs. With a sigh, she closed the album's well-thumbed pages and placed it aside, holding back tears that fell so easily these days.

"You have many lovely memories Jean" I whispered, trying to soften the blow. "Jack did have a wonderful childhood. Something I was never priviledged to enjoy," I told her.

"Oh, I am sorry Charles, I had no idea" she murmured."Can you tell me about it?"

"There's really not much to interest you Jean," I warned her. "Certainly nothing I'm proud of."

Apologizing, she went on. "I hope I'm not being tactless Charles, wanting to delve into your past?"

"No, not in the least" I assured her, "I've nothing to lose."

It was not too difficult for me cast my mind back, to a childhood of rejection and pain. Especially when one is abandoned by their mother in infancy, and institutionalized. Never during my early years was there ever any recollection of a loving parent, I told her. Or indeed, if one ever existed. From so called self-righteous nuns in whose clutches orphan children were placed, no spark of love was seen to manifest itself. Masked by an impenetrable cloak of religion the outside world viewed these so-called pious folk with angelic reverence, unaware what went on behind those convent walls.

Digging deep into my memory during our conversation that evening, I told Jean many things I hadn't dare mention to anyone before. When for instance, the emotional shock I experienced as a thirteen year old. In front of my school friends who were well aware I was an orphan, the head teacher at the school I attended, remarked; "Your mother wants you to go home."

There are many childhood memories secreted away in the furthest corners of my mind, refusing to fade with the passing of time. Often surfacing to haunt me, when least expected.

Listening attentively, Jean was shocked to hear the suffering I endured as a child, both mentally and physically. Chatting well into the night I almost forgot the time, for the hour was late.

"I'll have to be getting back to my ship now Jean, I said," hoping I had not outstayed my welcome.

"You will come and see me tomorrow, Charles?" she pleaded.

Standing outside her house on the side of a hill, a panoramic view of the City of Wellington lay before me. Arc lights aboard ships berthed in the harbour below, cast a luminous glow in the night sky. The clattering sound of ship's steam winches echoed through the darkened night, as longshoremen worked on discharging the vessel's cargo.

Bidding Jean goodnight, I headed back aboard my ship in the harbour below. Closing the portholes in my cabin to shut out the noise, I plugged my ears with cotton wool and turned in. Leaving workers to pursue their nightly task, unloading cargo from the ship's holds.

Throughout the remainder of my stay in Wellington, every free moment was spent in Jean's company. Meeting her many friends who arranged sightseeing tours and picnics, we enjoyed the long summer evenings together at various social gatherings. With so many places to visit, the time slipped quickly by. It was during a farewell dinner on our last evening together that Jean looking a little sad took me by surprise, when asking; "Would you consider staying in New Zealand with me Charles?"

Whilst my heart said yes because I felt so sorry for her, my head instinctively said no. I had a fiancee waiting for me back home and a sister whom I'd made several attempts at finding, but without success. The outbreak of World War Two in September of 1939, had forced me to abandon the search for her. For the time being I had no option but to wait until hostilities ceased, certain in the belief that at sometime in the future, my sister and I would meet.

Thanking her for her hospitality, I told Jean it was nice of her to invite me to stay in New Zealand, but I had an obligation to meet. And felt honour bound to return home.

"Haven't you had enough of war, Charles," she sighed. "There's nothing for you to go back to England for. Besides, I could get you a nice comfortable job here in the Post Office."

"Maybe I should have told you at the outset, Jean," I replied. "I'm engaged to be married, and I must continue the search for my sister."

I saw the look of sadness in her eyes, and placed an arm about her shoulder. Drawing her to me, I kissed her on the cheek. "I'm sorry Jean but I must go home," I told her, "much as I would have loved to remain here with you."

Hiding her disappointment she readily agreed with me, the circumstances required it best I should return home.

Inside the harbour next morning a gathering of sailing boats from the local Wellington yacht club, set off for the open sea. Flags fluttering astern, I watched as each in turn raised their sails as though in some form of salute. Aboard my ship the M.V.Port Huon, the Blue Peter flew from the foremost yardarm. A customary procedure required of all British merchant ships, signalling their intent to leave the port within twenty four hours. By late afternoon the last slings of cargo had been dispatched into the ship's holds, and all was made ready for the vessel to leave port. Without warning a number of cars arrived at the far end of our berth, and from them tumbled a group of young ladies. Amid shrieks of laughter they strolled down the quayside toward our ship, carrying flags, rattles, and coloured streamers. Leading them was Jean McDonald, intent on giving me a good send off.

Secured to the vessel fore and aft, attendant tugs eased her away from the berth, to the sound of our well wishers shouts of goodluck and bon voyage. As the last of the ship's mooring ropes were heaved inboard, they burst into song. Crisp and clear the words of the Maori's Farewell, "Now is the Hour," drifted across the harbour. This I imagined, was Jean's way of saying goodbye, as my ship sailed out of Wellington harbour. With emphasis on the words: "While you're away, oh please remember me. When you return, you'll find me waiting here."

Facing the open sea our pilot dispensed with the services of his tugs and was then himself transferred from the ship onto a pilot launch, and whisked ashore. Ceasing to pace up and down his bridge the Captain entered the wheelhouse, and hurriedly pushed the lever on the engine room telegraph forward. The vessel began to shudder as her twin screws began to thrash the water, and sprang into life. Like a greyhound straining at the leash, she knifed through the clear blue waters of the Pacific, and once again we found ourselves alone in a world of blue. Standing out on deck there was only the ocean, the sky, and small cotton wool clouds drifting overhead, helped along by trade winds.

Since leaving Wellington we had seen no ships or even a smudge on the horizon in this vast stretch of water to attract our attention, apart from a lone albatross. Ever patient it hovered overhead, waiting to scavenge scraps of food tossed over the ship's side. Hopefully it would stay that way, until we reached Panama.

With ample time to spare during off duty hours, there was little to occupy one's idle moments. Games of Chinese checkers in which all members of the crew indulged, were something of a novelty at the start. But when played day after day with monotonous regularity, they soon became boring. To occupy their spare time many seamen took up hobbies. Sandy Wilson busied himself with making rope mats whilst Harris who fancied himself as a modern day Van Gough, passed the idle hours away with his water colours. Painting scenes from memory.

Shifty Walker as usual continued his long running feud with old Morgan, the Chief Engineer, who liked nothing better than to sit alone on deck, puffing away on his pipe.

Going out of his way to antagonize the old chap, Shifty in passing retorted; "Blimey, what yer smoking chief. It smell's like Camel shit."

A normally placid fellow, Morgan turned on his tormentor;

"It's your underpants that stink, son," quipped the old man. "Why don't you put them in dry dock."

Mouth agape, Shifty was stuck for words. Old Morgan had at last, managed to turn the tables on him. Grimacing as though in pain, he ambled off to the after end of the ship. Leaning on the stern rails he joined his mates, boasting of feminine conquests at various ports of call.

En route for Panama we passed within hailing distance of Pitcairn Island, nestling amid the Pacific's sundrenched waters. Said to be populated by no more than one hundred and fifty inhabitants, many of whom were descendants of mutineers from Captain Bligh's infamous ship the Bounty.

Some of her original crew who took possession of Pitcairn, married Tahitian women from among the neighbouring islands of Henderson, Ducie, and Oeno. Each one a place of tropical beauty, with plentiful supplies of sweet potatoes, oranges, bananas, and cocoa nuts.

With the wind on our starboard quarter we made good progress at a steady thirteen knots, heading towards the equator. As the days grew hotter, the wind dropped. Soon, we were in the doldrums. Were it not for the movement of the ship slicing through the ocean's stillness to cause a breeze, there would have been scant relief from the day's choking heat. Temperatures in our cabins reaching anything from eighty to ninety degrees, were cooled by sudden squalls stealing up on us without warning. Banks of cumulus clouds in various hues would gather on the horizon, and as it neared the ship you could see the squall coming. When it seemed the clouds were almost kissing the sea, down came the rain. Like pennies from heaven it splattered over the ship's decks, sweeping all before it. And just as quickly the wind dropped and the rain subsided, leaving everything fresh and clean.

Leaving the doldrums, winds coming from the southeast picked up; a rare treat after the scorching heat we had to endure. Now and then silvery blue flying fish measuring eight to twelve inches long, would suddenly leap from the ocean. Skimming a few feet above the water, they travelled on for maybe a quarter of a mile before disappearing below the surface. Many among them were unfortunate to land on deck to be seized by the ship's cat, who hurried away to enjoy a tasty meal. If nothing else, this helped ease the sheer monotony of our long journey toward Panama.

Stepping out on deck when night fell, it was so black I had to wait a few minutes before my eyes became accustomed to the dark. Only then would I be aware of the stars and pick out the southern cross, lying upside down. As the wind increased so did the speed of my ship, creating an illusion of hurtling through the dark like an express train. Astern of us the ship's wake is like a phosphorescent stream that lights up the inky blackness, a glowing ribbon of frothy bubbles.

At daybreak on a morning some six thousand odd miles from New Zealand the sun was slow to rise, appearing like a yellow orb, creeping above the far horizon. Caught in the warmth of it's orange glow our first sight of land for many a day, could be seen in the distance. A shout of "Land Ahoy" from the lookout man in the crow's nest, brought the duty officer hurrying from the chart room to the wing of the bridge. We were fast approaching the Galapagos Islands a wild life sanctuary lying off the north west coast of Ecuador, home to colonies of seagulls, cormorants, and other aquatic creatures. Guano, the excrement of sea birds found in large quantities on this island, is exported from these shores. It's use as a valuable fertilising agent are well known, being rich in phosphate and ammonia. Among the many land animals are the giant tortoises, at times weighing up to five hundred pounds. These beautiful islands, unspoilt by the ravages of entrepreneurs from the outside world of commerce, and protected by the Government of Ecuador, are a modern day Garden of Eden to any nature lover.

Leaving the Galapagos far behind us, sweltering in a temperature of 120 degrees, we set course for Panama. Arriving days later at Balboa following a trouble-free voyage from New Zealand, our cool ocean breezes suddenly changed. We soon found ourselves embroiled in temperatures exceeding one hundred and twenty degrees, where it was possible to fry an egg on the ship's steel decks. With the setting of the sun, evening shadows brought little relief from the day's blistering heat. Bereft of the slightest breeze as darkness fell, the humidity made life unbearable. This however did not deter Shifty Walker, Limpy Roberts and the rest of the seamen from taking advantage of their limited time in port. On leaving the ship for a night out they caught sight of old Morgan the Chief Engineer, conversing with Quiggley the ship's Chief Steward. To derisive cheers from his mates, he taunted old Morgan; "We're going ashore for a leg up Chief," mocked Shifty. "Why don't you join us."

"It'll take that kink out of yer back" laughed Limpy, "you look like a bloody S hook."

"Have you nothing better to do than dash off to the brothel," sneered Quiggley. Who in the absence of a doctor on the ship was responsible for handing out medicine to members of the crew. "Don't come to me with a sore dick, because you'll get nothing," he told them.

As young Harris reached the gangway Morgan pulled him to one side. "You don't want to follow their example son, they'll get you in trouble," he confided. "They've got no sense."

"No, because their brains are in their dicks," said Quiggley.

Ignoring their good advice Harris marched boldly down the gangway, heading for Dirty Doris's Bar in the red light district.

A thin ribbon of silver etched along the far horizon, heralded a new dawn. From a cluster of small dwellings on shore, wisps of pale grey smoke rose steadily in the still morning air. Below deck on the M.V.Port Huon a chorus of protests from irate crew members was silenced by the Bosun's urgent call; "Show a leg there. C'mon me lads, let's be avin yer," he hollered. Urging his men to come out on deck. "We've got to get away from this stinking heat."

"Aw hell, I can't move," moaned Shifty Walker. "Me bloody back's killing me."

"Serves yer right for dipping yer wick last night" the Bo'sun sneered. "We don't all have money to waste on ladies of easy virtue."

"Yer mean whores, don't yer," laughed Lofty.

With some reluctance they left their quarters and trudged silently along to the fore'castle head, where they set about hauling in the mooring ropes. Moving smoothly away from the berth at Balbao, we proceeded on our journey through the locks at Miraflores and Pedro Miguel into the Culebra Cut. Sailing across Gatun's artificial lake we moved gently through it's system of locks. Literally sailing over mountains, we slowly descended to ocean level. Arriving at Cristobal on the Atlantic coast at dusk after an arduous eight hour journey through

Panama's man-made canal, we stayed overnight at Colon to replenish our fast diminishing supply of provisions and fresh water. Never one to miss the chance of a night ashore, Shifty Walker and his motley crew headed for the nearest bar. Drinking their fill of the local fire water they sought the company of nubile young maidens of ill-repute, who had long since lost their cherries. And were only too willing to lavish their favours, on the drunken seamen. Pie-eyed and legless they remained ashore throughout the night, in the arms of their chosen companions.

Morning brought it's unpleasant reminders of the price they would have to pay for their folly, in the aftermath of the night's entertainment. At the first light of dawn a group of bedraggled seamen with Shifty in the lead crept stealthily along the wharf, hoping to slip aboard unnoticed. An early riser in the shape of old Morgan the Chief Engineer watched closely, as Shifty and company staggered up the gangway. With perfect timing he stepped from his cabin nearby, to intercept them.

"Been for a night's drift, have you lads?" he said, with a wry smile.

"Yeah, and we've all got sore bloody heads. Wot's it to you?" demanded Shifty.

A chuckle of sheer delight escaped old Morgan's lips. "It's not your heads, it's your dicks you should worry about boyo's" the old chief jeered, in his lilting Welsh drawl.

"I suppose it's like they say is it," he quipped."Any port in a storm."

A wall of silence met the old man's final caustic remark. He had evidently managed to turn the tables on his crafty young adversaries. For the time being at least, he had the upper hand.

Approaching midday, Carruthers, the company's agent ashore, a tall sunburnt individual, clambered slowly up the gangway. A faded open-necked blue shirt, bleached white by the tropical sun, stuck like a limpet to his scrawny back. Removing a huge sombrero protecting his bald head, he mopped his brow as he stepped on deck and hurried toward the Purser's Office.

Placing a heavy package containing the ship's papers and a quantity of mail for the crew on the desk in front of him, he slumped down into a nearby chair. Producing a multicoloured handkerchief that had seen better days, he wiped his sweating palms.

"Phew, that damned heat is enough to kill you," he moaned. "Is there a drink handy?" he asked the Purser.

Motioning his assistant Purkiss to fetch a drink, he handed it to the scruffily attired individual sprawled out in front of him.

"Is there nothing stronger?" Carruthers enquired, looking distastefully at the glass of iced water.

"Sorry old chap we're clean out of booze at the moment" came the apologetic reply from Stevens the Purser. Watching the man shift uncomfortably in his chair he felt no sympathy for him, as beads of perspiration continued to roll down his face, soaking his shirt. An ardent teetotaller himself, Steven's was reluctant to waste liquor on scroungers in the shape of company rep's from whatever quarter they came. Placing his half finished glass of water beside him, Carruthers struggled to his feet. "I'll be going then," he said tersely.

Without so much as a backward glance at either of the two men, he sauntered off down the gangway, hurrying ashore. Sifting among the mail he brought on board I came across a letter from my fiancee, enclosing news of the family. Quite understandably, there was no mention of the war situation back home. Of many whispered plans mentioned in connection with the invasion of Europe while we were in New Zealand, nothing had materialized since our departure. Reading my fiancee's letter I knew I'd made the right decision, in declining Mrs McDonald's generous offer to stay with her in Wellington. I could now resume my search for Catherine, the sister I'd yet to meet, as and when the occasion presented itself.

Nevertheless, fond memories of my stay in New Zealand will remain with me forever. Remembering the hospitality of our many friends and their emotional send off. Listening to the strains of the Maoris Farewell, as we parted, brought a lump in the throat and a tear to many an eye. It's haunting melody tugs at the heartstrings, as one listens to the words of the song. The kindness, generosity, and above all the comradeship of it's people, lingers on in my thoughts to this day.

Preparations were now under way for our departure from Panama. The evening sky glowed a bright yellow then turned several shades of red, as the setting sun dipped below the horizon. Shrouded in semi-darkness we slipped unobtrusively out of Colon harbour into a South Atlantic sea swell, for the final leg of our journey home. With the sinking of the German Battleship Scharnhorst in December of 1943, the last vestige of enemy surface raiders were removed from Allied shipping lanes. But even though the U-boat menace had decreased somewhat, the utmost vigilance was still absolutely essential.

Our progress across the South Atlantic during the first week, was maintained at a steady speed of thirteen knots. Warm southerly trade winds blowing from astern gave the vessel fresh impetus, as she sliced her way through a sea as smooth as glass. Sighting very few ships from the time we left Panama on our journey of over four thousand miles, it seemed strange to have to avoid so many vessels around the English coast.

Approaching St George's channel, a Sunderland Flying Boat patrolling home waters, swept over the ship several times. From somewhere inside the huge body an Aldis Lamp flickered, requesting the vessel's name and destination. Satisfied our credentials were in order it bid us safe passage, allowing us to continue on our journey north. A brisk south westerly met us head on entering the Irish Sea, buffeting the ship around. Forcing her to pirouette about like a ballet dancer. Frequent heavy showers lashed the vessel as the weather turned nasty, obliterating our view of the shoreline when reaching the Mersey Estuary at daybreak. A discolouration in the water marking a line of demarkation between the Mersey River and the Irish sea, was seen as an imaginary boundary, where the two waters met. Arriving at Point Lynas on the North Wales coast we picked up our pilot and sailed on up the river Mersey to Liverpool, second busiest port to the Port of London. Traditionally used to handling most of the country's imported raw cotton, it also imports cargoes of sugar, grain, oilseed, minerals and crude petroleum. Exporting manufactured goods of all kinds, the port of Liverpool is the main outlet for manufactured goods from Lancashire and West Yorkshire, since the port itself came into prominence during the Industrial Revolution. The City's present Town Hall built in 1676 was reconstructed by James Wyatt, after it had been severly damaged by fire. A coat of arms showing Neptune and Triton standing beside a Liver Bird, dates back to 1797. Underneath is the motto; Deus Nobis HVBEc Otia Fecit. When translated it reads: God has given us these Blessings.

Anchoring abreast of Princes Pier the centre piece to a seven mile system of docks, one is attracted to an array of fine architectural buildings along the city's waterfront. In the foreground stands the white fronted offices, of the Mersey Docks and Harbour Company. By no means overshadowed, the Liver Building lies in the background. A pair of Liver birds, perched on it's central dome. Legendary creatures, from which the City of Liverpool inherited it's name.

Around midday we received orders from the Dockmasters' Office to heave up our anchor, and proceed to our allotted berth. Aided by attendant tugs we eased our way through the lock gates, into our berth at Huskisson dock. Here for me at least, ended a truly enjoyable voyage lasting several months. Among some of the most friendly people, one could wish to meet. Nevertheless, my life could have changed completely, had I taken advantage of the generous offer to remain in New Zealand.

Out of touch with the war while away on the other side of the world, soon after arriving we heard plans were already in progress for the invasion of Europe. When signing off the ship we were warned, there was every possibility any leave due to us could be cancelled at a moment's notice. With this in mind, I rushed through the formalities of clearing customs. Saying farewell to the many friends I'd sailed with over the past months, and hurried ashore. Without a backward glance I took a waiting taxi to Liverpool's Pier Head, where I boarded a ferry across the River Mersey to Birkenhead.

It was from here that Benedictine Monks from the Birchen Head Priory operated the first Mersey ferry in 1330, when granted passage to Liverpool by Edward III. Untouched by the ravages of the Industrial Revolution in Liverpool and other North Western Cities and distanced by the River Mersey, Birkenhead remained an agricultural area until the advent of a steam ferry service in 1820. With ready access from the City of Liverpool opening up, it's rapid growth as an industrial centre began. The towns vast shipbuilding yard of Cammel Laird employing thousands of local men, playing a large part in repairing British Naval and Merchant vessel's throughout the second world war.

Delighted to welcome me back home my dear old landlady Mrs Godfrey fussed around me, like a mother hen guarding her chicks.

"How long are you home for, Charles. And did you have a good trip." Were the first question's she asked.

She seemed quite upset when I told her my leave might be cut short, because of the impending invasion of Europe.

"But why do you have to go" she said, "you've only just come home?"

"All able-bodied men are liable to be dragged in this second front Mrs Godfrey, they'll need every ship they can muster and the men to man them. Just think of the people who are suffering in Europe, waiting for the Allies to drive the Nazi invaders out" I replied.

"Yes I suppose it is hard for them," she said with a sigh. And left me to finish unpacking my bags.

Visiting my fiancee later that evening we discussed the present situation concerning my possible recall to take part in the invasion, and decided to bring plans for our forthcoming marriage forward. Choosing her birthday on the first of May, no more than a week away, we were told we would need to obtain a special licence. Leaving my fiancee's family to take care of arrangements for her wedding dress and those of the bridesmaids, I attended to other important matters such as the church service, ordering flowers, and the hotel reception.

In a flurry of excitement, all was ready when the day of our wedding arrived. On this special occasion the weather relented, blessing us with sunshine and cloudless blue skies. Nerves a little on edge I made ready for the church service, set to take place that afternoon, at the village church in Oxton. My landlady Mrs Godfrey, generous to a fault, did her best to calm my ruffled nerves. "Why don't you try a drop of whisky to steady you up, Charles," she pleaded. Declining her offer, I duly arrived for the ceremony some ten minutes before it was due to start.

Moving on past a crowd of well wishers, I entered the church. Taking my place at the head of a small congregation of friends, and family of the bride. Shifting uneasily from one foot to another whilst waiting for my bride to appear, I felt butterflies cartwheeling inside my stomach. Then a murmur from the rear of the church, caused me to cast a hurried glance over my shoulder. Seeing her walking confidently up the aisle, eased the tension building up inside me. Her smile when our eyes met assured me all was well, ensuring our wedding went off as planned.

Waiting to greet us outside the church, members of the family and friends alike showered us with rice for good luck, as we hurried off to our wedding breakfast. It was late afternoon before we managed to slip away unnoticed, from the reception at the Central Hotel. Gathering our luggage we sped off to Llandudno, a quiet seaside resort on the North Wales coast. Overlooking the beach our hotel lay in the shadow of rugged mountains and green valleys, an ideal place to spend a honeymoon.

Days of warm spring weather with an abundance of sunshine amid cloudless skies of blue, were our's to enjoy on this our first week of married bliss. We thrilled to the raucous cry of sea birds along the shore, swooping down into the sea to snatch up whitebait from the incoming tide. On walks down country lanes one caught snatches of song from the blackbird and thrush foraging in hedgerows, while high above lush green meadows, the skylark warbled a joyful tune.

Nothing untoward happened to disturb the peace and tranquility of our time together, until midway through the second week of our honeymoon. The spectre of war, which until now had been pushed into the background, once again raised it's ugly head. On the tenth of May 1944, a telephone message from my father-in-law sent us scurrying back home. It seemed our honeymoon was to be short lived, at least for the foreseeable future.

On the hall table waiting for my return, was a letter marked urgent. Bearing the all too familiar stamp O.H.M.S, I had a sneaking suspicion it was from the Ministry of Shipping in Liverpool. Brief and to the point, it requested I report back for duty immediately, with all necessary documents plus my lifeboat efficiency certificate. I had a jolly good idea that something big was afoot, having been warned beforehand, my leave could be cancelled.

Midway into the month of May, I bid goodbye to my beautiful young wife of just a few days, and took passage on a ferry across the Mersey's busy waters to Liverpool. Alighting at Princes Landing Stage I walked past the remnants of our old Shipping Office at Canning Place, destroyed during the blitz of 1941. Admired as a fine example of Gothic architecture in bygone days, the beautiful white granite stone blocks covered in dust and grime, appeared to have lost their colour.

Beside a disused Customs office adjacent to a row of bonded wharehouses at Canning dock, I found the Shipping Federation's makeshift headquarters. A group of young men huddled together in animated conversation stood outside, to cast questioning glances in my direction as I entered the building. A cold and uninviting place with paint peeling on the dust coated walls, added to an atmosphere of doom and gloom. Seated behind a large desk in a faded blue serge suit that had seen better days, old

Repp the shipping clerk whom I'd crossed swords with in the past, gave a sardonic grin; "So, we've roped you in again" he leered, as I handed my credentials to him.

Pointing to a door marked conference room, he requested I enter. Inside I joined a group of men waiting to receive orders, from a uniformed naval officer. In a calm voice, he went on to say; "You have been chosen to undertake special training, in preparation for the Liberation of Europe. When you are ready you will be assigned to one of several hospital ships, being fitted out for the task."

Bidding us safe journey and God speed, we each of us were told to rendezvous at Lime Street Station, next day.

Boarding the train with the rest of my group at the railway station next morning, we left enroute for the Scottish town of Inveraray, lying at the head of Loch Fyne. Whilst there we were given a two week period of training in first aid, and the use of a specially designed ambulance launch aboard the S.S. Naushon. A small hospital ship stationed in the area, for that specific purpose.

Built in America, these specially designed craft constructed of five ply timber, had an overall length of thirty feet. Their purpose was to operate from ship to shore, ferrying wounded from the battle front. Each capable of transporting twenty one injured personnel, at any given time. These launches were powered by a six cylinder Chrysler Marine engine, with a large supply tank capable of carrying fifty gallons of fuel, fitted to the stern. Should the hospital ship be put out of action, this would enable the craft to return to their base at Southampton.

Split into groups of eighteen, when our training finished, I joined a party assigned to a hospital ship at South Shields, lying at the mouth of the River Tyne. Here a close-knit community of people lived in tiny houses adjacent to obsolete coal mines and a ship repair yard, that had lain idle for many years. Their usefulness having long since, ceased to exist. One of many ports in Britain allowed to fall into decline during the recession of the twenties and early thirties, only now were they beginning to recover from years of neglect. Reopening the shipyard at the start of World War Two, brought much needed employment to a hard pressed people.

Arriving at the dock in South Shields on the afternoon of the 29th of May 1944, I boarded the S.S. Prague in the dockyards' fitting out basin. Joined by an eighteen strong compliment of specially trained merchant seamen to crew the ambulance launches, we prepared ourselves for battle.

Requisitioned by the Ministry of Transport, the role of the S.S. Prague as a cross channel ferry in peace time, had undergone a complete transformation. She was now being made ready to serve as a hospital ship, for the invasion of Europe. Like a thing of beauty etched on an artist's canvas, her shining white hull and brilliant red cross on the funnel, brought hope anew to the area's unemployed. Her very presence in the tiny shipyard, be as it may a war was in progress, breathed new life into a long neglected ship building industry.

Normally associated with endless hours of sunshine, the month of June burst on the scene with gale force easterly winds, impeding our progress as we left the dock at South Shields. Entering the North Sea at dawn on the morning of June 2nd mountainous seas tossed the vessel about like a cork. Like a ballet dancer she skipped over the crest of each giant wave, courting disaster every time she plunged headlong into a deep trough. Within sight of land on our run down Britain's east coast, we journeyed south in the direction of the English Channel to an unknown destination.

Switching our navigation lights on as dusk fell, we found ourselves abreast of the white cliffs of Dover. Suddenly, from across the channel in the direction of Calais, came the unmistakable sound of gunfire. Flashes of light were seen as German shore batteries opened up on us, and shells whined overhead. Asking the engine room to give him all possible speed, our Captain ordered all lights to be extinguished, and sailed away from the danger zone.

Arriving off the Isle of Wight at first light, the hospital ship S.S Prague entered Southampton waters on the morning of June the third. Moving cautiously among a vast armada of vessels waiting there, we berthed close to several hospital ships in the port's huge system of docks. All waiting to play their part in the Invasion of Europe, when the weather subsided.

On the morning of June the fifth, gale force winds and rough seas that had hampered shipping, eased enough to allow the invasion fleet of over six thousand ships to set sail. Protected by a naval escort of battleships, cruisers and destroyers, they sailed from ports around England's south coast toward the beaches of France. Following some distance astern of the main body, hospital ship's S.S Prague, and Duke and Duchess of Argyle brought up in the rear. Throughout the day we inched towards the Normandy coast, in a movement both conspicuous and daring. Yet in this age of communication by radar and reconnaissance planes, our approach had gone unnoticed by anyone on the German side. At night an overcast sky afforded the convoy ample cover, until a break in the cloud around two a.m allowed a full moon to light up this vast armada of ships. Silhouetted against an angry dark gray sea they were sitting ducks, but there was no attempt by the enemy to intercept them.

The Battle for Omaha

The night's angry black sky had disintegrated into uneven patterns by dawn's early light on the morning of June the sixth 1944, nominated as the day of deliverance for the oppressed peoples' of Europe. Preparing to meet the enemy head on, the invasion fleet moved ever closer to it's objective, the beaches of occupied France. It was almost unbelieveable that a huge armada of ships such as this, was allowed to sail from England unhindered. Right under the noses of the German High Command. If just one Nazi patrol boat had been in the vicinity of the English channel at the time, it could have given them ample warning. But it was not to be.

Long before the first assault waves of British and Canadian forces hit the beaches at 6.25 a.m, Allied warships lying off the French coast, went into action. Firing salvo after salvo from their sixteen inch guns toward German coastal batteries, the noise echoed across the wind swept waters of the English Channel. The sound of approaching aircraft suddenly developed into a deafening roar as Squadrons of Spitfire, Mustang, and Thunderbolt fighter-bombers, passed overhead. Beneath the wings and fuselage of every allied aircraft one saw distinguishing marks of broad white stripes, setting them apart from the enemy. In a never ending stream, they flew toward the coast of France. Their objective was to destroy fortified enemy positions along the Normandy beaches, where the German High Command were reported to have amassed battery's of 155-millimeter guns, overlooking the beaches.

Abreast of beaches code named "Juno, and Gold," a section of the invasion force carrying British and Canadian troops left the main body. Following up behind the main invasion force, the hospital ships Duke and Duchess of Argyle anchored some half a mile off shore, as the first invading party landed opposite the town of Caen. Battling against strong head winds showing little sign of abating, the rest of the invasion force moved on in the direction of Cherbourg. Pitching and rolling in seas threatening to swamp us, the hospital ship S.S. Prague anchored at a safe distance from the shore, abreast of the American beachhead at Omaha.

It was here at first light on the morning of June 6th the American forces fought the bloodiest, and most desperate battle of D-day. Facing them on cliff-tops 100 feet high at either end of Omaha the Germans had sighted their weapons, so that every inch of the beach was covered. Protected by concrete walls three feet thick the enemy waited, high velocity 75mm and 88mm guns ready with a heavy fusilade of fire to sweep the entire American beachead.

As the first landing craft touched down on a mist shrouded beach at 6.30 that morning, the young G.I's heard a tattoo of machine-gun bullets hammering on the ramps of their LCT's. Within ten minutes of hitting the beach, the first assault force had become leaderless. Every officer and sergeant, either killed or wounded. Opening up with 88-millimeter howitzers, heavy mortars, and machine guns in positions on the cliff tops, the enemy pinned down what little remained of the American assault force behind a sea wall. Following the first wave ashore, further assault units of American troops found the enemy waiting, decimating them before they set foot ashore.

It was now obvious a pre-emptive strike by Allied bombers on German positions covering the Omaha beachhead some hours earlier, had been unsucessful. Hampered by low cloud and bad visibilty, and fearful of hitting American troops in the landing area below, planes sent to straffe the area were forced to eject their bombs further inland. Leaving enemy positions along cliffs above the Omaha beachhead, almost unscathed. Wreaking havoc among invading American forces, all attempts by them to land on the beaches was forstalled by the enemy, the situation looked desperate indeed. Fortunately for those G.I's trapped on the beach a miracle was about to happen, in the shape of a U.S. destroyer.

Seeing the plight of the assault force, the Captain of the U.S. destroyer Frankford moved his ship as close to the Omaha beachhead as he dare, in an effort to help American troops pinned down by the enemy. Shortening the distance between himself and the shore gave his gunnery officer a clear view of his targets, on the clifftops above the beachhead. Using telescopic sights they blasted away at pillboxes, machine gun nests, and heavy mortar batteries. Seeing the action taken by the Frankford, others in the squadron moved closer and joined in. As fortifications on this section along the cliff-tops began to fall apart, German troops came out with their hands up, surrendering to the advancing Americans.

In the sky to our right the morning cloud had lifted somewhat, and from the Cherbourg Penninsula bursts of anti-aircraft fire punctured the air. Then as if prearranged by the gods of war, the weather relented, and out came the sun. Aided by a strong wind it pierced a heavy smoke screen filled with the dust of battle, laying bare a scene of mayhem that lay all around us. On the boat deck of the hospital ship S.S. Prague, I watched with bated breath as an attack developed. Allied fighter bombers returning to the scene of carnage, were able to get a clear view of their targets. Moving in en-masse, they rained missiles down on the hapless German mortar and artillery positions on the clifftops.

Backed up by the fourteen inch guns of the American battleships Arkansas and Texas, whose shells whined over vessels anchored off shore, allied fighter bombers pounded the targets mercilessly. Within a short space of time enemy resistance inside fortifications along the cliff tops, was silenced. But for the odd sniper yet to be winkled out, all opposition ceased. By 10.am invading American forces pinned down by German shore batteries from the outset, were able to sweep ashore in their hundreds. Scrambling up the steep cliffs, they took over whatever was left of enemy positions.

Although the price paid was high, the hand of fate had prevented what might have been a massacre. On the clifftops of

Omaha's beachhead columns of thick black smoke were seen to rise skyward, from the burnt out remains of German 88 millimetre batteries. A pulverising attack of Allied sea and air power, had reduced it to a heap of rubble. Aboard our hospital ship, the pungent smell of cordite from exploding shells on the shore drifted toward us, in the aftermath of that merciless Allied attack. A defeat on the beaches at Omaha, that would have jeopardized the entire invasion, was somehow miraculously averted.

By now the fierce storms that caused so much confusion over the last two days, had eased off somewhat. Nevertheless a heavy sea swell and raging surf continued to pound the beaches, preventing ambulance launches on board the waiting hospital ship S.S Prague from being used. It was therefore found necessary to call upon the aid of American water transport known as Duks, to transfer wounded soldiers out to the vessel. With the weather improving a little during the next day or so, our hospital ship moved closer inshore.This gave the vessel an opportunity to use her ambulance launches, which up until that time were immobilized, to begin ferrying badly wounded soldiers from first aid stations ashore, to the ship. With some difficulty we managed to lower three of our launches on the leeward side of the ship sheltered from the wind swept waters, proceeding with all possible speed to the Omaha beachhead.

Approaching the shore, I gazed in horror at a scene of utter carnage that lay before me. It seemed we had entered hell itself. Columns of dense smoke from burnt out vehicles strewn across the beach directly ahead of us formed an impenetrable black curtain, hampering our vision. Mindful of fast receding tides in the area, our ambulance launches moved quickly inshore. Easing past a collection of wrecked tank landing craft and Duks bouncing around like corks in the raging sea swell, we looked for signs of life, but found none. All had apparently been abandoned by their occupants, and left to drift aimlessly about. Others among their number engaged in fierce combat with enemy shore batteries, lay useless hulks of twisted metal.

Caught fast in the sand, disabled tanks spewed out oil that had somehow caught fire, and now burned furiously. Along the beach burnt out trucks, bulldozers, jeeps and half tracks littered the shore. Floating about in the water, were corpses of countless numbers of young soldiers. Trapped in a merciless fusillade of machine-gun fire, their chances of survival limited. Some, chopped to pieces at the waters edge mutilated beyond recognition, lay among the debris. Their burnt out vehicles, scattered far and wide along a bloodsoaked sandy beach. Many cut down in the water simply floated back and forth in the foaming surf, a pinkish hue running along it's three mile stretch. The sea itself was littered with the bodies of young GI's, who'd breathed their last.

Oblivious to the roar of gunfire on the clifftops above them, crews of the burnt out wrecks who managed to survive the initial onslaught, lay on the beach badly wounded. The spectre of war or impending doom, could have been light years away for all they cared. What they badly needed was medical attention. Horrific scenes of mindless killing and unnecessary bloodshed, were nothing new to battle-hardened seamen among our ambulance crews. They'd seen it all before. So it was not without some misgiving and a feeling of revulsion for the horrors of war, they volounteered to take part in the invasion of Europe when asked to do so. Fully aware the road ahead, was fraught with danger.

In spite of having to reckon with magnetic mines and sunken objects obstructing their way ashore, ambulance crews from the hospital ship, S.S. Prague, stuck to their task. Giving first aid to all in need, both friend and foe alike. Throughout the days and nights ahead hundreds of wounded were transferred from the beachhead to hospital ships lying off shore, in a never ending stream. Ambulance launches dodging in and out of supply ships anchored nearby continued to carry out their duties, in the midst of enemy air raids.

Whilst the toughest fighting was undoubtedly at Omaha beachhead, an American assault force at Utah lying to our west, was making good progress. As reinforcements poured onto the beaches, the American XIX and V Corps joined forces to face the German defences at Cherbourg. Nonetheless, spirited resistance by the German garrison denied the Americans possession of the town, who's capture was of great importance to the Allied cause. It's ultimate surrender provided a landfall for PLUTO the undersea pipline, that was to supply millions of gallons of fuel oil to the Allied armies.

Picking up casualties in and around the port had now become part of daily life for crews on board the hospital ships, during cross channel forays between Cherbourg and Netley Hospital, at Southampton. Waiting inside the harbour to allow a column of American supply ships carrying young GI's aboard to enter Cherbourg, I watched their approach through my binoculars. Packed together like sardines, they sat astride a collection of tanks secured to the deck of each vessel. All eager to join their comrades who now had a foothold at the battle front, waiting to come to grips with the enemy.

No more than half a mile from the port entrance a huge explosion rent the air, tearing the leading vessel apart and setting her on fire. A pall of black smoke billowing skyward, was all that remained of the stricken vessel as it sank beneath the water. Even as we watched the vessel disappear, our hospital ship S.S Prague left the harbour to pick up survivors. Speeding toward the wreckage strewn area, we saw no signs of life. Just the sickening spectacle of mangled bodies floating aimlessly about in oil covered waters, that told us our task was hopeless. Lowering the launches, we endeavoured to pick up their corpses. Many mutilated beyond recognition, were taken back to Southampton for internment.

Within a short space of time naval minesweepers arrived to sweep the area clean, before the remaining ships could safely reach their objective. Meanwhile reports coming through following the disaster, indicated enemy minelaying submarines had been operating in the area the previous night, dropping magnetic mines. Slipping through our defence system during the hours of darkness, they were responsible for the total destruction of many unsuspecting landing craft, and their personnel. Seeing so much carnage and unnecessary waste of young life, sent a wave of nausea surging through my body. I gave an involuntary shudder and turned away from the gruesome spectacle, of so many lifeless bodies lining the deck. Offering a silent prayer for these young GI's who had made the ultimate sacrifice, I paused and reminded myself; but for the grace of God, there go I.

While the operation had started so disastrously for the American troops at Omaha, a break through came after much bitter fighting, by forces commanded by General Joe Collins' V11 Corps. By seizing the important fortress Port of Cherbourg from it's German Commander, Lieutenant General Karl von Schlieben, the Allies effectively slammed the door shut on any hope the Nazi's had, of driving the Allied forces into the sea. Mopping up operations in the area continued for a short time, GI's having to winkle out a few German diehards who remained hidden in underground bunkers. Clearing up the wreckage of sunken ships and other debris cluttering the harbour was quickly undertaken, allowing hospital ships the use of numerous berthing facilities now available to them. This in turn provided the allied forces with easier access, transporting wounded back to hospitals in and around Southampton. Eventually dispensing with the services of ambulance launches, that had carried out such sterling work in retrieving many hundreds of casualties from the beaches of France.

In a concerted air bombardment the Allies sent a large force of Liberator and Flying Fortress bombers to the Normandy area of Saint-Lo towards the end of July, which resulted in entire German defence systems being wiped out. Breaching enemy lines provided an opening for columns of American tanks to surge through the gap, causing total confusion among dispirited bands of fleeing German soldiers. As the tide of battle turned in favour of the Allies, who by the month of August were rampaging through France at will, large ocean going hospital ships were now able to move freely in and out of captured

French ports along the English channel. The need for small hospital ships such as ours, had now diminished.

Having served our purpose during the initial assault on the beaches of France, the hospital ship S.S. Prague and it's Merchant seamen crew, were recalled to the U.K. At the end of August 1944 I reported to the shipping office in Liverpool, and was granted a two week period of leave. Welcomed home by my wife, she readily agreed this would be an opportune moment for the two of us to travel south in search of my mother whom I had not set eyes on, since returning from sea prior to the outbreak of world war two. Conscious of the danger we faced from buzz bombs when passing through London, I wanted to visit mother's last known address in the Surrey area of Merton, in the hope of finding her. Bearing in mind, she was the only person who knew the whereabouts of my sister Catherine.

The train for London slowed to a crawl on it's approach to Liverpool's Lime Street Station, a ribbon of white steam issuing from the squat funnel as it ground to a halt. Joining the train were a group of young servicemen returning to barracks after a spell of leave, carrying with them their kitbags, haversacks, and rifles. With a loud snort the train jerked forward, pulling away from the bomb scarred city of Liverpool, where shattered buildings stood out at crazy angles against the morning sky.

As the train rumbled on, we passed the ancient city of Chester with it's Tudor style houses and old Roman walls, amid tranquil waters of the River Dee. Moving into the delighful Cheshire countryside, we viewed it's many charming villages and thatched cottages. Unseen by the traveller crossing the Wirral Peninsula into neighbouring North Wales, there lies a land of exciting mountains and majestic castles.

Some thirty miles on we pulled into the town of Crewe, a major railway junction and important manufacturing centre, home of Rolls Royce and Bently cars. Built on a greenfield site by a railway company in 1842, it was here in 1904 that Mr Henry Royce son of a miller and a well -established engineer of the Manchester based firm F.H. Royce & Co, met the Hon.

Charles S. Rolls, son of a wealthy landowner. And so the production of the Rolls Royce, a motorcar way ahead of its time was launched, with a silver lady as it's mascot. An observation of the worldly wise Mr Royce, being; "The quality remains, long after the price is forgotten."

Staying long enough to pick up a sizable amount of mail and a number of passengers, the train crossed the Cheshire border into the neighbouring County of Staffordshire, an area rich in deposits of iron and coal known as the Black Country. Surrounded by tall factory chimney's spewing out industrial waste we viewed the town of Stafford, noted for it's china and ceramics. A pall of dense smoke hung over the area like a black curtain, and in the background, slag heaps reared their ugly heads. A blot on the landscape, man had made no attempt to disguise.

Closing our carriage window to stop smoke and grit from the engine blowing in, the train reduced speed on entering the town. Smoke blackened pottery kilns gave way to rows of dingy back to back terraced houses, overlooking the railway. On the station platform a group of servicemen squatted down among a mountain of kit bags, haversacks, and rifles, squinting up at the departure indicator apprehensively. As though it were some kind of roulette wheel, about to decide their fate. Others stared disconsolately at the train, as it slid to a halt. Were it not for the uniforms, one could excuse them for their lack of concern, over a war that had gone on for five long years. Not until passengers had embarked from the train did the waiting soldiers jump to attention, when ordered to do so, by their N.C.O. With a great deal of reluctance they gathered their equipment, and shuffled on board.

From beneath it's belly the giant locomotive let out a sudden hiss of steam, and with a grunt she was off. Leaving Stafford behind we gathered speed and journeyed on south, catching a brief glimpse of the cathedral City of Lichfield. It's spires, gleaming in the late autumn sunlight. Crossing Stafforshire's border into Warwickshire, with it's castles of Kenilworth and

Warwick, we caught sight of the River Avon, birth place of William Shakespeare, flowing through the town. By-passing the industrial cities of Birmingham and Coventry, we arrived at the market town of Rugby. In addition to it's well known Public School, manufacturing industries in the area include electrical engineering, motor and aircraft pattern works. A timely delay here enabled me to slip onto the platform, to purchase two penny bars of chocolate from a red painted machine, and amble back to my seat on the train.

An elderly railway porter holding a green flag, glancing up at the station clock, advised me to hurry back aboard as I passed him by. From my carriage window I looked on as he withdrew a watch suspended on a long silver chain, from his waistcoat to examine it. Suddenly a shrill blast on a whistle from the far end of the platform, injected some life into him. Hoisting his green flag aloft, he waved it in majestic fashion. His garbled message to the engine driver went unheard, silenced by a gushing of steam from beneath the belly of the train as we moved off.

Displayed at intervals along the railway platform, posters advertising Bisto gravy, Andrews Liver Salts, and Gold Flake Cigarettes, were suddenly hidden from view by a trail of white vapour, as the train gathered speed. Over the border of Warwickshire and into the county of Northamptonshire, one glimpsed quaint little villages as the train rattled on past the river Nene and the town of Northampton itself, noted for its shoe manufacturing industry. An enforced delay at St Albans in Hertforshire saw the train arrive late that afternoon at Victoria Station, London, ending an exhausting journey for my wife and I.

A shaft of late Autumn sunlight poured through great yawning gaps in the bomb damaged station roof, shedding a ray of much needed light into this sadly neglected area of the nation's capital. Moving along among a crowd of passengers headed for the exit, our tickets were hurriedly snatched from us, by a frustrated railway official. Outside the station the city streets were as busy as ever in spite of being threatened by the enemy's latest instrument of war; the V-2 rocket, otherwise known as the flying bomb. Outlined against the backdrop of a bright blue sky one saw the remnants of burnt-out buildings standing at crazy angles. Buzz bombs as they were nicknamed, struck fear into many a poor soul, leaving widespread death and destruction in their wake. Not since the blitz of the early forties, did Londoners have to suffer such disruption to their daily lives.

Leaving Victoria station we found touts and spivs hanging about outside, on the lookout for a soft touch. One seedy looking individual in a faded blue serge suit, sporting dinner stains of yester-year down it's front, accosted my wife and I. Standing directly in our path, he whinged;

"D'yer wanna cab lady?"

Sidling up to me, he pointed to a rust laden car standing at the kerbside; "Ere yah mister, we'll take yer wherever yer wanna go "he grinned, showing his tobacco stained molars.

Crouched behind the steering wheel sat an unkempt looking individual, wearing sun glasses. His face, half hidden in the turned up collar of his overcoat. Obviously not wishing to reveal his identity. Without further ado I said; "No thanks, we'll take the train."

Leaving the disgruntled spivs issuing a torrent of curses in our wake, my wife and I moved quickly out of earshot. Anxious to get away from the inner city area as soon as possible and the threat of flying bombs, saw us hurrying to Victoria Underground Station. From there we caught the train to Wimbledon. Famed the world over as the mecca of lawn tennis. It's internationally famous playing courts, lay but a short distance from where mother once lived. Our problem of seeking suitable accomodation in the area, was quickly solved with the help of the local constabulary. From a list of local residents offering bed and breakfast to the weary traveller, we chose a boarding house run by a Mrs Clarkson, which suited our requirements. Retiring early that night I had but one thought in mind, a determination to find the whereabouts of my family if that were humanly possible, before my leave expired.

A rumbling sound one normally hears with an approaching thunderstorm, wakened me in the small hours of the morning. Sitting up in bed I listened for the inevitable downpour of rain, I felt certain would follow. In the distance, I heard a series of explosions. Mingled with the sound of anti-aircraft fire, it served to shatter a morning stillness. Was this another enemy V.2 rocket attack on the city, I wondered. London had seen more than their fair share of them, since the D-day landings in June.

Careful not to disturb my wife who lay sleeping, I left my bed and stood by the window. Through a chink in the bedroom curtains I watched a tiny orange glow spread like wildfire, along the distant horizon. Fingers of light stabbed the darkness, as searchlight batteries swept the night sky, and anti-aircraft guns opened up. Working in unison they sort to destroy pilotless missiles homing in on the city, before another projectile found it's target.

On the far horizon, blue lights flickered in and out like jets on a gas burner, setting light to everything in their path. With each successive attack, fires raged out of control, forming an iridescent display of colour where the missile landed. Not until long after midnight, when the raid had ended, did I go back to bed. Thanking my lucky stars, I decided against staying in London overnight.

Downstairs in the hall a Grandfather clock chimed the hour, and somewhere in the vicinity church bells called the faithful to morning prayer. Shaking my wife gently by the shoulder, I whispered; "It's eight o'clock dear, and time we were up."

Opening her eyes, she looked at her strange surroundings and asked; "Where are we?"

My response was interrupted by the melodious sound of a gong, calling boarders to breakfast. The aroma of freshly made toast drifting up from the kitchen filled my nostrils, as I opened the bedroom door. Coaxing me to hurry, with my ablutions. Meals were served each morning from eight thirty, until ten o'clock, by Mrs Clarkson. A well proportioned woman in her late forties who, since losing her husband at Dunkirk, eked out a living by taking in boarders.

"Good morning. Did you sleep well?" she asked, as we entered her cosy dining room.

"Why yes," I replied. "That is until the rockets arrived in the early hours. I'm afraid some poor devils in the city, caught a packet."

At the breakfast table all was quiet as we sat down to our meal of cereals, fresh milk, and new laid eggs from the nearby farm. Followed with generous helpings of toast and marmalade. Eager to resume her conversation as the meal ended Mrs Clarkson went on to say; "Your wife tells me you once lived in this neighbourhood, Mr Ashford. I do hope you'll enjoy your visit."

"Oh, I'm sure he will," my wife remarked, and begged to be excused from the table. Neither of us, wishing to divulge the nature of our visit.

Anxious to make an early start in the search for my mother, my wife and I left Mrs Clarkson's boarding house soon after breakfast. Informing her we would not be back, until late that evening. Hand in hand we arrived at the bus stop and waited, as a Green Line coach slithered to a halt in front of us. Scattering red and gold leaves in all directions. The vehicle's destination to Sutton via Merton, brought to mind the times I'd travelled this same route with mother, on weekend shopping trips.

Alighting from the bus on reaching the village of Merton, deep in the Surrey countryside, the spicy scent of new mown grass reached my nostrils. Partly hidden by horse chestnut trees, two rows of neatly painted houses caught my eye. Plainly visible among them, stood the house where my mother had lived. The sight of it took me back in time, to a bitterly cold morning in March of 1936. When as a seventeen year old radio operator, I was about to embark on my first sea voyage. A journey that took me half-way round the world, lasting over two years.

Saying our goodbye's, I remembered seeing a look of sadness on mother's face turn to alarm, as I begged of her to tell me where my sister was living. The hurt I felt when she refused my request, was nothing in comparison to the shock I received on my return from sea. She had disappeared, without a word of goodbye.

"Is this where you used to live?" my wife asked, a hint of sadness in her voice.

It was more than I could do to reply. I felt a lump in my throat, and a feeling of sadness came over me. I was back in time and the hurt of years ago returned, while I floated between what might have been and reality.

Feeling her hand on my sleeve, I turned to face my wife, and by the look on her face must have understood how I was feeling.

"Let's go dear," she said. "I don't think we've anything to gain by staying here."

Without a backward glance at the only home I'd known as a boy, I took my wife by the hand and set off in the opposite direction. Anxious to continue searching for my sister, I decided to pay a visit to the Council Offices where mother used to pay her rates. Lying in the shadow of a railway bridge spanning the main road, the office appeared to be much smaller, than it did in those far off days. It seeemed like only yesterday, that I played beneath it's huge archway as a young boy. Inside the office, the staff responded in a most helpful manner, to the many questions I put to them concerning my mother. But they gave me no information that might have helped me trace her whereabouts. Thanking them I made a few enquiries among the local shopkeepers in the village of Rose Hill where she was well known, but again drew a blank.

This was to be our last day in Wimbledon, and we realised that any further search for mother's whereabouts was like looking for a needle in a haystack. It was at this point I mentioned an aunt of mine living in the village of Downham, Kent, and suggested we visit the place. But my wife simply shook her head, saying;

"Yes dear, that was a long time ago. The person you are looking for, could be dead and gone for all we know."

I had to admit, too much water has passed under the bridge, and whatever chance I had of finding mother, was long gone.

"If she has survived the war years," said my wife. "She could be anywhere. We might just as well go back home, dear."

Victory in Europe.

During the early part of September 1944 all resistance to the Allied forces sweeping through Belgium and Holland had crumbled, our armies were now reported to be fighting on German soil. Desperate to stem the tide of war that had suddenly turned against him, Hitler retaliated by unleashing the first of a series of V-2 rockets on the city of London, in an all out attack of indiscriminate bombing. Elsewhere, advances were made on several fronts by Allied forces, who occupied the strategic city of Athens on mainland Greece.

The speed with which the Allies advanced across Europe was the subject of an urgent request to the United States for further shipments of war supplies, in support of our front line troops. With increased naval power, control of waters in and around the western approaches of Europe passed into Allied hands, and as a result the U-Boat menace slowly diminished. It was now adjudged unnecessary, to shepherd large convoys across the Atlantic. Instead, ships were given a combined sea and air escort for a period of only two days, which was considered to be sufficient.

Back home after an unsuccessful search for my mother in the south of England, it came as no surprise to find a letter from the Ministry of Shipping waiting for me. My leave had expired some two days earlier and as expected, I was asked to report back for duty. As usual my luck had run out for I was sent to join the S.S. Benbry, an old tramp steamer I'd sailed on before. This relic of yester-year offered little comfort to myself and those who'd sailed on her, on that never to be forgotten voyage across the North Atlantic in the winter of 1940.

Running head on into a cyclone we faced hurricane force winds, and fought for our very existence. Battered by mountainous seas that left her decks awash, all four of the vessel's lifeboats disintegrated, and like so much matchwood, were swept away. At one stage she stood on her beam ends, and almost capsized. Her maximum speed of six knots in calm seas, was of little use against the fury of a North Atlantic storm in mid-winter. But with the odds of surviving stacked against her, that floating heap of scrap iron with more moves than a limbo dancer, staggered on. Eventually limping into her home port of Liverpool, after leaving the Canadian Port of Halifax some twenty eight days earlier.

It was with a feeling of trepidation, I stepped aboard this heap of junk once again. Why I chose to do so, the Lord only knows. Suffice to say, old Creswell the ships Bo'sun whom I'd sailed with on this same vessel in 1940, encouraged me to stay, saying;

"Stick with her son, she's a stout old lady. She'll see you through, mark my words."

Taking the old seadog's advice I sailed in the Benbry for the next six months, along with the cockroaches and weevils who'd made it their home. During a period from late October of 1944 until early in May of 1945, the old tub carried thousands of tons of much needed war supplies from the U.S, to various ports along Europe's western seaboard. Approaching home waters in early May 1945, we were overjoyed to hear Germany had capitulated. Their humiliated and demoralized army forced to surrender on the eighth of May, 1945, brought an end to World War Two. Peace officially declared at one minute after the midnight hour on that day, sent a feeling of jubilation throughout the vessel. For me, however, the celebrations were short lived, as I paused for thought. In that brief moment, I remembered my comrades on the M.V.Waimarama who had made the supreme sacrifice, for a starving population on the beleagured island of Malta.

Not wishing to spoil the festive spirit the Captain chose to remind all on board, the cessation of hostilities did not come into force until after midnight. Therefore, none of us could afford to relax. Vigilance was necessary he insisted, if we were to come through unscathed. Late that evening I spoke with Cowdrey our navigation officer, who reckoned we'd make landfall within forty eight hours.

"I guess it's the last voyage this old tub will make," he grinned sardonically. "She's destined to return from whence she came, the scrap yard."

"What will Creswell, the old Bo'sun do?" I asked. "This heap of junk is his home."

"He's part and parcel of the blooming ship," laughed Cowdrey. "He'll have to be cut away from her."

It was now the end of May and summer had, it seemed, come early to England's northern hemisphere. Outlined beneath skies of blue on the eastern horizon, the City of Liverpool's cathedral spire bathed in bright morning sunshine, welcomed us home. Given advanced warning of our arrival, the pilot waited to board the vessel at the estuary of the river Mersey. Proceeding up river, familiar landmarks appeared. The huge dome of the Liver buildings and nearby Harbour Company offices on the city's waterfront, had come through the war unscathed.

In the background, the Cotton Exchange stood empty and forlorn, just a burnt out shell. Like many old buildings in the area, it had been torn apart during enemy air raids. Sailing past Liverpool's seven miles of docks, idle cranes and empty warehouses were the result of heavy losses suffered in our Merchant Fleet. Thankfully, the shadow of war hanging over our country for the past five years, with it's trail of wanton death and destruction, had now been lifted. With this in mind, I prepared to leave the rusting hulk that had been my home for the past six months, to spend a brief period of well-earned leave with my wife.

Saying goodbye to my fellow travellers aboard the S.S 'Benbry, I made a point of seeing old Creswell the ship's Bo'sun, whom I found sitting in his cabin staring into space. Rising from his chair he shook me warmly by the hand, saying;

"Well son, the old girl made it, just as I predicted."

A far away look in his eyes, the tough old seadog who many said joined the vessel when her keel was laid, shrugged his shoulders when I put the question to him; "What will you do, when the old tub is sent to the breaker's yard?"

Leaving him with his thoughts, I slipped down the ship's gangway into a waiting taxi that took me through Liverpool's Mersey Tunnel, to my home on the outskirts of Birkenhead. Driving along country roads with fields of ripened corn and quaint thatched roofed cottages, I arrived at the tiny village of Oxton. Where my wife waited, to welcome me back home.

Sandwiched between the river Mersey and the Dee, the village of Oxton lies on the Wirral Peninsular, accessible by way of the Mersey Tunnel, the Ferry, or by an underground system of trains running from Liverpool to Birkenhead. An alternative route to the area from outlying places on Merseyside and Cheshire, is the M.53 Motorway, running from north to south of the peninsular.

While on leave my wife and I journeyed to the City of Chester, no more than twenty minutes away by car. A visit to this ancient City of Roman Walls and timbered Tudor houses, and nearby beauty spots in North Wales, took up the greater part of my leave. All too soon I found myself at the shipping office in Liverpool reporting back for duty, and was promptly told to travel to London where I would join a ship on a special assignment.

Arriving at Tilbury docks I was taken on board the Royal Mail Steamer M.V. Highland Monarch, a vessel of about fifteen thousand tons with a top speed of sixteen knots, capable of accommodating several hundred passengers.

Among many rumours running rife on board the ship was her ultimate destination, which according to the galley wireless, was said to be the Middle East. Having spent much of my time at sea in this theatre of war, during the invasion of Italy, I had no desire to renew my acquaintance with Egypt's pyramids. Much less inhale a thousand and one obnoxious odours from wandering tribes of nomads and camel droppings, left to ferment along it's shores. It was with much foreboding, I prepared myself for whatever challenge lay ahead.

June 3rd dawned bright and sunny, although a slight breeze ruffled the murky waters of the River Thames. Aboard the M.V. Highland Monarch on that particular summer morning our destination was still the main topic of conversation, a sort of guessing game among the ship's crew, as she slipped away from her berth at London's Tilbury Dock and entered the river. Among many familiar sights missing along the Thames were the silver barrage balloons on their long thin wires, positioned at strategic points along the river in time of war to deter low flying enemy bombers. Passing Southend-on-Sea on our way to the Estuary, holiday makers sunning themselves on the pier looked on in silence as we sailed by. Rounding the North Foreland lightship into the North Sea, we set course for the English channel. Steaming at a steady fifteen knots in calm weather, Dover's white cliffs loomed up on our starboard hand. Tall and majestic they sat there, guarding the entrance to the Straits. In a never ending stream, ocean going freighters and coastwise vessels forced to sail in convoy throughout the war years were now free to ply their trade around British waters, without fear of attack from enemy aircraft or submarine. As darkness fell along Englands channel coast, a rare sight presented itself. Illuminations on pleasure beaches of seaside towns that for so long had been blacked-out, lit up the night sky.

Passing the Isles of Scilly at daybreak the Highland Monarch altered course toward Ushant on the French coast, northernmost point of the Bay of Biscay. Seeing the Red Ensign fluttering from the vessels stern, fishermen aboard a fleet of French trawlers waved excitedly. Free from German occupation their gratitude came to the fore with shouts of, Vive Angletere.

Well known for it's stormy weather the Bay of Biscay lay calm as a millpond, encouraging off duty members of the crew to bask in warm sunshine. Abreast of Cape Finistere my worst fears were realized when the vessel continued to hug the coastline along Spain and Portugal's western seaboard, down to the Straits of Gibraltar. Throughout the night hurried changes to the ship's course were carried out in order to avoid fouling the nets of inshore fishing fleets, an exercise the officer of the watch did not relish.

Within hailing distance of the Rock at break of day, the silhouettes of three naval vessel's patrolling the area, appeared on the far horizon. Picking up his binoculars Fullbright, the duty officer, stepped out onto the wing of the bridge and studied them closely.

"Oh it's just a couple of our naval craft returning to the Rock," was his nonchalant comment. Receiving no more than a grunt from the Captain, in response.

Passing through Gibraltar's narrow Straits into the Mediterranean later that morning, one viewed the Rock in all it's glory; a formidable obstacle for any opposing enemy to overcome. Overshadowing the landscape for miles around dwarfing the City of Gibraltar and Spanish border town of La Linea, stands Gibraltar's massive Rock. A giant of nature, acknowledged as guardian of the Western entrance to the Mediterranean Sea. Steaming at a comfortable speed of fifteen knots the sun grew hotter by the day, with temperatures soaring well over one hundred degrees at midday. Approaching the Island of Malta, strong southerly winds blowing from the direction of the Libyan Desert into the Mediterranean, caused no more than a ripple on the sea's glassy surface, as the vessel continued her steady progess toward Port Said.

Strategically placed between Gibraltar to the west and the Egytian port of Alexandria to the east, the island fortress of Malta, was a thorn in the side of would-be German invaders, throughout five long years of World War Two. Appearing as no more than a dark smudge on the horizon one became aware of the Suez Canal's proximity, long before catching sight of this gateway to the east. A pungent aroma of Oriental spices and Camel dung, savaging the nostrils. Our arrival signalled a spontaneous movement by advance parties of West Indian soldiers stationed in the area, who were ordered to board the ship. Before nightfall a further compliment of fifteen hundred of their number had embarked on board the M.V. Highland Monarch, awaiting transportation to their respective homes around the Carribean Islands. Could this I wondered, be the special assignment we had been chosen to carry out. Was there really any need for all the secrecy in performing such a task, in a cloak and dagger exercise.

If indeed our hasty departure from London was merely to transport West Indian troops back to their homeland from the Middle East, it turned out to be a most enjoyable experience. As darkness fell each night we had nothing more to contend with than to listen to a harmonizing of native voices as they sang of home, keeping time with their special kind of bongo music. So much easier on the ears, than the horrific rumble of explosions, as ships were torpedoed and sunk, a daily occurrence throughout five years of war. Our leisurely sojourn around these sun-kissed tropical islands, lasted but three weeks. During which time, batches of West Indian soldiers were discharged ashore to their homeland in Barbados, Trinidad, Bahamas, Antigua, and St.Lucia. At Belize the capital of British Honduras in Central America, our main contingent of troops disembarked.

Believing our mission was completed and we were about to return to home to England, a wave of disappointment ran through the ship when we received orders to proceed south to Buenos Aires, capital of Argentina. An air of mystery surrounded this latest order. Why should we be visiting a country who stabbed us in the back, aiding and abetting our enemy at the outset of World War Two, when things looked black. Arriving at Rio de la Plata the estuary between Argentina and Uruguay, silhouettes of two large naval vessels were seen cruising up and down on the far horizon. Anxious to discover their nationality, Vicary, the ship's third officer, clapped a telescope to his eye. Studying them for a moment he lowered the eyeglass and turned toward Captain Richards standing nearby;

"Looks like the Argentine Navy is having a day out," he scoffed.

Making no response, the Captain left the duty officer standing on the port wing of the bridge, and entered the chart room. Taking a map from the pidgeon hole he spread it out on the table, studying it intensely. Entering the estuary we picked up the pilot and continued our journey up river, berthing close to the shopping centre in Buenos Aires. Within a matter of minutes rolls of heavy wire netting and lengths of stout timbers were loaded on board, and placed at various points around the ship's deck. Shortly after midday carpenters arrived on the ship, and fenced off sections around the vessels second class passenger accomodation. It was at this point the mystery deepened; "What on earth is going on," was the question on everyone's lips.

Rumours aboard the M.V Highland Monarch were now at fever pitch, ranging from the sublime to the ridiculous. At sunrise the following morning the arrival of a British Naval destroyer caused more confusion to a puzzled ship's crew, when a compliment of marines was seen to leave the naval vessel and board our ship. While the local populace were enjoying their daily siesta, several coaches arrived alongside the ship, escorted by a sizeable number of local gendarmerie. Under the watchful eye of these gun-totting senors, the occupants of the coaches were quickly shepherded on board. Once again everyone was left wondering who these people could be, as the vessel made ready to leave port. Our mysterious passengers confined in wire cages on the second class deck were at first thought to be illegal immigrants from the U.K, but the mystery was solved some hours later when we were informed they were the crew of the notorious German Battleship, Admiral Graf Spee. Scuttled on orders from Hitler, when cornered by the British Navy on the thirteenth of December 1939, during the Battle of the River Plate.

Under cover of darkness the Highland Monarch slipped out of Buenos Aires harbour, our naval escort following some way astern. Outside international waters we rendezvoused with the

Royal Naval cruisers Ajax and Achilles, who played an important part in the sinking of the German battleship, and now had the task of escorting the prisoners back from whence they came. Faced with a shortage of fuel oil, the vessel called at Freetown Sierra Leone on the West African coast. Our arrival was seen to attract a gathering of natives to the ship, anxious to sell their bananas, oranges and limes.

Refuelling took place until well after dark when hordes of mosquitoes and other nocturnal creatures buzzing around, refused to leave us in peace. Long before dawn's early light streaked across the far horizon to herald a new day, the M.V. Highland Monarch and her escorting destoyer were well out to sea. Sierra Leone's palm fringed coastline of dense green jungle had all but faded from view as the morning sun, appearing as a ball of orange fire, began it's heavenward climb. With little wind other than that produced by the speed of the ship itself on a sea of glass, the sweltering heat of an equatorial day became unbearable. Behind a barrier of chain link fencing, separating them from the rest of ship's company, a sullen faced group of Germans looked on as seamen hosed down the vessel's wooden decks. Regular sluicing was maintained during the heat of the day, in an effort to cool fast melting seams of tar. Seeking cover from the sun in order to escape it's sweltering heat of one hundred and twenty degrees, I heaved a sigh of relief when the last vestige of Africa's fly blown continent slipped below the horizon astern of us.

Weather-wise the temperature cooled off considerably as the ship arrived off the Portugese coast, Lisbon our next port of call being a short distance away. Rubbing his hands together gleefully Conroy, a young seaman barely out of his teens, gave old Dobson the ship's Bo'sun a knowing wink.

"I guess wer'e O.K for a leg up ashore tonight," he grinned.

Dobson smiled sardonically. "Don't count on it son, we might only be here for a short while," he replied.

"Aw c'mon boss don't be a spoil sport," Conroy chided. "I suppose the lead has run out of your pencil," he teased.

"It's a pity you dont use your energy up scrubbing the decks" Dobson sneered, turning his back on the cocky young fellow.

A call for all hands to stand by stations as we entered port, put paid to further discussion between the two. At the mouth of the River Tagus which spirals eastward right across Portugal, we picked up our pilot. Much to the disappointment of many in the ship's company hoping for a spell of shore leave, the vessel lay at anchor inside the harbour. Seamen Conroy, who felt sure the ship would berth alongside the wharf, cursed his luck. His well-laid plans of spending the night ashore locked in the arms of some amorous Portugese maiden in the city's red light district, no more than a dream.

Sneaking off to his quarters on the afterdeck Conroy cursed his captain, and lay on his bunk gazing toward the shore, through the open porthole of his cabin. Letting off a stream of abuse he accused the pilot and ship's captain of being reponsible for his misfortune in having to remain on board, and eventually fell asleep dreaming of what might have been. Midway through an imaginary tete-a-tete with a young senorita, he was wakened by the Bosun bellowing in his ear; "C'mon me lad, let's be having you."

Conroy rubbed the sleep from his eyes, and crawled out of his bunk. Shading his face from the glare of the afternoon sun as he stepped out on the open deck, he found old Dobson the ship's Bo'sun, waiting for him. Grinning from ear to ear like a Cheshire cat he placed a friendly arm around Conroy's shoulder, and teasing him, said:

"There'll be no dipping yer wick tonight son, our passengers have just arrived. As soon as they've embarked we'll be on our way."

Turning a deaf ear to the Bo'son's remark, Conroy seized the mooring rope passed up to him from a launch arriving alongside the vessel. Securing it to a nearby bollard, he sauntered off towards the accomodation ladder. Sullen faced he watched as members of the German Legation in Lisbon who were being repatriated, struggle up the ladder with their luggage. Cursing them under his breath he refused to lend a hand, leaving them to get on board as best they could. As soon as the last of our German deportees were safely on board, the Highland Monarch slipped from the harbour, rendezvouing with an escorting destroyer out at sea. Heading in a northerly direction the vessel was forced to alter course several times during the hours of darkness, to avoid the nets of Portugese sardine fishermen, stretched out in never- ending lines along the coast.

Passing Cape Finisterre on a warm sunny morning in late July we entered the Bay of Biscay, which can be violent at times, but now appeared as flat as a mill pond with hardly a ripple on it's surface. Some twenty-four hours was to pass before we sighted the island of Ushant on the French coast, and altering course entered the English Channel. Picking our way passed numerous ships of all shapes and sizes, something we had not seen for many years, we set course for Dover. Abreast of Dover's White Cliffs we entered the North Sea steering a course for the Elbe estuary and the City of Hamburg, or what remained of it, following months of sustained air-raids by the Allied Forces.

At the mouth of the Elbe the vessel slowed down long enough to pick up a pilot, and proceeded on her way up river. Lining up on either side of the ship's deck the erstwhile crew from the sunken German Battleship, Admiral Graff Spee, looked on in horror, at unbeliveable scenes of utter destruction to their homeland. Proceeding on up river toward the port of Hamburg, the M.V. Highland Monarch weaved her way in and out of the wreckage of sunken vessels lying in her path, along an eighty five mile stretch of the river Elbe. With uncanny skill on the part of the pilot overcoming such hazzards, our arrival at the port of Hamburg was greeted by a wall of silence.

Unlike in Hitler's glory days, there was no brass band to welcome the crew of the German battleship, Graf Spee, who slipped ashore unnoticed as soon as the vessel berthed. Scenes of total destruction were in evidence wherever one chose to turn.

317

People wandered aimlessly around bomb scarred streets in a hopeless search for food, that simply did not exist. With such utter desolation staring you in the face you could not but feel sad to see ill-clad children attempting to sneak on board, looking for scraps of food from the ship's garbage bins. I was more than relieved to leave this shattered city of rubble, choosing instead to remember the proud city of Hamburg in happier times.

Disembarking the last of our disillusioned German prisoners ashore, the M.V. Highland Monarch having completed her mission, faced the difficult task of navigating past the remnants of sunken vessels on the river Elbe once again. Reaching the North Sea we set sail for England.

As in those far off days before the outbreak of World War Two, the North Sea was the scene of non-stop activity, fishing trawlers from Hull and Grimsby exchanging greetings with colliers sailing out of the Tyne. Ocean going freighters and passenger liners sailed the seven seas as before free to come and go unhindered, without fear of being torn asunder by enemy U-Boats or dive bombers. Counting myself one of the luckiest among my seafaring comrades to have survived those dark days of war, a prayer of thanks escaped my lips when my ship sailed up the broad reaches of the River Mersey. Entering the port of Liverpool with it's seven mile stretch of docks one cannot but admire the unmistakeable city skyline, the twin towers of the Liver Buildings and the waterfront offices of the Mersey Docks and Harbour Company most prominent.

Abreast of Gladstone Dock, lying at the north end of the city's dock system, the Highland Monarch was taken in tow by tugs from the Alexander Towing Company, who shepherded the vessel into her berth. Having already made up my mind this would be my final voyage to sea now the war was over, I was most anxious to sign off the ship and be on my way home. As soon as the berthing of the ship had been completed I wasted no time in collecting my belongings, said a hurried goodbye to my friends, and hopped into a waiting taxi. Unable to inform my wife I was on the way home, the look on her face when seeing me on her doorstep unannounced, was one of sheer delight.

"Oh Charles," she murmered as we embraced, "its so nice to have you back home."

"Hopefully this time will be for good" I replied, "I've no intention of going to sea again, if I can help it."

"Oh, that will be wonderful dear" she cried, holding me tight, "but what will you do?"

"Let's go in the house," I said, taking her by the hand.

"Then I'll tell you what I have in mind."

Over a cup of tea I told her I'd been promised a job with the Mersey Docks and Harbour Company following a visit to their office in Liverpool, prior to leaving on my last voyage. The gentleman who interviewed me said I was to report to him on my return, providing I was still in the same frame of mind.

"But what about your leave, dear," my wife asked. "You have a couple of weeks coming to you?"

"If I'm offered the job, I'm quite prepared to sacrifice whatever leave is due," I told her.

At the end of August 1948, I received my discharge papers from the Merchant Service. Taking a copy of the document with me I visited the Harbour office, and was informed a vacancy existed at the Huskisson Dock, in the North End of Liverpool. Although I lived some distance away from the place, I told the Harbour Master I was quite prepared to travel, if given the job. Signing an agreement to abide by the Company's rules and regulations, I was asked to report for duty to the Dockmaster at 8am on the Monday morning. Hurrying home I gave the news to my wife, who was overjoyed to hear I'd given up my career at sea, and taken up a permanent job ashore.

My initial two week period of training was spent at the Huskisson system of locks, which lay to the north end of the city's water front. I took to my new job like a duck takes to water, and was shown how to operate the hydraulic machinery to open and close the lock gates. Small shallow drafted vessel's such as barges and coasters sailed in and out of the system each day, four hours before and four hours after high water. While large ocean going cargo freighters moved in and out of the dock system for a limited time, prior to high water. Periods of duty were made up of three shifts, of eight hours duration. Working on a rota system, the hours worked were similar to those carried out at sea.

Engrossed in my work I hardly noticed the passing of time, until I was ordered to fill a vacancy at the company's Alfred dock system across the river in Birkenhead. Saying goodbye to the many friends I'd worked with over the past five years, I reported for duty at the Alfred Dockmaster's Office, and was promptly placed on the night shift. Stationed at the east end of the eighty foot lock adjacent to the river on a bitterly cold night in late November, my first week of duty was spent pacing up and down in an effort to keep warm. I was however to spend many a cold winter's night stationed out on that same waterfront during the next twenty years at the Alfred Dock. Living reasonably close to my work was a great advantage, whereas working at the Huskisson system of docks in Liverpool, was time consuming and expensive.

I settled into my job as an established member of the Harbour Company, and now had an opportunity to renew the search for my mother. Spending alternate summer holidays in the Surrey area where she used to live, my wife and I would wander around her old haunts in an effort to find her. Right up to the time my daughter Susan was born in 1955, every other year of our annual summer holiday was spent combing the same old ground over and over again, but it was like looking for the proverbial needle in a haystack. Driven on by a desire to see my sister Catherine I had first to find my mother, knowing she was the only person holding the key to her whereabouts. But as elusive as ever she had cleverly covered her tracks leaving no trace of her movements. Houdini could not have done better. Undaunted by these setbacks I decided to try another route in tracing this elusive mother of mine and placed an advert in a couple of the Sunday newspapers, on the off-chance someone in this land of our's might read it and get in touch with me. Time and time again failure stared me in the face and as the years rolled by, that tiny spark of hope still burned within me, that some day my sister and I might meet.

During my twenty-fifth year of service with the Harbour Company I gained promotion to Marine Supervisor, a position that carried a great deal of responsibility. Absorbed in my work I enjoyed life to the full with my family, which left little time to dwell on the pain and heartache caused by mother's determination to keep my sister and I apart. Knowing little about her other than she was a few years younger than me, I would often think of her and wonder where she was. Had she managed to survive the perils of World War Two. Was she married and like me happy. A thousand and one thoughts would flash through my mind, whilst allowing myself to drift into a world of make-belief. Day-dreaming, I would in my mind's eye, imagine her looking just like her mother who when young, was very beautiful, but all too soon those idle moments that time itself could not erase, would drift away, then I'd find myself back to stark reality.

Midway through my thirtieth year of service with the Harbour Company, a further step up the promotion ladder was within my grasp, when an old war injury put paid to my career. Going to the aid of one of my men who was struggling to heave a ship's mooring rope ashore I felt a searing pain in my back and found I was unable to walk, and had to be taken home in an ambulance. My family doctor came to the house and examined me the following day but could do little other than prescribe a course of painkillers, and arrange for me to visit a specialist. His report to my employer advised them I was suffering from a damaged vertebrae in the lower half of my back, and would be unfit for work in the forseeable future.

Following a six month period of sick leave, I was fitted with a corset by the physiotherapist at the hospital, which enabled me to walk again. Shortly after, I received a letter from the Harbour Office in Liverpool requesting I attend an interview with a company representative. Concerned for my future welfare, the company felt it best that I be placed on the retirement list. A handsome amount in severance pay being awarded to me in respect of my years of service with them, plus a monthly pension.

My employment with the Mersey Docks and Harbour Company would be terminated, the gentleman informed me, as from the 30th of June 1976. Signing the necessary documents severing my service with the company I thanked the gentleman, and hurried home to give my wife the news. I returned to the dock office a couple of days later to pick up some personal belongings and say goodbye to my many friends, and left without a backward glance. So here I was aged fifty-seven, being put out to grass because of an old war injury. For this, I was awarded a full disability pension of approximately five pounds a week by the British government in 1943, who saw fit to take it from me when I patriotically volunteered to go back to sea.

In the months following my early retirement I received a course of physiotherapy, which enabled me move about with greater freedom. Far from allowing the grass to grow under my feet, I carried out minor repairs to the lovely home I shared with my wife, in the Cheshire countryside. Soon I was fit enough to travel wherever I pleased, and made arrangements for us to spend a two month winter holiday basking in Mediterranean sunshine, on the beautiful Spanish Island of Majorca. On a cold wet morning in January of 1979 my wife and I boarded a plane at Manchester airport, and took off to our island in the sun. Winging our way over the snow capped mountains of the Pyrenees, separating France from the Iberian Peninsular, we arrived some two hours later at Palma the island's capital, in blazing sunshine. Hurriedly divesting our winter woolies on leaving the aircraft, a coach arrived to whisk us away to our hotel.

No more than a stone's throw from the beach, the Riu Bravo a four star hotel, had everything we needed. Air conditioned rooms with balcony facing the sea, an indoor swimming pool and restaurant. Buffet styled meals were served at breakfast from eight to ten a.m and dinner from seven to nine p.m, allowing guests time throughout the day to explore the island. Taking full advantage of the opportunity my wife and I visited many wonderful sites the island of Majorca had to offer, such as the pearl and leather factories and the Caves of Drac. In between trips around the island much of our time was spent lazing in the sun, listening to the gentle motion of warm Atlantic waters lapping the sun-kissed beach. All too soon our time on this sun-drenched paradise isle ran out, and before long we found ourselves back at Manchester's wet and windy airport.

Having enjoyed ourselves so much we returned to sample the good life on the nearby island's of Ibiza and Minorca, taking our daughter's family with us for their summer holidays. As a special treat for my wife who's one wish was to visit America, my daughter and I arranged for her to spend our next holiday at Fort Lauderdale in Florida, on her birthday in May of the following year. Leaving a watery sun trying to force it's way past heavy rain clouds at Manchester Airport, we boarded a Laker Airways flight, and flew off into the wide blue yonder. Arriving at Miami Airport, as dusk was falling. The heat outside was unbelievable, as we left the cool atmosphere inside the aircraft and hurried into an air-conditioned arrivals lounge, where we cleared customs and were taken to Stouffer's beachside hotel in Fort Lauderdale.

Shortly after settling into our hotel we visited one of the many car hire companies and booked a vehicle to carry five of us in comfort, then set about planning our visit to Disney Land. Rising early we took breakfast at a nearby restaurant and heading onto a motorway known as the turnpike, drove leisurely along in the direction of Orlando. From an assortment of motels along the way advertising vacancies, we chose one named Larson's Lodge, with a swimming pool and sauna, which offered it's residents a free breakfast. Booking in for our four-day stay we had a base to work from, then headed for Disney Land.

Aboard a paddle steamer, taking us across to the Magic Kingdom, my wife sat starry eyed, and listened to the haunting melody of "When you wish upon a Star." A truly unforgettable moment, in her life. She sat there as though back in childhood days, taking in scenes she had only read about, never imagining for a moment her dream of a lifetime would come true. As is often said, nothing is forever. It was time for us to leave Disney's world of make-believe and return home, taking with us memories of a holiday we were to enjoy many times in the years to come. Arriving at Manchester Airport, where believe it or not the sun was cracking the flagstones so to speak, we picked up our car and headed home. With nothing to do but plan for our next winter holiday in the sun.

It was during our holiday on the Spanish island of Majorca in the winter of 1988 my wife fell ill, and we were obliged to return home to seek medical treatment for her, not wishing to trust the diagnosis of the local physican. Some two days later she visited her family doctor, who diagnosed her problem as an irritable colon. For a time the medication helped to ease the pain from which she suffered, whilst we continued to enjoy both summer and winter holidays on the Mediterranean and Canary Islands, with alternative jaunts to Florida in the U.S.A.

Booked to fly off to the Canary Islands on a winter's morning in March of 1990, my world fell apart when my wife was suddenly taken ill and admitted to the local hospital. Undergoing a series of tests covering a period of five weeks, she waited for the specialist's report. At her bedside on that particular morning I sat watching the white coated figure of the hospital's resident doctor talk with several patients in the ward, accompanied by the sister-in-charge.

"Have my results come through, Doctor?" my wife asked him, as he approached her bed.

He stood in silence for what seemed an eternity, then in a voice barely audible, replied; "I'm sorry Mrs. Ashford, there is nothing we can do for you."

Outwardly calm, my wife bravely asked; "How long do I have, doctor?"

Somewhat reluctant to answer he shrugged his shoulders in a gesture of hopelessness, saying; "It's in the hands of the Lord, Mrs Ashford. It could be days, weeks, or months."

As I listened to the doctor's diagnosis, the strength drained from my body, and as the tears ran down my cheeks unchecked, there was nothing I could do to comfort her. I sat there immobile staring into space, unaware the doctor had already left my wife's bedside, until I felt someone touch me on the shoulder. Turning round I found myself face to face with a young nurse, and noticed the look of compassion in her eyes.

"Doctor would like to see you in his office, Mr Ashford," she said in a hushed voice. "Would you please come with me."

Leaving my wife's bedside I followed her from the ward, and was ushered into the doctor's office. Motioning me to be seated he finished wrapping a small package before handing it to me, saying; "This is your wife's medication Mr Ashford, make sure she takes it each day as directed. There will also be frequent visits made to her at home by a member of the McMillan Nursing Order, who will attend to all her needs."

Fighting back the tears I somehow managed to put on a brave face, while inside me my stomach turned cartwheels. Thanking the doctor for his kindness I left the office and returned to collect my wife from the ward, and took her home.

A change of environment seemed to work wonders for her; showing a slight improvement in her state of health. Whether it was due to the homely atmosphere or the medication I could not be sure, suffice to say within a few days she was her old self again enjoying life as before. The transformation was simply remarkable, which led me to ask myself, could the wrong diagnosis have been made. Her condition continued to improve with each passing day. Eventually she was able to accompany me on shopping trips, as the weather began to warm up a little with the approach of spring. Arriving a little earlier than usual that year the sun's warmth encouraged the forsythia to leave it's winter retreat, displaying brilliant yellow blossom. In parks and gardens, crocus, snowdrops and daffodils peeped from their earth brown nurseries, exhibiting a riot of colour.

Halfway into the month of April, Easter a special time of the year for us both, was almost upon us and as usual, we were treated to spells of sunshine with intermittent showers. Memories of our first meeting some forty-six years ealier back in 1943, were always a cause for celebration. Still as beautiful as she was on our first date all those many years ago, when I presented her with a bouquet of yellow tulips, the march of time had treated her kindly. She was such a dainty young thing: slim of build, with auburn hair and a pair of laughing brown eyes. Our friendship blossomed into romance some months after our first meeting, resulting in marriage the following year, on her birthday, the first of May. That we would be suddenly torn apart came as a terrible blow. I could not bear the thought of losing her. Yet somehow sensing there was no escape from the illness ravaging her body and with the time left to us all too short, I was unprepared to face the inevitable when it came.

With the passing of time her condition worsened and began to take it's toll, tiny furrows appeared on her temple, but the laughing brown eyes never wavered. Her indomitable spirit always evident, refused to succumb to her incurable illness. In the weeks since leaving hospital I was taken by surprise, with the speed of her remarkable recovery. Brushing aside so many disappointments that we as mere mortals, on planet earth, grappled with throughout our lives, she had no fear of tomorrow's unknown. Accepting with dignity, whatever lay ahead. At peace with herself and living life to the full, her radiant smile and an outward calm emanating from her person gave little sign if any, our time together would be short-lived.

A time of Sorrow.

Whatever time the good Lord chose to allow us, we sought to enjoy each precious moment at our caravan home on the beautiful island of Anglesey. Driving along the North Wales coast road enroute to our enchanted hideaway one passes villages and white-washed cottages, nestling amid the green hills. From the Welsh mainland we crossed Telford's suspension bridge over the Menai Straits, on to the Isle of Anglesey. A short distance from the town of Beaumaris, the island's capital, lay our holiday home near the village of Penmon. From the Coastguard Station at Black Point, one has a bird's eye view of Puffin island, lying less than a mile from the shore.

Strolling along a deserted beach that evening, a gathering of sea birds wheeling around in the clear blue sky overhead, caught our attention. Shadowing shoals of mackerel pursuing a large school of whitebait on the incoming tide, they watched and waited as the hunters circled around in a frenzy gorging themselves. Then all too soon the hunters became the hunted, as flocks of herring gulls swooped in for the kill.

Recognized as a former stronghold of the Druids whose cult was stamped out by the Romans in A.D.61, the Isle of Anglesey carries a stark reminder of their presence. Running through the centre of the island's seaport town of Holyhead, the remains of a high walled Roman fort stands to this day. Sailing from the harbour of Holyhead throughout the summer months, local passenger sevices run to the U.K, Ireland, and the Isle of Man, carrying thousands of tourists to roam at will around the island. The island's rugged coastline with mile after mile of sheer cliffs and dangerous reefs has claimed hundreds of ships that foundered there, in south-westerly gales during the winter months. Elsewhere on the island largely given over to heathland and rough pasture, smallholders are content to rear pigs, black cattle and geese. Sturdily built whitewashed farmhouses of rough-hewn stone in which the local people live, are often buffeted unmercifully by howling gales, sweeping in from the Irish Sea.

As with most towns and villages in North Wales, Sunday is kept strictly as a day of observance, with young and old in the ancient town of Beaumaris attending chapel. Although not of the same denomination as the local people, who are for the most part Welsh Methodist, my wife, an ardent churchgoer, insisted on attending the Sunday morning service with them. Since in many communities throughout the area the church is, and always has been apart from anything else a storehouse of information and local gossip, I felt a reluctance to enter it's hallowed portals. Understandably, our entrance into their holy of holies was a signal for the tiny congregation to turn their heads as one, and gaze suspiciously at the intruders in their midst. Within such an independent and close-knit community, strangers arriving in town were tolerated with a certain amount of caution. Nevertheless, one could forgive their peculiar behaviour and offhanded attitude to outsiders, when listening to the beautiful voices of their church choir raised in song. Echoing throughout the hills and valleys of this Welsh countryside, their lilting refrains would charm the birds from the tree tops.

Five months had elapsed since we took our leave of the hospital in the town of Birkenhead, to spend time at our holiday home on the Isle of Anglesey in North Wales, when my wife was informed there was nothing they could do for her. This allowed us for the time being at least, to forget the dark cloud hanging over our heads. In the lovely Welsh village of Penmon an abundance of early spring colour had no sooner faded from view, before summer's wild flowers began to appear, covering banks and hedgerows throughout country lanes. Passing village gardens where neatly clipped lawns were bordered by beds of geraniums, and edged with blue and white lobelia, one caught the heady perfume of roses in the morning air. Appearing high above the countryside's green, brown, and summer-gold patchwork landscape, distant Holyhead Mountain the islands highest point, rises to a height of 720 feet.

Enjoying days of endless sunshine, we chose to wander hand in hand along the island's country lanes and sandy beaches. Combing a rocky shoreline we discovered tiny coves echoing to the sound of the inrushing tide, sweeping past banks of sea-washed shingle. Changing direction we wandered through dense woods within sight of elegant old Tudor-style houses along Anglesey's southern shore, where the Menai Straits separates the island from the Welsh mainland.

Nearing the end of our second month on this wild and beautiful island, I noted a gradual change in my wife's health. Although tanned by the sun her face appeared pale and drawn, but it was her loss of appetite that caused me the greatest concern. Helpless to alleviate the awful pain and suffering she endured, other than give her medication, she steadfastly refused to allow me to take her back home.

Sadly our time together on this charming island, was suddenly cut short. Overcome with fatigue during one of our daily walks, I succeeded in getting my wife back to our caravan home, where she collapsed exhausted on the settee. Alarmed by this sudden decline in her well-being, a need for us to return home immediately was of the utmost importance. Fighting our way through dense traffic in and around the town of Bangor, during the midday rush hour, was an absolute nightmare. Skirting seaside towns Conway, Colwyn Bay, and Llandudno to avoid being caught in traffic hold-ups, enabled us to reach our home in the village of Oxton by nightfall, where my daughter Susan waited to meet us.

"Is everything alright Dad?" she asked, a worried look on her face.

"Your mother's very ill dear" I gasped, holding the car door open. "You'll have to help me into the house with her, she's hardly able to walk."

Thoroughly exhausted by the long journey, and extremely weak with the illness from which she suffered, between us my daughter and I carried her gently upstairs to bed. Making her as comfortable as possible I waited at the bedside for a while until she had dozed off, then left her sleeping peacefully to return downstairs. In the lounge I sat talking with my daughter for a while and decided there was little we could do at this late hour of the day, as the doctor's surgery had long finished.

"Try not to worry Dad" she whispered, taking her leave. "Give me a call if you need me."

I heard the front door close behind her, and watched from the lounge window as she disappeared from view. Finding myself all alone I felt as though I'd suddenly been transported from light into darkness, leaving our island paradise to face the unknown. Drained both mentally and physically from the long journey home I crept quietly upstairs, before much needed sleep overwhelmed me. Careful lest I disturb my wife who now slept soundly, I slipped into an adjoining room. Leaving the door ajar I undressed in total darkness and literally fell into bed, seizing the opportunity to close my eyes and snatch a few hours rest. But sleep would not come, I just lay there listening to the sound of laboured breathing from my wife's room. Tossing and turning well into the small hours, I finally dropped off into a fitful sleep.

Waking long after the sun had soared high into the morning sky, I withdrew my bedroom curtains and peered out. It was a beautiful summer's day, the scent of orange blossom drifting up from the garden below filled the morning air. From the branches of a nearby horse chestnut tree the trill of a blackbird drifted through the open window of my room, and as if in answer to it's tunefull song, the bells in the village church struck the hour of eight. Worried lest the noise disturbed my wife who lay fast asleep in the next room, I closed my bedroom window, and peeped in on her.

Her heavy breathing, and poor state of health, worried me greatly. For a while, I stood gazing down at the pain-wracked face of the woman I loved, with a longing to help her in her hour of need. Helpless to do so, I became angry with myself for feeling so useless, and tip-toed quietly downstairs into the kitchen below. Closing the door behind me, I busied myself preparing breakfast. Moving silently across the hall, a sudden cry of pain sent me rushing to my wife's aid. At the top of the stairs, I gazed in horror as I looked toward the bathroom and saw her emaciated body, lying on the floor in a crumpled heap. She lay unconscious. My first thought was to gather her up in my arms, but fearing complications might set in, I hesitated to do so. Instead I placed a pillow beneath her head and covered her with a blanket in an effort to keep her warm. Then phoned for the doctor's help.

Arriving at the house he examined her, and within a short space of time, announced: "Your wife must go to hospital, immediately."

Between the doctor and myself, we lifted her gently from the bathroom floor and carried her into the bedroom, where she slowly regained consciousness. Pale and drawn she gazed at me through pain filled eyes, and whispered;

"Don't worry dear, I'm going to be alright."

Sitting by her side I could not but admire the courageous manner in which she made light of a life threatening disease, in her weakened state.

"Dear Lord" I murmured to myself; "if only what she says, were true."

The mournful sound of an ambulance siren could be heard long before the vehicle arrived at the house, where with amazing speed and efficiency, she was quickly transferred to the local hospital at Arrowe Park. On my own, albeit surrounded by a sea of loneliness, I remained by the window, unable to take my eyes off the vehicle until it was out of sight. Then sinking to my knees I prayed to the Lord, for her safekeeping.

"Was this to be the end," I kept asking myself? "Did the good Lord spare me from certain death those many years ago, to suffer a catastrophe such as this. Had he seen fit to desert me in my hour of need?"

Swirling emotions careered subconciously through my mind, leaving me in a state of utter confusion. Tears I'd forcibly withheld for so long began to fall unashamedly, when in the midst of my prayer an outward feeling of calm descended upon me. It's purpose, to leave me at peace with the world once again. Rising unsteadily from the bedside where my wife had been lying, I returned downstairs to the lounge, and telephoned my daughter.

"Your mother was taken to Arrowe Park Hospital a short time ago dear," I told her.

A note of alarm in her voice, she gasped; "Why, what has happened Dad?"

"I was in the kitchen preparing the breafast and heard your mother moving about in her bedroom. There was an anguished cry of pain, then all was silent. Hurrying up the stairs, I found her unconscious on the bathroom floor. But don't worry dear, she's in good hands" I said, "there was nothing more I could have done for her. We must call at the hospital to see her, so I'll come and pick you up as soon as I can."

Before I'd set foot in my daughter's driveway, the front door opened and my granddaughter Stacey, ran to meet me.

"Oh Grandad, is my Nana alright. She's not going to die, is she?" the child asked.

Fighting back tears, I held her hand whilst trying to comfort her. Knowing it was far from the truth, I did what I could to allay her fears, saying; "Your Nana's going to be alright, my dear."

Willing myself to believe what I was saying to Stacey, I knew in my heart of hearts, the end was near. But as a drowning person clings to a straw, deep within me a spark of hope remained, that my wife might somehow recover. Refusing to believe otherwise, I was in all honesty afraid to face the truth, when accompanied by my daughter to the hospital. Although the day was bright and sunny it could have been mid-winter for all I cared, as we sped along the motorway. My thoughts were for the woman I loved.

Surrounded by a sea of green in our local park, the hospital looked cold and uninviting. As I stepped inside, a strong smell of disinfectant assailed my nostrils.

"Could I see Mrs Ashford?" I asked the young nurse who came to meet me.

"She is under sedation and sleeping at the moment, but you may go in," she said. "You'll find her down the corridor, in ward two."

Curtains partly drawn inside the room to keep out the morning sun, did nothing to improve the cold and cheerless appearance of the place. My daughter and I walked to the far corner of the ward where my wife lay, and together we sat in silence at her bedside. Helpless to comfort her, I watched the pale face twitch spasmodically, every time the pain surged through her weakened body. As I took her hand in mine, the eyelids fluttered and, misty-eyed, she looked up at the ceiling. Turning toward my daughter and I sitting at her bedside, a smile of recognition spread across the beautiful face that looked gaunt to the point of being bony, now ravaged by an incurable disease. For an instant her eyes remained focused on the two of us, then slowly closed. Surrendering to the effects of a pain killing sedative, administered some time earlier. Numb with grief I was on the point of leaving but hesitated, when my daughter seemed reluctant to move away from her mother's bedside.

"There is nothing more we can do, dear," I whispered;

"Shall we go home.?"

Rising from the chair my daughter stretched her aching limbs, and placing an arm around my shoulder to comfort me, we left the hospital together and stepped out into the morning sunshine. Fear, bordering on panic, gripped me, as I walked over to my car. I felt as if a part of me, had been torn away. Although the day was hot, when sitting in the car, I began to shiver, and found it hard to concentrate on the road ahead. Some twenty minutes later we arrived back at my daughter's house, where my granddaughter threw her arms around me, and asked; "Is my Nana alright, Grandad?"

As the tears threatened to cascade down my cheeks, I whispered: "The Lord is watching over her."

Taking leave of my daughter that morning I noted the sky was suddenly overcast, and storm clouds rolled in. Flashes of lightning swept across a darkening sky, as peals of distant thunder drew ever closer, bringing rain in it's wake. The downpour lashed against the windscreen of my car as I drove home along the motorway, forcing the wipers to work overtime. As the storm progressed the wind increased in velocity, tending to make driving difficult. No sooner had I reached home and stepped inside my front door, the telephone started ringing. Lifting the receiver from it's cradle, my hurried "Hello" was answered by a young lady.

"May I speak with Mr Ashford?" she asked.

There was something in the tone of her voice that caused my body to stiffen. "Why, yes, I'm Mr Ashford, I replied" rather hurriedly, "what can I do for you?"

"This is Arrowe Park hospital calling you, sir," was her response. Which startled me.

Fearing the worst I interrupted her in mid sentence, to ask: "Is anything wrong?"

"It's your wife, Mr Ashford," she went on. "I'm afraid there is nothing more we can do for her here. We have just transferred her to a hospice at Clatterbridge, where they are better able to give her the special care she needs."

The words sent shivers down my spine, as I fought off a dizziness that threatened to swamp me.

Again I heard the young lady's voice. Only this time it seemed rather distant; "Do you have transport to take you to the Hospice?" she asked.

A sandpaper dryness clutched at my throat, preventing me from answering the question immediately. Garbled noises issued from within me, until I managed to reply, saying:

"Yes, I have a car. I'll get there as soon as I can, and thank you."

Replying she said, "your wife will be well taken care of at the hospice, Mr Ashford, and on behalf of the hospital staff may I say - we are sorry."

There was a brief silence, then the line went dead. I put the receiver back on it's cradle and made ready to visit my wife. Putting aside a need to stop for lunch I called at the local florists to purchase some flowers, so as to brighten her day. Then drove as fast as I dared along the motorway, toward the tiny village of Clatterbridge.

On arrival at the hospice I was shown into a spacious ward, curtained off into small sections. Differing in many respects from the dismal place she had just vacated at the Arrowe Park hospital, each room was tastefully decorated in bright pastel shades. Reaching my wife's bedside I placed the flowers on her table and although fast asleep, she appeared to sense my presence when I sat down at her bedside, for she opened her eyes. But her welcoming smile could not disguise the terrible pain from which she now suffered, in spite of her determination to put on a brave face.

Hunched up among the pillows, she looked a mere shadow of her former self. Deep furrows lined the pale face, revealing how months of pain and suffering had taken their toll. Her breathing, slow and painful at times, gave way every now and then to slight convulsions. I somehow feared the end was near for the love of my life, and realizing I was going to lose her, broke down and cried. There was nothing I could do to stop the avalanche of tears, cascading down my face.

With great difficulty she reached out to me, and I felt her hand close on mine. Drawing me closer to her, she whispered; "You have your life to live dear so please don't grieve for me, there is someone out there waiting for you."

Exhausted by this effort, she lay back on her pillow and closed her eyes. Her every move dictated by what little strength was left in her frail body. Was this the ramblings of a sick person I asked myself as I sat there, or could she, being a devout Christian, have been granted some supernatural power by the good Lord. Thus enabling her to predict something that would come to pass in the future, before she passed on.

Before leaving her bedside, I stood for a while gazing down at the woman I loved. A feeling of great sorrow came over me as I turned to leave, for I knew there was litle I could do to help her. At the doorway leading from the hospital a young nurse approached me, and asked; "May we have your telephone number, Mr Ashford?"

"Yes of course" I replied, reaching in my pocket for a notebook, I always carried with me. Tearing a sheet out, I wrote the number down and handed it to her.

"We'll call you if there's any change in her condition Mr Ashford," she promised. Then bidding me goodnight, said:

"Try to get some rest sir."

Thanking her I left the hospice, and stepping into my car, headed along the motorway for home.

Rain that began early in the morning continued to fall unabated, making driving difficult on the greasy surface of the motorway. Not until I was well on my way home did I realize I was shivering, and switched on the heating. When I arrived, the house was in darkness. A note from my daughter Susan pinned on the front door, asked if I would call her as soon as possible. Picking up the phone from the hall table I dialed her number, and waited for her response.

Before the sound of her "Hello" had faded, she stammered;

"Dad, where have you been?" I've called you several times and received no reply. I was getting quite worried that something had happened to you."

"Oh, I'm alright dear, it's your mother. They've taken her from Arrowe Park to the hospice at Clatterbrige" I replied, somewhat shakily. Then I heard her quick intake of breath.

"Oh, Dad" she whispered, fearing her children were listening. "It's not serious, is it?"

"I'm afraid so," I replied. "They've asked for my telephone number, and said if there is an emergency they will call me. So all we can do is wait and pray. Meantime, try not to worry, dear, I'll call you in the morning."

As an afterthought I added; "Please don't let the children know, it will only upset them. Goodnight dear, and once again, please don't worry, it's in the hands of the Lord."

I heard a faint click as the phone went dead, so I placed the receiver back on it's cradle and went into the kitchen looking for something to eat, remembering I had not eaten since early morning. Whilst no feelings of hunger were evident I realized only too well one had to eat if one was to keep mind and body alert, so set about cooking myself a meal. Exhausted by the day's events I wasted no time in climbing the stairs, gave myself a lick and a promise of a washing, and almost fell into bed. Sleep, however, was not to be; my mind was in a whirl, fearing what a new day would bring. I tossed and turned for a considerable time, before sleep finally came.

The rat-a-tat of driving rain lashing against my bedroom window, was loud enough to wake me with a start. Through red-rimmed eyes I peered at the clock on my bedside table, and heaved a sigh of relief. It was eight thirty in the morning and the night had apparently gone well, for I'd slept like a log. Slipping downstairs I put the kettle on to boil, and drawing the curtains in the lounge looked out on a new day. Beneath a formation of dark clouds I watched the angry morning sky splashed with streaks of red, spread across the far horizon. Back in the kitchen the eerie silence was broken by the ringing of my telephone, sitting on the hall table. My "Hello" was answered by a softly spoken young lady, saying: "This is Clatterbridge Hospital calling you Mr Ashford."

Pausing a moment, she said; "We regret to inform you, your wife passed away early this morning." Adding; "may we offer you our deepest sympathy."

Her carefully chosen words, hit like a hammer blow. I felt the strength ooze from my body, and in that instant a part of me died. Grasping the telephone table for support, I slumped into a nearby chair. In stunned silence I sat immobile, staring at the receiver in my hand, without realizing the caller from the hospital was still talking at the other end. Hearing a garbled noise coming through, I put the receiver to my ear once more and heard the young lady asking; "Are you alright, Mr Ashford?"

Struggling to release my tongue stuck fast in the roof of my mouth, I swallowed hard and managed to say; "Yes I'm alright now thank you," knowing it was far from the truth.

There was a momentary pause, then the young lady spoke again; "Will you be coming to the hospice, Mr Ashford?" she asked.

Suddenly I found my voice, and with a measured degree of urgency responded, saying; "I'll come as soon as possible, and thank you so much."

"That's alright, Mr Ashford," she replied, "we'll wait for your arrival."

For the first time in forty six years, I knew the meaning of loneliness. It all seemed so unreal. Gladys, my lovely wife, dead. How could I go on without her? I asked myself over and over. What was I to do? Then, forestalling a need to press the panic button, I began to reason with myself. She wouldn't have allowed this I said. No, in spite of it all, life must go on.

With a supreme effort I pulled myself together, and picking up the phone, rang my daughter. Hearing her "Hello," at the other end of the line, I swallowed hard. Hesitating for a moment, I found enough courage to say; "The hospice has just informed me, your mother passed away early this morning, dear."

I heard her sharp intake of breath, as she sobbed;

"Oh no, Dad."

Allowing a little time for her tears to subside I asked if she would come to the hospice with me after breakfast, to which she readily agreed. Within the hour I drew up outside her house and, having seen the children off to school, we were free to make our way to the hospice at Clatterbridge. Little if anything was said between us during the journey, the shock of losing a loved one left us with our own silent thoughts as we reached the hospital.

Ushered into the room where my wife lay, I stood gazing down at the still form, and realized it was just an empty shell. I had seen death so many times before in various guises, but I was not prepared for this.

Suddenly it appeared as it really was. There was nothing attractive about it. A shrunken white face with sagging jaw, and hands hanging limp and lifeless. I sat by the bedside and took in every little detail, knowing it would be forever imprinted on my mind. A moment I would always remember.

Close to an emotional display of tears I rose unsteadily from the bedside, and taking my daughter's arm we left the ward. A need for us to linger would serve no useful purpose now, for death had placed an insurmountable barrier between us. Paying a silent tribute to a loving wife and mother we tried to comfort each other, whilst walking along a corridor, beyond. Our footsteps beating a tattoo on the cold marble floor until reaching the entrance to the hospice. Outside in the parking area, we slipped into our car. Minutes later we were heading for the motorway, on the way home.

The funeral took place in the early days of September. By special request it was a simple affair, with the family and a few close friends in attendance. Seated in a tiny church within the cemetery grounds, I listened to a moving epitaph from the young vicar who conducted the service. His voice, gentle and moving. While in close proximity to the coffin, a strange sensation of spiritual togetherness came over me. Even as the purple curtains came together to close her off, I still felt her presence. Moving from the chapel into the tiny churchyard after the service had finished, this feeling of nearness persisted, until the hearse departed. Our many friends attending the service, offered their condolences and discreetly slipped away. Leaving myself and the rest of my family to return home.

Having survived many periods of great emotional stress and exceptional disappointments during my life, none ever affected me more profoundly than the loss of a loving wife. But where does one find comfort and hope, when an incurable illness invades their personal lives, and claims a loved one. My wife's passing left a void I found impossible to fill. At times, it seemed that life itself had no meaning.

Wandering around on unsteady legs and looking through unseeing eyes, with faltering step I'd place one foot in front of the other, as though in a dream. Groping in the dark, I had to somehow try and pick up the threads of my life. This awful feeling of emptiness deep within me, made everything seem so unreal.

Deeply shocked with my loss, my faith in the Lord who had come to my aid during many critical moments in my life, never wavered. With the passing of time I somehow felt he would surely intervene on my behalf, easing the pain and deep sorrow a bereavement causes. Overcome with grief, little did I realize then my life would soon be filled with unimaginable joy and happiness in the days to come, when I set about the task of preparing myself to face the future without her. But it was not until the latter part of November 1990, almost three months since my loss, that I had any inclination or desire to visit the house we had shared together. Refusing to step outside my daughter's house since the funeral, she finally succeeded in coaxing me to venture into town.

"You can't spend the rest of your life cooped up here Dad, mother wouldn't have wanted that," she chided. "Let's go and check out your house, just to make sure it's safe. Then we'll carry on into town."

In every neighbourhood you'll find friends are willing to keep an eye on your house whilst you are away on holiday, and on occasions, when for one reason or another you have business to attend to. There are also those who love nothing better, than an opportunity to pry into other people's business. In this respect the tiny village of Oxton in Cheshire, was no exception. Behind lace curtains my return home after three months absence was witnessed by several pairs of inquisitive eyes, wondering what I had been doing whilst I'd been away. Making certain inquiries around the village during my long absence was none other than old mother Mason, my next door neighbour.

An elderly widow of immense proportions she was square of jaw with protruding teeth and sharp beady eyes, and as deaf as a post. Her husband an inoffensive little weed of a man whom many say married her to win a bet, had died some years previously. Many believe the cause of his death, described by the coroner as heart failure, was due to her unnatural demands on him. Anxious to find out what I'd been up to she emerged from her hiding place behind the lace curtains, and waited until I had stepped from my car. In a gesture of mock surprise at my sudden appearance, she shouted; "Why, hello Charles, I haven't seen you for some time, is everything alright?"

In neighbourly fashion I acknowledged her friendly gesture, saying; "Oh, I'm fine thank you, Mrs Mason."

Determined to prolong our discussion and squeeze further information from me, she asked; "Is there anything I can do for you?"

"No thank you, Mrs Mason" I replied, endeavouring to be rid of her. At the same time, muttering to myself; "I wish she'd mind her own damned business, for a start."

Hurrying inside the house to avoid further questions I was faced with the job of sorting out a huge collection of mail, my daughter Susan had picked up off the vestibule floor.

"She's such an old busybody" I told my daughter, who busied herself in the kitchen making a cup of tea. "Why can't she mind her own business, she's like a vulture waiting to pick the bones of it's prey."

Susan, laughing out loud, tried to pacify me, saying;

"She's only trying to help, Dad. There have been a few burglaries in the area," you know. "So it's maybe just as well she's keeping an eye on things."

Not to be put off I retorted; "There are too many pairs of inquisitive eyes watching us right now, that's the trouble dear. The house is fitted with a burglar alarm, why should I need their help. They're too damned nosey." Gathering up my mail I placed it on the dining-room table, where it remained until an inspection of the house was completed.

Meantime, Susan went around checking each room on the ground floor, opening windows to let in a breath of fresh air. For my part, I did likewise, to bedrooms and bathroom upstairs. Nothing had apparently been disturbed during my absence, although the air was somewhat stale and the house badly needed airing.

Among a huge collection of mail that had accumulated over the past month or so, most of which could only be described as "bum fodder," were three buff coloured envelopes. Printed on the front of each letter in large black type were the words, ON HER MAJESTY'S SERVICE. All expressed a similar request, asking for the return of my wife's pension book. Whilst sorting out some begging letters, adverts, and junk mail, I came across the undertaker's bill which I placed aside. Dumping the rest, in with the household garbage.

Before the onset of winter, November's weather turned much colder as the month petered out. Night temperatures dropped way below zero, covering the ground in a blanket of white frost each morning. To prevent the water pipes throughout my home from freezing, I felt it necessary to leave the central heating system on day and night. Thus ensuring every room in the house was sufficiently warm, should the weather worsen, while I was at my daughter's. Having no desire to return home, at the present time.

Gathering up my letters and a few personal papers that belonged to my wife, I joined my daughter in the lounge.

"Why it's lunch time, Dad" she exclaimed, looking at the clock. "Let's eat in town, I don't feel like cooking. It will do you good to get out and about again."

Arriving at the restaurant we noticed it was crowded with lunch time customers and the sound of their voices exchanging idle gossip, was lost amid the clatter of knives and forks. Seated in one corner of the room I took in the spectacle before me. It's atmosphere combining warmth and friendliness, went a long way to dispel a feeling of depression I'd allowed myself to fall into, since my wife's death. By the time our lunch arrived I somehow felt more at ease, having just exchanged greetings with one or two old friends. It was at this point our conversation centred on one of my neighbours, old mother Mason the local gossip. Adjudged by villagers living in the area, to know everybody's business for miles around, they decided to nickname her "The News of the World."

Catching me unaware, my daughter popped the question;

"Will you go back and live in your house when things are settled down, Dad?"

"After this morning's performance from her next door, would you expect me to?" I asked."It's far too big for one person to manage, and furthermore, I don't need four bedrooms. How could I escape being pestered to death by that old windbag, forever quizzing me as to my movements. No, I've made up my mind. The property will be put up for sale."

A Dream Comes True.

After a long discussion with my daughter Susan, as the month of October 1990 drew to a close I decided to sell the house my wife and I had shared, and called at the estate office of Messrs Jones & Chapman in the town of Birkenhead. Speaking with one of their real estate agents, I asked if my property could be placed on the market. Taking my name and address, he agreed to view the house later that week. A day or two after, the agent arrived to inspect the house and proceeded to take down details of alterations I had carried out, to modernize the property.

Built in 1917, the house constructed of red glazed bricks from which mortar tended to crumble with age, required large area's on the outside walls of the house to be repointed. A job I undertook to do myself, some two years earlier. A damp course of silicone had been injected into bricks around the foundation of the house, where none previously existed when the property was built back in the early nineteen hundreds. Oak beams supporting the slate covered roof sagged beneath the weight, causing considerable leakage onto the ceilings inside the house. The whole structure was eventually taken down and replaced with Marley tiles, with a lifetime guarantee of twenty years. Wooden joists, fastened beneath the ground floor, had succumbed to wet rot, due to rising damp. It was therefore necessary to replace the flooring in the lower part of the house. Finally, all windows in the house were eventually fitted with double glazed units, instead of the draughty old shuttered type that rattled in the wind, also installed was a modern central heating system.

Satisfied my property was in good saleable condition, the estate agent from Jones & Chapman phoned to tell me they had put my house up for sale. At the same time, reminding me not to expect them to dispose of it right away, because the market was inclined to be rather slow at this time of the year, and added: "One never knows in this business. You could get a surprise caller."

It was now early December. Morning frost and bitterly cold east winds reminding us winter was upon us, with the possibility of worse to come. Heeding the weathermen's warning, I felt it necessary to check the temperature in my house, mindful not to be seen by my next door neighbour because of questions she was certain to ask. As night fell I slipped into the house unseen by prying eyes, to attend to the central heating system. Drawing the lounge curtains together, I switched on the lights and checked the temperature in each room, increasing it to a minimum of fifty five degrees, which I felt was high enough to prevent the water pipes from freezing. Satisfied they would be warm enough to combat the winter weather I switched off the lights and drew back the curtains, and prepared to leave the house.

Outside in the street, old mother Mason from next door was in ernest conversation with a neighbour, rambling on about the festive season of Christmas, and the expense one incurred in buying presents. Seeing me she screeched; "Hello Charles, I see you've got a for sale sign up there. Are you leaving the area?"

"I'm afraid so" I replied. "This house is far too big for me to manage on my own." Then begging to be excused, said: "I'm sorry I can't stop to talk with you. I have some urgent business to attend to," and breathed a sigh of relief as I drove off.

Some four days before Christmas I received a telephone call from estate agents Jones & Chapman, informing me of a prospective buyer wishing to view the property. Would I be kind enough to make myself available at 3 p.m. that day, to show the person around the house. My arrival at two o'clock that afternoon did not go unnoticed by my neighbour. A slight movement of her lace curtains told me she was on sentry duty, when I opened my front door. Among a heap of correspondence lying on the vestibule floor, a buff coloured envelope caught my eye, stamped with the usual heading OHMS in large black letters.

Ah! another one of those damned questionnaire's I said to myself, picking up the envelope from among a jumble of letters, and went to deposit it in the waste bin. At that particular moment, my front door bell rang, and slipping the letter into my

345

back pocket I answered the door. Standing there, his face wreathed in smiles, a neatly dressed young man, extended his hand.

"I've come to view the property, may I come in please?" he asked.

"Yes do" I answered, and stepping aside, allowed him to enter. Closing the door I ushered him into the lounge and from our conversation, learned he was a doctor from South America, attached to the Liverpool School of Tropical Medicine. While looking around upstairs he made a particular note of the four bedrooms, suggesting the smaller one at the rear of the house would be suitable for his study. He was obviously pleased with the property, and asked; "But why do you want to sell. It's a lovely house?"

"Yes, I have to agree with you," I stammered; "But having lost my wife some three months ago, I have no further use for it."

Apologizing profusely, the young man took his leave, promising to return at a later date. From the lounge window I watched as he disappeared from view and sat down on the settee, to collect my senses. It was then I felt the bulky letter I'd thrust into my back pocket, and looking at it noticed it was sent from Newcastle-On-Tyne. Now why would someone from that God forsaken place write to me, I asked myself. My curiosity aroused, I slit the envelope open. Inside was a heavily sealed plain white envelope bearing my name, with a letter addressed to me dated December 17th 1990 from the Social Services Investigation Department, in Newcastle. What on earth had I done to get caught up in an investigation? I wondered.

Briefly, the letter read; "Dear sir, we have been requested to forward this sealed envelope to you; "it's contents, of which we are unaware, are of a personal nature."

A signature scribbled across the bottom of the page, was unreadable. Leading me to believe, the letter could be nothing more than a practical joke. I just sat there, afraid to open the sealed envelope bearing my name, wondering what dark secrets or surprises lay within, that someone would choose write to me in this manner. I had, to the best of my knowlege, done nothing that warranted an invasion of my privacy, especially at a time when I mourned the loss of my wife. Undecided whether to open the letter or simply destroy it, nothing more than curiosity found me ripping the envelope open, unaware the information inside would leave me in a state of deep emotional shock, and thereafter change the course of my life. A letter inside from the Salvation Army Social Services' Investigation Department in London, read as follows;

Dear Mr Ashford,

You will perhaps be aware of the Salvation Army's work in the realms of family relationships, and especially in circumstances where for some reason there has been a loss of contact. We are attaching details relating to one of our current inquiries, and are writing to you in the hope that you may be the person sought. If you believe that the information given may refer to you, we would be most grateful to have your reaction to this inquiry, and to know whether you might wish to be put in touch with the inquirer..

If you have any hesitation about disclosing your present whereabouts, may we suggest that we invite the inquirer to write a letter which we could then forward to you - provided, of course, that you supply us with your address. We would give you our assurance that this will not be divulged to anyone else, without your prior consent.

If for any reason contact is not desired, please inform us accordingly in order that we need not trouble you again. If this communication has reached you in error, kindly accept our apology for any inconvenience which may have been caused.

Our reply-paid envelope is enclosed for your response, and we look forward to hearing from you.

Yours sincerely,

J.Beech, for Colin Fairclough

Major, Investigation Secretary.

The type-written note pinned to the back of the letter, left me speechless. For it read; "Your sister, Mrs Catherine E. Wilson, nee Ashford, wishes to get in touch with you."

The message set my pulses racing, and my mind in a whirl. Was this the person my wife spoke of, before she passed away, saying: "don't grieve for me, there is someone was out there, waiting for you?"

Overcome with excitement I felt the room spinning around, and became entangled in a sea of emotion. Following my bereavement the news proved too much for me to comprehend. I lay down on the settee, and passed out. Drifting from reality into the mists of time, I recalled days of my childhood, where convent life for an orphan was full of ups and downs. Then, as a shocked and bewildered boy of thirteen, I heard the mother superior saying to me; "Your mother wants you to go home."

Stepping off the train at London's Victoria station, I saw my mother running towards me. Lost in the warmth of an embrace, I hardly noticed her tears caressing my face. Again, as though it were only yesterday, Grandmother sought to appear. Catherine is your sister, she whispered, then her picture slowly faded.

Weightless, I floated aimlessly into space. Held fast by a spiritual force beyond my control, wrapping itself around me. Wakened by an incessant ringing of the telephone, I fumbled around the now-darkened room, and lifted the phone from it's cradle.

My hurried "Hello," was answered by my daughter, asking somewhat anxiously; "Are you alright, Dad. What's happening, you've been there an awful long time?"

"Oh, I must have dropped off to sleep, dear. I'm a little overtired with all the running around."

"Did the gentleman view the property?" she asked.

348

Why of course, I assured her. "I'm on my way home now, so I'll tell you all about it when I arrive."

"Alright Dad," she replied. "Be careful won't you, it's quite dark now. Bye bye."

In a dazed condition I replaced the telephone on it's cradle and sat for a moment trying to recall what had happened that caused me to pass out. Somewhat vaguely, I remembered reading a letter from the Salvation Army which mentioned my sister, but where was it. Groping around the darkened lounge I switched on a table lamp, and drew the curtains. My attention was drawn to a piece of paper on the floor, no more than six inches square. It's typewritten message, simply said; Your sister, Mrs Catherine E, Wilson, nee-Ashford, wishes to get in touch with you.

A wave of excitement swept through my body. So it wasn't a dream after all, I said to myself, reading the note over and over again, until the words grew so large they seemed to leap from the paper, to touch me. But of the letter that came with the message, there was no sign. It was most important I look for it. A frantic search brought it to light, from behind cushions on the settee. Excited as a young schoolboy I studied the letter carefully, with not a doubt in my mind, I knew it to be genuine. The notepaper on which the letter was written, bore the Salvation Army crest. Enclosing their telephone number, they requested I ask for a Miss C. McDowell, when calling their office, Monday morning.

How had they managed to find my sister Catherine after all these years, I wondered, and in so doing, make a dream of a lifetime, come true. Overjoyed, I felt an all-pervading calm, quell my turbulent emotions. Gone was the feeling of loneliness, I found hard to shake off, since the loss of my wife. I now had something to live for.

Prepared to face the future anew, I made ready to visit my daughter. Putting the letter from the Salvation Army into an inner pocket of my jacket, I took to the road with a song in my heart.

"Where on earth have you been, Dad?" my daughter asked, as I stepped from my car. "I expected you home hours ago."

"I'll explain in a moment" I answered, and placing an arm around her, we hurried inside a brightly lit lounge, where I relaxed in a comfortable armchair.

"My goodness, Dad, what on earth's happened to you?" my daughter gasped, as I sat down. "Your face is quite pale, you look as though you've seen a ghost."

Taking the letter I received from the Salvation Army from my pocket, I handed it to her, saying; "Read this dear, I'm afraid it will shock you.

Reading the letter, her face showed no sign of emotion until she saw the little note pinned to the back, and I watched as the colour drained from her face. Her eyes opened wide in disbelief, and a strangled cry escaped her lips;

"Oh Dad, I can't believe it" she gasped, "can this really be true? How on earth has your sister managed to find you among the millions of people living in this country, after all these years."

"That's something I cannot be sure of until I hear from the Salvation Army on Monday morning," I replied.

"But who else knew you had a sister?" she asked.

"The only person other than yourself, was your mother."

"Sadly, she is no longer with us. She would have enjoyed this wonderful moment."

Throughout the long week-end I sat waiting to call the Salvation Army's office in London, eating enough to keep a mouse alive and hardly able to sleep a wink. By the time Monday morning arrived I felt like the wreck of the Hesperus, and my nerves were on edge.

Long before the first light of dawn streaked across a sullen morning sky, I felt beneath my pillow, just to satisfy myself the letter from the Salvation Army, was still there. As my hand brushed against the envelope's smooth texture my heart skipped a beat, for never in my wildest dreams did I expect to be in touch with my long lost sister. But how long had she been aware of my existence. Had she gone to live with mother after I'd left to go to sea, I wondered.

There was nothing I could do to quell the excitement coursing through my body that morning, when I slipped into the bathroom to hurry through my ablutions, and creep quietly downstairs into the kitchen. Breakfast consisted of nothing more than a cup of tea and a slice of toast, which I forced myself to eat. Not wishing to add further expense to my daughter's already large household bill, I decided to telephone the Salvation Army's office from my own house a short distance away.

Giving myself ample time to make the journey I drove at a steady pace along the motorway, toward my home in Oxton. It was shortly after eight fifteen when I parked my car in the driveway and hurried inside, where the air was heavy with the scent of pot-pourri, almost to the point of being overbearing and stuffy. Without attracting too much attention from the neighbours, I opened a window in every room, for some much needed fresh air, and sinking down in the comfort of my favourite armchair in the lounge, tried to relax.

Watching the clock as the minutes ticked slowly by, I sat there trying to figure out how on earth my sister had managed to find me. But where had I gone wrong in my search for her all those years ago, and where was she living now. I had not long to wait before finding out. As the hands of the clock pointed to the hour of nine on that morning of the 23rd of December 1990, I had a pencil and piece of paper, ready to jot down her address.

My pulses began to race, and I felt my heart beating ten to the dozen when I picked up the phone and dialed the number of the Salvation Army's Headquarters in London. Agog with excitement, I could feel the tension building up inside me, waiting for someone to reply.

The response came much sooner than I anticipated, catching me completely off guard.

"This is the Salvation Army," said the voice of a young lady at the other end of the line. "Can I help you?"

351

Tongue-tied I remained silent, listening to the pounding of my heart. The lips moved, but no words of mine would come out. Panic-stricken, fearing they might cut me off, I forced myself to stammer incoherently; "This is Charles Ashford calling. I received a letter from your London office on Saturday 21st of December, informing me my sister Catherine Elizabeth Wilson-nee-Ashford, wishes to get in touch with me." Almost breathless I rambled on. "The letter requested I ask for a Miss C.McDowell, could I speak to her please."

"One moment Mr Ashford," came the brisk reply. "I'll go and fetch her."

My whole being trembled with excitement, waiting for Miss MacDowell to come to the phone, which seemed an eternity, but was actually no more than half a minute. Why were they taking so long, I wondered? Couldn't they find a copy of the letter, or was the letter I received, not from them after all. All kinds of excuses and nonsense ran haphazardly through my mind whilst listening to the rustle of papers, mingled with the chatter of female voices at the other end of the line. I held my breath as the young lady broke the silence, saying;

"Hello Mr Ashford, sorry to keep you waiting." Pausing for a moment, she said; "This is Miss MacDowell speaking to you. I have your sister's letter in my hand, would you like us to get in touch with her, on your behalf?"

"Er, no thank you Miss," I spluttered nervously. "If you would oblige me with her address, I'll write to her today."

"Just as you wish Mr Ashford," she replied good-humouredly. "If you have a pencil handy, I'll read it out for you."

As she spelt out my sister's name and address my eyes misted over and uncontrollable tears of joy fell unashamedly, in great big blobs on the writing paper. Nothing could check this tide of emotion sweeping over me. At the other end of the line, my stifled sobs must have caused the young lady some concern, for she promptly asked; "Are you alright Mr Ashford?"

"Er, yes Miss I stammered," wiping the tears from my eyes.

"I understand how you feel sir, so please take your time. There is no hurry."

"I'm alright now Miss" I replied, brushing aside the tears that had fallen on my notepaper. Then continued to write my sister's address, as it was spelt out to me.

There was a brief silence, then she asked; "Do you have that all down now sir?"

"Yes thank you, Miss" I answered, breathless with excitment.

"Very well Mr Ashford," she responded, "good luck and may God bless you both." Then the line went dead.

I sat there in a daze for some minutes before replacing the phone back on it's cradle, my pulses banging against my ears. Examining the tear-stained notepaper in my hand a feeling of elation such as I had never experienced before, swept through my body with electrifying speed. Over and over again I read my sister's address, until I suddenly realized she lived thousands of miles away in the far reaches of Western Canada.

Once the shock wore off I put aside any disappointment, knowing my sister and I lived miles apart, grateful to the Salvation Army who were responsible for putting us in touch with each other. Slowly I felt a cloak of loneliness draped about my shoulders since the loss of my wife, finally slip away, now that my dream of a lifetime had come true.

A never to be forgotten moment of the most extrordinary magnitude was about to change my life, in knowing somewhere in Western Canada my sister waited to hear from me. An unimaginable feeling of joy surged through my body, leaving me weak at the knees. I flopped down on the settee; the excitement had proved all too much.

It was the persistent ringing of the telephone, that wakened me with a start. Picking it up from a nearby table, I lifted the receiver and said: "Hello."

There was a slight pause before I heard my daughter ask somewhat anxiously; "Is everything alright, Dad. Have you spoken to the Salvation Army. Did they give you your sister's address?"

"Why yes", I replied excitedly, and read it out to her.

"My goodness she's in Western Canada," Susan gasped in surprise. "That's on the other side of the world, Dad." And as an after-thought she said. "But that's no problem, you can call her on the phone."

"There is an eight hour difference," I reminded her. "We'll have to make sure we're not disturbing her in the middle of the night," I laughed. "It's a few days before Christmas, so I'll slip down town right away and send a Christmas card, that should surprise her. I know it's late, but better late than never."

"Alright then Dad," she replied, "I'll see you later."

"Cheerio for now."

Pushing my way through a crowd of Christmas shoppers looking for bargains, I purchased the best Christmas card I could find from what little remained in the store. Slipping into one of the many restaurants in town I found a quiet corner to sit down, and wrote a letter to my sister.

One cannot described the feeling of joy and sheer delight I experienced when receiving your message, through the good services of the Salvation Army. It was, I wrote, by chance I learned of your existance during a visit to grandmother, who lived in the Peckham area of London. I was just thirteen years of age at the time, and could never understand why mother denied me an opportunity of meeting you. Why she did this, I shall never know. It is, however, nothing short of a miracle you were able to get in touch with me, in the twilight of our lives. In closing I wish you every happiness for this, the festive season, and hope and pray after all the painful years of waiting, we shall meet in the near future. Posting my letter to her that morning I could do nothing more but wait for her reply, which I hoped would arrive early in the New Year.

Never before had I wished a Christmas to be over and done with, but time stood still. When the festive day finally did arrive, with a turkey and plum pudding dinner followed with helpings of mince pies, I'd lost my appetite, and sat watching the clock as the day dragged slowly by. When my head touched the pillow that night I heaved a sigh of relief and looked forward to the dawning of a new year, with the realization a letter from my sister Catherine living in Canada would make a dream of a lifetime come true.

As the old year drew to a close, a change in the weather brought ominous black clouds scurrying across the sky, casting an impenetrable curtain across the landscape. Easterly winds sweeping in caused temperatures to drop quite dramatically, bringing our first snowfall of the winter.

Down it came in huge flakes, swirling around like mounds of white spume in a boiling sea, covering the ground in a thick carpet. On and on into the New Year light snow showers continued to fall, playing a game of hide-and-seek as they swirled around the rooftops.

During the second week of January the weather abated, enabling the postman who we had seen little of during this period, to resume his daily round. Then like manna from heaven the letter I'd been waiting for from my sister in Canada, duly arrived. From the lounge window I watched as he shuffled through the melting snow to my front door to pop it through my letterbox, and let out a whoop of delight as it fluttered gently to the floor. Picking up the letter, a smile creased my face as I read the opening lines of this my first ever letter from my sister Catherine, which read as follows.

Dated the 28th of December, it began;

"My dear Charles,

When I received your lovely Christmas card and letter today, my first thoughts were, who do I know in Liverpool?" I just cannot believe this miracle that has happened, making it possible for us to finally contact each other after so many lost years. Our thanks must surely go to the Salvation Army for a task well done, despite searching a trail that had long gone cold. Although I received no indication they were prepared to carry out a search for you, I was of course, only able to give them your barest details. Such as where you were born, and the date. In spite of this, they managed to track you down. How they ever found you among so many millions of people living in Britain is amazing, beyond comprehension.

Strange as it may seem, I was totally unaware of your existence until October of this year, (1990). I had already, through the kind services of a Genealogist living in Lakefield, Ontario, a well-known author on this subject, secured mother's birth and marriage certificate. Unable to obtain her death certificate, I hired the services of a Researcher in Whitstable, Kent, England, who not only produced the long-awaited document, but also your birth certificate.

In finding you at last, sadness creeps into one's very heart, realizing mother would not tell you of my whereabouts. That in itself is distressing. But, it is the time we have lost in the knowing and growing up together in family life, that is so devastating. We have both missed so much. The urge within me now, compulsive as it may sound, is the need for us to meet before more years pass us by. I simply don't have another forty six years to spare. This Charles, is the time it has taken me to search for my parents. Neither of whom did I ever meet, or know. According to our birth certificates you and I and our younger sister Elizabeth, were born in the same place, but your brother and elder sister were born elsewhere. So what happened to you. Where were you brought up? I have so many questions to ask, and I sincerely hope, Charles, you will be able to answer most of them for me. One big one I'll ask you now. Do you have a picture of mother? This has always been my greatest wish, never having had the privilege of meeting her.

When you next write, will you give me all the news on your life and where you spent it. Also whether you kept in touch with mother until she passed away in 1952. I do know she was buried at St John's cemetery, in Margate. In reply to your letter, I will relate our story to you, which I must warn you is a very long and traumatic one, which describes the strict way in which we were brought up. Also a distressing experience encountered by myself, when endeavouring to search for mother. Sad to say, I spent almost a lifetime completely on the wrong trail, tramping the streets in the East End of London looking for family, but to no avail. Seeking help from various Roman Catholic Societies whom I later learned possessed the information I sought, yet persistently refused to help me, and slammed their doors in my face. Insisting, I let sleeping dogs lie. I do hope Charles, you will come over for a holiday and meet me. Spend some time with me, I'll spoil you!

Welcome to the family, and let us meet soon. My best wishes to you and your family for a good Christmas and New Year. I send you my love and affection, — Catherine.

With a feeling of profound gratitude I wrote a letter of thanks to the Salvation Army for putting my sister in touch with me, a brother she was unaware of. Appealing to them for help when all else failed these truly wonderful people came to her aid, at a time when one particular charitable organization saw fit to slam the door in her face. This remarkable act of human kindness was all the more appreciated when one considers the length of time my sister spent searching for her family, over a period of forty years without success. On the other hand I knew of her existence at the age of thirteen, some sixty two years ago. But was never priviledged to meet. It is only now, that I find myself no more than a telephone call away from her, for the first time in my life. Yet even as I wait to put in a long distance call to her, across the other side of the world in Western Canada, I find it hard to believe this is actually happening to me after a lifetime of waiting, and ask myself: Am I dreaming.

Because of an eight hour difference in time between us I decided to wait until that evening to call Catherine, and bursting with excitement sat watching the clock, as the minutes slowly ticked away. Striking the hour of six the grandfather clock in the hall, set my pulses racing and my heart beating like a trip-hammer, when lifting the receiver to dial her number. Fidgeting nervously with the lines of a speech I'd written, I tried to memorize them. A persistant buzzing at the other end of the line ceased abruptly, followed by a short pause. At the sound of her first "Hello!" I knew for certain the voice at the other end of the line, was that of my sister's.

In that instant I experienced sensations of varying degrees from emotion to ecstasy coursing through my body, and a sense of warmth and belonging came over me. Drumming at the temples, my pulses beat time with the pounding of my heart. There was no doubt in my mind the voice on the telephone was Catherine's and I wanted so much to speak to her, but the tension proved too much for me. A speech I'd so carefully prepared beforehand slipped from my grasp onto the floor, leaving me tongue-tied.

In a state bordering on panic I forced myself to speak, and spluttered; "Hello Catherine, this is your brother Charles calling," then waited for some response.

I heard a startled gasp at the other end of the line, followed by an excited cry of; "Charles my dear, what a lovely surprise. Tell me is it really you, and I'm not dreaming? Welcome to the family."

Pausing long enough to catch her breath, she asked;

"But where have you been all these years, please tell me, what have you done with your life?"

"I've so much to tell you Catherine but I don't know where to begin, and it would take far too long over the telephone. So I'll have to be brief and write to you later, giving you a chapter by chapter rundown on my life so far." I then told her how I'd been cruelly treated whilst in a convent, until mother came to take me home with her, when I'd reached the age of thirteen.

"You were with mother"she cried out loud. "But, where were you living Charles?"

"In the Carshalton area of Surrey," I replied. "Did you know it, Catherine?"

"Why of course" she said, "I know it well."

Not wishing to go into further detail I promised to write to her in the next day or so, giving details of my life thus far.

"I'll look forward to that," she said, I'm dying to know all about you." Pausing a moment, she asked; "Do you have a photograph of mother, Charles?"

I'm awfully sorry Catherine, but I haven't," I replied.

"Oh, what a pity," she sighed. "But never mind Charles, it's been wonderful just to be able to talk with you. Goodbye my dear, I'll look forward to your letter."

Our First Meeting

Long after the line went dead I sat day-dreaming, with the telephone receiver pressed to my ear. It was the operator reminding me my call had finished, that brought me back to reality.

I had just spoken to my sister who lived a world apart in Western Canada, for the first time in my life. Like a couple of excited school children we talked for over an hour, swapping news and views about our lives. Briefly she spoke of St Anne's convent where she'd spent her childhood, under the watchful eyes of Sisters of Mercy, in whose care she was entrusted. A cold and heartless group of people showing neither love or kindness to orphaned girls, whom they looked upon as outcasts of society. Leaving the convent in her teens, Catherine was pitchforked into a strange new world. A place which the nuns talked little of, or failed to warn her about. Left to fend for herself in unfamiliar surroundings, she struggled to survive.

Only by denying herself some necessities of life was it possible, she told me, to pay for her lodgings or purchase clothing to keep herself warm. With little money left from a miserly wage she earned helping the war effort, she could ill-afford to buy nourishing food. With no one to whom she could turn for assistance, she fell ill whilst working in an aircraft factory, and collapsed. At the hospital where they attended her, she was found to be suffering from malnutrition, and her employers, Vicker's Aircraft, were informed she could no longer do heavy work, but should be put on light duties.

If only mother had let us meet when we were young, I reminded Catherine, there would have been no need for you to have suffered so much pain and misery, as a teenager.

I told my sister that I had also suffered the same hardships she encountered, at the start of my working life. It was no act of kindness on mother's part when she took me home with her shortly after my thirteenth birthday from the convent, where she abandoned me as an infant. I soon found life at home, was not a bed of roses. My stepfather insisted I work after school hours, to supplement the family income.

During our conversation over the telephone Catherine warned, there were a few surprises in store for me when next she wrote. When her letter did arrive, it fair took the wind out of my sails. Dated January 15th 1991, It read:

My dear Charles,

It will no doubt come as something of a shock when you examine the birth certificates of the four of us, which I will be sending to you in my next letter. So what I will do here, is fill you in with some of the details. You will note on Margaret's the father's name is different, whilst Harry's certificate has always been of a questionable nature. My own appears to be quite straightforward, as does Elizabeth's, with the exception of her father's name. Since we are getting down to brass tacks, so to speak, I will send you mother's certificate of marriage to Edgar Reginald Ashford, also her divorce papers from him, and a second marriage to a John Brandon. It has taken me over forty-five years to secure these documents, unaided by any member of the family. I'll send you these papers to start with, Charles, as I have no wish to shock you completely, in that you may not want to hear all the facts surrounding mother. I didn't know her, as you did, so I can be impartial to a degree, while at the same time, not wishing to upset you. That would not be my intention, believe me, but I feel you should know the truth, don't you?

Must close now Charles, I'll write again soon,

Much Love, from your sister Catherine.

Hardly had I recovered from the shock of her first letter than a second dated 22nd January arrived, with the documents she mentioned in her previous correspondence. In writing to me, she says;

My Dear Charles,

I have, with this letter, enclosed certificates of mother's birth, her marriage in 1915, and divorce from our father E.R. Ashford in 1926. There is also the marriage certificate I mentioned in my last letter between mother and a John Brandon in December of 1919, along with birth certificates of Margaret, Harry, Elizabeth, and myself. We all have reason to believe that the names used, Ashford, Brandon, Hinks and Marsden, all belonged to mother. Your expression, mother was rather 'wayward,' is comparatively mild compared to some of the Canadianisms I could use, to vent my anger at the way we have all been treated. However it would serve no useful purpose to behave like this and as you say, who are we to point an accusing finger at her since we are not aware of her circumstances. What has happened is over and done with, but, for the sake of social history our story should be told. It's complexities alone, make for interesting reading. It would I am sure, take many a Sherlock Holmes to unravel a web so tightly woven.

Catherine's letter ends with words I can only describe as most appropriate, for the way mother behaved toward us all. Bringing to mind a well versed phrase, and I quote;

"Oh, what a tangled web we weave, for those who practice to deceive."

In the letter she asked; "Are you in possession of a Baptismal certificate, Charles?" Elizabeth our youngest sister has indicated there was every possibility you may have been baptized at St George's Cathedral. This being the closest church to mother's home. In summing up the situation, I must admit Charles my dear, the story becomes more bizarre the deeper we delve into our family history.

Of one thing however we can be certain, mother has left us in a terrible mess. It's not surprising therefore, after forty years of agonizing search, we are still trying to unravel some of the mysteries she left behind. Many of which I doubt we ever will. I don't suppose in your wildest dreams you imagined, when finding us, we would throw you into such a turmoil, which sadly I regret doing. Thank God, you are an understanding man, and did not choose to turn your back on us. Finding you Charles has made all the heartaches, pain, and suffering worthwhile. Wishing you and the family every happiness for the coming year,

My Love to You,
Catherine, xxx.

Sifting through several marriage and birth certificates sent by my sister, I now had the unenviable task of trying to piece together details of mother's early life, following the break up of her marriage to my father E.R Ashford in 1926. According to these records I have to hand, he was a petty officer in the Royal Navy at the time of his marriage to my mother in 1915. My birth certificate states I was born on the 29th of January 1919, father Edgar Rowland Ashford, mother Caroline Elizabeth Ashford nee-Adams.

Information supplied by the naval authorities as to the whereabouts of my father at the time of my birth, lists him as stationed in Salonika on a two year draft aboard H.M.S Wildfire. Not content to wait for him to return home my mother formed an association with John Brandon a first class stoker also of the Royal Navy, in July 1919, some six months after I was born. On the 17th of December that year, they were married. From this relationship a daughter named Margaret Brandon is recorded as born in July 1921, at the North Lambeth Hospital in the County of London. The father named as John Brandon and mother Caroline Florence Brandon, formerly Hinks, were living at 25 Lambeth Square, Lower Marsh, North Lambeth.

I was two and a half years old at the time and apparently unwanted by the man she had just married, also a burden to my mother who now had another child to care for. To overcome this problem mother had me baptised into the catholic faith at St George's Cathedral in London, on the 6th of November 1921.

Entered on the baptismal certificate my name was given as Ronald Brandon born on the 29th January 1919, father John Brandon, mother Caroline Brandon, nee Hinks. On December 20th of that year I was taken from the place where I was born, to a convent many miles away on England's southern shores. There I was handed over to be cared for by nuns of the Franciscan Order where I lived in fear of those in charge, who ruled with a rod of iron. Hidden away in this place where no one would ever find me, I spent the next ten years of my young life in what I can only describe as hell on earth. My mother was now free to indulge in her pursuit of pleasure with her new husband John Brandon.

In 1924 she gave birth to another child, a son whose details are recorded as follows; Name William Harry, born on the twenty-first of February. Father Edward, R Ashford a petty officer in the Royal Navy, mother Caroline Elizabeth Ashford, late Brandon, formerly Hinks. It is quite feasible John Brandon received word my father was about to be discharged from the Royal Navy around this time, and left my mother in the lurch. With two children to care for whose father had flown the coop, so to speak, mother although not of the same faith, once again solved her problem by having them placed in a Catholic Institution.

Picking up the threads of her marriage with my father E.R. Ashford on his return to civillian life in 1925, she gave birth to a little girl named Catherine. Recorded as born on the twenty fifth of September, father Edward R. Ashford, Petty Officer Royal Navy (retired), mother Caroline Elizabeth Ashford, formerly Adams. While there are no records of what might have transpired after this event to break up their marriage, my father must have found out mother had committed adultery while he was away in the navy and filed for divorce on the 22nd of June 1925.

Knowing mother was six months pregnant with his child at the time, my father chose to desert her, long before the print on his application for divorce was dry. No sooner was the decree nisi finalized he married Sarah Elizabeth Ring a widow who came from Plymouth, Devon, with whom he had presumably been associating. The break-up of her marriage left my mother destitute, without a roof over her head and little means of support for her infant child. Having no-one to whom she could turn for help, her situation became desperate and as happened on previous occasions, she simply abandoned her child, who was taken into care by the Romney Marsh Union in Kent, in 1928.

Free once more to pursue a life of ease this beautiful looking mother of mine now in her mid-thirties, chose a path one can only describe as being fraught with pitfalls. By all accounts she simply drifted around for a while like a ship without a rudder, falling into the arms of some silver tongued gigolo, to whom she gave her favours.

In 1927 she had another daughter named Elizabeth, whose birth certificate named the father as Edward Ashford. But according to information in my records, it shows him as having married a Sarah Elizabeth Ring on November the 20th 1926. Because of mother's complete disregard for the welfare of her child, this unfortunate mite also ended up in the same institution. Along with her other four children, she chose to abandon. Then like a rolling stone she again foolishly chose to tread, what had proved for her a rocky marital path, after two broken marriages and the birth of five children.

Following her progress along the matrimonial path in search of wedded bliss, she met and married Edwin Thomas Marsden in 1928. From this union which according to my records was her last, three sons were born. With three children to care for and a husband unable to provide enough food for her family, my mother decided it was time I left the convent, to which I had been abandoned some ten years earlier. It came as the biggest shock of my young life when the mother superior at the convent, said to me; "Your mother wants you to go home."

With a cynical smile I'd seen so many times before, when those in charge tried to cover up their mistakes, she simply waved my protestations aside. At the end of July 1932 I left the convent and was put on a train to London's Victoria Station where I met my mother, who welcomed me with open arms and took me home with her. My experience of home life was not a happy one, in that I was forced to go out to work to help support the family. I remember rummaging around in mother's sideboard in the diningroom, one day, looking for some writing paper, and came across the picture of a young man in naval uniform.

"Who is this mother" I asked? showing the photograph to her.

Turning a whiter shade of pale, a look akin to fear, crossed her face. Then somewhat sadly, she answered:

"That is your father, Charles."

"But where is he, I asked."

"He died from war wounds," she hurriedly replied. Evidently not wishing to discuss the subject.

While browsing through the records it came as something of a shock to note mother was divorced from my father in January of 1926, after having me believe he was dead. There is no doubt she lied to me when I questioned her about him, knowing full well if he were still alive I'd want to meet him. This, I felt sure, was one of many reasons why she could not allow me to meet my sister Catherine, fearing we might learn of her murky past. Yet, despite her every effort to keep us apart, she would turn in her grave if she knew we finally met in the twilight years of our lives. With so many episodes of mother's wayward life now coming to light, I doubt if the whole truth will ever be known. Suffice to say she felt reasonably safe in not having to answer awkward questions, taking her secrets with her to the grave. While I found it hard to forgive her for the suffering my sister and I endured throughout our childhood, we made a special journey to England on a bitterly cold day in March of 1993 and visited her grave.

Putting the finishing touches to the ups and downs of mother's life, I put away the many family documents sent to me by my sister, that had taken her a lifetime to collect. Among them were mother's marriage certificates, the birth certificates of her eight children and her divorce papers from my father. Over the years, my sister had worked tirelessly gathering this information from genealogists and researchers in England, costing her thousands of dollars and hours of painstaking study. Looking back to a period of mother's early life in the aftermath of the first World War, times were hard and unemployment was rife. There was no such thing as unemployment benefit or social security for the needy, so one could sympathize and understand the hardships she must have suffered, in the troubled times of the 1920's and early 1930's.

Having spent endless hours over the past couple of months pouring over a wealth of information in relation to mothers past life from my sister Catherine, much of which shocked and saddened me, I realized why mother herself used so many aliases to cover her tracks. Now at least, I thought, her ghost had been laid to rest, but sadly I was wrong. No sooner had I put my pen aside,than another skeleton appeared out of mother's cupboard.

In early May of 1990 my sister wrote;
My Dear Charles,

Once again I write asking a favour, hoping all is well with you and the family. I am enclosing a copy of Grandfather's death certificate, signed by his son, our Uncle Ernest, whom you visited with mother when just a boy. Would you Charles, please secure the services of Mr J,D.Wilks the researcher living in the county of Kent, England, who was instrumental in sending mother's documents to me. Ask him if he would trace Uncle Ernest, or his survivors. This I hope, will finalize a long drawn-out search I have undertaken over the last forty-five years, in an effort to find my family.

In your last letter you mentioned the property market was at a standstill, I do hope things will pick up now that spring has arrived. So try and come over as soon as your house is sold. You will love Canada. More especially the beautiful areas of British Columbia where I live, with it's sub-tropical climate. The city of Victoria and the impressive Empress Hotel overlooking the harbour, is no more than a short journey by car from my home. Wishing you every success with the sale of your property, and in your efforts to trace Uncle Ernest. Take care dear, and do give my love to the family,

Loving you as always, Your sister Catherine. xxx

Contacting a Mr. D.J.Wilks of Kent by telephone, he agreed to carry out a search for my Uncle Ernest. Forwarding his asking fee of two hundred and fifty pounds sterling and the necessary death certificate, I waited for his response.

Some three weeks passed before I received word from him, in the form of a letter which read:

Dear Mr Ashford,

Upon receipt of your letter I carried out a thorough search for your missing uncle but without success. I will however give you a telephone number to ring, that would most certainly be to your advantage. Wishing you luck in your endeavours

Yours sincerely, D. J. Wilks, (Researcher)

With little to work with, other than a telephone number, I waited until that evening, and picked up the phone. My call was answered by a gentleman who asked me to hold the line, and passed the receiver to his wife.

"Can I help you," she asked.

"I hope so," I replied, "I am trying to trace my Uncle Ernest who may have lived in the area."

"Yes he did," she said. "We purchased this bungalow we live in from his wife a Mrs Phyllis Adams, a couple of years ago. I believe she has since past on, but if it's any help I'll give you the phone number of her niece."

Thanking her, I rang off and called the number the lady had given me. This time my inquiry was answered by an elderly woman who seemed quite agitated, when I asked if she knew of my aunt Phyllis.

"Who are you" she said, "and what do you want with her?"

"My name is Charles Ashford" I replied, "and I am looking for any living relative of my uncle Ernest Adams."

"Oh well, I don't think I can help you," she muttered. "Maybe someone will call you" she said, and rang off.

Working on my word processer up in the bedroom some two hours later, I received a call from a lady, who asked; "Are you Mr Charles Ashford?"

Her question puzzled me, so I answered; "Yes, I am that person, but what can I do for you?"

"Can you tell me the name of your mother, and anyone else in your family," she went on.

This is rather strange, I said to myself. Who on earth can this person be, who wants to know my family history.

Hesitating for a moment, I agreed to talk to her, saying: my mother's name was Elizabeth Ashford - nee Adams, and my Uncle Ernest lived in Downham, Kent."

The lady's response went through me like an electric shock, when she said, "Yes I remember you coming to my house as a young boy in short pants." And giving a chuckle, added;

"I am your first cousin, Elizabeth Markham. Your mother and mine, were inseparable sisters.

Shaking with excitement, I pleaded with her; "Do you have a photograph of my mother. I have a sister in Canada who would love one."

"Yes," she replied, "I have photographs of the whole family. I'll post them to you if you give me your address."

There followed a brief period of silence, and when next she spoke it left me speechless, for she said; "You know Charles, you are not your mother's first born."

Startled, I gasped; "What do you mean, Elizabeth."

She then told me my mother had married a man named Antonio Capolongo in 1910.

My God, how many more times had she been married, I asked myself. That's her fourth.

We chatted on for some considerable time, until Elizabeth said she had to go. Promising to send the family photographs and keep in touch, she said: "My it was a surprise hearing from you Charles, give my regards to your family and until next time, goodbye and good luck."

Wasting little time I telephoned Catherine in Canada, telling her I'd found a first cousin living in Sussex who will provide us with a photograph of mother. She was over the moon to hear the good news, and cried: "Oh thank you so much Charles, you've done a wonderful job. I can't wait to see this picture of mother."

Meanwhile a steady flow of correspondence between my sister and I, continued across the Atlantic throughout May at an alarming rate and on, into flaming June. A month failing to live up to it's reputation. Arriving rather cool and somewhat damp it was not until we approached the middle of the month, traditionally accepted as the Summer Solstice, that we felt the sun's warmth. This sudden change in the weather sent prospective house hunters flocking to estate agents offices looking for bargains, and there were many to be had with the market having sunk to an all time low. But as time moved on I despaired of ever ridding myself of a property I'd offered for sale almost twelve months ago and had to sell off, before I could plan a trip to Canada.

But when all seemed lost, a telephone call from the estate agents Jones & Chapman, took me by surprise. They informed me the South American doctor interested in buying my property back in December of 1990 had made a new offer, much nearer my original asking price.

"Would you be willing to sell now, sir," the gentleman asked?

Seizing this golden opportunity to be rid of the four bedroomed house I'd lost interest in since my wife passed away,

I instructed the agent to go ahead with the sale. By the end of July documents transferring the property to the new owner were duly signed by both parties, leaving the way clear for me to arrange a long awaited trip to Canada. With the holiday season at it's height travel agents were inundated with would-be travellers booking flights, to the more popular Mediterranean resorts of Majorca and Ibiza. I did however manage to raise a few eyebrows, when I asked the young lady at Pickford's Travel Office:

"Could you book me a flight to British Columbia."

"Ah, let me see now" she said, taking a reference book from a drawer in her desk."

Not wishing to upset her unduly, I replied; "It's Western Canada, Miss."

Consulting with her supervisor she returned to her desk and smiled apologetically, confessing she was unaware they had flights to that particular part of the world, having just joined the company.

"What part of British Columbia do you wish to book your flight to, and how long will you be staying sir?" she asked.

"I would like to leave for Vancouver Island as soon as possible for a period of three months," I replied.

"Then you will need to book a flight from the mainland to Vancouver Island's International Airport," she said with a smile.

Taking a flight with British Airways, due to leave the following afternoon, I telephoned my sister informing her of my time of arrival. Then wandering around town I purchased a few odds and ends I might need, during my three month stay in Canada. It was late afternoon when I arrived back at my daughter's, with whom I'd been staying since the sale of my property, and slipped up to my bedroom. Whilst packing some presents in my bags ready for tomorrow's journey a wave of excitement surged up inside me, and a feeling of belonging encircled me. For within a few short hours I would meet my long-lost sister. It was well past the hour of midnight when my head touched the pillow, and still sleep would not come. I simply lay there in the darkened room listening to the beating of my heart, holding back a tide of pent up emotion waiting to burst.

Suddenly the darkness had turned to light and through the open curtains in my bedroom I watched the sun rise above a whiteness of cloud, to turn from pink to gold. Morning had broken on this the 31st day of July 1991 and as my mantle of grief from past months slipped away, I looked forward to the joy awaiting me as I prepared to leave. As though in a dream I found myself being driven along the motorway in the direction of Manchester Airport, a hive of activity at this time of the year because of large crowds of would-be travellers.

Accompanied by my daughter Susan and three grandchildren who had come to see me off, I eased my way through the maddening crowd to reach passport control. With my family bidding me a safe journey and God speed I passed on into a waiting lounge, before boarding my flight for Vancouver. Yet even at this late stage I had to ensure myself this was not a dream, that within a few short hours I would for the first time in my life meet my sister, whom I thought was lost forever.

Seated at the window of a British Airways 747 on that summer evening, I held my breath as it taxied along the runway, ready for take off. With a thunderous roar the engines burst into life and as it gathered speed and took to the air, a silent prayer escaped my lips. In that short space of time an eerie feeling of weightlessness claimed me, while I watched the cold grey waters of the Atlantic Ocean receding beneath me. Reaching an altitude of twenty thousand feet the aircraft levelled out as the roar from the giant engines faded to a gentle hum, hardly audible above the sound of passenger's voices, as we sped into the wide blue yonder. One heard a clicking of seat belts being unfastened, and all was momentarily stilled when the lights dimmed, and the large cinema screen came to life. Beneath a blanket I curled up in my seat, seizing the opportunity to catch up on some much needed shut eye.

Sunlight streamed through the window of the aircraft when I awoke, for night had turned into day.

"You'll have to fasten your seat belt," my fellow traveller advised. "We're due to land shortly," he grinned.

Struggling to raise myself into a sitting position I noticed the empty food tray in front me, and gave him a questioning look.

"You were having a such a good old snore, it seemed a shame to let the grub go to waste. I guess you weren't hungry, Buddy, or you'd have surfaced."

"Oh, that's alright I'm not hungry, I lied." But all the while my stomach craved for sustenance, to stop it turning cartwheels.

It was shortly after midday when the aircraft began it's descent. From my seat by the window I watched air flaps slide out, checking our approach. With both engines in reverse as we hit the runway, the plane shuddered to a halt outside the arrival's lounge at Toronto's International Airport. With little time to get my bearings I was fortunate to have been able to book my luggage through to Vancouver, before leaving Manchester. Easing past waiting crowds and traversing many lifts, I boarded my flight to Vancouver. A smooth take off and I was heading up and away into Canada's heartland, the wheat growing Provinces of Manitoba, Saskatchewan, and Alberta. Ahead lay snow capped peaks of the Rocky Mountains, stretching along Canada's west coast from Alaska into the U.S.A and Mexico. Panoramic scenes of unspoiled natural beauty en route to British Columbia left me spellbound, a spectacle I shall never forget. On alighting from the aircraft at Vancouver, I hurried to the arrival's bay to retrieve my luggage. Waiting patiently as suitcases, canvas bags, and an assortment of cardboard boxes passed by on the carousel. Picking up my belongings and clearing customs and immigration, I telephoned my sister on Vancover Island.

"Where are you Charles?" she cried, her voice bubbling with excitement.

"I'm at Vancouver Airport" I replied, "waiting to catch my plane to Victoria."

My telephone call was cut short by an announcement on the tannoy, asking would-be passengers to prepare to board. Within minutes we had taken off, and rose steadily into a cloudless sky of blue. Banking slowly as if in some form of salute the tiny aircraft made a sharp turn on leaving the mainland behind, winging it's way to Vancouver Island. Skimming low over sheltered bays and inlets, with yachts bobbing gracefully at their moorings. Within sight of Victoria's International Airport, I heaved a sigh of relief that my long journey had ended. With no more than the slightest bump our tiny aircraft touched down and taxied along the runway, coming to a halt outside the arrival's terminal at the airport. A tremendous feeling of excitement gripped me, as I walked from the tiny aircraft.

A dream of a lifetime was about to come true as the doors of the arrival's lounge slid open. Among the crowd waiting inside, I recognized my sister immediately. She was standing alongside a group of people waiting to meet their loved ones, and ran to greet me. Her welcoming smile, reminded me so much of mother. Taken by surprise, I could have sworn it was her who had come to greet me, instead of Catherine. The likeness to mother was perfect in every detail. For a split-second I remained rooted to the spot, afraid to move, then fell into her arms. No words of mine could describe the feeling of delight I experienced, as we embraced. Overcome with emotion on this our first ever meeting, I was speechless. There was so much I'd planned to say on this wonderful occasion, but try as I may, words of welcome I'd rehearsed so often, failed me.

Oblivious to those watching, we remained in a loving embrace for some minutes. Reluctant to break the spell, I gathered my luggage from the carousel as it circled round, and left the arrival's lounge. Outside we stepped into a waiting taxi and sat holding hands, as we drove off. The journey took us along winding country roads edged with stately pine forests sweeping down to the sea, where the clear blue waters of the Pacific Ocean tumbled over the island's sandy beaches. Dotted here and there among dense green foliage one glimpsed rows of brightly painted dwelling houses, set back off the road. As suddenly as it began my journey ended, when we arrived in the driveway of a neatly painted ranch-style bungalow in a quiet cul-de-sac. Retrieving my luggage from the taxi Catherine showed me the house where she lived, which was less than a stone's throw from the town's shopping centre.

Inside the house everything was neatly set out, albeit with her mother's eye for beauty and comfort. In the bedroom she'd made ready for my arrival I unpacked my clothes, putting them away inside the closet and chest of drawers. Waiting until I'd finished Catherine invited me to join her for a cup of tea, and ushering me into the lounge, suggested I take a seat. Sitting beside her I could see a perfect likeness between my sister, and the mother she had never known. Even to her facial expressions, I remembered so well as a boy, and her infectious smile. "Reluctant to break the spell of this magic moment, I simply sat there, and asked myself;

"Is this for real, or am I dreaming?"

About the Author

One of a large family, Charles. G. Ashford was born in London, England, after the first World War. Completing his education at St. Joseph's Academy, London, he then went on to train as a radio operator and joined the Merchant Service in March 1936, at the age of seventeen. A sea career spanning thirteen years enabled him to travel extensively to many countries throughout the world, until leaving the Merchant Service in 1948. He then joined the Mersey Docks and Harbour Company in Liverpool, and after twenty five years service was promoted to the position of Marine Supervisor. In 1976 an old war injury forced him to retire from the company, at the age of fifty seven.

Married in 1944, his wife Gladys passed away in August of 1990.

Mr. Ashford now lives in British Columbia.

Printed in the United States
765400001B

9 780759 638822